# AMERICAN
# TERROR

# AMERICAN TERROR

## THE FEELING OF THINKING IN EDWARDS, POE, AND MELVILLE

### PAUL HURH

STANFORD UNIVERSITY PRESS · STANFORD, CALIFORNIA

Stanford University Press
Stanford, California

©2015 by the Board of Trustees of the Leland Stanford Junior University. All rights reserved.

No part of this book may be reproduced or transmitted in any form or by any means, electronic or mechanical, including photocopying and recording, or in any information storage or retrieval system without the prior written permission of Stanford University Press.

Printed in the United States of America on acid-free, archival-quality paper

Library of Congress Cataloging-in-Publication Data

Hurh, Paul, author.
 American terror : the feeling of thinking in Edwards, Poe, and Melville / Paul Hurh.
 pages cm
 Includes bibliographical references and index.
 ISBN 978-0-8047-9114-4 (cloth : alk. paper)
 ISBN 978-1-5036-0418-6 (pbk. : alk. paper)
 1. American literature—History and criticism. 2. Terror in literature. 3. Edwards, Jonathan, 1703-1758—Criticism and interpretation. 4. Poe, Edgar Allan, 1809-1849—Criticism and interpretation. 5. Melville, Herman, 1819-1891—Criticism and interpretation. I. Title.
 PS169.T47H87 2015
 810.9'3552—dc23

2014042839

ISBN 978-0-8047-9451-0 (electronic)

Typeset by Bruce Lundquist in 10/14 Minion

*To Aileen*

## CONTENTS

Acknowledgments — ix

Abbreviations — xi

**Introduction:** Reopening Darkness — 1

1. **Awakening Terror:** Hellfire Preaching, Jonathan Edwards, and the Logic of Revivalist Affect — 31

2. **Critical Terrors:** Poe's Aesthetic Terror and the Claims of Art after Jena — 75

3. **The Air of Analysis:** Resolution and Composition in Poe's Sublime and Confessional Tales — 119

4. **The Uneven Balance:** Dialectical Terror in Moby-Dick — 161

5. **Dread:** Space, Time, and Automata in The Piazza Tales — 203

Afterword: "Some Dim, Random Way" — 245

Notes — 251
Works Cited — 273
Index — 291

## ACKNOWLEDGMENTS

The composition of this book would not have been possible without many kinds of aid from many generous people. I owe a special debt to Samuel Otter, upon whose insightful wisdom, invaluable feedback, and dependable wit I relied at every stage of the book's composition. I am also especially grateful to Stuart Davis, who encouraged me to develop the project, nearly two decades ago, that shaped the animating interests of this study. And for the steady and inspiring editorship of Emily-Jane Cohen—who offered celerity when I had no time and patience when I took it—I am deeply thankful.

It is reported that Jonathan Edwards once likened his pleasure, in his youthful reading of Locke's *Essay Concerning Human Understanding*, to that of "a greedy Miser in gathering up handsful of Silver and Gold from some new discover'd Treasure." My own miserly hoard was provided by several smart and selfless readers, whose advice and criticisms I treasured as gold. I trusted Mark Allison and Penelope Anderson with the earliest and roughest of drafts, and they responded with alacrity and illumination, showing me where to find stable ground in what was a formless chaos. The first readers of the whole manuscript, Jennifer Fleissner and an anonymous reader at Stanford University Press, offered a wealth of expertise in both detailed, comprehensive critique and generous encouragement. No less valuable were the many expert readers who read individual parts of the manuscript or earlier drafts: Charles Altieri, David Bates, Mitchell Breitwieser, Frederick Crews, Edgar Dryden, Allison Dushane, Jerrold Hogle, Matthew Kundert, Maurice Lee, Ayon Maharaj, John Melillo, Scott Selisker, Lynda Zwinger, and an anonymous reader at *Nineteenth-Century Literature*.

Multiple communities and institutions have supported me throughout this project. My colleagues in the English Department at the University of Arizona, in particular Edgar Dryden and Lynda Zwinger, have been ardent supporters and invaluable guides. Amy Hungerford, Peter Chemery, and their family were incomparably gracious hosts during my research trip to the Beinecke Library. Gigi Mark and Friederike Sundaram at Stanford University Press ushered the manuscript through production, and Christine Gever's careful copyediting made it both more precise and more graceful. Experts and archivists generously lent their aid when research led me into unfamiliar terrain: Carol Clark with Charles Deas, Robert Wallace with Melville's prints, Kenneth Minkema with Edwards's cryptographic handwriting, and the staff at both the Shelburne Museum and the Weill Cornell Medical College with permissions for archival materials. This book has also benefited in diverse ways from both colleagues and friends, among whom are Aaron Bady, Kate Bernheimer, Daniel Clinton, Alan Drosdick, Peter Goodwin, Kristine Ha, Hsuan Hsu, Joseph Jordan, Cody Marrs, Slavica Naumovska, Hoang Phan, Carolyn Porter, Chris and Claudia Price, Robert Schipano, Ernesto Tanjuan, and Leonard Von Morzé. My earliest friends in Tucson—Megan Campbell, Andrea Dallas, Juan Diaz, Allison Dushane, Uriah Kriegel, Clint McCall, Ander Monson, Manuel Muñoz, Jonathon Reinhardt, and Charles Scruggs—cheered me with both intellectual stimulation and welcome diversion through the toughest and hottest stretches of research and writing.

A portion of Chapter 3 was originally published in *Nineteenth-Century Literature*, and I am grateful for the editors' permission to reprint it here. The Shelburne Museum granted permission to reproduce the Deas illustration. The University of Arizona Provost's Author Support Program helped defray the cost of publication.

My family has been a constant support in all my endeavors, and I thank dearly the families of Tracy and Robert Prescott, Patrick and Marnie Hurh, and David, Liana, Nick, and Meredith Feng for their patience and encouragement. I am especially grateful for the support of my parents: Gloria Hurh, who first taught me to write and think critically, and Won Moo Hurh, whose life of philosophy and deep care continues to guide me even after its conclusion.

Finally, my most heartfelt gratitude goes to Aileen Feng, for intellectual acuity in moments of confusion, for unwavering belief in moments of doubt, and for affection through it all.

# ABBREVIATIONS

## Edwards
| | |
|---|---|
| MI | The "Miscellanies" |
| PW | Letters and Personal Writings |
| RA | Treatise on the Religious Affections |
| SP | Scientific and Philosophical Writings |

## Poe
| | |
|---|---|
| CP | Collected Poems |
| ER | Essays and Reviews |
| TS | Tales and Sketches |

## Melville
| | |
|---|---|
| C | Correspondence |
| M | Mardi: And a Voyage Thither |
| MD | Moby-Dick |
| PT | The Piazza Tales and Other Prose Pieces |

# AMERICAN
# TERROR

# INTRODUCTION

## Reopening Darkness

**IN HIS 1850 REVIEW** of Nathaniel Hawthorne's tales, Herman Melville intimated that American literary genius derives its force from a terrific "power of blackness" (*PT* 243). The metaphysical terror of the obscure blackness—the "short, quick probings at the very axis of reality" (*PT* 244)—that Melville finds in Hawthorne is paired, in the essay, with a plea for the recognition of genius in American literature. In reasserting the call for a national literature through an appreciation of a distinct tone, Melville diverges from the conventional view of American literature as defined by the furniture of its settings: its wild forests, its native peoples, its colonial heritage. Instead, what Melville's essay encourages is a new view of American literature afforded by pressing its philosophical stakes, a view in which the aim is not to give provincial imitations of foreign masters but rather to force, "covertly, and by snatches," glimpses of a great transcendent "Truth" that hides itself in our "world of lies" (*PT* 244). That this hidden truth is figured as a terrible blackness may strike us now as pessimistic, but in raising its stakes, Melville advocates for literature's power to address, to compel, the hard task of piercing through the "world of lies" to an absolute truth. Shifting the field of American literature by putting Hawthorne, instead of the more popular Irving or Cooper, at its center, Melville's essay advances an implicit hypothesis: that Hawthorne's power of blackness, his terror, designates the signal contribution of American literature. For Melville, the new possibilities for literary art afforded by the new nation and new culture allowed the American author to better sound the depths of human experience and excavate the dark, difficult truths from under the polished and fair, but for all that, still disguising and obstructing, literary conventions of inherited traditions. Why Melville thinks these truths are dark and terrifying is, as this book explores, tightly bound up with the imagined demands of detached objectivity informing his claim for American originality: that to see truth, one must first escape the fatal touch of influence or subjective preconception.

The distinctive tone of terror in American romantic literature has been, since Melville's review, one of the most compelling, persistent, and definitive concerns for American literary criticism. These concerns have evolved from decade to decade, joined by their intuition of some obscure and new "darkness," a new feeling of terror, an anxious or pessimistic undertone, in the literature of American romanticism. Since Melville, critics of antebellum American literature have often either pointed toward this darkness as the defining trope of American literature, or away from it as its polar negative, a cringing fear inherited from older traditions that sets off and prepares the way for the emergence of a healthier, properly American and democratic literary tradition. It has been tempting, since F. O. Matthiessen hypothetically apportioned American literature into categories of optimistic "thesis" and tragic "antithesis" (179), to assume two tonal traditions in American literature—one bright and optimistic, organized around Emerson and expressed in the possibilities and desires of Whitman and Thoreau; the other dark and pessimistic, organized around Poe and expressed in the cynicisms of Hawthorne and Melville and in the more troubled lyrics of Dickinson.[1] The "bright" side has been explained as informed by the democratic spirit, essentially progressive, and central to the development of pragmatism as the distinctive turn of the American mind. The "dark" side, in contrast, is assessed as essentially regressive, the revenge of the psychologically repressed guilt of America's puritanical religious heritage, or the nightmarish manifestation of a national conscience haunted by slavery. The neat, if overgeneralized, division still appeals; readers can still "feel" that Poe's dark pit and menacing pendulum is just, well, *darker* than Emerson's liberal eyeball enjoying its original relation to the universe. But what is behind this feeling of darkness? Is there a way to analyze and define this darkness without either falling into tautology (the "darkness" is there because we feel it to be dark), or translation (the "darkness" is political or ethical belief melted down into the fluid language of emotion)? Dissatisfied with descriptions that merely assert darkness's obscure profundity or seek to explain it away by rephrasing it as nonterrifying propositional belief, I aim in this book to reopen discussion about this often-observed, rarely defined tone. Such a reopening depends upon a preliminary hypothesis: that the model of symptomatic interpretation most often adopted by explanations of literary terror may be compromised by the special problem terror poses to it.

When Melville first recognized the "power of blackness" in Hawthorne, he not only framed the problem of this tone for literary criticism of the early twentieth century, but he also ventured what would come to be accepted as its best explanation: the influence of early America's "Calvinistic sense of Innate Depravity and Original Sin" (*PT* 243). Melville's review, and his neat distinction between the positive, optimistic, and affirmative mode of literature and Hawthorne's profound darkness, grounded the early formation and criticism of "classical" American literature. Many influential readers of American literature in the first half of the twentieth century—such as D. H. Lawrence, Charles Feidelson Jr., Harry Levin, William Carlos Williams, and Leslie Fiedler—found darkness as American literature's enduring trait, an "inner diabolism" (Lawrence 89), a Puritanical "primal darkness" (Levin 29), a "literature of darkness and the grotesque in a land of light and affirmation" (Fiedler 29). In contrast to Matthiessen, who dismisses Poe from his canon-forming study on grounds that Poe "was bitterly hostile to democracy" (xiin), William Carlos Williams describes how Poe is foundational to American literature by clearing and cutting it a new field: "a field of cold logic" (228). These midcentury readers may have been drawn to the moral murkiness of American literature's darkness out of the disillusionment with universal progress and moral evolution wrought by global war. When they looked at American literature, they looked hardest at the writers of darkness and saw in it the strange ghosts of America's past: the cold demands of a determinist religious orthodoxy and the equally cold prospects afforded by the logic and objectivity of a new scientific era.

Informed by Fiedler's claim that "[i]t is the gothic form that has been most fruitful in the hands of our best writers: the gothic symbolically understood" (28), critical approaches following the midcentury critics grew to identify darkness and terror in American literature as a subset of the gothic, a genre in which literary fear can be read allegorically.[2] Fear in literature, approached as gothic convention, is thus read as a symptomatic expression of various historically specific repressions. Perhaps most influential in this vein is Toni Morrison's seminal argument that the darkness of American literature is a symptom of the psychological and social demands exerted by slavery: "What rose up out of collective needs to allay internal fears and to rationalize external exploitation was an American Africanism—a fabricated brew of darkness, otherness, alarm, and desire that is uniquely American" (38). Teresa Goddu similarly focuses on how the gothic expresses the repressed content of foundational national narratives: "By resurrecting what these narratives repress, the gothic disrupts the dream world of national myth with the nightmares of history" (10). For Morrison, Goddu, and others, the terrors of the American gothic are symptomatic irruptions of specific historical repressions, particularly slavery, that haunt the collective American unconscious.[3]

In a wider Western context, this expression/repression model of historical interpretation sees gothic fears as outgrowths of a broader encounter between religion and reason in the Enlightenment. For some, literary fear critiques the limits of Enlightenment thought by expressing as horror the irrational outside of its bounds, as Cathy Davidson remarks: "[T]he Gothic challenges the primacy of the individual mind and the claims of reason. . . . The sleep of Reason, as Goya noted, begets monsters" (320).[4] Responding to this thesis, other critics have hypothesized that the expressive horrors may not critique reason as much as they complement it. In this sense, the gothic becomes the repository and outlet for moral or supernatural psychological needs that the Enlightenment paradigm could no longer satisfy, thus serving as "an indispensable corollary to Enlightenment liberalism which ultimately served to protect the liberal view of human nature" (Halttunen 99). Recasting Goya's *The Sleep of Reason Produces Monsters*, Diane Hoeveler finds that "the uncanny gothic dream world of superstition, magic, and demons continues to exist only when the subject sleeps and his reasonable faculties are dormant. And it is precisely in this historical gap—between the decline of magic and the rise of science—that the gothic imaginary emerges" (8). Whereas Davidson's reading implies that monsters intrude from the irrational outside of reason, Hoeveler's adds the qualification that the monsters were always, in a sense, already there—in the problem of evil and in transcendent religious belief that had to be reworked and given expression through the gothic imaginary. Summing up this complementary thesis, Hoeveler claims that "the gothic needs to be understood, not as a reaction against the rise of secularism, but as a part of the ambivalent secularizing process itself" (6).

The most recent discussions of the function of literary fear continue to pivot on what, exactly, it signals as repressed content. Updating and clarifying the complementary thesis, Victoria Nelson reads the gothic as a dark repository, where religious energies were "forced underground" (*Secret Life of Puppets* viii) until our own postmillennial present, in which those energies flower again in what she calls the "bright" gothic, a "normative supernaturalism" (*Gothicka* 18) that would "transform this dark template into a sunnier, more all-embracing spiritual framework" (*Gothicka* 17). Yet this view, in turn, has been challenged by Mark McGurl, who argues that the gothic does not suppress religiosity but rather *realism*. Pointing to the advent of scientific modernity as a threshold moment in Western culture's disenchantment with religious supernaturalism, McGurl reads the gothic as "one way of managing our intuition that the material world, writ large, may be utterly indifferent to human ends, so indifferent that it might as well be malevolent" ("Dark Times"). Nelson sees the gothic as the repressed (and eventually expressive) site of religious drives. McGurl sees it as the site of repressed intuitions about our insignificance in deep time. From Calvinism to slavery, from irrationality to liberalism, from supernaturalism to realism, the connecting thread in the long history of competing interpretations of literary fear is the shared assumption of its repressive function.

But in McGurl's posthuman-inflected turn of the question, there is an opportunity to question the repression/expression model itself. For, if terror manages and represses a depressing new reality (about our insignificance in the universe), it is curiously not defensive; this fear does not indicate a preference to return to a prior, unafraid state, but rather it itself shapes the attitude by which we may access as affect the extreme posture of objectivity demanded by the Enlightenment. By expressing a repressed reality, fear itself would ratify the ground for explanations of what it is "really" about. Terror, then, may be a special case that complicates the repressive/expressive model by which literary fears are often understood.

Justine Murison, in her recent study of anxiety, has come to the same conclusion. According to Murison, anxiety drives contemporary historicist criticism by "produc[ing] the discursive traces of repression constantly in need of exposure" (173) and thus becomes criticism's blindspot: "The role 'anxiety' plays as both discursive source and its result, however, complicates literary historicism by resisting causal relationships: 'Anxiety' stands metonymically for the motivation behind which analysis cannot go" (8). In other words, perhaps the persistent explanatory model of repression/expression—through which literary terror is viewed as an expression of repressed racialized guilt, repressed religiosity, repressed liberalism, or even repressed realism—may be ill equipped to describe an aesthetic effect that underlies the repression schema from the start. What if terror is not the sign of repressed trauma but rather an approximation of an experience unmediated through the normative assumptions that enable our interpretive diagnoses of repression? In such a case, terror would not simply manage "our intuition that the world, writ large, may be utterly indifferent to human ends" but rather more fundamentally constitute that very intuition. To read terror in such a way would take more seriously the generative verb, *producer*, in Goya's *The Sleep of Reason Produces Monsters*: the monsters are neither reason's threats nor its complements but its dreams.

The complicated relation of terror to a symptomatic strain of historicist interpretation, however, does not mean abandoning historical research entirely. Recovering the intellectual, biographical, and social contexts of terror in the current study, I find the stories of these American terrors lead consistently to a common event and discourse: the invention and formalization of universal method in the Enlightenment's definition of thought. Yet because of its resistance to interpretive explanation, terror is not finally reducible to this discourse but rather would extend it in an aesthetic realm and interrogate it in a philosophical one. To reopen a discussion of America's tradition of literary terror requires bridging historical and aesthetic modes of literary criticism in ways that neither explain the aesthetic by way of the historical nor subordinate historical particulars to a universal aesthetic. Such balancing is not merely in line with recent calls for a renewed aesthetic criticism[5] but, moreover, a method adapted to meet the challenge of terror's own unique dynamism, its operation along that crucial boundary between the world of thought and the world of nature.

In formulating an approach that seeks to balance historical context and aesthetic form, my study draws from two recent and related turns in literary theory. The first is the recent swath of interest in the study of affect across the humanistic disciplines referred to as affect theory.[6] The renewed sense of affect as more than propositional belief, as ontologically both securing and troubling distinctions between subject and object, self and world, prepares the ground for a study such as this one: one that would consider the significance of literary tone while paying attention to political alignment, historical context, and biographical anecdote. Buttressed by studies in cognitive science and psychology that have used fMRI scans of brains to complicate and question the always troubled division between self-possessed conscious reason and uncontrollable passion, affect theory begins with the idea that emotions can no longer be bracketed as simply fuzzy beliefs or irrational bodily irruptions but rather should be understood as core instruments of cognition, understanding, and consciousness.[7] The second recent strain of discourse pertinent to my study is the attention to the history of science as an extraordinarily powerful shaping influence on cultural production. Known as "science studies," this approach defamiliarizes science's ahistorical and transcendent pretensions by restoring the narrative of its development and exploring its political and aesthetic consequences. In a very general sense, affect theory has worked to make emotion more objective, more scientific, while science studies have exposed how the story of objectivity is more subjective, more affective.[8] From these two developments, I have constructed the hypothesis of this book: that what is distinctive about American terror is its aim to produce the peculiar affect of scientific objectivity, the feeling of thinking.

I assert that terror is the feeling of thinking with the following qualifications. First, I am not talking about all terror, or all instances of fear, but rather the particular strain of terror that operates so powerfully in American literature. Perhaps it would thus be better to define it as modal terror, procedural terror, terror of process, or logical terror. This terror is more tonal and atmospheric than directed; we rarely feel terror *for* the characters of Poe's stories, for instance, but rather shudder at the particular worldview that Poe constructs through them. Second, I don't mean all thinking. Thinking here refers to the process and method of intellectual inquiry largely determined by the undeniable advances in medicine and technology enabled by the scientific method in the eighteenth and nineteenth centuries. The terror of Poe's recurrent motif of premature burial, for instance, does not arise out of any immediate threat of pain but rather inheres in a certainty, figured as an enclosure, from which there is no escape.

The feeling of thinking is a special affect, for it would circumscribe the very activity, the intellection and interpretive procedure, by which it would usually be explained. What I gain from this reversal of priority is not, however, a critique of reason. Just as Jonathan Edwards depicts the horrors of hell not to make hell less plausible but actually more so, the writers in my study return again and again to the terrors of thinking not to undermine reason's power but rather to show its power. This is not, however, to say that thinking is "just" a feeling. The extremity of terror instead registers the demand of reason, even in the felt insufficiency of the mind to meet that demand. Thinking is a special function of the mind, one that admits and orients the self to the world in a special way; we believe that the world out there obeys conventions and laws that are "outside of us," as it were, and that in order to know this world genuinely, a set of conventions and laws must be adhered to in the operation of our rational mind. The truthfulness of this situation might be able to be proven according to those same laws, but underwriting the truthfulness of those laws is something else altogether. It is this something else that the writers in my study outline in terror—a self-justifying emotion that demands and threatens, that does not rest in compromise, that presents us with an "outside" yet refuses to be hemmed in by the aesthetic conditions of the sublime or the utility and flexibility of pragmatism. For Edwards, it is the content of a true experience of God; for Poe, the legitimate deduction of the soul; for Melville, the heartless immensity of a palsied universe stripped to its bitterest particulate objectivity.

If the "power of blackness" is ultimately best understood as an aesthetic associated with thought itself, we may then return to the generalized and provisional distinction between "bright" and "dark" traditions in American literature in order to both challenge it and reconsider its consequences. For even though Emerson is most often taken as championing a kind of aesthetic mode of thinking through his essays, one that eventually flowers in the liberal and progressive philosophy of pragmatism, Branka Arsić's recent reading of Emerson's philosophy emphasizes what might be called its darker aspects, the way the Emersonian individual is less an atomistic, stable, and self-determined subject and more a conflux of forces, palpable through "the abyss of the impersonal within us" (*On Leaving* 15). In the same vein, Arsić notes Emerson's method of always leaving positions, of refusing comfort in a persistent act of turning away: "[W]e can stay, repose, and live a lie, or we can depart, gaining truth only by experiencing the restlessness of living in the oppositions and aporias that make our being swing" (17). Like Melville's enjoinder that American literature should ceaselessly uncover truth in our "world of lies," this Emersonian restlessness proceeds through maneuvers and evasions that correlate with the "dark" tradition's more skeptical, less assured vision of the world. So whereas Arsić's recasting of the skeptical ground of Emerson's eventual optimism troubles the essential distinction between "dark" and "bright" traditions from Emerson's side, my study proceeds from the other direction: what if the terror that had previously been seen as an expression of deeply buried anxieties was not essentially repressive and conservative but rather a new tone calibrated to the very same intellectual crises as those of the "bright" tradition? As Arsić's reading of Emerson uncovers the fragmentary, chaotic abysses in the classical American philosophy of the individual self, my study would consider those literal abysses, those literal scenes of fragmentation and destruction, populating the darker strand of American literature as constitutive of a deep affective commitment to the project of completing thinking through aesthetic feeling.

Yet the tonal discrepancy between Emerson's leave-taking and, say, Poe's dramas of desperate escape or criminal evasion does make a difference. While the philosophical reading of the "bright" tradition links it to the evolution of pragmatism, I will conclude that terror in the "power of blackness" eventuates in the different, though related, philosophical tradition of poststructuralism. To say that the difference between pragmatism and poststructuralism is primarily tonal is not, however, to diminish their distinction. As both philosophies make clear, affective states as well as aesthetic properties are conceptually significant, irreducible and inseparable from the content of propositional thought. Thus, to say that terror is the feeling of thinking is to emphasize how the texture of terror—its urgency, its fear, its certainty—neither merely attends thought nor merely arises from it but rather informs the thinking itself. So, while pragmatism becomes associated with optimism in the face of impossibility or failure, terror does not then entail a skeptical rejection of or resignation from the project of thinking the world. Instead, it can be seen as a distinctive reshaping of that project and a commitment to it that is powerful not despite impossibility but because of it. In tracing a prehistory of poststructuralism through the terror of American literature, this book thus seeks to help complete the still-emerging story of American literature's contribution to philosophy.

## Thinking Feeling

Why would humans want to scare themselves? Of what artistic value is terror? For as far back as Aristotle's *Poetics*, these questions have regularly been addressed as calling for a theorization of fear's purpose. Aristotle's *catharsis*, for instance, explains dramatic fear as addressing a human need to purge itself of negative energies.[9] We seek to be frightened in a movie theatre, or by a chilling novel, so that we may be less susceptible to fright in our "real" lives—the passions of poetry are of use to us by becoming the repository of emotional states that would otherwise disrupt our rational lives. Philip Fisher, substantially revising this account, writes a history of the aesthetics of fear that would not essentially separate passion from lived and willed experience but join them. Because fear, for Fisher, leads to pity and sympathy, the "aesthetic importance of fear . . . has the unmistakable prominence it does precisely because of the political imagination that locks our own state into play with the state of another—or of many others—and invents in fear an unexpected but crucial kind of civic energy" (156). In Aristotle's account, the desire for becoming scared by art is to release fears in a safe direction away from our civic life.[10] In Fisher's account, that desire is concomitant to leading a healthy civic life; our fears are not threats to sociality but rather the glue. Despite this opposition, both accounts conclude that it is finally in action, in the political state, that the purpose of the aesthetics of fear finally resides. This route to the political consequences of terror in art exerts its hold upon our imagination because in the original question—"Why would humans want to scare themselves?"— is the assumption that humans only want what is, in some way, beneficial to themselves and the social order. Terror, in these accounts, may be explained as functioning within, in Aristotle's case, or grounding, in Fisher's case, our political and social psychology.

But explaining fear in art by positing its social purpose runs the risk of resolving too quickly the intricacy of its texture into broad political instrumentality. For one of the chief elements of the distinctive terror in American literature is that it defamiliarizes the self's relation to its world and that it opens, in glimpses felt rather than in propositions understood, a vision of the universe in which the causal narrative that would make sense, make purpose, of phenomena is estranged from the experience of the frightened self. In this case, fear resists, or more properly derives itself from, purposive accounting. Poe's carefully elaborated theory of perversity, which underpins his tales of psychological terror, makes the case that humans feel compelled to take actions because they *know* they should not—and, moreover, that this very faculty of perversity is so difficult to recognize because it doesn't make any sense in psychological accounts that begin with the assumption of rationality and purposive self-preservation. As Poe writes, "It would have been wiser, it would have been safer to classify, (if classify we must,) upon the basis of what man usually or occasionally did, and was always occasionally doing, rather than upon the basis of what we took it for granted the Deity intended him to do" (*TS* 2:1220). For Poe, perversity acknowledges that much of human action is taken against rational self-interest, against political or social benefit, not from wayward whim or misunderstanding but from a self-destructive impulse. According to such a philosophy, the desire for artistic terrors and horrors may not be wholly explained by how that desire accommodates or enables what we grant as the ends of self-interest. Perversity, as itself a site of terror, resists functionalist explanation. Poe's terror upsets rubrics of explanation that would fix its final purpose and projects its peculiar feeling as radiating from that very drama. Moreover, Poe's definition of perversity suggests that terror is directed at the urge for purposive accounting itself, that what is really scary is not only that such narrative explanations are inadequate but that all explanations, by reason of their reason, may be incapable of accounting (if account we must) for their own demand to provide an account.

The problem with accounting for the terror of the inadequacy of accounting is not limited only to feelings of fear. The question of how to talk about aesthetic feelings without reducing them to propositional beliefs about self-interest or social function is a wider issue within philosophies of affect. Resisting the way Martha Nussbaum defines emotion as a *"cognitive appraisal"* that relies upon "the idea of *one's own flourishing* or *one's important goals and projects*,"[11] Charles Altieri emphasizes that the essential attribute of affect is that it is irreducible to articulated beliefs, that "[i]f we seek only explanations for actions, we tend to ignore everything that might give such particular expressions distinctive vividness and force" (*Particulars* 126). One of the things that give expressions force is the ability for feeling to reciprocally affect belief: "In fact the beliefs may be themselves influenced by the specific flow of feelings, so rather than helping us identify the emotion they become aspects of complex states that are quite difficult to characterize" (*Particulars* 11). In the problem of Poe's perversity, it isn't just that feelings influence belief but that they flow in a direction diametrically opposite to it, and thus to define those feelings through belief is to miss their distinctive force. Although the tendency, when thinking about feeling, is to try to explain it in relation to a world governed by causes and effects, the special case of terror shakes not only the assumption of a rational order but also, in the cases I consider in this book, the grounding imperative that informs explanation itself. That is, attempts to explain the purpose of aesthetic fear run the risk of missing the way its peculiar force is predicated upon the failure of those very efforts to reason it away.

The shortcomings of accounts that funnel aesthetic emotion into propositional belief, especially in the case of terror, may be clarified by analyzing

Nussbaum's reading of Alfred Hitchcock's *Psycho* (1960). Nussbaum holds that "we seek out painful literary experiences, as Aristotle argued, for the understanding of self and world that they offer. While the understanding itself is painful . . . it is, on the other hand, a valuable and a pleasant thing to acquire understanding" (244). Taking the shower scene as her illustration, Nussbaum claims that, as a viewer, she experiences real fear on three levels: (1) for the character, Marion Crane; (2) for women in general, as potential targets of sexual assault; (3) for herself, Martha Nussbaum, embodied as female. At each level, the film thus offers "a safe context," in which "we allow ourselves to investigate a fear that at some level accompanies us everywhere we go. What we want from such works is the opportunity to explore these fears in a context of immediate safety" (246). Nussbaum emphasizes how the "safety" of the view is tantamount to allowing the viewer to experience not only "sympathy for Leigh [Crane] and rage at the predator who stalks her," but more importantly, "sympathy for women who are raped or assaulted and rage at their attackers" (246). She notes how the moral is complicated by Hitchcock's manipulation of the viewer's perspective as the killer, but even this sadism is explained as "the exhilaration and delight of learning something about ourselves, disturbing though this knowledge in some respects is" (247). For Nussbaum, who in many ways updates the Aristotelian account of aesthetic fear, the terrors that *Psycho* elicits are all functional, or potentially functional, and could lead to real ethical action. Real fear is transformed into both educative lesson and felt delight.

What enables Nussbaum's translation of fear into propositional belief (about the vulnerability of women in America) as well as positive emotion (delight) is the key term "safety." Because we know we are safe, we can investigate and explore the lessons that fear can teach us about ourselves and the world. But then, is this still "real fear"? For in Nussbaum's positing of safety as the essential context in the appreciation of aesthetic fear, she adopts Kant's condition of the sublime as requiring, for its educative experience, that the subject be safe: "since he knows he is safe, this is not actual fear" (*Critique of Judgment* 129). Yet what occurs when the bracketing potential of safety is itself targeted as the cause and essential element of terror?

For Kant and Nussbaum, the belief that "I am safe" is necessarily attendant to appreciations of painful or threatening aesthetic experiences. For Poe's narrator of "The Imp of the Perverse," however, it is that very phrase "I am safe" that haunts his consciousness and becomes the cause of his eventual self-destruction. In this tale of perversity, the narrator, having committed an undetectable murder, becomes delighted by his safety: "It is inconceivable how rich a sentiment of satisfaction arose in my bosom as I reflected upon my absolute security. For a very long period of time, I was accustomed to revel in this sentiment" (*TS* 2:1224). That very delight, however, precipitates his eventual fall: "I would perpetually catch myself pondering upon my security and repeating, in a low, under-tone, the phrase, 'I am safe.'" (*TS* 2:1225). His unwilled utterance becomes a perverse compulsion, and he is finally undone by his own performative speech: "'I am safe—I am safe—yes—if I be not fool enough to make open confession!'" (*TS* 2:1225). The feeling of safety, in this tale, becomes the agent of its own dissolution. What fear the tale elicits is thus pointed at one's psychology, at the possibility that in our safest and most secure moments what threatens us is a recognition and delight in that security itself. The consciousness of safety is itself a threat, capable of perversely causing that which it protects against.

What makes "safety" such a problematic concept in determining the appreciation of aesthetic fear is that it would bracket and refit terror into a predetermined scheme of self-knowledge and self-possessed reason. But, Poe's perversity shows, the safety of knowledge can itself become a type of threat. It is not because we are not "really" safe that we are in danger, but rather that because we *are* really safe, we are in danger. Obviously, we are in some irrational waters here. But what makes Poe's perversity so compelling, the secret of its terror, is that it follows a bizarre order that nevertheless makes some kind of sense, validated by an affect that fills in for reason's hiatus. To return to the shower scene in *Psycho*, then, is to see that the ideal viewer experiences real fear in which the fictiveness of the performance is not a diminishment or limit but rather an integral part. Our beliefs about the threats facing women in our society might inform our fear, but the experience of fear in that moment is not reducible to such beliefs. The greater terror emerges when the fact of our feeling comes to play havoc with our beliefs about the boundary between fictiveness and reality, when our sense of safety becomes somehow estranged from our own consciousness (when Poe's narrator "catches himself" repeating the phrase), when through our complicity—we went to the theatre, we paid the admission, we sit passively watching—our desire to feel fear cannot be separated neatly from the fear itself. If we hold on to the possibility that the feeling of fear troubles hard and fast boundaries between fiction and reality, between safety and danger, then the terror of that moment can be a recognition of just how permeable, how ultimately ineffective, those barriers, like the flimsy shower curtain that Marion clutches and finally bears to the floor with her, really are.

To say that our knowledge of safety enables us to enjoy this moment is to miss the powerful indictment of our feelings of safety that the shower scene makes, both in its overt symbolism—the resolution to come clean, the shower curtain drawn, even the sanitary crackle of the wrapped bar of soap—and in its resistance to generic conventions. According to the expectations of genre, Marion should have been "safe" as the lead actress, and especially safe midway through the film. The very conventions of safety that are at issue in the shower scene emphasize Altieri's point that the Aristotelian account of aesthetic emotions tends to overplay the distinction between the "real world" and the "imaginative world" of the text, especially in cases in which "fictionality is not simply a contractual state but an inescapable feature of how we produce and respond to affective intensities" (*Particulars* 126). We cannot understand the effectiveness of the shower scene without accounting for the pressure it forces upon its own "fictional" and therefore "safe" conventions. Any definition of terror in American literature thus has the challenge of refusing explanations that would see terror as beneficial to human subjectivity from a safe distance, because the distancing effects of explanation are at stake in the terror itself.

With the consideration that terror not only resists explanation but also perversely gains from the very attempts to explain it, the peculiar feeling tone of American literature can be contrasted against two adjacent aesthetic categories, the sublime and gothic horror. While both categories, the sublime and the gothic, are sites of continued critical interest, neither term is quite adequate to account for the recursive contours, the perverse sway, of the terror of Edwards, Poe, and Melville. The sublime, as noted above, has in its Kantian definition the feeling of estrangement and being overwhelmed by infinitude—it is the philosophical account of the feeling of perceiving the vastness of nature, the limits of one's own perceptual understanding. Certainly such a concept could apply to Edwards's portrait of God's infinite wrath, or Poe's terrific whirlpools, or the immensity of Melville's white whale. However, for Kant, the sublime is always perceived in safety, and its consequence is, like Nussbaum's delight in understanding, a recuperation of the power of the individual subject. Because we cannot fully comprehend what is communicated in the sublime, Kant writes, its feeling thus confirms in us the unlimited ability in our own nature: "[T]he subject's own inability uncovers in him the consciousness of an unlimited ability which is also his, and that the mind can judge this ability aesthetically only by that inability" (*Critique of Judgment* 116). Even when Kant describes how the sublime is a feeling of inadequacy, he prepares the way to recoup that inadequacy as evidence of an even greater power of mind: "For although we found our own limitation when we considered the immensity of nature . . . we found in our mind a superiority over nature itself in its immensity" (*Critique of Judgment* 120).

Such recourse from sublime terror to the promotion of the individual subject, of one's own powers of mind, would be incomprehensible to Edwards, who professed the individual's nothingness and ultimate dependence upon God, as well as to Poe and Melville, who through their fictions consistently locate their sublime-like terrors as originating in and ultimately challenging the sanctity of individual subjectivity. From Kant's definition to its current definition as aesthetic category, the sublime carries with it this sense of recuperation and empowerment, and does so by emphasizing the essential condition that it be regarded in safety.[12] Therefore, it is inadequate to describe the terror I chart in this study, because for these American authors, the power of blackness does not derive from its ability to be appropriated instrumentally for the satisfaction of an individual subject but rather from its uncompromising demand that such appropriations are possible deceits and evasions from a real, not fictional or framed, threat. This distinction of terror from the sublime might be formulated, then, as follows: terror is the sublime stripped of its subjective orientation; it is the sublime without safety, without the aesthetic judgment that would rescue the threatened ascendency of the rational subject.[13] But to this must be added the complicating addendum explored earlier: what keeps terror from being reframed as the sublime is that terror seems to be *about* the impulse to refit its fear into rational and purposive categories.

A clue as to how terror resists the bracketing and purposive impulses of the sublime might be gained by distinguishing it from those gothic horrors with which it has often been confused. The tradition of the gothic genre consists of a set of conventions—old castles, threatened maidens, perfidious histories, vengeful ghosts, murderous madmen—that seek to instill fear. The fear raised by these conventions, however, I would designate as primarily horror before terror, for chief among the conventions of the gothic is that of the locatable horror (the monster, the specter, the crazed monk, etc.), which comes to symbolize or express a real-world anxiety.[14] Stephen King suggests in his study of the genre that cultural preoccupations—from the Cold War to acne—become manifest in the monsters of horror: invading spacemen for Soviet Sputnik (12), the disfigured face of teenage Frankenstein for the juvenile horror of acne (47–48). Symptomatic horror is different from terror in that it relies upon some perceived deviation; one can feel horror by being confronted by a hideous, many-tentacled, and drooling monster, just as one can feel horror by hearing about atrocities committed by a dictator upon his people. Horror is thus closely associated with outrage in its normative assumptions, the sense that something is out of place and that the anomaly must be assimilated or destroyed. Once manifest or projected as an identifiable threat, the horror of that anomaly consequently becomes available for symptomatic interpretation. Horror, in its symptomatic function, accordingly proceeds from two assumptions: (1) the world is fundamentally a good and stable and desirable order, and (2) something has trespassed on that world and must be destroyed or assimilated to regain what is threatened.[15]

Terror, on the other hand, operates in a more subconscious register. Rather than the world being known and stable, terror occurs when the world itself becomes out of place. In this, it isn't the external monster threatening an Apollonian universe but rather a glimpse of the possibility that the Apollonian universe is actually quite brutal and inhuman, threatening existential anomie in which one's self becomes the monster in an unfamiliar world.[16] This is the terror that Frankenstein's creature feels, in comparison with the bare horror of Frankenstein himself. Terror creeps out of horror because the monstrous, when considered upon the scales it imposes, threatens to expose the terror of the radical contingency of our deeply held assumptions about the world and our place in it.[17]

Horror and terror are not essentially distinct as much as they are different frames for the imagined consequences of the fearful. What I identified as the implicit bracketing impulse in the sublime is also found in the orientation of horror—fear locates an aberration, a threat to our operative paradigm that we would seek to overcome, either through philosophical translation of that fear as productive or by restoring the threatened world by destroying the threat. But in most moments of horror, there is also the possibility of latent terror, that what the horror indicates is not an aberration but rather some deeper truth of the instability of our worldly paradigms, that a world which could allow a horror is not one that is hospitable to the human subject. Ahab can be said to chase the whale because he finds it a horror, "'for forty years to make war on the horrors of the deep!'" (*MD* 543), but in the demand that he eliminate the horror, he begins to recognize a deeper terror, one of self-estrangement: "'What is it, what nameless, inscrutable, unearthly thing is it; what cozening, hidden lord and master, and cruel, remorseless emperor commands me; that against all natural lovings and longings, I so keep pushing, and crowding, and jamming myself on all the time; recklessly making me ready to do what in my own proper, natural heart, I durst not so much as dare? Is Ahab, Ahab?'" (*MD* 545). In horror, the whale is the unnatural thing that needs to be eliminated; in terror, it is Ahab's own impulses to destroy the whale that are unnatural, that are finally monstrous. In horror's frame, the monster is object; it is locatable in the world and in the text; it is capable of being destroyed or rehabilitated; and perhaps most importantly, it is interpretable in a fairly straightforward symptomatic way. In terror's frame, the monster is subject; it is only gestured at by the world of the text; it can neither be destroyed nor rehabilitated; and most importantly, it resists interpretation because it takes to task the very categories and assumptions central to the impulse to explain away, to rationalize, to ameliorate fear.

The difference in these frames is not as simple, however, as simply distinguishing between subject and object. For while objectively oriented explanations of aesthetic fear work from the assumption of a rigid subject/object division and hierarchy—Aristotle, Kant, and Nussbaum all resolve fear as of objects and instrumental to the subject—terror destabilizes those distinctions. The differences between subject and object, between self and world, between the real and the fictional, are not reinforced, as they are in the gothic horror, or recuperated, as they are in the sublime, but rather are taken themselves as affective incitement. What is necessary, then, is a term that designates the operation by which this binary is destabilized. I find this in Sianne Ngai's definition of *tone*. Ngai, addressing the problem of where the feeling of a text occurs (in the text? or in the reader?), theorizes tone as arising centrally from the subjective/objective problematic of emotion itself: "Tone *is* the dialectic of objective and subjective feeling that our aesthetic encounters inevitably produce" (30). As tone, then, terror belongs not just to a certain figure in the text (as in objective accounts of gothic horror's taxonomy of conventions), but neither is it found only in the reader's experience (as in the case of the sublime, in which the subject regains superiority over the world of the objects of sense). Instead, terror disrupts categorization by being an aesthetic orientation, an effect, of the very categories of subject and object. That which experiences "tone," in Ngai's sense, cannot be either just subject or object itself—our affective capacities come to open a new mode of apprehension, one in which the experience of aesthetic effect dislodges the subject/object binary. Given the unique structure of terror as I have defined it above—as emerging from and being recursively amplified by the self's own struggle to rationalize it—the ambiguity built into the concept of tone will allow a discussion of terror without either refitting it into subject/object schemes or abandoning those schemes entirely.

Terror's tonal quality is thus resistant to the most inherent structural principles in reason. But this does not lead us back to terror as a response to Enlightenment reason; it is neither a complaint about, nor a functional complement to, the universalizing sway of methodic reason as it colonizes and evicts superstition, myth, and fear. Rather, terror is inimical to reason, as Horkheimer and Adorno express: "Enlightenment is mythic fear turned radical" (16). In their critique, the dream of Enlightenment reason is born from fear: "Man imagines himself free from fear when there is no longer anything unknown"; so that through its efforts to dispel fear, the fearful is deposited into a single taboo category of exteriority: "Nothing at all may remain outside, because the mere idea of outsideness is the very source of fear" (16). The Enlightenment's commitment to rationality, as they theorize, demands that it regard with terror all that it cannot explain according to reason and self-preservation, including its own origins: "The mythic terror feared by the Enlightenment accords with myth. Enlightenment discerns it . . . in any human assertion that has no place in the ultimate context of self-preservation" (29). Even though the Enlightenment would dispel fear by leaving it no mystery to hide in, the fact that reason develops in response to fear means that it bears its traces.[18] We hear in the terror of that which cannot be explained through the "context of self-preservation" the secret of Kant's sublime or Nussbaum's flourishing, for their inversions of the aesthetic of terror from bewildering fear to confident delight are informed by just such an impulse for self-preservation. But what exactly is reason itself, if we are to regard it as a faculty capable of having a tone?

## Feeling Thinking

Jonathan Edwards is the first and most forthright of the three authors of this study to trouble the distinction between emotion and reason, through his pithy note, "the mind feels when it thinks" (*SP* 345). We have seen above how difficult it can be to think about feeling, especially when the feeling itself, in the case of terror, is oriented toward the very operations that would produce knowledge. But just as we need the fluid term "tone" to handle such ambiguity, we also need to consider our definition of what counts as "thinking." For the authors of this study, thinking is not a self-evident process or faculty. From Edwards's interest in logic, Poe's literary experimentation with the terms of analysis, and Melville's continued obsession with epistemological skepticism, all three authors engage with thinking *about* thinking, and find in logical method the clearest articulation of what thinking, as object, might be. Abstracted into sets of methodological principles and rules, thinking, for these American authors steeped in logic and epistemology, might be made apprehensible by feeling.

To regard thinking in this way is to submit the figure of scientific method to aesthetic apprehension, where the trace of mythic fear postulated by Horkheimer and Adorno becomes visible in aesthetic objects.[19] It is to find the feeling of what George Levine has identified as the narrative of scientific epistemology, that "continuing aspiration to get it straight, to understand what it means, to transcend the limits imposed by the limiting self" which curiously, "depends on the elimination of the self" (2). Levine's study seeks to recuperate the objective demand that the knower get outside himself or herself—"dying to know"—by showing how Victorian narratives reveal how that bleak demand "is a condition of intellectual exchange and of social life; and it is a perilously saving condition toward which the intellectual, moral, and aesthetic ventures of Western society have occasionally inched" (15). What is compelling in Levine's study is the way it uses narrative, a literary element, in order to reframe the problem for objectivity that Thomas Nagel defines, namely, that one must stand outside the world in order to know it. If the objectivity problem is read as a narrative, then the shape it takes, the "sound" of its rhetorical attitudes and enabling assumptions, can render aesthetic tone.[20]

Both Levine and Amanda Anderson defend the aspiration for a distanced, detached view, on the grounds that, even if such a perfectly objective and unsituated viewpoint is impossible, the aspiration itself should not be dismissed, or regarded as a politically suspicious instrument of hegemony. If these powers of distance, worked out in American literature, yield a potentially disturbing terror, it would at first seem to be a tacit critique of objectivity. But I argue that just as it is not a critique, neither is it a celebration of objectivity's "progressive potentiality" (5) as Anderson finds in its Victorian context. On one hand, beginning with Edwards, terror itself is an aspiration; one aspires to religious terror, for such an experience is vital and truthful in a way that would shrug off the mediated relations of self to world. The capacity for objectivity, for its demand to see the world from outside the self, to generate terror in fact confirms its claim. On the other hand, whether or not the aspiration to critical distance issues in "progressive potentiality" would seem, in terror, to be more ambiguous. Potentiality for whom? Progressive in what direction and for what reason?

In a perfect state of self-annihilation, knowledge can be gained, but the self and those sets of beliefs for which that knowledge might be useful would be suspended. If, for Victorian literature, the narrative of scientific epistemology and its aspiration of detachment retains a saving and progressive potential, that same narrative, worked out in the terrors of American literature, rejects as its outcome the conservation of threatened ethical imperatives and the presumption of progress toward an emancipatory ideal. Terror's aim would thus have more in common with recent ecocritical theorizations of the "world-without-us," a hypothetical conception, brought about by awareness of global climate change and natural disasters, of the world as an indifferent "nebulous zone that is at once impersonal and horrific" (Thacker 6).[21]

Feeling thinking here means that the terror which coincides with the scientific narrative and the paradox of objectivity can in some ways better describe those logics than bare accounts of them. In this way, my study treats literary affect as a philosophical mode and joins an ongoing discussion about American literature's relation to philosophy. The call to interpret American literature within a philosophical context sounded by Stanley Cavell at the end of *The Claim of Reason* has been answered by critics who have pinned American literature's philosophical contribution to the emergence of pragmatism.[22] These studies reflect the mood of Cavell from the start, his enduring concern with the crisis of skepticism and its sophistication, and the mood or attitude that he consistently adopts, which is more hopeful than skeptical, more cheerful than frightened. When Cavell looks at Emerson and Thoreau he discovers the outline of the "'sacred Yes'" of Nietzsche ("Thinking of Emerson" 133), an answer to skepticism that reconstitutes its attitude of self-defeat. Cavell seeks a way to inhabit the skeptical position, a way of allowing skepticism's premises while at the same time refusing the character of its consequences—nihilism, self-defeat, cynicism, or what he finds in Poe as "the will to be the monstrous" (*Quest of the Ordinary* 141). Yet even when Cavell claims most forthrightly the need to think skepticism positively in order to salvage or rescue a deep and moral conception of the human, he at the same time recognizes that "the wish to escape the conditions of humanity . . . is itself only human" ("Thinking of Emerson" 146–147). Nevertheless, Cavell's is a humanist skepticism, and when he confronts those places in American literature where the "sacred Yes" gives way to "NO! in thunder" (*C* 186), he pathologizes the "will to be monstrous," reading Poe's terrors as essentially parodic and ironic.[23] For Cavell, even if we cannot achieve the impossible ideal of the transcendentalist, the perfect human subject, "we aspire to this man, to the metamorphosis, to the human—hence that we can be guided and raised by the cheer of thinking" ("Thinking of Emerson" 130). Similar to Anderson's claim for the progressive potentiality of objective aspirations, Arsić's Emerson for whom leave-taking may "set us on the journey of a life worthy of keeping" (*On Leaving* 23), and the ethical issue of Nussbaum's "flourishing"—Cavell's "cheer of thinking" would adopt a tonal posture of optimism, even in the acknowledgment of impossibility.

In some respects surprisingly, since Cavell himself resisted the idea of calling Emerson a pragmatist, several recent studies, beginning with Joan Richardson's *A Natural History of Pragmatism* (2007), have extended Cavell's reading by tracing a pragmatist throughline in American literature, centralized around Emerson, and connecting Jonathan Edwards, the Jameses, Wallace Stevens, Gertrude Stein, John Dewey, and Ralph Ellison.[24] For Richardson, Edwards first, and then a line of American writers, "sought out and studied timely scientific descriptions in order to be able to imagine the moving structure in which they lived" in order to "provide the signals for positive action" (11). Reading American literature through pragmatism emphasizes both its adaptation to environment and its activity in producing and altering that environment. Thinking in these accounts becomes something more impersonal, more dynamic, less what we do with the world and more what the world does with us. Thus, for Richardson, the American aesthetic obtains in linguistic distortions that "are mimetic of feelings entertained, animal responses to what exists as matter of fact" (10). These pragmatist readings illuminate how American literature employs language to break down distinctions between fact and feeling, and thus re-imagines the potential for productive thought and action in the wake of skepticism's challenge to individual autonomy. "Thoughts are actions in American literature," Andrea Knutson writes, a conflation that necessitates "the articulation of a habit of thinking in order to guide that movement which results in cultural revision" (12).

Whether moving toward cultural revision, getting "to possibilities of personal or cultural renewal" (Poirier 11), or performing a ministerial function "requisite to keeping a community together" (Richardson 3), these studies return a renewed appreciation for the complex communitarian and progressive strategies associated with an optimistic strain of American literature. Yet perhaps because of pragmatism's emphasis on instrumentality and action, this positive emphasis has had less to say about the other skeptical, apparently pessimistic strain in American literature. Richardson bypasses Poe, Hawthorne, and Melville because she wants to concentrate on American writers free to experiment with the ability to move forward as a community.[25] Hawthorne and Melville are dragged down by their "outworn" religious dispensations, and Poe is clearly a puzzle, since, despite his reading in science and his influence on the pragmatist Peirce, he "did not express ministerial purpose" (12). One significant exception to the pragmatist avoidance of American literature's more skeptical authors is Paul Grimstad's recent study which inserts both Poe and Melville into the evolution from Emerson to James.[26] Grimstad shows how, on a linguistic and compositional level, Poe's and Melville's deployments of experience as experiment coincide with the broader pragmatist function of "wording the world into something shareable and meaningful" (14). Thinking about experience as publicly conditioned rather than an autonomous affective encounter, Grimstad brackets tone to better account for composition as procedural, as a dynamic that flowers out of the tension between general and particular in the act of writing. Yet this might still be brought round to terror, for if, as Grimstad concludes concerning Melville, "the relation of writing to experience shifts from faithful portraiture to the making sensuous of the way one thing can be made to stand for another" (89), then what might it mean when those exchanges are couched in anxiety, skepticism, or terror?

The pragmatist readings of American literature give a much-needed and developing argument for the philosophical outcomes of the optimistic tradition. Through pragmatism, one gains a sense of how those authors engaged with and offered complicated yet dynamic alternatives to the dark cynicisms and dreadful authority of Calvinist predestination and epistemological skepticism. In this Emersonian evolution, the mood of thought is always cheered and "the task of onwardness" (Cavell, "Thinking of Emerson" 138) presses forward toward a forever-unfolding hope that abandons despair. A skeptic, such as Melville in his darker moods, might call such an evolution a utilitarian compromise, a quailing before the admittedly unfairly advantaged God and Nature. A pragmatic idealist, such as Emerson, would see Melville's alternative—the framing of philosophy's mission as radical agon—as a commitment to despair, as a deliberate madness, or at best, as a pathological residue of fossilized religious doctrine. Melville, in fact, made the incommensurability of these two perspectives the thesis of his most famous book: whether one sees Ishmael, in his pragmatic shuffling of beliefs, or Ahab, in his single-minded and doomed epistemological quest, as the hero of that narrative in large part reveals, like a personality test, whether one considers philosophy as a tool that we use or a demand that we must answer.[27]

But even Ishmael and Starbuck can feel the tug of Ahab's madness. And Cavell's essays on Poe's skepticism as well as Grimstad's recognition of pragmatic practices in Poe and Melville make apparent the proximity of the skeptical tradition to the pragmatist one. What remains necessary is some way of accounting for the significance of the tonal difference from the other direction, a way of thinking about the skeptical tradition's "darkness" without translating it into a resigned "despair." Whereas the development of philosophical pragmatism through the thesis texts of American literature has recently been given a compelling narrative, this book's attention to the antithesis texts, and especially to the formation and consequences of their unique tone of darkness, arrives at a rather different outcome. Instead of pragmatism proper, with its connotations of instrumentality and smooth exchange, American terror feeds into the dimmer and less ethically secure modes of poststructuralism. For, although the initial figures of poststructuralist thought emerge from twentieth-century France, they inherit their moods from Baudelaire and Mallarmé, and from them, Edgar Allan Poe. But I do not aim to fully rehearse the lineage from Poe to Derrida, because that story of influence would distract from this book's major purpose: to better define the particular character and consequence of terror as tone. While Richardson would seek to understand how feeling can open new accounts of fact, my insistence on feeling's unique claim on fact leads to a transposition: it isn't the fact that we feel but rather the peculiar feeling of factness that is central to the subjects of my book.

My study is thus informed by scholars who have been drawn toward the skeptical and darker elements of American literature and find in it poststructuralist tendencies. Perhaps as a feature of its intense concern for difference and particularization, some of the most influential scholarship in this line, John Irwin's *The Mystery to a Solution* and Colin (Joan) Dayan's *Fables of Mind*, avoid totalizing claims about American literature, yet at the same time indicate the germ of a tradition in their shared interest in Poe. Dayan sets Poe up as Emerson's opposite, a thinker who, along with Edwards, insists upon the "severe relation to an immutable cosmic plan, and as a result had to replace blind faith with a difficult, dark skepticism" (7). Irwin defines in American literature an "ontotheology (the metaphysical quest for the Absolute)" that becomes "the epistemological question of *figuring* the absolute, that impossible task of imaging something that, because it is infinite, cannot be bounded by a line" (*Mystery to a Solution* xvii). In contrast to the shiftiness of a pragmatist American literature, a poststructuralist American literature dwells upon fixity, in both the inhuman universe and philosophical practice. Or, perhaps more accurately, its dynamic is not marked by forward progress but by the dive of infinite recursion, a repetition of the same within the same. Though the poststructuralist heyday in American literary studies may be past, it would seem to me that its attempt to uncover an American thought that "originates in its own *irony*" (Riddel 44) is better positioned to account for how terror returns more than simply skepticism.[28] What we can recover from poststructuralist readings of American literature, then, has perhaps less to do with linguistic structure and more to do with aesthetics, with the affective experience of thinking.

I do not want, however, the affiliations I notice between terror and poststructuralism to explain terror *as* poststructuralism. On one hand, such philosophical flattening would threaten to lose the particular curve that literary affect gives to an idea. On the other, by only privileging twentieth-century theorists, it might lose the compelling historical story of how their theories themselves are embedded within the intellectual context of the period. That is, my study aims to satisfy both Elizabeth Duquette's call for "philosophical reading," a methodology that finds "key critical concepts, theoretical problems, or structural paradigms *within* texts, rather than importing them from elsewhere" ("Making an Example" 346) and Maurice Lee's call for the "historically minded" to "read within philosophical history . . . not to attenuate theory or cultural studies but rather to advance them through an effort of synthesis that does not exclude philosophy from the domain of politics and culture" (*Slavery* 9). What this book adds is an attention to the darkness itself, the tone of terror, as an analyzable element central to the literary intervention upon philosophy. Whereas earlier poststructuralist readings concentrated on the ideas and logical paradoxes manifest in the language and art of American literature, I seek to write about the feelings, the affect, located somewhere between the portrayals of terror on the page and the feelings of anxiety in the reader. My hypothesis, that this feeling is, in some obscure way, directed toward and delivered over from the methods of logical thinking, raises the methodological problem of how to think about a feeling that is about thinking.

## Methods and Map

In the prior two sections, I have sketched two preliminary lines of argument, the first about how terror disrupts our usual ways of thinking about feeling, the second about how terror may be read as a feeling adapted from a historically specific structure of thinking. The chiastic nature of these moves, shuttling emphasis between the literary affect of terror and the discourse of scientific logic, will hopefully gesture at the immanence of both orientations, even if we must inhabit each position sequentially. In a similar fashion, this book tells two complementary stories about each of the three authors: one which attempts to reveal the historical context of each author's unique evocations of terror, and another that considers the particular aesthetic effects of their works as contributions to those intellectual contexts. By looking at each author in two ways, I try to balance the relation between terror and thinking that emerges from their work.

A word here should be said about my choice of authors and texts. There is terror in other works of American literature across the 125 years my case studies span. I am not trying to make an exclusive argument. For instance, in early projections of this book, familiar names such as Hawthorne and Dickinson were included, and less familiar names such as Charles Brockden Brown and George Lippard competed for attention. That they do not command chapters themselves owes to two factors. First, it would not have been practically expedient. The method of applying close readings for theoretical content alongside recovering historical contexts already strains the size of the chapters, so some omission is necessary. Moreover, arranging the chapters in more topical, less author-specific fashion might have enabled a wider coverage, but at the expense of the particular understanding of each text. I want to make general claims, but to ground them in specific evidence, in the historical and textual particulars of the literature, and that requires a density of ground that would subvert the sweep of a general historical study.

So why these three? What joins Edwards, Poe, and Melville is not only their evocation of terror in many of their literary works but, moreover, their interest in the methods of philosophy and metaphysics and, most importantly, in terror itself. Whereas Brockden Brown and Lippard were interested in political philosophy and ethics, and Hawthorne and Dickinson were more attuned to the subjective construction of the individual in society, Edwards, Poe, and Melville all shared a deep, though strained, regard for epistemology and existential questions of metaphysical speculation. They posed similar philosophical questions in their literature—What is the nature of self? Can the will be free? How do we ascertain truth in a world of appearances?—and they each found some version of a response in the complex affect of terror. But most importantly, these three writers not only used terror, but they theorized it. Whereas Hawthorne and Brown and Lippard each generate terror in their works, Edwards and Poe and Melville write *about* terror, about the power of that feeling, and actively work to gain for the strange passion a greater legitimacy. In this book on terror in American literature, I have chosen the three writers who not only best exemplify the particular and unique terror that American literature offers, but who also themselves offer the richest theories about terror.

This book begins with Edwards and a reassessment of the terrors of orthodox Calvinism. Most accounts of the "darker" tone of American literature sense a connection between that tone and the centrality of the fear of hell in the Puritan culture of early New England. By comparing the hellfire sermons of earlier generations of Puritan ministers with those of the Great Awakening, my first chapter shows how the significance of terror in the religious and communal life of New England turns from being a cautionary and practical rhetoric of avoiding evil external influences to, in later generations, being an immanent and ideal rhetoric of confronting the evil in oneself. Sponsoring this turn in terror is a concurrent shift in the significance of affect, and in affective experience in general. The central figure to the paradigm shift is Jonathan Edwards, the philosopher-minister who not only wrote some of the most effective terror sermons, but who also built an entirely new philosophy of affective identity to endorse them. In his debate with Boston conservative Charles Chauncy, Edwards defends the methods and manner, the totalizing terror, of the Awakening; and what the defense culminates in—the philosophy of affective identity—bears the residual structure of its foundational affection, terror. Thus, the first half of the chapter shows not only how unique Jonathan Edwards's religious terror was, but also how important that new terror was to his philosophical thought.

The second half of the chapter addresses how Edwards's early idealism and deep interest in logic and metaphysics shaped his unique vision of affect. It is no new revelation that Edwards's theology is inflected by the idealist metaphysics that marks his early writing. However, by considering the sources for his metaphysical speculation, the influence of the *Port-Royal Logic* and other logic textbooks, I show how the new terror defined in the first half of the chapter obtains a structural resemblance to the abstract space of geometry and the method of thinking more essentially. Edwards was attracted to the metadiscourse of method, the idea that the way one thinks affects what one comes to know. And as the Calvinist beliefs in the lack of free will and total dependence upon God drew from a rigorous rethinking of intellectual method, so too may Edwards's strange new terrors—the terrible tone of damnation and hellfire—be seen to bear, in grasping after the infinite and in portraying the affective subject reduced to nothingness, the tone of objectivity, or more precisely, the tone of the impossible task of objectivity, carried out through method and authorized by the feeling of first principles.

The second writer of my study, Edgar Allan Poe, was born nearly fifty years after Jonathan Edwards died. In the interim, the American Revolution, the new republic, and the widespread escalation of manufacturing and industrial capacities made Poe's United States a radically different context than Edwards's colonial New England. Still, one context was similar: just as the Awakening revivals inscribed the importance of emotion to Edwards's communities, so too did the renewed rhetoric of sentiment and sensation, the cult of feeling, in Poe's United States reawaken affect and an interest in aesthetics. Poe's horror stories at first seem merely to exploit these new feelings, operating as sensational mechanisms meant only to evoke lurid feelings. However, a closer study of his so-called dead woman tales reveals a calculated structure that raises aesthetic feeling by reflecting upon it, a recursion reminiscent of Edwards's infinite terrors. In the second chapter, I define this structure, showing how it develops alongside Poe's interest in the aesthetic theory of the Jena school. The constructiveness of Poe's aesthetic, his belief in an absolute homology between form and effect, turns his tales into something like alchemical formulas—their terror, he asserts, is the terror of the soul. Charting the operations of soul and mind, Poe's dead woman tales, in their recursive plot of return, gain effectiveness by destabilizing the metaphor of mind as enclosure. Attempts to know, figured as operations of framing the object, are doomed in Poe's fiction. The terror, though, does not come just from the failure of the framing operation but from the note, continually struck in Poe's work, that this failure is in some sense inherent in the operation itself. No perfect enclosure, say a perfect burial or a perfect crime, can ever be final, because of the trace of its framing. As I turn, in the following chapter, to Poe's later fiction, particularly those horror stories associated with his less emotional but more rigid detective tales, I show how the method of Poe's fiction (putting the frame into its own frame) anticipates poststructuralism's critique of disciplinary knowledge.

The horrors of mind, in the recursive plot of return, inform Poe's interest in analysis as literary object. The third chapter turns from the abstract and inchoate terror of philosophy in the dead woman tales to the analytical and logical terrors of his detective fiction and his later sublime and confessional tales. Drawing upon analytical method's division of thinking into two steps, resolution and composition, Poe explores the possibility of dramatizing thought as narrative structure. An early precursor to the more formalized detective tales, "The Man of the Crowd" adopts as both its plot and theme this doubling and reciprocal narrative structure. Understanding how that tale's failure to produce stable knowledge despite its adherence to method sheds light on both the innovation responsible for the detective tales' success (the separation of the narrative voice from the analyst's) and the stakes of Poe's confessional and sublime tales, which similarly depend upon the sound and conditions of analytical method. The final sections of the chapter show how the patterns that connect mind and terror—the centripetal and centrifugal tendencies of method—shape both the natural and the psychological oscillations in his sublime and confessional tales.

The two chapters together read Poe's tales as not, or at least not only, critiques of the limits of reason but rather as experiments through which he imagined a literature modeled upon objective method. That these tales are frequently terrifying, however, should not be taken as a sign of their shortcomings but, as in Edwards's terror of conviction, as a display of their truth. Poe's strange detective fiction may have become the darling of poststructuralism for its austere arrangement of analytical postures, but by recovering the fundamental terror through which that pattern of oscillating and self-defeating thought was developed, these chapters on Poe help define what Rei Terada calls the "feeling in theory"—the affective yet nonsubjective basis for deconstructive critical methodology.[29] Ultimately, what endorses such a critical methodology cannot be any local or political action that issues from it but rather, at heart, the feeling of reason's implacable demands of objectivity.

If for Edwards terror became a mode and model of certain knowledge, and for Poe that terror enabled the literary exploration of the methods underlying that knowledge, Herman Melville finds in this epistemological terror, and in the paradoxes of its doubled pattern, the agonistic character of the metaphysical subject/object divide. Whereas Edwards and Poe extrapolate from the intellectual method of Enlightenment logic, Melville's charged acquaintance with German metaphysics helps determine the darkening philosophical mood of the works from the middle of his career. The fourth chapter of this book provides a stronger context for his relationship with George Adler, the professor of German literature with whom Melville bonded during his influential trip to Europe in 1849. Through Adler, Melville would have been impressed with both the stakes of post-Kantian philosophy as well as the fearful and paranoid tenor of someone who would live by their commitments. Dialectical method, as an answer to the problem of ground in subject/object logic, informs the dialectical treatment of philosophy as balance, the transcendentalist attitude of Ishmael and the stoic attitude of Ahab, in *Moby-Dick* (1851). The multiple terrors of the book thus arise not as against any particular philosophical outlook but rather from the application of dialectical method to the problem of dialectical method itself. The way this study, routed through Edwards and Poe, appraises *Moby-Dick* emphasizes how the problem of knowing becomes the situation of terror, how even the balanced tolerance of a transcendentalist and dialectical position leads to a fear of the uneven certainty it occludes.

My final chapter performs a unified analysis of the discrete tales that make up Melville's *The Piazza Tales* (1856). Whereas Melville had noticed the terrors of uneven balance corresponding to dialectical method in *Moby-Dick*, it is in his later short fiction that the phenomenon of that terror underwrites specifically human encounters between felt subject and perceived other. Looking at the origin of difference that empowers dialectical method, then, Melville's tales come to parallel, in their privileging of fear, Kierkegaard's and Heidegger's theorization of dread as the baseline ground of subjective experience. Melville's several manipulations of the categories of space and time in *The Piazza Tales* can thus be read as ways to get at that phenomenological dread which precedes sense experience. The final text of this study, "The Bell-Tower" (1855), brings together the tropes of dread of the other tales—the distorting effects of space, the absolute mark of time—with a common gothic motif, that of the automaton. What I argue is that, contrary to expectations, Melville's fatal automaton does not in the end represent the human as object but rather as the perfect human subject whose very possibility and recognition is felt by the dread of our difference from it. Whereas this book begins with the terrors of objectivity, of the bitter yet irresistible fruit of reason's authority, it ends with a portrait of the terror of subjectivity, perfectly idealized in the figure of the inhuman automaton.

The depth of the textual and historical analysis of these authors' changing engagement with matters of mind and terror enriches an often-felt, but not yet narrated, thread of influence between American literature and the development of poststructuralism. If, to combine at once the claims of Matthiessen and Cavell, the thesis of American literature is its commitment to democracy and the prelude to pragmatism, the antithesis of American literature, as I argue here, is its commitment to the aesthetics of paradox and the prelude to poststructuralism. From Edwards to Poe to Melville—three writers who felt a similar pull to analyze the methods of mind through forms of feeling—this book charts the development of the "powers of blackness" in American literature against the development and abstraction of method as the formal mode of philosophy. The arc of my study follows the history of an idea—that terror is the special feeling of objective truth—as it emerges in Edwards's logic-based hellfire, is schematized in Poe's materialist aesthetics of formal horror, and finally coalesces in the dread of Melville's portrait of inhuman subjectivity.

I come at the end of this introduction to a bizarre problem, for I want to say something about what one might learn from this book's story, to what use its thesis might be put, how it might benefit the shared mission of humanist scholarship. But it is through resistance to this very urge for purposive accounting that terror constitutes itself; to say that knowing this story may help us in the future would be to verge on a translation of terror that elides what makes it distinctive. Yet, to say that this book is useless to others would be perverse, soul crushing. The commonsense answer would be that this book does not itself belong to the works of terror that it analyzes; it relates a chapter of American literary history in which a set of influential authors, driven by historical circumstance and philosophically informed aesthetic conviction, sought to reframe thought through terror as an artistic device. The book shows how literary tone can be philosophical and provides an instance of how an aesthetic effect explains thought and is not wholly explained by it.

But the more ambitious answer would try to honor the recalcitrance of terror, the way that it implicates, to a degree, the criticism that would fit it into a progressive narrative. Any message then would be conditioned by Poe's imp: what interests us is not always that which benefits us. Yet, as the feeling of thinking, terror additionally asserts that the rift between an economy of interest and an economy of utility is not irrational but rather what reason itself exacts (reason as a means that works insofar as it brackets ends). If terror helps us, it will be in ways that we cannot predict, for its genetic signature is one of exploration, of disinterested study, of objective truth. Thus, to be unable to specify at the outset the final benefit of terror directs us to a space where "pure" science and "pure" art meet: in an ultimately contingent account of the human's estrangement from both perfect subject and perfect object, where voyages are braved, thrills are pursued, and books are written, not wholly for our sakes nor for their own sakes only. What deeper engine, what more intractable ghost, then inspires? In the darkness of American literature, the answer is neither an enduring presence nor a distressing absence but rather a tone that reflects the thought that asks.

# 1

## AWAKENING TERROR

Hellfire Preaching, Jonathan Edwards, and the Logic of Revivalist Affect

**IN EARLY SEPTEMBER 1741**, the twenty-five-year-old itinerant preacher James Davenport found himself in the house of New Haven's long-established minister Reverend Joseph Noyes, defending his claim that Noyes was a "[w]olf in Sheep's cloathing" (Clap et al. 2) to an audience of Noyes's supporters. According to Davenport, Noyes was too lenient in explaining away the distresses of his parishioners. Noyes had, according to Davenport, assuaged the fears of a woman who had deep convictions of her own sinfulness, had "deadened" the passions of awakened persons with his preaching, and had suggested that a view of one's own sinfulness is easily accomplished (3). Davenport's accusations, along with Noyes's responses, were recorded and the informal gathering prepared to adjourn. What happened next might best be described as prayer-crashing. According to witnesses, Davenport began praying aloud: "[W]ithout any Notice given, while divers in the Room were talking loud, and others smoking and some with their Hatts on, he began a Prayer, but there being so much Noise in the Room he was hardly heard at first, many kept on talking, others cryed out stop him, the Rev. Mr. *Noyes* spoke once or twice and said, Mr. *Davenport* I forbid you Praying in my House without my leave; but he persisted and went on in the midst of the greatest Noise, Confusion and Consternation, and declared Mr. *Noyes* an unconverted Man, and his People to be as Sheep without a Shepherd" (3). After being subjected to censure in his own house, given by an upstart young preacher twenty-eight years his junior and a stranger to his community, Noyes told Davenport to leave and not come back.

This relatively tame episode in the spectacularly tumultuous religious crises of American history now known as the Great Awakening illustrates the clash not only of differing doctrines but of different modes of discourse. Noyes and his followers invite Davenport to explain his criticism of Noyes, sequestering him in a private meeting with the elite learned men of the parish. Such a remove would favor the conservative Noyes; Davenport, the outspoken evangelist, was known as a crowd favorite, capable of exciting whole congregations with his passionate sermons and histrionics. Noyes sought to corner Davenport into a rational debate according to a long-established tradition of inquiry and evidence in settling congregational disputes. And at first, this is what occurred. But what happened next, Davenport's breach of decorum and his condemnation of Noyes, was of a single impulse; Davenport's behavior didn't just attack one minister but refused the entire set of assumptions that underlay the mode of the inquiry itself: the boundaries between private and public, between theory and practice, between religious theology and lived social life—in short, the whole orthodox hierarchy of the congregational "New England Way."

Yet for all their generational and political differences, the specific difference between Noyes and Davenport comes to a head over the significance and place of one single emotion: terror. Noyes considers the fears of his parishioners to be unfortunate states that it is the task of the minister to mitigate. In this, Noyes is only voicing the traditional Puritan stance toward fear—that although fear of eternal damnation can be useful in awakening the hardened, dwelling on those fears is to make much of symptoms and to ignore the causes. Davenport, however, attacks Noyes for downplaying fears and passions. For him, as for the majority of "New Light" revivalists, the affections, and terror chief among them, were not symptoms or secondary qualities of religion but religion itself. Thus it was the minister's job not to "deaden" passions but to raise them to feverish pitches.

And raise them Davenport would. As one shocked churchgoer reported, Davenport's preaching style was no less imprecatory than his parlor manner:

> At length, he turn'd his Discourse to others, and with the *utmost Strength* of his Lungs addrest himself to the Congregation, under these and such-like Expressions; viz. ["]You poor unconverted Creatures, in the Seats, in the Pews, in the Galleries, I wonder you don't drop into Hell! It would not surprise me, I should not wonder at it, if I should see you drop down *now, this Minute* into Hell. You Pharisees, Hypocrites, *now, now, now,* you are going right into the Bot-

tom of Hell. I wonder you don't drop into Hell by *Scores*, and *Hundreds* &c.["]
And in this *terrible Manner*, he ended the Sermon. (qtd. in Chauncy, *Seasonable Thoughts* 98)

Not only does Davenport single out the audience for especial concern—"in the seats, in the pews, in the galleries"—but he offers little consolation to them. We can hear the auditor's surprise at the sermon's truncated ending as much as at the content of the sermon; hellfire sermons were nothing new to the colonies, but they always had, to greater or lesser extent, a happy ending—an application, a call for a change of behavior, or even a dire warning. They didn't merely damn the congregation and leave it wallowing in its damned state.

Instead of comforting his audience, what Davenport does instead is to perform, in a kind of inarticulate dance, the experience of inhabiting such a state: "Then he came out of the Pulpit, and stripped off his upper Garments, and got up into the Seats, and leapt up and down sometime, and clapt his Hands, and *cried out* in those Words, the War goes on, the Fight goes on, the Devil goes down, the Devil goes down; and then betook himself to *stamping* and *screaming* most dreadfully" (qtd. in Chauncy, *Seasonable Thoughts* 99). Descending from the pulpit, Davenport aligns himself with the congregation and leaves absent the apparatus of authority. Leaping and dancing half naked, along with the congregation, in the pews was shocking behavior for a man of God, and its shock registers its symbolic import: rather than use fear to warn, to caution, and to direct from the pulpit, Davenport, and the revival in general, saw fear as a state to inhabit, the religious feeling of that renegotiation of power from pulpit to pew.

Scholarship on the Great Awakening has focused on its antinomian and latently proto-republican aspects.[1] Davenport, the populist voice disrespectful of decorum or establishment, shouting down the established Noyes may be read as an instance of what Nancy Ruttenburg has termed democratic personality, "a process of individuation unconnected to the concept of citizenship, announcing itself through the exercise of an authoritative, public voice unconnected to rational debate in a Habermasian public sphere" (*Democratic Personality* 3). Although Davenport's supporters will eventually lose the local battle, this compelling reading of the period holds that the latent populism of the revival would prepare the way for the articulation of democracy. In such an account, Davenport and the revival that he participated in would be both socially and politically significant—as harbingers of the populist republican sentiment to flower later in the revolution.

But in moving to the political ramifications of these antinomian episodes, scholarship on the revival period has had less to say about the particular content and ostensible cause of the dispute. Davenport, remember, charges Noyes with ignoring vital terror, and his own sermons come under fire for their stark use of terror. The traditional reading of this terror would say that terror is of the past, a holdover from the hellfire and humiliation sermons of a more orthodox tradition. But even if, or especially if, Davenport's unorthodox conduct presages the democratic revolution, the conventions and modes by which he operates, the inciting and championing of terror, may be subject to revaluation. How can we read Davenport as both liberal—as champion of the individual popular voice—and at the same time radically conservative—inciting the fears of hell that would seem to belong to an older, more archaic tradition? To make sense of how this terror could point in two directions at once, how terror finds itself at the center of a dispute with not only religious but political and social implications as well, requires not only the testimony of an eyewitness or the explanation of a religious historian but also the speculation of a philosopher attuned to the peculiar state of emotion.

It isn't George Whitefield, Gilbert Tennent, or James Davenport—the famous itinerant preachers of the time—but Jonathan Edwards, now known best for his own terror sermon "Sinners in the Hands of an Angry God," who comes to theorize terror by defending it. Witness to the revival, minister of its most famous sermon, and philosophical defender of its legitimacy, Jonathan Edwards found himself, in order to defend terror preaching, completely reconceptualizing the place of emotion in psychological and religious identity. Edwards's relation to terror, however, has been a topic of some disagreement. Perry Miller, who in the middle of the twentieth century probably did the most to secure Edwards in the literary canon, initially saw Edwards as laced through and through with terror, writing: "[T]he terror he imparted was the terror of modern man, the terror of insecurity" (*Jonathan Edwards* 147). In the early 1980s, Norman Fiering tempered the claim, suggesting that Edwards's obsession with terror is, on the surface at least, incompatible with the personality that emerges from his less fiery work: "How could a man as deeply sensitive and tender as he appears to have been, . . . dwell so unflinchingly upon the most excruciating and unimaginable horrors?" (201). Fiering's answer is that the hellfire in Edwards was the hellfire of Edwards's fathers, and his repeated turns to it were part of a psychological struggle in which he attempted to convince himself of doctrine which he and his age had begun to doubt. More recently, in

2005, Norton Anthology editor Philip Gura has suggested that the important Edwards, the one that should be anthologized, is not the terrible one of "Sinners in the Hands of an Angry God" but the sensitive and sympathetic one of *The Life of David Brainerd*. Edwards's hellfire, for Gura, is "atypical" and makes Edwards seem "a curious artifact of a lost century, not a vital part of America's literary tradition" (92). Terror, at first the vehicle for Edwards's introduction to American literature, has seemed to have aged into an outdated eyesore, an obstacle to Edwards's rehabilitation in the literary canon.

Turning away from terror and toward Edwards's philosophy of experience, one productive strain of recent criticism has encountered a more progressive Edwards, one who seeks to reconnect the mind with the world and whose insistent deprecations of an autonomous self serve to foreground a more pragmatist interleaving of thought and environment. Elisa New privileges *consent* in Edwards's philosophy, a term she takes as smudging sharp distinctions between a human's will and God's, offering instead affectionate correspondences that privilege "adhesive attachment and connectedness" (*The Line's Eye* 243). As the autonomous self dissolves into a flux of worldly and divine forces, what comes to the fore is "a metaphysics of greater fullness than one either driven by subjects or driven by objects" (63). Filling out the scientific contexts for this pragmatist Edwards, Joan Richardson similarly finds, in Edwards's reading of Newton's optics, a theory of light that would enrich the perceptual basis of this consensual exchange, one that, by "reconceiving dependence, not as submission and passivity . . . but as the activity of consent," ultimately "optimiz[es] the choices for successful survival of the spirit" (60). This emerging pragmatist version of Edwards is considerably brighter and more ethically progressive than earlier accounts; his unrelenting hell-borne attacks on any conception of self-sufficiency become preparatory to a fuller Emersonian tradition of action and belief within one's environment, a continuous unfolding that constitutes a "[g]lory never divided because always joining" (New, *The Line's Eye* 295).

As central as Edwards becomes to pragmatism's foundation in this narrative, one may still wonder about Edwards's more orthodox commitments—his sense of sin, his hellfire preaching, his use of terror—that are remaindered in the transition to Emerson. Just as one could imagine Edwards appreciating the superabundance in a universe within which the human and the natural are in a continually shifting state of mutual definition, one could also imagine Edwards fretting about the secularizing consequences of pragmatism and the drift toward the transcendental, in which someone might blasphemously think that becoming part and parcel of God might be achieved in any way other than through an unrelenting sense of one's own worthlessness and sin.[2] Michael Colacurcio, for instance, also notices the similarities between Edwards's and Emerson's idealisms but marks a crucial difference: "[T]he opposite sort of power" of Edwards's idealism "ultimately contrived to hand the whole world, including its own consciousness and that of every other man, over to *God Alone*" (97). Thus when Edwards finally takes down material "reality," it is not to open positive potentialities or the space for a new ethics but to hollow out once and for all the negative lack at the center of original sin. In Colacurcio's reading, sin is the site of Edwards's last stand against the pantheism toward which he felt his idealism leading.[3] For all the flexibility and adjustment in Edwards's system, it depends ultimately upon an absolute, the concept of sin that, as Marilynne Robinson notes, "is the little mote that makes him create a pearl" (3). Perhaps Edwards takes this stand in sin because sin is where difference belies smooth identifications, where negation snags loose a thread in the pragmatist weave of God, self, and nature.

In the same vein, Sharon Cameron, outlining the furthest consequences of Edwards's "hard-core commitment to impersonality" (214n), shows how the very vehicle of idealism—the self's dependence and nothingness—unravels any conception of correspondence between heaven and world, God and natural man. What she calls the "disalignment of Edwards's presence-chamber [heaven] and world" (49) is a disabling disproportion. Set at a distance, the human and the divine unhinge, and a late-career Edwards pursues "an ideal, indifferent to the fact that, according to Edwards's characterizations, it could not be implemented" (214n). Paradoxically, even perversely, committed to working out an idealist impersonality beyond the point at which it stops being useful, this Edwards would evacuate the self not into the plenitude of dynamic nature and experience but rather into the harshest scarcity of rule-bound and static quantitative abstraction. Colacurcio and Cameron would check a too-smooth adoption of a pragmatist Edwards, reminding us of the rigorous, uncompromising orthodox minister whose sense of sin—the individual's disalignment from God—and radical impersonality eclipse recoverable outcomes for action or ethics in this world. In other words, if "a metaphysics of greater fullness" is taken as Edwards's contribution, that metaphysics must constantly be reminded of the hole at its heart, the vital site of nothingness that not only drives its fricative unfolding but also, considered rigorously, renders that fullness finally and categorically inaccessible to us as persons.

This chapter builds on Colacurcio's and Cameron's case by exploring how Edwards's negative "opposite sort of power" develops through a historical and theoretical engagement with the affect of terror. Without constructing Edwards as a one-note firebrand, I argue that terror is not opposed to sensitivity, and that to ignore or de-emphasize the power of his terrors is to miss what originally drew attention to Edwards in the first place. What is needed is not more sympathy and less terror, but a deeper regard for what makes Edwards's terror special and how it organizes the affective revolution in the revival. The first part of this chapter qualifies Fiering's assumption, that Edwards's terror is inherited seamlessly from an older Puritan tradition. To that end, I reconsider the difference in hellfire preaching between the late seventeenth century and the revivals of the early eighteenth century. I then go on in the second part of the chapter to address Gura's intimation that Edwards was not really as obsessed with terror as the sermon "Sinners in the Hands of an Angry God" would portray. In order to ascertain just how atypical his hellfire is, I survey Edwards's sermons and situate his own brand of hellfire as central to the period's changing conceptions of affect. The third part of the chapter considers Edwards's defense of terror in his debate with Charles Chauncy during the Awakening. I argue that the structural logic of terror informs Edwards's turn to affect as a mode of direct religious knowledge. By recovering these contexts for Edwards's terror, this chapter turns, in its final section, to the relation between terror and Cameron's sense of Edwards's impersonality. Forged through the crucible of the revival, Edwards's concept of terror becomes the affective corollary to the fundamental site of sin in his theology, a feeling of truth that rejects the very thing that feels it.

### Inhabitable Terror

In today's parodies and satires, the figure of the hellfire preacher is a sign of the old conservative Puritan patriarchy. But what did that figure, cut by Davenport—whose own popularity in newspapers of the time is a mixture of reverence and ridicule—mean to his own audiences? Hadn't those unforgettably named Puritan divines, Increase and Cotton Mather, preached terror as well? The Mathers may have refrained from disrobing in the pews, but wasn't the substance of their terror and Davenport's—the fear of being damned to hell's fires—basically the same?

The question of the significance of Puritan expressions of terror, and especially the changing nature of that expression over the seventeenth and eighteenth centuries, has been the site of influential studies that use the jeremiad sermon as an index to the period's cultural dynamics. The changes in the jeremiad's traditional imprecatory form, according to these studies, reflect wider social and theological tectonics. Perry Miller, for instance, points to a shift in 1652, when the jeremiad's list of God's punishments comes to include the sinfulness of the people themselves. According to Miller, in this turn inward, "the subjective preëmpted the objective: a universal anxiety and insecurity had become no longer something, which, being caused, could be allayed by appropriate action, but rather something so chronic that the society could do nothing except suffer" (*From Colony to Province* 28). The effect on the jeremiad was that, for the next forty years, its terrors became the expression of a people caught between an absolute theological imperative and an emerging capitalist expediency. The jeremiads, in Miller's view, thus become accommodating and cathartic; through them the New England society found "a method for paying tribute to their sense of guilt and yet for moving with the times" (51). Yet, instead of reading the terrors of the late-seventeenth-century jeremiads as thus pharisaical, false shudders merely servicing future crimes, Miller reiterates in sweeping language that the New England people "had not closed their eyes to the illogical and unconfinable terrors of the universe" (*The Seventeenth Century* 489) and more generally, that whenever people confront such "gigantic power . . . they invariably must find means of coming to terms with it, of bringing it into friendship," not just for themselves or for their human ends, "but for that of the lawless, brutal force itself" (490). Terror, in Miller's view, pulses behind the paradoxes and contradictions, obviating any easy elision of economic and psychological histories.

Qualifying Miller's claims by pointing at the jeremiad's paradoxical optimism, Sacvan Berkovitch finds its terrors corrective rather than confessional. Subtly marked by the shift in tone consequent on substituting "anxiety" for "terror," Berkovitch emphasizes hellfire's positive function. Making "anxiety its end as well as its means," the rhetorical heat of the jeremiads functioned "to create a climate of anxiety that helped release the restless 'progressivist' energies required for the success of the venture" (*American Jeremiad* 23). Where Miller had seen an enduring contradiction and incoherence, Berkovitch finds a smooth junction wherein structures of feeling endorse an ideological consensus that issues in the growth of an "increasingly pervasive middle-class hegemony" (xiii).

The stakes of terror's significance are thus tied to scale. For Miller, terror is the counterweight to economic progress, and it seeks to eclipse worldly concerns by widening the scale of value to the universal absolute, to a radically exploded view in which the "illogical and unconfinable terrors of the universe" are momentarily acknowledged. For Berkovitch, terror is the handmaiden to social progress, and by redrawing the scale as cultural history, the appeal to the universal absolute becomes functionally an adaptation to the new pressures of an industrializing world. Remarkably, put in such terms, this difference between Miller and Berkovitch is emblematized within the balance of consolation and terror in the jeremiads they study. On one hand, inculcating a constant sense of anxiety fuels a progressive turn in American culture, underwrites American proto-nationalistic tendencies, and validates imperialist violence.[4] Yet, on the other hand, terror is, as Miller finds, more fundamental than functional, and its outscaling of historical and cultural concerns threatens its reformative and progressive functions. That is, if the jeremiads of the late seventeenth century tried to tame the terrors of hell in service of progressive outward action, then perhaps the explosion of concern over terror preaching in the revivals of the 1730s and 1740s marks the functional limit of a constantly inculcated anxiety. To determine this question further, I want to consider the rhetorical differences in the depictions of hell and terror between the late-seventeenth-century sermon and its revivalist counterpart.

Turning to the hellfire sermons published during the two generations preceding the Awakening reveals both similarities and discontinuities.[5] While it is true that some aspects of hell are eternal—hell is always hot and uncomfortable, it is almost always infinite in duration, it is where sinners go, and so on—its figuration during the period does vary, and with the minute adaptations of figuration, so too does its purpose. For the late-seventeenth-century ministers—including Increase and Cotton Mather, John Webb, and Edwards's grandfather, Solomon Stoddard—the first and foremost outcome of preaching terror was reformed behavior. They preached what might be considered the basic jeremiad: things are getting worse and there's hell to pay, therefore change your behavior or else. For the cadre of later revivalist, "New Light" preachers—including Whitefield, Israel Loring, Gilbert Tennent, William Cooper, and Jonathan Edwards—the outcome of preaching terror was not reformed behavior but conversion. To this end, the jeremiad might be seen as inverted: things are getting better, and if you don't get on board soon there will be hell to pay. For the imprecatory sermons of the Mathers, the danger is one of crashing the collective bus—of somehow abandoning or mishandling the divine errand. For the awakenings of Edwards and Tennent, the danger is one of missing the bus altogether—of the millennial fear of being left at the station.

One indication of this shift in purpose is a subtle redirection of the hellfire sermon's intended audience. For the elder Mather, Increase, hell was best used to threaten specific groups of sinners off their characteristic sin. To drinkers he says: "Drunkards, tremble at this! Do you not see Hell gaping for you, and opening her mouth wide to receive your Souls, when once they are out of your Bodies?" (*Wo to Drunkards* 26). To naughty children he says: "You Children that disobey . . . the ravens are like to feed upon you" (*The Wicked mans Portion* 210). From rowdy drinkers, to misbehaving children, to women who preen over their "false Locks . . . like *Comets*, about their heads" (*Heavens alarm* 37), the targets of Increase Mather's sermons are types of the fallen and rough synecdoches for the community. But the specific audience for the sermon is always to a degree delimited by the occasion. The drunkards, for instance, are lectured after a tavern burns down. The children, receiving the brunt of an execution sermon, are asked to imagine themselves as the corpse of the executed, being eaten under the gallows by the ravens circling the scene. And, proving that there is no figurative stretch too great for the elder Mather, the warning to women with false curling, comet-like locks comes after a spectacularly bright comet is seen in December of 1680. Increase's typological bent sees fearful signs everywhere, but in parceling them out, he apportions each horror to its deserving sin and its offending sinner.

The artful pairing of condemnation to the individual and occasional sin in Increase Mather's and other ministers' late-seventeenth-century sermons may be understood as belonging to the "gentle way in punishment" theorized by Michel Foucault as developing between the older forms of torture and the soon-to-be forms of disciplinary and corrective reform.[6] What distinguishes this mode of punishment is that "[i]t is an art of conflicting energies, an art of images linked by association, the forging of stable connections that defy time" (104). And in order to do so, the punishment imagined must "be transparent" to the crime such that "it will be infallibly the sign of the crime that it punishes" (105). What Foucault notices in the evolution of punishment situates the theoretical stakes of the reciprocal punishments offered by early colonial hellfire sermons. These sermons work in the realm of representation; they set up stable links between crime and punishment and thus fantasize (since the punishments here are *not* visible) the notion of the individual as the "subject of law, through the reinforcement of the systems of signs and representations that they circulate" (128).

If, in this "gentle way," the tortures of hell became linked to social crime, and their contemplation turned sinners into the signs of the law, then one of the effects is to reinscribe a division between the interpretive community and the external sign of sin to be read. As a corollary, the dangers of hell and sin are insistently figured as outside the church. As Urian Oakes notes in the introduction to one of Increase Mather's more inclement sermons: "The design of this Discourse is . . . to get into the Gap, and make up the Hedge, that the Evils threatened and approaching may not break in upon us, but there may be a lengthening out of our Tranquility." It is "their" bodies that blaze out, not "your" bodies, as they will become in the terror of the revival. Or, to be more precise, although hellfire sermons throughout the period use the pronoun "you" to address those in danger of hell, in the earlier sermons the "you" is always understood as an unfortunate subsection, the drinkers or the misbehaving children, of the whole. The "you" of the later sermons is much more abstract. Davenport's audience—"in the seats, in the pews, in the galleries"—allows no space for evasion even as it makes terror accessible to all. In contradistinction to the universalizing trend in the revival, the hellfire sermon of the late seventeenth century was manifestly exclusionary: a call to arms against encroaching forces of evil, to "get into the gap" and seal the threatening breaches. As Andrew Delbanco argues, these third-generation Puritans, cultivating a theme of ends, discard earlier accounts of the privative nature of sin in order to find evil in the outside world, "sin as excrescence, disease—the threatening other—against which the community of purist selves builds barricades" (*Puritan Ordeal* 221).

One effect of the late-seventeenth-century hellfire sermon's outward and exclusionary rhetoric is an emphasis on reformation in which the horror of hell is a deterrent to social and public behavior. No one would dare charge Increase Mather with Arminianism, the belief that doing good works might "earn" one a place in heaven, but in *Heaven's Alarm to the World* (1682), he comes close to that heretical notion by ending on an imperative to reform behavior: "And there is one thing more, that should in special be remembered by us; a thing that hath been much talked of, but little hath been done in it, that is, *Reformation! Reformation!*" (36). Reform is the driving force of Increase's hellfire sermons, and the fear of hell should make not only for more frequent prayer, but more importantly, for a better society: "Ah! *New-England*, . . . shall there not be so much as an *external Reformation* of those things that provoke the glorious eyes of Heaven?" (37). Just as the audience of the sermon was determined by external behavior and social station, so the result of the hellfire message is registered in "external reformation."

Reforming sins in the personal and the social becomes the ultimate outcome of Increase's often-republished hellfire sermon cycle, *The Greatest Sinners* (1686). *The Greatest Sinners* depicts Judgment Day in its particulars, arguing that it will be a "fiery day" (74) and that sinners will tremble when they hear the sentence that they must "be thrown *alive* into the lake which burns with fire and Brimstone" (76). The final "use" of the sermon would seem a pietistic one—to engage in secret prayer. But notice how that private will shades into public action:

> O be much in prayer, especially in *Secret* prayer, and you shall be rewarded *openly* in the Day of Judgment. Alas, there's many a wretched man that will think with himself *at that day*, Oh if I had spent that time in secret prayer and Communion with God, which I spent in vain Company, in unprofitable discourses, in Taverns, in mad merry meetings; my soul might have been saved . . . whereas now, because I have been an unprofitable Servant, I must be cast into outer and Eternal Darkness. Oh then, Let every man practice *Now*, as he will at that DAY wish he had done. (94)

In this all-important directive, the turn inward becomes a turn outward, and private considerations of future estate become public actions of the present day. One can hear, layered in the language, an economic undertone—spending and profit circulate through Mather's imperative such that personal religious feeling (my soul might have been saved) becomes enterprising action, taken for the profit of a wider and greater interest (to be a profitable Servant). The fires of hell may scorch sinners into private repentance, but also, and more importantly, to public practice, to "external Reformation" of the corporate body of the New England congregational community.

The assumption of reformation through terror is made explicit in the most complete pre-Awakening defense of terror preaching made by Edwards's grandfather, Solomon Stoddard. In "The Efficacy of the Fear of Hell" (1713), Stoddard seconds Increase's demand for reform, and points out the "*great benefit to many Men, if they had more of the fear of Hell*" (14). Stoddard names as fear's beneficiaries sets of social identities: "*[i]t would be a great benefit to Parents*" (15), for they would teach their children to behave, for example; or "*[i]t would be a great benefit to Buyers and Sellers*" (20), because it would keep them from bargaining falsely. After explaining how the fear of hell may be used to improve social behavior, Stoddard launches into a fairly conventional description of hell: "*The Miseries of Hell will be exceeding great*" (23), "their *Bodies and Souls* will be *Vessels of wrath*" (24), "Men, Women, Children, all like *light Torches*, . . . Scream out and Roar" (25). Despite the ferocity of image, the significance of those screams is mundanely utilitarian: do not price-gouge your flaxseed.

But even as Stoddard extols the reformative uses of terror, his contemporary, Cotton Mather, begins turning terror inwards. The execution of an ax murderer in 1717 becomes the occasion of one of Cotton Mather's most popular sermons, *A View of the Unseen World*, later published under the title *The Valley of Hinnom*. Like his father, Cotton Mather solicits fear as a deterrent: "Such a *Dread* of the Divine Displeasure whereto our Sin Exposes us, as to Compel our *Flight* unto the only SAVIOUR from *Sin*" (*Valley of Hinnom* 38–39). But Mather also adds a second use, one which corresponds with conversion rather than correction: "The *Fear of GOD* infused into the *Heart*, will make a *New Heart* of it, and a clean One!" (40). Dread, as a deterrence, is the occasion of sin—"whereto our Sin exposes us"—and thus depends on a system in which sin leads to dread and dread leads to flight from sin. But the fear, as a conversional element, is abstracted from its occasional and proximate use and comes to be "infused" into the heart as a purifying agent. We see here the logic by which the local and signifying rhetoric of hellfire begins to give way to a more immanent, abstract, and universal one. Fear inspired by the dread of occasional and specific sins, which before had been directed against the specific types of sinful behavior that caused it, becomes the abstract model and universal method for a psychological transformation of the individual's self, or "heart." Reformation of specific behavior is no longer only accomplished by shaping fears symbolically linked and marked with those behaviors but rather turns toward converting the deeper principle of the individuals who consistently will them.

Mather's sermon thus occupies a threshold moment in the shift in the imprecatory sermon's chief aim. We see this no better than when, in a Franklinian moment of methodic self-improvement, the sermon concludes by turning terror into an incentive for making a to-do list. Mather implores his audience "[t]o Think seriously, *If I were to Dye this Day, how should I wish that I had ordered my Life?* Then take up steady Resolutions to *Live* accordingly, and so to *walk in the Fear of GOD!*" (*Valley of Hinnom* 43). Composed and preached during the period directly preceding the revivals, Mather's sermon appears transitional between the earlier use of hellfire as promoting good behavior— "live accordingly"—and the later use of hellfire as a constant psychological experience—"so to walk in the fear of God!" Fear thus can be organized into a set of resolutions that would direct behavior, a clearly external reformation, but this behavior will carry within its every motion the fear that was its motive. Mather's list made in fear is a method by which terror may be made to interpenetrate all aspects of lived life, even when the actor no longer feels the immediate demands and claims of the emotion. The sway of Mather's published sermons, especially during the decade of the 1710s, drifts from warning to invitation, keeping to some extent the pragmatic aims of his father's thunderings but shifting emphasis from individual action to the inculcation and maintenance of terror as an omnipresent experiential state.

Cotton Mather's balancing between treating terror as an occasional symptom of external influence and treating terror as an internalized habit or practice of mind indexes how the scales will tip, in the revival, from the former to the latter. During the revival, William Cooper modifies the role terror plays in both conversion and action: "[W]e *may*, and have *need* to call in and improve the consideration of the torments of hell. *This motive* the sinner usually feels the force of at his first conversion, in the beginning of a religious life; and it is of use to us thro' the whole of our christian course" (111). The torments of hell, for Cooper, are not just the force of the first conversion but a portable vesture for Christian action "thro' the whole of our Christian course." Israel Loring's "Serious Thoughts on the Miseries of Hell" goes even further in imploring its audience to dwell with terror: "Inure yourselves then to the thought & contemplation of these things. Attend to the fearful representation of Hell, which God hath been pleased to exhibit in his Word. Frequently revolve in your minds the fearful and astonishing Miseries of it" (22). Rather than an occasional use of hellfire, to frighten the flock to action elsewhere, Loring's sermon hovers over the fear itself, suggesting that one needs to "inure oneself" to hellfire, to carry it with oneself, to "attend" to it not only by paying it attention but by tending its maturation. If terror is the alarm clock of the Awakening, Loring would have his parishioners ponder its sound rather than turn it off.

So does this turn toward the individual psychology and emotional state of the sinner and away from his or her behavior still aim for the reformation of sinful practices? It is important to note that these later sermons do not abandon the reformative impulse. But rather than considering reform an exertion of the act of the will—a preventive ideology that flirts with the heresy of Arminianism—the revivalist's interest in affect proceeds from a sense of the will as itself determined by emotion and habit. In this approach, changes in occasional external behavior are secondary. The primary goal is to turn human beings into the kind of people who don't sin at all, who don't refrain from sin because they rationally fear hell but because the fear of hell is constitutive of their being. This process from inherently evil to inherently good is, for the revivalists, the nature of conversion, and their use of hellfire would thus be less to reform behavior than to reform the soul.

Such an outlook on the mediatory function of the human will was not new. From Thomas Shepard on, the New England Puritan theology had developed a relation between the individual will and experience that made spiritual conversion the sine qua non of correct action.[7] The question then is why it took so long for the imprecatory sermon to catch up: why did earlier uses of hellfire threaten the punishment of outward social action when Puritan theology always held that such sin was not located in the occasional will but in the unregenerate individual? One answer is that the communal stakes of sin may have tended to gear sermons toward the most immediate contexts of daily social life in the colony.[8] If individual sin was a community issue, then the calls by Oakes and the Mathers to "get into the gap" and defend the community from encroaching sin might be explained as the earlier period's concern for applying individual soteriological principles to the wider narrative of the New England experiment. The change then—from the direct and occasional relationship between the hellfire terror and the sin, which sought to reform the community in the same fashion as public legal punishments upon a scaffold or wearing a mark of the sin, to the omnipresent immersion in which terror is not projected outward but inhabited—may testify to the changing relation of the individual to the community. It isn't Reverend Noyes, who had served and lived in New Haven for twenty-five years, but James Davenport, who had been there less than a week, who answers the hungers of the New Haven parish in 1741. As what counts as community across the colonial strand bends to that change in the public sphere facilitated, as Michael Warner has shown, by the emergent modes of print discourse, the compact bonds between sin and punishment, between individuals and their local clergyman, yield to more diffuse conceptions of community, and thus the communal functions of divine fear are paradoxically internalized.[9] The call to inhabit terror as a conduit to individual conversion, then, reframes the stakes not from community to individual but rather from the individual as part of a local community beset by invasive sin to the individual as part of the sin encroaching upon a wider, more imaginatively constructed community always elsewhere (of which Davenport would thus be an emissary rather than invader).

In the Awakening revivals of the 1730s and 1740s, anxieties lay not with outside influences, then, but with inside ones, with the unconverted ranks of the congregation, swelled by the "half-way covenant" that allowed unconverted children of converted parishioners to remain in the church, and with the ministers who seemed unable to lead them to conversion.[10] Thus, while hell for Increase Mather was always "out there," for Edwards it had been imported into the very church building, burning invisibly under the pews themselves. "There is reason to think," Edwards says to his audience at Enfield, "that there are many in this congregation now hearing this discourse, that will actually be the subjects of this very misery to all eternity. We know not who they are, or in what seats they sit, or what thoughts they now have" (*Sinners* 416). Edwards may be speaking to the unregenerate in general, but rather than specify like Increase Mather, he instead uses an ambiguous proposition—"we know not who they are"—to obscure the signifying distinctions between "we" and "they," between saved and damned. Rather than identifying sinners as essentially knowable and distinct, readable signs that reinforce the law, Edwards's sermon casts into doubt the nature of all of the auditors. Thus, when he continues more pointedly to lecture "those of you that finally continue in a natural condition. . . . You have reason to wonder, that you are not already in hell" (416), he has already yanked the security out from under those who otherwise would imagine themselves exempt. The "you" of Edwards's imprecations is not a recalcitrant sinner of the audience, or even the unregenerate portion of it, but the whole of it, unsure of their neighbor in the seat next to them as they are equally unsure of themselves: "[I]t may be that they are now at ease, and hear all these things without much disturbance, and are now flattering themselves that they are not the persons, promising themselves that they shall escape" (416).[11] Suggestive of the uncanny logic of Poe's theory of perversity, the idea that feeling oneself as safe is itself a threat, Edwards's imaginative projection of those "at ease" leaves no room for escape, either from the sermon's surveillance or from the hell that it describes.

Thus, despite their many similarities, revival hellfire is different from its predecessors in that it severs the "corrective" function and redistributes the source of the perceived threat. Untethered to moderation, comfort, and communal activism, the revival hell is absolute and outstrips the covenantal promise that had made anxiety profitable during the last half of the seventeenth century. Inhabiting terror thus testifies to a new conception of emotion as self and at the same time enacts an endlessly skeptical attitude toward our access to it. If terror is the end, not a means to an end, then it cultivates a paranoid imaginary within which framing narratives and comforts can only be seen as further signs of depravity. If in 1657, as Miller pronounced, corruption became a scourge, a visitation of wrath, in the shifts preceding the Awakening in the early eighteenth century security itself became a corruption. Thus, expressions of hell would match the unconfinable nature of terror and describe an attitude toward a universe that could accommodate the human only by writing the human out of the equation.

Turning back to Davenport's controversial sermon, then, we see that what the shocked critic was noticing was an index to the changes in hellfire preaching in general. First, the sermon was directed outward toward the entire audience, using deixes such as "you" to indicate not a discrete subgroup of revelers or prideful women but instead the congregation itself—there was, as it were, nowhere to hide. Second, Davenport left out the traditional third part of the sermon, the "use" or "application" that would turn description into prescription; he ends the sermon by informing the congregation that they are falling—there was, as it were, nothing to be done, no practical or external reformation to make. And finally, when he descends and dances, clapping and carrying on, his behavior exceeds the intentionality and compartmentalization of language, performing terror and inhabiting it. There was, as it were, nothing more to say. American terror emerges in the revival as ontologically prior to the will and the understanding, and to defend its new form would be to define a radically new significance for affection in general. Thus, when Jonathan Edwards takes on the task in his *Treatise Concerning Religious Affections* (later published as *Religious Affections*), his most influential claim—that affect is an inhabitable experiential state and a true mode of perception central to religious conversion—bears in both its marks the impress of terror's new form. But his theoretical defense is drawn not only from the context of hellfire's changing role but also from his own practice of it. Through his own hellfire sermons, Edwards begins to confront the epistemological problems engendered by the new use of hellfire. And in thinking about the problem of how terror works, Edwards shapes it into a mental activity allied with the methods and power of abstract thought itself.

## Edwards's Early Hellfire

It is true that Edwards does not preach many hellfire sermons of the type that "Sinners in the Hands of an Angry God" falls into—a relentless and focused depiction of hell that never shifts topics. Yet, to read Edwards's sermons from the beginning is to see hellfire everywhere, laced throughout his early sermons rather than concentrated into any single one of them.[12] With the expanded availability of Edwards's surviving sermons provided by the Jonathan Edwards Center's ongoing editing project, we are now in position to correct the misleading assumption that Edwards rarely preached on the terrors of hell. In fact, Edwards often preached on hell, on God's wrath, and on the torments of sinners. An overview of Edwards's sermons—their doctrines and texts—suggests that no less than 78 of the earliest 650 sermons (preached between 1722 and 1741) in the archive address hell, the wrath of God, the future estate of sinners, and so on. When we further consider that Edwards oftentimes introduced hellfire rhetoric into sermons ostensibly about heaven, that number may be estimated to be somewhat larger.[13] Still, it is probably best not to oversell either claim: Edwards was neither exclusively obsessed with hell and damnation, nor did he habitually avoid it. By recovering the development of his hellfire rhetoric, I hope in this section to show how it comes to fulfill the tendency of the hellfire sermon in its conversional goals and its inhabitable terror. Furthermore, his attention to the paradoxes of hellfire—why it can't be described, why it is ineffective, why it is completely different from bodily punishment, how it can be both proportional and infinite—press the abstraction and quantification of hell into epistemological questions that will have consequences upon his entire religious philosophy.

Although Edwards uses the earlier tradition's conventional figurations of hell and its terrors in many of his early hellfire sermons, such as *The Value of Salvation* in 1722,[14] a reading of his career indicates that what sustains his interest in hellish subjects is not a one-to-one application of punishment to crime but rather the way such figuration ultimately fails. In 1727, Edwards seems intent on writing an imprecatory sermon in *Warnings of Future Punishment Don't Seem Real to the Wicked*, but becomes derailed by the rhetorical problem of preaching hell; the persistence of sin in the face of fiery demonstration indicates that the hellfire sermon just does not seem to work. Edwards observes that "[i]f it seemed real unto men that there is a hell of everlasting burnings that all that die impenitent and unconverted must immediately be cast into as soon as they die, and never be delivered from, it would be impossible in nature and a self-contradiction that they should be easy and merry . . . as impossible as it is for a man to love pain and to delight in being miserable" (*Warnings* 204). Since Edwards sees merriment abound in the unconverted, he is forced to the conclusion that, despite the fiery demonstrations of their preachers, hell still does not seem "real" to them. To fix the hellfire sermon, then, Edwards thus sets out to solve the preliminary problems: the psychological question of what "real" belief requires and the expressive problem of how to furnish that quantity.

Edwards posits two criteria as necessary for the "realizing" of things. In order for a thing to seem "real to us," Edwards claims that we need to (1) believe in the truth of it and (2) have a sensible idea or lively apprehension of it. It is this sensible idea of hell that wicked men lack: "They believe it as the Papists do transubstantiation and purgatory, because so their fathers believed, and so the church believes. But they never, since they were born, were properly convinced that it was really true" (*Warnings* 202). In the economy of terms Edwards uses here, one could believe that hell exists yet at the same time not know that hell is real: "Their belief is not a belief upon evidence shown to their minds, but only a yielding in some measure to education and example" (202). If this is the case, then, Edwards would seem to set an impossible task for the hellfire and brimstone sermon, since telling wicked men about hell would seem to be able only to produce the belief of education, not experience: "They hear that it will be intolerable, exceeding dreadful, that [it] will fill their souls with misery, that it will be like fire and brimstone and the like; but they nevertheless seldom think what is meant by these expressions. They never felt none of it, and never saw anybody under this punishment or that ever did endure it, and so they have no notion how dreadful it is—no, not of the hundredth part of the greatness of that misery—and so they are not terrified and affrighted by it" (203). The problem of hell is that it isn't attainable in rhetoric; how does one present an immediate sense of hell given that it is only available, in this world at least, to the senses mediately?

The sermon thus ends up in a difficult position. Edwards has suggested the need for an immediate and lively apprehension of hell, but has also admitted that "[h]ell is in another world, and it is invisible" (206). At the end of the sermon, he lays out an ambitious yet abortive argument about why one should believe that hell exists, arguing from a point of worldly ethics instead of scripture. If there were no divine retribution, Edwards argues, there would be no enforcement of morality; "[m]ankind would devour one another" and "the earth would be turned into a hell" (208). Following this theoretical argument, Edwards half-heartedly attempts to finally provide a more "lively sensible apprehension of this punishment," but ends up retreading many of the tired metaphors that had been adorning the imprecatory sermon for two generations: it is a place of the "blackness of darkness" where the sinner will see "nothing but horror, amazement, and torment there" (210). His return to scriptural descriptions of hell, following his scriptureless argument for the moral necessity of hell, beats a hasty retreat from the psychological problem posed at the start.

But the problem defined—how to provide a lively apprehension of that which is invisible—will inform the tactics of his evocations of terror in his later career.

By 1729, in a sermon on the doctrine "It is a strange punishment that God has assigned to the workers of iniquity," the description of hellish punishment through hyperbolic worldly metaphors no longer suffices. "[I]t is very different from all punishments that Are Inflicted by men," Edwards notes. "[T]here is a Great variety in these but none of them are like the Punishments of hell fire. . . . [M]en are sometimes by Earthly Judges Condemned to suffer perpetual Imprisonment but this is very different from being shut up in the Prison of hell[.] [S]hut up with more than Gates of brass & bars of Iron this will be a more dreadfull Confinement than to be shut up in the most loathsom dungeon" (L. 3r.).[15] It is the difference between worldly punishments, not in degree but in essence, that Edwards emphasizes. For while worldly punishments may affect the body, the terror of hell is that the punishment is directed toward the soul—"the superiour & more Essential Part of man" (L. 3v.). In turning from the hell of the body to the hell of the soul, Edwards begins to answer the question of how to express the otherworldly terrors of hell. Still, though, such a turn inward depends on the description of the outward; hell may be "very different" from a worldly prison, but still can only be described by dint of that from which it differs.

Searching for the expression of hell's intangibility, Edwards is drawn to the problem of its disproportion: "This Punish. —— is exceeding disproportionate to their strength. [T]he strength of man his ability to bear is but as the strength of a little worm but the wrath of G. which will be Inflicted on the wicked will be like the weight of a mountain" (L. 2v.). What makes hell inexpressible, its disproportion to one's senses, is related to its terrors, its disproportion to an individual's strength. When Edwards is forced to describe hell's sense of prison as "very different" from ordinary senses of prison, this isn't simply a negative analogy but a quantification of disproportion. In order to generate the sense of never-ending and exponentially aggravated increase in disproportion, however, Edwards would still require a more "realizing" rhetoric, one he finds in the language of abstract mathematics and recursive functions.

Edwards connects the quantified and disproportionate nature of sin's exponential increase directly to the problem of expressing hellfire adequately in one of his earliest sermons, written on the text "God sometimes punishes sin by giving men up to sin" (1722–1723). The somewhat paradoxical doctrine for the sermon, that sin's punishment is more sin, allows Edwards to build a case for why hellfire-

and-brimstone sermons may fail: "[T]he oftener they [sinners] hear Gods threats and are told of hell, the less they Regard and all that Can be said to Awaken them Out of sleep does but harden them" (L. 2v.). That is, one of the punishments for sin is that it hardens sinners against hearing the awakening sermon that would save them, which in turn becomes the route to more sin and thus to more punishment. Edwards is not saying just that sinners can't hear sermons but rather the more complicated indictment that hearing more about hell actually makes the sinner less likely to avoid it. Articulating the physics of such a recursive structure four years later, Edwards compares the growth of sin, the way it seems to increase itself, to the acceleration of falling bodies: "[Sin] Grows as a Grain of mustard seed" (L. 3v.). Edwards begins with the analogy to the mustard seed but instantly converts that natural metaphor into a more abstract one—the fall of a body through space—the difference being that one is not accustomed to seeing or hearing about mustard weeds growing "so violent that nothing can withstand [them]," but is capable of imagining such in the abstract world of quantified physics.

The problem of expressing hell directly to the soul in these formulations is not solved by coming up with the right real-world analogy but rather by presenting a recursive mathematical equation that could be apprehended in the abstract. Around the same time as Edwards conceives this possibility, in late 1729, he begins working out its solution through this recourse to quantity in a sermon bearing the doctrine "The torments of hell will be eternal." A close study of this, perhaps Edwards's most schematic and extended description of hell, shows the turn from psychological problem to mathematical solution that underlies his break with the external hell of the older generation. In order to get hell inside and to make it real, Edwards will lay hold of the powers and limitations of thought in the consideration of infinite quantities.

Thus Edwards begins "The torments of hell will be eternal" by restating the general problem but with a telling change: Why do sinners sin in the face of knowledge of eternal damnation? Here it is not hell's misery but its temporal quantity that is selected as being the obstacle to realization: "But this Eternity of torment is a thing that when they seriously think of they Cant Get over" (L. 2v.). In order to address the problem of realizing the eternity of hell, Edwards must also consider the root cause, the inability to conceptualize eternity in a positive sense at all. His very first point in the sermon, then, points up the metaphysical impasse:

> 1. thing viz what is meant by Eternity. The thing is what we Cannot Comprehend nor perfectly Understand for this Plain Reason. because that that is Infinite

> Cannot be Perfectly Comprehended by that which is finite. . . . [O]ur Idea of it is only negative[.] [O]ur way is to Run out a Great length in our minds & when we have done and Gone as far as minds Can Go thence to deny any end. (L. 3r.)

The best finite humans can do is to conceptualize eternity in a "negative" way, to proceed through a process of quantification ("run out a Great length") and then recoil when we have reached only our natural limit ("to deny any end").

Put this way, the problem facing the preacher of hellfire would seem insurmountable. We cannot have a positive conception, a realization, of eternity by the limited nature of our finite minds, so how would the preacher be able to make the eternity of hell, its most awful feature according to Edwards, a factor in the day-to-day decisions of lived religious life? Edwards's answer is remarkable in that he attempts to turn the inconceivability itself into a positive sense, so that though we cannot comprehend, we can at least feel the lack. Thus, Edwards proceeds to provide his audience with several thought experiments, not to make eternity more comprehensible but rather to emphasize its incomprehensibility:

> [A]nd because it is such as that we Cannot Comprehend or define it maynt be amiss [to] help in Concieving [sic] of it to mention some of the Properties of it. [T]hose properties that I shall mention tho they may help our Conceptions so as to subserve to our Practice yet they are so far from Giving us a Comprehensive understanding of it that theyll only show us our Ignorance & make us to see that the nature of it is mysterious & Incomprehensible. [T]he Particulars that I shall mention will be but so many Paradoxes. (L. 3v.–4r.)

Edwards's list of eternal properties allows him to apply his speculative metaphysical interests to the rhetorical problem of making hell real. The features of eternity he goes on to list—that it cannot be divided, that it cannot be measured in periods, that it denies proportion—are each close in spirit to the rangy idealism of his early-career philosophical musings collected in "The Mind." But these practices of the mind, considering "so many Paradoxes," only serve to make eternity less familiar, more "mysterious & Incomprehensible." In trying to make the eternity of hell more real to his audience, Edwards comes to the unlikely conclusion that he needs to make it more incomprehensible to them.

The vehicle of eternity's incomprehensibility is mathematical quantification, or more precisely, the assertion of the failure of mathematical quantification, demonstrated through the portrayal of unfathomable, yet certainly possible, sums. Sinners will never reach even a "tenth Part or a thousandth or a millionth Part of their Continuance in hell," since "we Can as soon by Reckoning or multiplying Come to the End of Eternity. [A]nd Reckon up the whole of it as we Can Come to the thousandth Part because indeed there is no such neither as an End nor a thousandth Part of Eternity" (L. 4r.–4v.). In such failing calculations, the standard practice of hellfire sermons, to make proportional analogies between grains of sand and years, also fails:

> [A] Great while or a long Period. bears no Greater Proportion to Eternity than a little while a thousand years or a thousand Ages bears no Greater Proportion to Eternity than a minute or which is the same thing a thousand Ages is as much Less than Eternity as a minute is a minute Comes as near to an Equality or You may take as many thousand out of Eternity out of that whole as you Can minutes. He that has lived but one day his Age is as near an Eternity as he that has lived the Longest life. [I]f the utmost skill in arithmetick Reckon up a Great number of Ages & should Rise by multiplication to never so Prodigious numbers. should make as Great Leaps as he Could & should rise as fast as he Could & should spend all his life time in multiplying. the Product of all would be nearer Equal to Eternity than one minute. & therefore those that understand most Are as far from a comprehensive knowledge. as Angels. (L. 4v.–5r.)

What makes Edwards's description of hell's eternity so unique is not only that it mobilizes and depends upon a process of reckoning that at the same time declares itself as insufficient, but that it appears to work opposite to the usual, conventional way of describing eternity as a "running out." A minute, in this passage, is as much an eternity as a thousand years. Edwards is not saying that a thousand years is to eternity as a minute is to a thousand years—that would be the conventional way of extending infinity, by multiplying quantities in analogical proportion. Instead, Edwards is saying that a minute and a thousand years are the same thing—"an Equality"—with respect to eternity. The very problem of comprehending eternity, Edwards suggests, is that we think of it as a very long time, when the truth is that it is no time at all.

In order to show the negation of time, Edwards exhorts his audience to think almost only of time. All imaginable time comes to nothing in the infinite disproportion of eternity:

> [T]he Continuance of their Tormts Cannot be measured out by Revolutions of the sun & Planets or by Centuries or the Ages of worlds. they shall Continue suffering when this world shall be overthrown. they shall Continue suffering

> & tormented when the sun shall Grow old & dull & Cease to shine, when the [sun] & fix'd stars shall be moved out of their Places that they have held so many Ages & the heavens & the whole visibl [world] shall decay with age & Come to Ruin then the tormts of Ungodly men will be but Beginning. what will be Past of their sufferings will be but a Point to what Remains. . . . [T]he Past Part of their torment will [be] as disproportionate to the Remainder as the first minute. (L. 6r.; brackets in original)

Edwards exhorts his audience to "consider eternity" in reckoning that only serves to underscore the insufficiency of reckoning in order to become more sensible of hell's terrors. What mathematics allows, for Edwards, is the production of one side of a conceivable equation whose other side is unfathomable. We cannot comprehend eternity, especially by the instruments of arithmetic that it belies, but we can come closer to a sense of its incomprehensibility by considering the failure of those instruments.

When Edwards turns to the application of these lessons, then, he must reiterate their complete inadequacy, since their inadequacy is part of the lesson:

> [B]e Entreated to Consider attentively how Great & awfull a thing Eternity is. [T]ho You Cant Comprehend it anything the more for Considering Yet you may be made more sensible by it that it is not a thing to be disregarded. (L. 15v.–16r.)

Edwards draws a distinction here between comprehension and sensibility. By considering eternity attentively, no comprehension can be gained, but only a greater sensibility. But what is sensibility without comprehension? And how does one consider attentively something that will always escape comprehension? Edwards's example of what it means to consider attentively, in the very next sentence, suggests that it is to perform the kind of imaginative calculation he had earlier criticized as being wholly inadequate to the task of summing eternity:

> [D]o but Consider what it is to suffer extreme torment forever & Ever day & night from one day to another from one Year to another from one Age to another from one thousand of ages to another & so adding age to age & thousands to thousands in Pain in wailing & Lamenting Groaning & shrieking & gnashing of teeth with your soul full of dreadfull Grief & amazement with your body & Every member full of Racking torture without any Possibility of Getting Ease. (L. 16r.)

To "consider" is thus to perform the endless and utterly inadequate calculation of addition and multiplication, to address one's powers of quantification to the incomprehensible. This, Edwards states, will make one more "sensible" of the disproportionate situation—one will sense what one cannot understand by the very activity of failing to understand it.

But what kind of sense is this? Careful readers might anticipate Edwards's next turn, by which the sensibility of eternity becomes the sensation of hell:

> [D]o but Consider how dreadfull despair will be in such torment. how dismal will it be when you under those Racking torments to know assuredly that you never never shall be deliver'd from them. . . . [Y]ou may by Considering make your self more sensible than ordinarily you be but it is a little you Can Conceive what it is to have no hope in such torments. [H]ow sinking would it be to you to Endure such Pains as you have felt in this world without any hope & know that you never should be deliver'd from it. nor have one minutes Rest you scarcely Can now Conceive how dolefull that would be. how much more to Endure the mighty weight of the wrath of G. without hope. (L. 15v.–16v.)

Turning from considering "what it is" to "how dreadful," "how dismal," "how sinking," and "how doleful," Edwards suggests that the increased sensibility is associated with affective capacities. Sinners cannot "conceive" the whole affective experience of eternity but may be introduced to it by the feelings that they entertain as they, in their finite inadequate way, calculate it. Our affective sensibility is raised by our inadequate calculation; thus the more we think, the more we feel.[16]

Edwards explicitly comes to the point, drawing the activity of thinking together with the sensibility of feeling, in a conclusion that reorganizes hell from a physical punishment that incurs as a secondary result mental anguish to a mental anguish of infinite calculation supported by physical pain:

> The more the damned in hell think of the Eternity of their torments the more amazing will it appear to them and alas they are not able to help thinking of it, they will not be able to keep it out of their minds their tortures wont divert them from it but will fix their attention to it. O how dreadfull will Eternity appear to them after they have been thinking ont for Ages together & have had so long an experience of their torments. [I]f it were Possible for the damned in hell to have a Comprehensive knowledge of Eternity their sorrow & Grief would be Infinite in degree. (L. 17r.–17v.)

The more the damned "think," the more dreadful eternity becomes. Thus the fires, the pains, all of the torment that hell can unleash on the spiritual body, are all incitements to think upon eternity, to continue out the endless calculation of years upon years, ages upon ages, that Edwards exhorts earlier. The tortures "fix their attention," prevent any distraction from the endless and inadequate calculation that Edwards would have his gathered congregation consider for the duration of the sermon.

Even though comprehensive knowledge of eternity is inaccessible to living sinner and dead sinner alike, the sinner in hell "will have a vastly more lively & strong apprehension of it than we Can have in this [world]" because "their torments will Give them an Impression of it" (L. 17v.). Pain thus goes from being a sensation to being an inducement to sensation; we may sense pain, but its more important effect is what mental enlargement it achieves for one's sensibility of temporal paradox:

> [A] man in his Present state without any Enlargmt of his Capacity would have vastly a more lively Impression of Eternity than he has if only he were only under some Pretty sharp Pain of some member of his body & were at the same time were assured that he must Endure that Pain forever. [H]is Pain would Give him a Greater sense of Eternity than other men have. [H]ow much more will those excruciating tormts that the damned will suffer. & besides their Capacity will be Enlarged their understandings quicker & stronger in a future [state] & G. Can Give them as . . . Great a sense & as strong an Impression of Eternity as he Pleases to Increase their Grief & horrour. (L. 17v.–18r.; brackets in original)

The more pain, the more understanding. The more understanding, the more horror.

The brilliance of the hell that Edwards describes in "The torments of hell will be eternal" is that it finds a way around the problem of portraying that which cannot be experienced. He cannot "realize" hellfire for his congregation by telling them about it, or even through the series of analogies that hellfire preachers often used. Instead of making hellfire real, he makes it less crucial, merely an instrument for a greater torment, that of not being able to calculate infinity. And that torment he can engender, since it is the sensation of a process of thought, not a sensation of an object out of this world. By performing these thought experiments in the paradoxes of infinite time, one is actually experiencing, to a lesser degree, hell's torments already.[17] That is, in Edwards's hell, sinners are inflicted with pain so that they can never stop thinking about the doctrines of Edwards's sermons. Hearing the sermon feelingly, then, is like being given a little slice of hell in Northampton.

When Edwards revises the sermon in 1739 in response to Archbishop Tillotson's controversial and popular sermon arguing that hell cannot possibly be eternal, Edwards adds the argument that the eternity of hell is "proportional" ("The miseries of the wicked in hell" L. 2r.) to the infinite evil of sin. Since God is infinite, and since sin is an abrogation of infinite duty, then it is an infinite crime and must be punished infinitely. In this economy of infinites, Edwards thus begins to bring together the abstract and mental space of his hell of mind with a more positive view of God—for all of the same problems with conceiving the infinite nature of hell also apply to the infinite glory of God. In the early *Fragment: From an Application on Seeking God* ([1721–1722]), Edwards envisions the two as polar opposites: "[A]s in heaven there is nothing but pure love, one to another, so it will be directly contrary in hell; there will be nothing but perpetual, inveterate hatred" (386). Edwards is able to get at heaven through hell, and thus the more terrible the rhetoric on one side, the higher the excellency and holiness on the other. For instance, in his sermon *God's Excellencies* ([1722–1723]), Edwards cantilevers God's holiness by pumping the inexhaustible jack of horrendous sin:

> If he be such an excellent being, how dreadful is sin against [him]. There are very few that conceived what a dreadful thing it is to sin against the infinitely excellent, great, and glorious Jehovah. The aggravations of sin are really infinite, infinite in greatness and almost infinite in number, for it is committed against an infinitely great and powerful God, one that has infinite authority. (426; brackets in original)

In such a characteristic moment, the statement appears at first to be describing how "dreadful sin is." But it works the other way as well; as Edwards multiplies the infinite quantities of wrath sin incurs, the audience's ability to feel that sinking sense of being unable to escape, that nightmarish certainty that one has committed an eternal mistake, incontrovertible for eternity, becomes the figural ground for the transcendent and inexpressible divinity of God. The route Edwards takes to realize hell, then, becomes a possible way to realize God—and thus terror is not simply a response to the fires with which the hellfire preacher threatens but absolutely integral to the increased sensibility of Christian truth. Thus, when terror preaching comes under fire during the Awakening, Edwards's defense of it has higher stakes than simply its efficacy.

## The Revival Defense

Edwards's *A Faithful Narrative* (1737) and his letters to Benjamin Colman, his frontline correspondence regarding the revival, provide a seemingly discordant picture of religious revival. They depict a people at once so committed to religion and thoughts of God that they can barely perform their daily duties, but at the same time so deeply anxious and fearfully paranoid that they refuse to sleep for fear of hell.[18] Edwards poses the confluence of joy and terror in the same breath: "This town never was so full of love, nor so full of joy, nor so full of distress as it has lately been" ("Unpublished Letter" 104).

Edwards knew about the conventional order of conversion, laid out by Thomas Hooker in 1632 and modified only slightly by his grandfather, Solomon Stoddard.[19] In the conventional order, fear was traditionally the first stage in the coming to Christ, and would be replaced with consolation and mercy in later stages. Edwards had already been playing in his early sermons with the idea of terror being more intrinsically conjoined with religious delight: "The design of the spirit of God in these legal terrors seems most evidently to be, to make way for, and to bring persons to a conviction of their absolute dependence upon his sovereign power and grace" ("Benjamin Colman's Abridgment" 123). Here, the terror is not cautionary but fundamental; the terrors lead to a sense of "absolute dependence" upon God, in which there is no promise of mercy, no comfort or consolation, but instead a clearing of the ground in order to establish first the true relation of the individual to God. More constitutive of religious sense, terror thus increases rather than recedes in proximity to grace: "The awful apprehensions persons have had of their misery, have for the most part been increasing, the nearer they have approached to deliverance" (*Faithful Narrative* 161). In the attack on the revival and on terror preaching that was to come, however, Edwards would have to answer how the gradually increasing terror was capable of saving.

Charles Chauncy, a contemporary of Jonathan Edwards and pastor of the First Church of Boston, became the most outspoken critic of the Awakening revival. Always choosing to call it "enthusiasm" rather than a revival or religion, Chauncy developed in a series of sermons and in one definitive treatise a conservative critique that appealed to common sense. The main contention for Chauncy was that the enthusiasms that were rocking not only the eastern seaboard but the very bodies of the churchgoers were natural and biological, not divine. They were, for him, a kind of viral disease, in which the lower animal faculties of the body usurped the rightful place of reason and understanding, of restraint and civility: "*Reasonable* Beings are not to be guided by *Passion* or *Affection*, though the Object of it should be GOD, and the Things of another World: They need, even in this Case, to be under the Government of a *well instructed Judgment*" (*Seasonable Thoughts* 324). Chauncy operates from an already-outdated medieval conception of the human faculties. Reason stands at the top, and affection, a baser faculty, must be controlled and regimented by it.

For Chauncy, the fallen state of humanity is the corruption of reason: "You are, it must be acknowledged, in a corrupt state. The fall has introduc'd great weakness into your reasonable nature" (*Enthusiasm Described* 18). With no less vigor than the "New Lights" thunder about hell, Chauncy thunders about the dangers of the loss of reason, equating it with animal nature: "Be advised then to shew yourselves men, to make use of your reasonable powers; and not act as the *horse* or *mule*, as tho' you had no understanding" (18). The horses and mules of the Awakening, for Chauncy, are those that are being ridden by their passions rather than controlling and directing them. When Chauncy looked at the Awakening—and he looked quite a bit, visiting notable parishes, scrapbooking a massive archive of anecdotal evidence, and chronicling the embarrassments of the revival—what he saw was nothing less than an epidemiology of madness, a bodily disease of the "over-heated imagination": "The cause of this *enthusiasm* is a bad temperament of the blood and spirits; 'tis properly a disease, a sort of madness" (3).

In defending terror preaching and the revival, then, Edwards would have to challenge this commonsense distinction between emotional nature and disciplinary reason. In his 1741 response to Chauncy, *The Distinguishing Marks of a Work of the Spirit of God*, Edwards notes that Chauncy's method of considering the mechanical functions of the body as evidence against divine nature is to fail to inquire into "the nature of the operations and affections that persons' minds are under" (234). Edwards thus begins to pressure the term "nature," locating it not in the epiphenomenal act but rather in one's affective constitution. Edwards's illustrative example thus goes back to the question of terror and the way that its expression can be at once rational and natural:

> If we should suppose that a person saw himself hanging over a great pit, full of fierce and glowing flames, by a thread that he knew to be very weak, and not sufficient long to bear his weight, . . . what distresss would he be in? . . . [W]ould not he be ready to cry out in such circumstances? How much more those that see themselves in this manner hanging over an infinitely more dreadful pit, or

> held over it in the hand of God, who at the same time they see to be exceedingly provoked? . . . [N]o wonder they cry out of their misery; and no wonder that the wrath of God when manifested but a little to the soul, overbears human strength. (231–232)

We hear, of course, echoes of Edwards's later "Sinners" sermon here, but it is worth noticing how the case of dangling over a pit is put hypothetically here in order to legitimize crying out—it is in our nature. Equally in our nature is the volume at which we would cry out to save others. Edwards doesn't accept Chauncy's taking it for granted that vociferous and enthusiastic preaching styles are corrupt. Again, he adopts a fire metaphor, and again he moves from an example in the real world to the example of hell:

> If any of you that are heads of families, saw one of your children in an house that was all on fire over its head, and in eminent danger of being soon consumed in the flames . . . would you go on to speak to it only in a cold and indifferent manner? Would not you cry aloud, and call earnestly to it, and represent the danger it was in, and its own folly in delaying, in the most lively manner you was capable of? Would not nature itself teach this, and oblige you to it? If you should continue to speak to it only in a cold manner, as you are wont to do in ordinary conversation about indifferent matters, would not those about you begin to think you were bereft of reason yourself? (247)

For Edwards, the key term here is what "nature itself teaches," through which we begin to feel the difference between Chauncy's nature and Edwards's. For Chauncy, nature was the horse and the mule, the animal economy to be channeled and controlled by human reason. For Edwards, nature and reason coincide—if you were to calmly tell your child to come out of the fire, you would be "bereft of reason yourself." Thus, what nature itself teaches is the very content of reason. The distinction between reason and nature eased, Edwards is able to consider how affections could constitute a kind of reason, and reason conversely a variety of feeling.

Whereas for the older generations, terror was exceedingly useful for getting people to stop all their sinning, for Edwards, confronted with the attack on terror preaching from Chauncy on one hand, and witnessing terror in its operations within the Awakening on the other, terror becomes the inhabitable and communicable process of experiencing truth: "Why should we be afraid to let persons that are in an infinitely miserable condition, know the truth, or bring 'em into the light, for fear it should terrify them? 'Tis light that must convert them, if ever they are converted. The more we bring sinners into the light, while they are miserable, and the light is terrible to them, the more likely it is that by and by the light will be joyful to them" (*Some Thoughts* 390). Defining terror as the affective perception of light, Edwards fulfills the tendency in terror's evolution into the substance of religious experience. Comfort, in such a scheme, cannot come from anything but submission, from a complete evacuation of self before an all-powerful and incredibly incensed God. The minister's duty, then, is to increase terror by removing comfort:

> [A] man that sees himself in danger of drowning is in terror, and endeavors to catch hold on every twig within his reach, and he that pulls away those twigs from him increases his terror; yet if they are insufficient to save him, and by being in his way, prevent his looking to that which will save him, to pull them away is necessary to save his life. (391–392)

This remarkable figure of the minister methodically removing branches from the clutching grasp of the drowning man, attempting to save him by dispossessing him of everything he thinks might save him, illustrates the privative nature of terror for Edwards. Finding that ground, that reality, that anchorage, is to ask sinners only to "accept of a Savior . . . but not to make 'em think their present condition less miserable than it is, or at all to abate their uneasiness and distress, while they are in it; that would be the way to quiet them, and fasten them in it, and not to excite 'em to fly from it" (391). Here, to quiet miserable sinners is not to abate their distress but to "fasten them in it," to inhabit terror rather than fly from it.

The final step in the maturation of terror in Edwards's philosophy will come in his much later *Treatise Concerning Religious Affections* (1746). In this postscript to the revival, Edwards has given up the fight with Chauncy, and the tone is no longer argumentative in a topical sense. Instead, Edwards writes what the revival has taught him, the lessons coming out of his engagement in the terror debate. This leads to a much plainer and more streamlined recapitulation of the philosophical bases of his defense that Chauncy had either never understood or cagily refused to acknowledge. For instance, Edwards is able to say simply that "[t]he will, and the affections of the soul, are not two faculties; the affections are not essentially distinct from the will, nor do they differ from the mere actings of the will and inclination of the soul, but only in the liveliness and sensibleness of exercise" (*RA* 97). And he is finally able to make plain his disagreement with Chauncy about affect as merely a motion of fluids in the animal body: "[I]t is not the body, but the mind only, that is the proper seat of the affections. The body of man is no more capable of being really the subject of love or hatred, joy or sorrow, fear or hope, than the body of a tree, or than the same body of man is capable of thinking and understanding" (*RA* 98). The body is no more capable of feeling as it is of thinking, and thus affect finally becomes categorically related to thought—reason, it might be said, is nothing more than a feeling. In fact, as we've seen, Edwards had suggested as much years earlier in his unpublished "Notes on the Mind": "The mind feels when it thinks" (*SP* 345).[20]

Though Edwards's final comment on the revival severely limits and cautions what can be taken as true religious affections and true convictions of conscience practically, he still defends the theoretical prospect of terror that he had been developing since his very earliest hellfire sermons. Terror, finally, becomes the natural sight of God. A natural man, unconverted, has only the terror of God, but the converted, the saved, have all of the terror of the vision of God's awful majesty with only one thing more, a sense of its beauty:

> Wicked men and devils will see, and have a great sense of every thing that appertains to the glory of God, but only the beauty of his moral perfection. They will see his infinite greatness and majesty, his infinite power, and will be fully convinced of his omniscience, and his eternity and immutability; and they will see and know everything appertaining to his moral attributes themselves, but only the beauty and amiableness of them. (*RA* 264)

Edwards, coming out of the terror debates of the revival, finds himself armed with a whole new conception of the relations between affection and will and between terror and beauty. The difference between terror and grace, the only difference, is a sense of the "beauty of his moral perfection," which is not to say that the sinful man and the converted man are looking at two different things—rather, they are both seeing the same truth; the only difference is that natural man cannot sense the beauty of that which terrifies.

And herein lies what I believe to be the most important consequence of Edwards's engagement with hellfire, its innovation from its earlier cautionary uses into a more fundamental piece of the conversion puzzle: Edwards uses the new sense of terror, its efficacy as a mode of perceiving and knowing and *feeling* the truth of God's sovereignty, as the foundation for the highest state reserved in his theology. The final view of God, for Edwards, is nothing but sensing the beauty of the terror that we all inhabit.[21] Thus terror is integral to Edwards's philosophy, not just as an instrument or a step, not just as a cautionary tale, but as actually constitutive of his view of God and truth: "Not that a sense of God's greatness and natural attributes is not exceeding useful and necessary. For, as I observed before, this is implied in a manifestation of the beauty of God's holiness. Though that be something beyond it, it supposes it, as the greater supposes the less" (*RA* 266). Terror may be less than beauty, but beauty is nothing without terror[22]—it is through the gauntlet of terror, with its rigorous evacuation of self and its inward turn and its wrestlings with the infinite and the inexpressible, that we sense the beauty of God's complete sovereignty, not because he loves us, but because he doesn't have to. And the way to save oneself when drowning is not to grasp at branches but to throw one's hands up in the air—the only comfort is realizing that there isn't one.

## An Ardency to Be Emptied and Annihilated

What we have seen through Edwards's early hellfire and his revival defense is how terror returns, by a new route, to the privative nature of sin that had eroded in the late seventeenth century. What makes Edwards's route new is how it makes that privation capable of a positive sense, capable of being registered in the sinner's affective faculties as an empirical certainty, thus operating within an evidentiary sphere of rational methodology. The imbrication of emotion and reason in Edwards's defense of terror thus reflects the broader collision between religious piety and Enlightenment reason in the Great Awakening. Though many readers have often understood these forces as having opposite trajectories and thus found Edwards a divided figure, either internally conflicted or hopelessly trying to accommodate his theology to a materialist metaphysics, recent re-evaluations of Edwards's sources and success demonstrate how Edwards's commitments to science may have fit within an earlier pietistic tradition.[23] As Sarah Rivett has argued, Edwards's concept of the "indwelling light" became a "Christian solution to the Enlightenment's most pressing epistemological problems" by offering through the soul's affections "the necessary data to further a frustrated empirical inquiry into the essence of divinity" (292). Edwards's affection is not, therefore, a turn away from the modes and methods of reason but rather an attempt to offer new kinds of knowledge, affectionate knowledge, to the scientific endeavor. Affectionate pietism may return in Edwards's Awakening, but feeling is now no longer subjective, no longer mystical and personal; feeling becomes a new kind of fact, promising to break through the epistemological limits of Lockean empiricism.[24]

Terror, then, given its relation to the skeptical problems of infinity and nothingness, may be considered a special case within such an economy of affectionate certitude. If Edwards plays feeling to science's fact, it is not merely to give religious piety a scientific identity but rather to alter the shape of science from the inside. That is, in searching for a feeling that might yield new certainty, Edwards fixates on a feeling *of* certainty, a feeling that preserves the scientific doubt and harnesses its endlessly negative capacities. Edwards's infinite terror is special, as this section argues, for it would write into its own structure the tone of logical analysis, redrawing the anxieties of abstract skepticism into the inexhaustible wellsprings of religious affection. In order to get at this feeling, Edwards would return to the paradoxes of mind that he explored in his early scientific and philosophical writings, metaphysical thought experiments whose impossibilities not only constitute the cognitive limits that affection would surpass, but whose recontextualized grammar would throw off a particular affect of its own. Edwards isn't satisfied with merely an affectionate end around past scientific doubt. Edwards would go directly through it, making that doubt itself the recursive feeling of terror.

To illustrate how Enlightenment philosophy and terror converge in Edwards, I begin by comparing two lengthy passages, the first from one of Edwards's early pieces of metaphysical speculation, the second from his conversion narrative. In "Of the Prejudices of the Imagination," Edwards addresses the problem of conceiving the idea of nothing:

> When we go about to form an idea of perfect nothing we must shut out all these things. We must shut out of our minds both space that has something in it, and space that has nothing in it. We must not allow ourselves to think of the least part of space, never so small, nor must we suffer our thoughts to take sanctuary in a mathematical point. When we go to expel body out of our thoughts, we must be sure not to leave empty space in the room of it; and when we go to expel emptiness from our thoughts we must not think to squeeze it out by anything close, hard and solid, but we must think of the same that the sleeping rocks dream of; and not till then shall we have a complete idea of nothing. (*SP* 206)

In his much-later *Personal Narrative*, Edwards confronts the problem of conceiving his own sin:

> My wickedness, as I am in myself, has long appeared to me perfectly ineffable, and infinitely swallowing up all thought and imagination; like an infinite deluge, or infinite mountains over my head. I know not how to express better, what my sins appear to me to be, than by heaping infinite upon infinite, and multiply-

ing infinite by infinite. I go about very often, for this many years, with these expressions in my mind, and in my mouth, "Infinite upon infinite. Infinite upon infinite!" When I look into my heart, and take a view of my wickedness, it looks like an abyss infinitely deeper than hell. . . . [Yet] [i]t seems to me, my conviction of sin is exceeding small, and faint. It appears to me enough to amaze me, that I have no more sense of my sin. I know certainly, that I have very little sense of my sinfulness. . . .

Others speak of their longing to be humbled to the dust. Though that may be a proper expression for them, I always think for myself, that I ought to be humbled down below hell. 'Tis an expression that has long been natural for me to use in prayer to God. I ought to lie infinitely low before God. (*PW* 802–803)

When read against one another, the two texts on what appear to be vastly different subjects come to share the same preoccupation with an inexpressible quantity. The case of nothing, which can only be arrived at through a series of negative substitutions, is like the case of sin, which Edwards seeks to express through impossible calculations of infinity. To conceive of the magnitude of sin is to seek after an impossibly small state, a reduction to nothingness that would go lower than dust, that would aim at the "infinitely low" and even then despair for the remaining "infinite depths" still left in the heart. The "perfect idea" of nothing that Edwards would develop through a sequence of stages—body in space, space emptied of body, then space emptied of space, and finally the impersonal dreams of rocks—tries to get at a similar kind of impossibly distant perceptual state through subtractive substitution. The substitution of space for body, then dreams for space, puts each preceding stage under erasure just as Edwards's declaration of his sin as swallowing up all expression is then substituted for by the phrase "infinite upon infinite." The curious way this phrase is "in his mouth" echoes and amplifies the ongoing figural process of swallowing. Edwards's "infinite upon infinite" becomes both talismanic and material, verbal rocks to be endlessly swallowed, an abstract process of addition in being that would subtract from the self until it is "infinitely low" so that it might touch that perfect nothing that the sleeping rocks do dream of.

In a way, when Edwards exhorted ministers to methodically remove branches from the reach of the drowning man, giving him nothing by which he could deceive himself with security, he was reprising that same drama of deprivation that refuses to allow the mind, in conceiving of nothing, "to take sanctuary in a mathematical point." It is this compulsion to constantly remove and place under erasure all the points and powers of security or safety that would join Edwards's interests in the mind with his interests in terror. So, if we can glimpse how Edwards imports the abstract language of infinite calculation to substitute for descriptive expression of the terrors of sin, we can at the same time see how such calculation itself, at its furthest reaches (reduction to nothingness or extrapolation to infinity), must refuse sanctuary and pursue a course in a kind of terror, a course which takes as its ultimate goal a fully alienable and estranged perceptual state. Terror may be incurred and maintained by invoking the calculations of infinity, but that is because, as Edwards's examples emphasize, those calculations can be seen as propelled by the recursive logic of a fear of security; the perfect idea of nothing, like the man drowning without a branch, can only be achieved by facing and submitting to the terror of absolute insecurity.

Edwards's efforts to inculcate terror by annihilating himself become a key plot of his *Personal Narrative*. In it, Edwards recounts the development of his own conversion. Rather than a simple linear progression from sinfulness to grace, however, the *Personal Narrative* spirals, recoils, and continually returns: doubts become convictions that turn back to even greater doubts. In an early passage, even as this pattern begins to take shape, Edwards suggests that it yet falls short of what would seem to be its ostensible goal, terror:

> But God would not suffer me to go on with any quietness; but I had great and violent inward struggles: till after many conflicts with wicked inclinations, and repeated resolutions . . . I was brought wholly to break off all former wicked ways . . . and to apply myself to seek my salvation, and practice the duties of religion: but without that kind of affection and delight, that I had formerly experienced. My concern now wrought more by inward struggles and conflicts, and self-reflections. . . . But yet it seems to me, I sought after a miserable manner: which has made me sometimes since to question, whether ever it issued in that which was saving; being ready to doubt, whether such miserable seeking was ever succeeded. But yet I was brought to seek salvation, in a manner that I never was before. . . . My concern continued and prevailed, with many exercising things and inward struggles; but yet it never seemed to be proper to express my concern that I had, by the name of terror. (*PW* 791)

The "inward struggles" that Edwards names three times in the single paragraph are signified not by any explicit definition or example but by the action of the passage as a whole, turning on each "but" to add counterargument to every argument, qualifications for every conviction. Despite these turns, Edwards's inward struggles remain static and irruptive, prevailing only in that they continue, but seeming to fail in their production of affective states, the "affection and delight" of former experiences or the final "terror" that would exceed his concerns.

To consider its ultimate term, the winding logic of the passage apparently serves to answer a question that nobody asked: Why, in the final sentence, does Edwards protest that his concern should not be mistaken for terror, especially since, in the narrative to that point, Edwards had never mentioned terror? One possibility may be that he was distancing his own narrative, which would depend heavily upon the state of his affections, from the convention of terror as a sign of grace. Yet that would seem to fly in the face of his defense of terror and terror preaching throughout his career. A more likely possibility is that Edwards was noting a lack that contributed to the "miserable manner" of applying himself to seek salvation detailed before. In this reading, the inward concerns with which Edwards struggled did not come up to the bar of terror, thus signaling how crucial Edwards held the experience of terror to be.

What immediately follows the note on terror is Edwards's description of his struggles with the doctrines of eternal damnation and predestination: "[M]y mind had been wont to be full of objections against the doctrine of God's sovereignty, in choosing whom he would to eternal life, and rejecting whom he pleased; leaving them eternally to perish and be everlastingly tormented in hell. It used to appear like a horrible doctrine to me" (*PW* 791–792). For Edwards, as well as today's students coming to Edwards for the first time, the cocktail of eternal damnation and predestination proved difficult to swallow. But Edwards takes this difficulty and makes it the site of his depiction of the difference between a mere conviction of belief and an affective conviction of realization. His first conversion is merely reasonable: "But I remember the time very well, when I seemed to be convinced, and fully satisfied, as to this sovereignty of God, and his justice in thus eternally disposing of men . . . but only that now I saw further, and my reason apprehended the justice and reasonableness of it" (*PW* 792). Yet this reasonable conviction, the one lacking in terror, is one of only seeming. Edwards's second conversion moves from reason to affect: "I have oftentimes since that first conviction, had quite another kind of sense of God's sovereignty, than I had then. I have often since, not only had a conviction, but a *delightful* conviction. The doctrine of God's sovereignty has very often appeared, an exceeding pleasant, bright, and sweet doctrine to me: and absolute sovereignty is what I love to ascribe to God. But my first conviction was not with this" (*PW* 792). Just as his first conviction lacks terror, it also lacks sweetness. But then which is it? Is the doctrine terrible or delightful? Has Edwards completely bypassed terror in moving from a rational conviction to a delightful one?

Anticipating such a question, Edwards offers one of the stranger illustrations in his work—a description of his terror and delight of thunderstorms:

> And scarce anything, among all the works of nature, was so sweet to me as thunder and lightning. Formerly, nothing had been so terrible to me. I used to be a person uncommonly terrified with thunder: and it used to strike me with terror, when I saw a thunderstorm rising. But now, on the contrary, it rejoiced me. (*PW* 794)

Delight takes the place of terror; it does not do so by rejecting terror, however, but by accepting and submitting to it. Edwards's new behavior—"to fix myself to view the clouds, and see the lightnings play, and hear the majestic and awful voice of God's thunder" (*PW* 794)—prepares for the translation of the awful voice of God to the sweet singing Edwards would, if it is to be believed, perform in the midst of the tempest: "And while I viewed, used to spend my time, as it always seemed natural to me, to sing or chant forth my meditations; to speak my thoughts in soliloquies, and speak with a singing voice" (*PW* 794). From terror to delight, from thunder to song, Edwards's conversions here would mediate affective conversion through the submission and acceptance of terror, overcoming it only by being drenched in it.

Edwards's rendering of the feeling of grace from the substance of fear thus revisits the fundamental place of terror in the revival's conversion morphology. But what the personal narrative clarifies is the infinite and ongoing reduction of self in order to inhabit such a state. Consistently figured as an infinite smallness, a "swallowing up," the experience of one's immersion into the terrible and glorious is for Edwards a matter of becoming nothing: "The person of Christ appeared ineffably excellent, with an excellency great enough to swallow up all thought and conception. . . . I felt withal, an ardency of soul to be, what I know not otherwise how to express, than to be emptied and annihilated; to lie in the dust, and to be full of Christ alone" (*PW* 801). This desire to be swallowed up and emptied into nothingness is perhaps the most conspicuous motif of Edwards's narrative: "My heart as it were panted after this . . . that I might be nothing, and that God might be all" (*PW* 796); "to receive salvation of him . . . quite empty of self" (*PW* 800); "an ardency of spirit, and inward struggling and breathings and groaning, that cannot be uttered, to be emptied of myself, and swallowed up in Christ" (*PW* 801); "The person of Christ appeared . . .

great enough to swallow up all thought and conception" (*PW* 801). This desire for infinite reduction into nothing obeys, I argue, the same logic that attended Edwards's conversion of terror to joy—that inward struggle not to overcome the terror that threatens but to recalibrate one's conception of self so that one would, as it were, learn to love the terror itself. This infinite humility that Edwards everywhere desires in the *Personal Narrative*, as we will see, adopts its figuration from the metaphysical problem of nothing that Edwards had confronted many years earlier.

Sharon Cameron has illuminated the way Edwards invites impossible calculations in order to make accessible, or at least thinkable, a mode of perception completely alienated from one's person. Considering the impossible (for us) calculations that Edwards enjoins in his late-career treatise *The Nature of True Virtue*, Cameron argues that "Edwards makes the nothing that cannot be imagined available to imagining. But he makes it available through a limit case before which we must remain on the near side of the limit" (26). These paradoxes, like so many of the infinite-upon-infinite calculations that Edwards inhabits through continual figuration in his personal narrative, draw upon a discourse of mathematics and logic, the abstract space of quantity and proportion, made possible through metaphysical thought. Like the way in which Edwards asks us to erase both body in space and space between bodies, Cameron shows the way Edwards's quantifications erase both self as person and self as impersonal: "Edwards's quantifications reveal a simultaneous disappearance of the person (for whom they exist synechdochically, as emblems of what he is and can do) *and* of the impersonal, which is differently blanked out in a vacuum of absolute value" (40–41). Becoming nothing is thus an immanent experience achieved not at the end of calculation but through its constant maintenance, and makes visible, "one might almost say available, some impersonal universe in which thought and affect (though not our thought and not our affect) are made at once unrecognizable and intelligible. In the sleeping-rocks passage . . . nothing and everything are almost made perceptible, if perception could be reinscribed as a fully alienable phenomenon, as something not ours" (52).

What Cameron identifies in Edwards recalls the paradox of objectivity described by Thomas Nagel as the desire to attain a "view from nowhere" and discussed by George Levine as the trope of "dying to know."[25] Perfect knowledge would seem to require an absolute detachment. But whereas Nagel and Levine would fill out the assumptions and conditions such quantifications obscure, saving the pursuit of objectivity from the absolute skepticism that the paradoxes incur, Edwards would seek to combat skepticism in the same way that he engages with terror of God's infinite majesty, by calculating and figuring a more perfectly impossible perceptual nothingness. Levine identifies the trope as properly Cartesian, arising most conspicuously in Descartes's First Meditation. Edwards would seem to lift his understanding from the same source, as his early studies on the mind, on being and nothingness, bear the imprint of the Cartesian primer—the *Port-Royal Logic*—which would introduce the Cartesian method of logic to America.[26]

*Logic, or the Art of Thinking*, more commonly known as the *Port-Royal Logic*, was one of the most popular introductions to Cartesian method in the late seventeenth century. Edwards not only owned a printed copy of it but also a heavily marked-up manuscript transcription of it that had been passed down to him from his father, who had in turn received it from Warham Mather.[27] For Edwards, this new logic, with its focus on the training of abstract judgment, would come to replace the heavily schematized and meticulously gridded orders of the older Ramist logic.[28] It is through this text that Edwards would first come upon the definition of abstraction that would lead him to the much wider problems of being and nothingness.[29] The *Port-Royal Logic* describes abstraction as a matter of degrees, a patterning of inclusion: "Thus I can rise by degrees to extension itself [by abstraction]. Now in these abstractions it is clear that the lower degree includes the higher degree along with some particular determination, just as the I includes that which thinks, the equilateral triangle includes the triangle, and the triangle the straight-lined figure. But since the higher degree is less determinate, it can represent more things" (Arnauld and Nicole, Buroker trans. 38). This straightforward description of the categories of abstraction cleverly folds the *cogito* into what Cameron notices in Edwards's desire to rise up through levels of abstraction to a universe of impersonality. At its highest end, the authors note, abstraction dissolves into metaphysics: "There is also a genus that is not a species, namely the highest of all the genera. Whether this genus is being or substance is unimportant, and is more a question for metaphysics than logic" (41).

For Edwards, the metaphysical question is immediately answerable: the highest genus is being. In his manuscript copy of the *Port-Royal Logic*, Edwards's handwritten notes focus on this very question of abstraction and being: "The more General the more simple and abstracted the idea although the more Comprehensive. Therefore instance till we come to being. The more special the more comprehended" (Downame MS). Moving up the ladder of abstraction through "instance till we come to being" would sacrifice comprehension for comprehensiveness. The idea becomes more comprehensive as it moves toward being, but the mind becomes less able to comprehend it. Edwards would later articulate from this the problem of a perfect comprehensive knowledge: "Infinite knowledge implies a perfect, comprehensive view of a whole future eternity, which seems utterly impossible: for how can there be any reaching of the whole of this to comprehend it, without reaching to the utmost limits of it? But this can't be where there is no such thing as utmost limits" (*"Miscellanies"* 372). Edwards's translation of the *Port-Royal Logic* describes the fate of the pursuit of a "full extent of Knowledge" in terms that sound remarkably like the infinite prostration Edwards would advocate in his personal narrative:

> The most compendious way to the full extent of Knowledge is, not to toil ourselves in the Search of that which is above us, and which we can never rationally expect to comprehend. Such are those Questions which relate to the Omnipotency of God, which it would be ridiculous to confine within the narrow Bounds of our Understandings; and generally as to whatever partakes of Infinity. For our Understanding being finite, loses itself in the Labyrinth of Infinity; and lies overwhelmed under the Multitude of Thoughts contradicting one another. (Arnauld and Nicole, Ozell trans. 381)

At this outer end of the genus of being, where logic becomes metaphysics, the *Port-Royal Logic* advocates a blank confession of ignorance in the face of infinity:

> Can God make a Body infinite in Quantity; a Movement infinite in Swiftness; a Multitude infinite in Number? Is Number infinite, Even or Odd? He that should answer once for all, I know nothing of it, may be said to have made as fair a Progress in a Moment, as he that had been beating his Brains twenty Years about these Niceties. (Arnauld and Nicole, Ozell trans. 381)

Edwards, it would seem, reads this capitulation against the grain. If "fair progress" can be made by knowing nothing, then Edwards would begin there—not by just admitting that nothing is all he can know, but by trying to know nothing more positively by adopting wider and wider calculations and aiming at infinite reductions that would perform a calculus of perspective, achieving impersonality by approaching zero by infinitely minute subtraction.

Though the *Port-Royal Logic* advises one to admit ignorance in the face of infinity, it goes on to engage in several familiar paradoxical demonstrations of infinity, beginning with the infinite divisibility of matter—"[T]his part whose smallness is already incomprehensible to us, contains still another proportional world, and so on to infinity. So there is no particle of matter that does not have as many proportional parts as the entire world, whatever size we give it" (Arnauld and Nicole, Buroker trans. 231)—and ending with the conversion of Zeno's paradox of motion into the method of finding an area under a curve— "If we take half of a square, and half of this half, and so on to infinity, and then we join all these halves along their longest sides, we will form a space of an irregular shape that will continually decrease to infinity along one end, but that will be equal to the entire square" (232). Yet the authors of the *Port-Royal Logic* draw from these examples a negative lesson, the limits of the mind, "to make us admit in spite of ourselves that some things exist even though we cannot understand them. This is why it is good to tire the mind on these subtleties, in order to master its presumption and to take away its audacity ever to oppose our feeble insight to the truths presented by the Church, under the pretext that we cannot understand them" (233).[30]

The mastery that the paradoxes would achieve over the "audacity" of mind echoes the economy of humility that Edwards expresses in his accounts of thinking hell's eternity, but at the same time the exercises signal a greater desire for power and control ("to master its presumption"). This is an instance of what Levine has identified as the self-empowerment built into the strategy of self-humiliation: "The expressed humility, utterly necessary for the argument and representative of the ways in which the work of scientific self-legitimation proceeded in the centuries that followed, also works within a frame of almost overweaning ambition" (48). Yet what if this frame of ambition were itself subjected to humiliation—would it result in a greater pride, that would then have to be overcome in like manner? Such a recursion is precisely what we see in Edwards's repeated attempts to express his sin in terms such as "infinite upon infinite," a kind of humiliation that would direct itself even against the pride of successful humiliation: "It seems to me, my conviction of sin is exceeding small, and faint. It appears to me enough to amaze me, that I have no more sense of my sin" (*PW* 802). For Edwards, this structure of infinite recursion between humility and pride, the need to constantly abase oneself, works according to the structure of infinite division. Feeding on itself, the terrible reduction and infinite regress could approximate the impersonal only in its rededicated efforts to calculate oneself to nothing.

Such a pattern of infinite reduction and recursion, latent within the abstracting principles and methods of Cartesian logic and its model of ideal geometry, thus fuels the paradoxical, limitless energy of terror and hellfire in Edwards's affective psychology. It is the deep engine of what Richard Niebuhr has identified as Edwards's "open system," in which "[t]rue virtue must always be open to the possibility of greater and greater plurality" (41).[31] Terror is necessary and substantial, a means and a goal, for it continuously, like an infinite algorithm, dismantles those limits of security that would arrest one's continual fall into nothingness.

Edwards will play on the analogy between this quantitative reduction and the sinner's descent into hell in his most famous sermon, *Sinners in the Hands of an Angry God*, by lacing its dynamic everywhere with his favorite figure of swallowing up. The first three times he uses it, swallowing up is merely a figure for the destruction of hell: "[H]ell opens its mouth wide to receive them [sinners]; and if God should permit it, they would be hastily swallowed up and lost" (407); "hell is gaping for them, the flames gather and flash about them, and would fain lay hold on them, and swallow them up" (409); and "'tis nothing but his mere pleasure that keeps you from being this moment swallowed up in everlasting destruction" (411). But the final swallowing in the sermon points back to the attributes of infinite abstraction and paradoxical recursion:

> There will be no end to this exquisite horrible misery. When you look forward, you shall see a long forever, a boundless duration before you, which will swallow up your thoughts, and amaze your soul; . . . you will know certainly that you must wear out long ages, millions of millions of ages, in wrestling and conflicting with this almighty merciless vengeance; and then when you have so done, when so many ages have actually been spent by you in this manner, you will know that all is but a point to what remains. (415–416)

Thoughts swallowed up by perceptions of long forevers, Edwards's figure would situate in hell the kind of infinite calculation—never to conclude without the external aid of God's infinite mercy—that he would inculcate in his parish and himself.

Swallowing up, this annihilation and emptying of the self in the face of the infinite, is not only the threat that terror would fear, but the effect that terror would cause. In the following, Edwards gives as detailed an outline as he ever would of the psychological mechanics of terror:

> And the terrors which some persons have, are very much owing to the particular constitution and temper they are of. Nothing is more manifest, than that some persons are of such a temper and frame, that their imaginations are

> more strongly impressed with everything they are affected with, than others; and the impression on the imagination reacts on the affection, and raises that still higher; and so affection and imagination act reciprocally, one on another, till their affection is raised to a vast height, and the person is swallowed up, and loses all possession of himself. (RA 156–157)

Edwards here is trying to explain the causes of the self-violence of those under a conviction of their sinfulness. Terror is so powerful because it operates recursively, amplifying itself in a feedback loop of imagination and affection. Yet, though in the case of self-violence this outcome is tragic, this same recursive structure can accomplish what is in Edwards's view more desirable, namely, the loss of egoistic self through its humiliation.

The affect of terror that Edwards conceives in order to rebut the conservative critiques of the revival is one that is defined along the contours of logical abstraction and infinite calculation. Terror would approximate, in its endless dynamic and regressive potential, the inexpressible yet tantalizingly felt concept of nothingness at the heart of the Cartesian method—that always-deferred, impossible perspective of impersonality for which both the epistemological method and the soul-wracked sinner continually search. This theoretical point of nothingness (although not really a point, as Edwards argues) is a kind of zero-limit. I define *zero-limit* here in the sense of an asymptotic limit of a function in calculus, a hypothetical quantity of nowhere that the affect of terror could approach, through infinite sums of infinitely abbreviated distances. Thus Edwards clarifies the new terror of the Awakening from a manual on the art of the new thinking, and installs within the American intellectual and literary tradition an affective accommodation, terror, as the feeling of almost accessing that wholly alienated perspective of impersonality. Being swallowed up, then, is a way of getting at truth by losing oneself in that degree of nothing, and finding in it the dependency wherein one's infinite terror could converge with joy.

## 2

## CRITICAL TERRORS

Poe's Aesthetic Terror and the Claims of Art after Jena

**IT MAY AT FIRST SEEM A STRETCH** to turn from Edwards's divine terrors of God and hell to Poe's sensational terrors of revenants, premature burials, ghastly dismemberments, and homicidal insanity. Not only at a century's remove but also at a wide generic one, Poe's and Edwards's work seems written for different audiences and burdened with different stakes. Yet, though evidence of Edwards's direct influence on Poe is thin, the similarity of their habits of mind and their shared interest in terror have suggested strong, if indirect, affinities, especially in their aesthetic philosophies. "As philosophers who join a determination to know with a Calvinist dread of that knowledge," Colin (Joan) Dayan observes, "neither Edwards or Poe can accept the comfort of any abstract or general language of nature and mind" (6). The historical genealogy behind this sense of overlap is a philosophical one. It moves from Edwards's idealism as an affective-sensational response to Locke, through Kant's critiques and toward post-Kantian romantic philosophy, to which Poe's own unique aesthetic philosophy responds. Edwards's idealist philosophy, a more affectionally charged version of Berkeley's and Hume's, could be seen as part of the dilemma to which Kant responds. Poe's aesthetic philosophy, drawing from the German sources of romantic philosophy acquired through Coleridge, becomes a more radicalized version of post-Kantian idealism. Thus Edwards, before Kant, and Poe, after Kant, both explore the significance of affect within idealist metaphysics. The route from Edwards's logical terrors to Poe's more aesthetic ones thus goes through Kant's *Critique of Judgment* (1790) and the idealist aesthetic philosophy that emerged from its attempt to conceptualize terror through the sublime. But getting to the point at which Poe's terror may be read philosophically also means getting past its popular understanding, which, like Chauncy on the revival, would see it as derivative and pathological. Poe's theory of terror, like Edwards's, may best be seen through its defense.

Poe has become, in popular regard, less an author and more a brand indelibly associated with terror. Even the features of his daguerreotyped face—the tall forehead, sunken eyes, disheveled hair, and delicate moustache—have become cultural shorthand for the macabre and gothic. Like most popular reputations, this one deserves qualification. The caricature of a haunted Poe, writing obsessively from a drunken delirium, broadly misconstrues his terror as the whole of his personality, missing his other contributions to American letters—his literary criticism, his humor, his scientific pretensions—by reading him as if he were himself a character belonging within the popular horror genre that his work in fact shaped. Yet what is most misleading about this caricature is not that it leaves out the ranges of Poe's other interests but rather that it forecloses inquiry into Poe's terror as a serious trope. By portraying Poe as an author compulsively consumed by terror, the question of why he writes terror is most often answered by a species of diagnosis: what was wrong with Poe that he felt compelled to write this way? Or what is wrong with us that we read it? Seeking to account for what seems so unhealthy about Poe's morbidity, readers are led to interpret Poe's terror as a symptom of something else.

In 1835, trying desperately to land a job as an editor and writer for Thomas White's *Southern Literary Messenger*, Poe at the start of his career was pressed to defend the horror of his themes. He had sent White a number of pieces, both critical reviews and a short tale, to exemplify not only his writing facility but, moreover, his awareness of the emerging literary-critical discourse of periodical culture. The tale Poe sent White, "Berenice" (1835), is classic Poe: a grotesque story of premature burial, grinning corpses, and dental mutilation. White published the tale in the March number of the *Messenger*, but appended a note at the end of the issue, complimentary of the tale's style but complaining that "we confess that we think there is too much German horror in his subject" ("Editorial Remarks" [Mar. 1835] 387). White's jab at what would become Poe's popular reputation initiates a broader critique of his literary horror in general, roping it into the gothic genre (here signaled by its "German" origins) and suggesting its illegitimate or derivative quality. Many critical accounts of Poe's terror define terror in a similar way, reading it in order to discover the real fears of the period or of the man. The tales themselves, in these interpretations, become so many symbolic nightmares—nightmares of sexuality, of race, of Western enlightenment, of capitalism.[1] Terror, in each of these readings, is read as an indexical symptom which must be passed over in order to get at the real conditions that those terrors can be said to be about. Poe's defense of sensational fear in literature thus not only responds to White's misgivings but can be extended to the common hermeneutical interpretations of his horrors as well.

Poe responds to White's comment in multiple ways over the next five years, both directly, as in a letter he sends White apologizing for but also defending "Berenice,"[2] but also implicitly, through both his fiction and his literary criticism. Instead of retreating from "Berenice" and its horrific themes, Poe instead habitually revisits it, revising its plot of a female beloved's death and return in "Morella" (1835), "Ligeia" (1838), and "The Fall of the House of Usher" (1839). The tales mature with each revision, becoming increasingly complex yet still retaining the skeletal plot of "Berenice," as if Poe sought to exonerate the original tale. And when Poe collects those tales in *The Tales of the Grotesque and Arabesque* (1840), he again returns to White's criticism of terror, appending a preface defending his tales from "Germanism" and arguing for the legitimacy of terror. The coincident and entangled origins of both Poe's literary critical career and his sensationalist fiction form the signal consideration of this chapter. Poe, in defending the critical worth of terror, not only writes about terror in his criticism but raises criticism to a theme in his terror. Seeking to establish his critical name, and drawing heavily from the German romantic literary critics, Poe writes tales that incorporate the rising philosophical stakes of literary criticism, fables in which terror resists and reframes precisely those interpretive moves that would explain terror as an unhealthy symptom.

The preface to *Tales of the Grotesque and Arabesque* begins by referring to the "one or two critics" who have taxed him "in all friendliness, with what they have been pleased to term 'Germanism' and gloom" (*TS* 1:473).[3] Poe counters that if his tales are "Germanic," then that is only the "vein for the time being." He bristles at the suggestion that the "Germanism" is all he can do, and especially at the assumption that macabre themes must be the symptom of a disordered mind. Poe's broadest argument is not only that his terror is designed, but that it is philosophically legitimate:

> But the truth is that, with a single exception, there is no one of these stories in which the scholar should recognise the distinctive features of that species of pseudo-horror which we are taught to call Germanic, for no better reason than

that some of the secondary names of German literature have become identified with its folly. If in many of my productions terror has been the thesis, I maintain that terror is not of Germany, but of the soul, — that I have deduced this terror only from its legitimate sources, and urged it only to its legitimate results. (*TS* 1:473)

Poe adopts the rhetorical language of the metaphysical philosopher, posing terror as a thesis and describing its discovery through the language of analysis—*deduced*—as well as the language of compulsion—*urged*. Poe imagines his tales being read by "the scholar" rather than the moral critic or the mob, and he calls upon an analytical vocabulary to assert terror's legitimacy. This turn, then—from reviewer to scholar, from assumption to analysis, from Germany to the soul—seeks to reframe the value of literary terror in a philosophical discourse. It is not a local symptom of a disordered mind, nor is it the unconscious imitation of a mind under the influence of the "secondary names" of Germanic literature. Poe might give a similar response to the myriad other critical interpretations of his terror—as historical and cultural index, as psychological projection—for these interpretations all take the literary effect to be subordinate to the world which is its cause. What Poe urges instead is to consider terror as derived not from the world but from the mystery of the human soul.

In this chapter, I will outline how Poe's avowed "terror of the soul" in his dead woman tales takes as its thematic material the resistance that affects in general, and terror more particularly, pose to the critical interpretive paradigm. Poe's early-career terror, rather than being about some external cultural or biographical circumstance, can be more properly said to be about the conditions and processes of the criticism that would read terror as symptom. I begin at the end of Poe's dead woman series—"The Raven" (1845) and its companion piece, "The Philosophy of Composition" (1846)—to show how Poe's project culminates in the mirrored image of poetry and criticism, a reflective arrangement that enables a view of the dead woman plot as a fable of critical interpretation. With that in view, the chapter then turns to the tales, bookended by "Berenice" and "The Fall of the House of Usher," in which that plot develops. I show how Poe's terror is in fact under an influence originating in Germany—not the influence of the "secondary names" which he disparages, but the idealist post-Kantian philosophy of Fichte and Schelling and the literary theory of the Schlegels and their English translator, Coleridge.[4] Poe's terror emerges in works in which he presses the romantic demand that literature contain its own self-reflection, and thus what makes his terror so difficult to interpret is that it insists upon taking as its own object the compartmentalizing nature of interpretation. What Poe's terror is "really about," I will argue, is the impulse to reduce literary effect to being really about something else.

## Absolute Raven

Poe's reputation as a writer of terror and his career as a literary critic arise concurrently. He is, perhaps more than most American authors of the period, acutely attuned to the burgeoning importance of criticism to the maturation of literary prospects. At the *Southern Literary Messenger*, the young Poe gains a reputation for scathing reviews, earning him the epithet "tomahawk man," an epithet that imagines a native ferocity, a distinctly American brutality, in the quality of his reviews. Never humble when brash self-promotion might increase his fame, Poe collects the complimentary notices of both his reviews and his tales and republishes them in the columns of the *Messenger*. He thus constructs his authorial self in the reflexive and romantic mold of the writer/critic, claiming that "the less poetical the critic, the less just the critique, and the converse" (*ER* 5). As a critic, Poe works to install in America a more fastidious and objective criticism of literary art. As a writer, he incorporates the general aims of this new criticism, but crucially extends the critical project through experimental frames in fiction and poetry.

In doing so, Poe becomes both a practitioner and a theorist of the developing discourse of romantic-era aesthetic criticism. The stakes of aesthetic criticism having been raised by the idealist metaphysics of the German post-Kantian tradition, the practice of literary criticism became more and more indistinguishable from philosophical inquiry. Rather than merely publishing a reader's subjective opinion regarding the merit of a work or a summary of the work's contents, literary criticism began to model itself as a scholarly discipline, searching for essential meaning within aesthetic form. Poe, noticing this new character of criticism, calls it a "science": "That the public attention, in America, has, of late days, been more than usually directed to the matter of literary criticism, is plainly apparent. Our periodicals are beginning to acknowledge the importance of the science (shall we so term it?) and to disdain the flippant *opinion* which so long has been made its substitute" (*ER* 1027). In the same article, Poe objects to the "cant of generality" exemplified by Cornelius Mathews's claim that criticism "'dismisses errors of grammar, and hands over an imperfect rhyme or a false quantity to the proof-reader; it looks *now* to the heart of the subject and the author's design. It is a test of opinion'" (*ER* 1030). Poe prefers instead the analytical tradition of German criticism associated with the Jena school: "[W]hat need we say of the Germans?—what of Winkelmann, of Novalis, of Schelling, of Göethe, of Augustus William, and of Frederick Schlegel?—that their magnificent *critiques raisonnées* differ from those of Kaimes, of Johnson, and of Blair, in principle not at all . . . but solely in their more careful elaboration, their greater thoroughness, their more profound analysis and application of the principles themselves" (*ER* 1030). Within this analytical frame, and against the spirit of "Orphicism, or Dialism, or Emersonianism" (*ER* 1031), Poe demands criticism limited to the work itself: "A book is written—and it is only *as the book* that we subject it to review. . . . [I]t will be seen that criticism, the test or analysis of *Art*, (*not* of opinion,) is only properly employed upon productions which have their basis in art itself" (*ER* 1032). For Poe, the critic does not bloviate over general theses and opinionated assertions but rather dissects objectively, becoming an objective scientist who possesses above all "a talent for analysis and a solemn indifference to abuse" (*ER* 1032).[5]

Preferring German romantic critics, scientific methods, and textual analysis, Poe's definition of the new criticism helps us to see it as the spiritual inheritor of Edwards's logical idealism. Turning scriptural exegesis into a secularized hermeneutics and replacing theological truth with aesthetic judgment, Poe's romantic criticism repositions Edwards's epistemological questions in a post-Kantian domain. As Philippe Lacoue-Labarthe and Jean-Luc Nancy have shown, those Jena romantics that Poe singles out as exemplary derive, from German transcendental idealism, the influential theory that literature embeds and complicates philosophical idealism.[6] In this account, both empirically based assessments of beauty and prejudiced evaluations of morals are gradually replaced with a supplemental criticism, a criticism that, according to the logic of the Derridean supplement (a supplement that reveals an original lack), comes to perfect the work of art by supplying what it lacks. That is, before Schelling and the Schlegels, criticism would focus on either those formal matters that Mathews dismisses or the general moral opinion that Poe derides. After them, criticism becomes an integral part of the art product itself, reflecting and creating: "Construction (criticism) is art—or more precisely, the *entire* construction is the critical complement or supplement that the work requires in order to be a work (of art)" (Lacoue-Labarthe and Nancy 110). The addition of criticism to art thus seeks to complete the romantic project of literature, diverting the trajectory of philosophical idealism from those radical impasses of epistemology in which Edwards found the terror of divinity to a theoretically limitless project of installing within the work of art both "the 'auto-illumination' of the beautiful work" and "in every work, . . . the absence of the Work" (105). It is this doubled determination of criticism that Poe renders the theme of his most famous poem and its critical supplement. Poe, aware of the shifting modes of criticism, reprises Edwards's affective turn toward terror in order to inscribe the enduring negativity of the "absence of the Work." As Edwards had found in the radical deprivations of terror the posture by which the privations of hell and sin could be made dynamically accessible, Poe constructs a particular feeling-tone, the signature affect of "nevermore," that similarly seeks to complete romantic criticism by insisting on its fundamental deficiency rather than evading or ameliorating it.

Though "The Raven" is a poem that is clearly about loss and absence, it is only through the addition of his essay "The Philosophy of Composition" that Poe is able to describe that loss as a fundamental deficiency of art in general. Attesting that the composition of "The Raven" was a rational process, "The Philosophy of Composition" dispels any mirage of spontaneous genius by offering

> a peep behind the scenes, at the elaborate and vacillating crudities of thought . . . at the painful erasures and interpolations—in a word, at the wheels and pinions—the tackle for scene-shifting—the step-ladders and demon-traps—the cock's feathers, the red paint and the black patches, which, in ninety-nine cases out of the hundred, constitute the properties of the literary *histrio*. (ER 14)

Poe's shifting catalogue of props wheels out an elaborate machinery of literary effects, erasing the idea of an original fully formed aesthetic unity and interpolating a deconstructed array of material costume and stage direction. What follows, Poe's scarcely credible account of deducing every feature of the poem, from its length to its subject matter to its repetitive refrain, leads many critics to consider "The Philosophy of Composition" as a hoax or a burlesque.[7]

Yet when we compare the deconstructive aims Poe outlines above with the new function of criticism that Lacoue-Labarthe and Nancy consider, we notice a telling similarity. For the Jena romantics, the identity of the work of art is less imitation and more production, the generation of a new spirit that arises through the criticism that would penetrate (and thus contribute within) the formative process of the work of art:

> [C]riticism's inverse direction leads toward a penetration to the heart of the formative process, and toward the reconstitution of its efficacity. One can easily

see that this direction is no less idealistic than the first. One could say that it opposes to—or imposes upon—an idealism of manifestation another idealism, ... the idealism of production, of the conditions of production and of the exhibition of the conditions of production. ... From this point on, the genuine identity of art (of the work, of the artist) no longer depends on the relation of resemblance to another given identity (or on veri-similitude), but on the construction of *critical identity*. (Lacoue-Labarthe and Nancy 111–112)

"The Philosophy of Composition," with its stated goal of offering a "peep behind the scenes," might thus be seen as imposing an idealism of "the exhibition of the conditions of production" and the auto-generation of "critical identity." For "The Philosophy of Composition" belongs to "The Raven" according to the logic of criticism as essential supplement; it attempts (and here, it does not matter whether the history it tells is factual or not) to lay bare the machinery, the idealism of process, in order to re-install absence at the heart of the work. A critical idealism does not merely dismantle the pretensions of mimetic art but replaces them with a new source of identity, the reader's critical understanding, which lays claim to the meaning of the poem by recoordinating the particles of its dispersed wreckage. The poem does not exist wholly on the page but in the mind of its reader. In order for this idealist transaction to occur, there must be something missing from the work that the critic/reader would supply. But what if, Poe seems to ask, criticism installs the very absence that renders its own presence necessary? What kind of strange reflective arrangement might ensue if criticism found the absence it locates in its work inherent not really in the work's process of production but rather in its own analytical process? Rendering "The Raven" as feathers, paint, and patches, "The Philosophy of Composition" may seem to demystify the poem, but it at the same time allows the poem to mystify the criticism.

"The Raven," for all its themes of love and loss, of death and memory, is populated throughout with references to scholarship and criticism. The speaker is, after all, a "scholar" who turns to his "curious volumes of forgotten lore" in order to escape the sorrow, the affect, attendant upon the death of his beloved Lenore. His study, moreover, is appointed with a bust of Pallas, the goddess of wisdom who sprang from the head of Zeus fully formed. This symbol of thought becomes the sole perch for the raven, suggesting a chain of analogous associations. Where Pallas emerges from Zeus's head, the birth of wisdom and reason, what would emerge from Pallas's head is a more affective symbol of woe and darkness. The gods may generate thought, but thought itself would thus, associatively, generate something darker, a shadow that haunts and hangs over the intelligence that breeds it. Given such clues, the poem would seem to be not only about the dread of a man thinking about his dead beloved, but more generally about the dread arising from the intellectual act of thinking in general.

Thought, then, may be considered the origin of the poem's emblem of terror, a thematically appropriate image, since the scholar's own mind is responsible for his anguish. During the course of the poem, the scholar comes to realize that the bird can only repeat the sound "nevermore." Once he realizes this, he perversely formulates his questions in such a way as to produce from the raven confirmation of his own fears about the permanence of death and his own misery. "[I]s there balm in Gilead?" the scholar asks; "Nevermore" (*CP* 368) comes the reply. The self-torturing implication of these questions Poe explains in his essay: "The student now guesses the state of the case, but is impelled, as I have before explained, by the human thirst for self-torture, and in part by superstition, to propound such queries to the bird as will bring him, the lover, the most of the luxury of sorrow, through the anticipated answer, 'Nevermore'" (*ER* 24). The villain of the poem, then, is not the raven but rather the scholar, who tortures himself in transforming unmeaning birdsong into existential argument.[8] The poem might appear to be a dialogue but is in fact a monologue. What appeared to be an object of mystery (the raven and "The Raven") and an inquiring critic (the scholar and the speaker of "The Philosophy of Composition") resolve into a single auto-reflective work. What the poem would seem to be about, then, is the way in which intellectual attempts to divert, comprehend, or criticize loss come to recognize their own inherent complicity in that very loss, that the loss is not in the world but rather is projected onto that world by the very attempts to corral it.

In "The Philosophy of Composition," Poe offers an account of the compositional process of "The Raven" through an identical logic of ironic self-interrogation and manipulated discourse. For example, Poe attests that he began composing "The Raven" by first deciding upon its length. Considering that a poem too lengthy would entail a "loss of unity" by requiring more than one sitting, Poe imagines that "the extent of a poem may be made to bear mathematical relation to its merit" and "that the brevity must be in a direct ratio of the intensity of the intended effect" (*ER* 15). Having calculated mathematically, Poe reports that "I reached at once what I conceived the proper *length* of my intended poem—a length of about one hundred lines. It is, in fact, a hundred and eight" (*ER* 16). This has the air of deduction, with one glaring caveat: Poe already knew the poem was one hundred and eight lines long and so could obviously manipulate the aesthetic maxims to produce the answer he claimed followed from them.

The pattern of questions and answers that Poe uses as the method of "The Philosophy of Composition" thus reflects the suspicious and anticipatory logic behind the pattern of questions and answers in "The Raven." At times, the voice of "The Philosophy of Composition" falls into explicit conversation with itself, replaying the action of the poem:

> I asked myself—"Of all melancholy topics, what, according to the *universal* understanding of mankind, is the *most* melancholy?" Death—was the obvious reply. "And when," I said, "is this most melancholy of topics most poetical?" From what I have already explained at some length, the answer, here also, is obvious—"When it most closely allies itself to *Beauty*: the death, then, of a beautiful woman is unquestionably, the most poetical topic in the world." (*ER* 18–19)

Bracketing the flimsiness of the argument for the moment—more than one reader has expressed surprise at Poe's "obvious" assumptions here—what is interesting in relation to the place of criticism in "The Raven" is the way the rational process of composition recalls the dialectical back-and-forth between speaker and raven. By asking the right questions and tinkering with the aesthetic maxims that will answer them, Poe emerges victorious from the process with the theme of his poem, the death of a beautiful woman, which, of course, he could have predicted from the start. It is this deceptive cleverness that leads skeptical readers to designate "The Philosophy of Composition" as merely a similitude of analysis, a skinning of "The Raven" rather than an exposure of its soul.[9] Yet this trick itself is the most salient point of connection between "The Raven" and "The Philosophy of Composition": both poem and essay capitalize upon the same method of ex post facto proof, of manipulating questions in order to prompt predetermined answers.[10] As Leland Person, first noting the reflection, puts it, "While the raven ('The Raven') utters only a word—only itself—the student (the reader) manipulates the text in order to make it mean what he wants it to mean" ("Poe's Composition of Philosophy" 8).

Opening this analogy redirects attention back to the bird. For the essay treats the poem as the poem treats the raven; it gives voice to a nonrational object by making it sound like an interlocutor in rational argument.[11] The raven, even though it is able to learn "by rote" a lesson, is allegedly chosen, as Poe explains in "the Philosophy of Composition," *because* it is a nonreasoning creature. The raven is thus a reasoning blank. Its "words" are merely squawks. Yet, though it says nothing of itself, the student, by putting questions to it, makes it, as it were, speak. What he makes it say, however, is ironic, for in testifying in the enduring negative, it suggests that there is no afterlife, no escape from mental anguish, and that the inciting event of the poem, the speaker's turn to the forgotten lore, is insufficient to remove the sorrow he feels. Thus the student/lover has rendered from absence a message of eternal negation, one that refuses conclusion and ends with the suggestion that the dialogue will never end; the raven "still is sitting, *still* is sitting / On the pallid bust of Pallas" (*CP* 369). The irony, that the student/lover has determined this existential bleakness out of nothing, indicates a deeper paradox. The processes of reason are haunted by an emblem of enduring absence; the reading of scholarship and even the interrogation of the raven only exacerbate the melancholy effects of nothingness, of the permanent death and inaccessibility of the object of desire that they would displace.

The poem thus comes to reframe its critical supplement.[12] The romantic critical project of completing the work of art by installing an absence it would fulfill is rendered into an affective drama of loss, projection, and deeper loss. Aesthetic criticism, thinking about the material and formal causes of feeling, would thus turn inward upon itself. This is not so much a critique of aesthetic criticism, which in its banal form would be the claim that criticism makes the work say exactly what it has already decided upon, but rather its radical extension, explored in the idea that the productive emptiness of literary works corresponds to some persistent yet estranged negation at the origin of critical thought. Put another way, Poe's reflective works do critique one version of aesthetic criticism: the dream of enclosing, comprehending, and controlling feeling through the exertion of intellect. But this critique operates by pressing and thus offering another version of aesthetic criticism: an operation within which the work of art can open up the unstable gaps within thought's pretensions, but without mitigating its felt urgency. As Joseph Riddel notes, this "[i]nterpretation as critical performance . . . cannot in itself be theorized" because "that which is produced assumes in its alterity a certain priority, as if in a feedback loop" (156). In his own feedback loop, the poem's scholar is not able to give up thinking when he realizes that his method is responsible for his feeling of loss, for the feeling of loss is both antecedent and consequent to thought. In Poe's drama, thinking makes the hole that thinking would fill.

Reading the essay as a reflection of the poem raises the question of affect in a new way: if the essay turns the poem into a frame for criticism, then why is it so famously dark? We have to remember, then, that though the student initially seeks "surcease of sorrow" (*CP* 365), it is through the self-torture of pursuing answers to his existential questions that he generates a surplus of affect. The student/lover and the speaker of the essay actively court, seek, and produce the conditions by which that loss of essence can become a "luxury of sorrow." One may try to explain such desire as perverse—the self-torture of the student/lover and the radical unraveling of the essay may simply be unexplainable, or explainable only in terms of perversity as that "human thirst for self-torture"—but such an answer begs the question. The relation between the desire for self-torture and the method that produces it is elaborately figured, over and over again, within both works. The affective surplus that the scholar seeks to produce in himself and that the author seeks to produce in his reader is both a knowledge of absence and a knowledge of one's own complicity in the production of that absence.[13] That is, if effect is caused by literary *histrio*, and the causal agent in this case is the exposure of literary *histrio* in the first place, then the unsettling effect of the poem, of the raven, is a response not to existential nothingness in general but to the circular logic of a criticism that invents cause in order to validate effect. Like Edwards, Poe uses terror's implacable demands to forestall any claim for sufficiency or completion within our interpretive frames; yet at the same time, in terror, endless and recursive negation is felt as the heart of a hermeneutic process that seeks to recuperate nothingness as a positive value.[14] Poe's critical reflection here is dark, then, because it would press the romantic critical supplement and the idea of auto-reflection to a limit point at which the auto-reflective work does not supplant absence but preserves it as eternal negativity. Terror projects that absence as inescapable, but does not thus realign or recuperate its otherness, its alienness. It would preserve difference, but it would at the same time project the drama, the desire, of its overcoming the incongruity it itself projects.[15]

Criticism in the Jena tradition seeks to install and expose, through an exhibition of the conditions of production, a formative absence at the heart of the work. Poe's poem, seen from this angle, is thus a drama of that critical project, as the scholar would make the object speak of its own enduring absence and render from that absence a productive, unending wellspring of affect. The speaker searches for Lenore, the essayist composes a fantasy of calculation. The metafeeling, the feeling of criticism searching for and imposing meaning on unmeaning form, allies itself with terror because terror further provokes and demands the inquiry that is also terror's cause. Like the sublime, it outlines the subject's relation to nothingness, but unlike the sublime it returns only an inverted and emptied reflection of its own complicity within the projection of that nothingness. Elaborate tricks enable an illusion of another, external authority, but these tricks only emphasize that whatever external negation they probe, discover, and worry is but a reflection of a negation fundamental to the operations of critical thought in the first place.

The question that began this section was of Poe's engagement with romantic criticism, and now we see that through it he raises a more complicated question about the relationship between art's significance and the criticism that would explain and encapsulate it. Rather than merely criticize criticism as inadequate to the task or show how art succumbs to a critical gaze, Poe produces a dialectical arrangement between thought and the aesthetic absence that it would think. Illuminating the complicated reflection, the interaction between a work and its criticism that Poe achieves in his poem and essay, we are now in a position to turn to the question of affective specificity. Why *this* affect? To answer this, I turn now to Poe's early fiction, especially those tales of dead and dying women, in which he developed both the plot and affect central to "The Raven."

### The Excess of Fragment: "Berenice"

Poe's tales about dead and dying beloveds portray a gruesome plot of death and return against a backdrop of philosophical erudition and literary criticism. These tales, beginning with "Berenice," extending through "Morella" and "Ligeia," and culminating in "The Fall of the House of Usher," are each variations on a single fable: a woman falls ill and apparently dies, but then returns to haunt her male counterpart. Poe revisits this plot again and again, mirroring in his habitual returns the memory-wracked and tortured men who cannot (and inevitably do not have to) accept the loss of their beloveds. Each tale is steeped not only in sensational horror but in the atmosphere of scholarship, meditation, and metaphysics. At stake in these tales is not just the return of the dead woman to haunt the narrator but the suggestion throughout that the narrator's analyses of the beloved are in some way complicit in both her death and return.

As we have seen, this pattern culminates in the critical/aesthetic oscillations of "The Raven" and "The Philosophy of Composition," in which the beloved may not return physically but does return as a never-to-be-filled absence carved out by the scholarly inquiries of both the speaker and the critic. Given how the beloved becomes a symbol for the work of art in critical apprehension, I want in this section to turn back to the development of that plot in Poe's earlier tales, especially the first tale, "Berenice." Poe's plot of return may at first seem a kind of revenge of the repressed, a gendered revenge of the feminine affect of art on the masculine hubris of trying to classify or delimit it in reason. But, as we have seen in "The Raven" and "The Philosophy of Composition," positing an adversarial relationship between art and criticism, feeling and thinking, is significantly troubled by their interpenetration and their shared motives.[16] Considering the relation between Poe's first tale in this sequence and the post-Kantian aesthetic philosophy Poe drew from, this section reveals how Poe's plot figures terror as both product and producer of the slide from a reflective and idealist aesthetic theory toward a recursive and ironic one.

Poe's first of these dead woman tales is the same tale, "Berenice," that led to Thomas White's criticism of Poe's "German horror" mentioned earlier. A plot that Poe admits comes to the "very verge of bad taste" (*Letters* 1:58), "Berenice" is the story of a scholarly man obsessed with his ill wife's gleaming teeth. After she apparently dies, the narrator's dental fixation provokes him, in an amnesiac swoon, to exhume her body, extract her teeth, and deposit them in a small box on his library desk. The kicker of the tale, that Berenice is still alive and was presumably conscious during her mutilation, not only approaches the verge of bad taste but, for most readers, egregiously oversteps it. Responding to White's criticism, Poe writes him a personal letter, apologizes for the gruesome content, yet then defends "Berenice" on the grounds of sensationalism and literary precedent. Poe draws in his defense several hypotheses concerning literary popularity, sensationalism, and criticism, mounting two arguments in favor of the terror tale. The first is that, even if it is in bad taste, it is still good business: sensational, mystical, horrible pieces are the ones that command the most popular interest.[17] The second argument goes further, to question whether they are in bad taste after all, given the high esteem granted them by "first men" such as Edward Bulwer-Lytton and Coleridge: "Such articles are the 'M.S. found in a Madhouse' and the 'Monos and Daimonos' of the London New Monthly — the 'Confessions of an Opium-Eater' and the 'Man in the Bell' of Blackwood. The two first were written by no less a man than Bulwer—the *Confessions . . .* universally attributed to Coleridge—although unjustly. Thus the first men in [England] have not thought writings of this nature unworthy of their talents, and I have go[od] reason to believe that some very high names valued themselves *principally* upon this species of literature" (*Letters* 1:58; brackets in original). The qualification in Poe's argument raises a question: Why would Poe draw Coleridge, who didn't even, as Poe points out, actually write the anonymously published "Confessions of an Opium Eater," into the defense of "Berenice" and the sensational terror that Poe would continue to write? The clue leads us to the fact that Poe read and reviewed, in the same issue of the *Southern Literary Messenger* in which "Berenice" was published, a long essay published in the *North American Review* on Coleridge's life and thought.[18] Although much has been made of the apparent general influence of Coleridge on Poe, it is even more illuminating to focus on the essay *about* Coleridge that would serve as Poe's introduction to romantic critical theory and a crucial theoretical context for "Berenice" and the extended engagement with aesthetics, art, and thought in the sequence of tales that "Berenice" begins.[19]

Poe reviews the *North American Review* essay, published anonymously under the title "Coleridge" and probably written by George Cheever, in the April 1835 issue of the *Southern Literary Messenger*. In "Coleridge," Poe found literary criticism described as "a great science" (312), informed by a Kantian aesthetic which would connect "the science of the beautiful in all its forms with those psychological and moral principles, of which in truth it is but the expression" (312). This science of criticism discovers in art the expression of those hidden internal principles constitutive of individual psychology. Cheever's conception of Coleridge's aesthetics thus follows Kantian aesthetic theory by moving beauty from an objective quality (something the object has) to a subjective feeling produced by a kind of agreement between the form of the thing perceived and the cognitive powers involved in making judgments.[20] What the beautiful expresses, in the Kantian theory of aesthetic pleasure, is really an underlying harmony between apparently disparate internal psychological faculties: "For the basis of the pleasure is posited merely in the form of the object for reflection in general, and hence not in a sensation of the object.... Therefore, the harmony we are dealing with is only a harmony in reflection, whose a priori conditions are valid universally, between the presentation of the object and the lawfulness [inherent] in the empirical use in general of the subject's power of judgment (this lawfulness being the unity between imagination and understanding)" (*Critique of Judgment* 30; brackets in original). If we keep in mind that *imagination* for Kant is the faculty of making mental ideas out of physical sensations (*concepts* out of *intuitions*, in Kantian terms) and that *understanding* is the faculty of coming to knowledge out of those mental ideas, we see that what is at stake in Kant's aesthetics would seem to be nothing less than the relation between our sensations of the world and our knowledge of it. Feeling as expression thus proffers a way to suture the Cartesian gap between subject and object. Carrying out this Kantian scheme, the Coleridge of Cheever's piece enlists scientific criticism to discover unifying and abstract moral principles and thereby to bring the matter of objects under the a priori rules of subjective psychology. For Poe, dreaming of changing the nature of literary criticism in America, the philosophical stakes of Coleridge's aesthetic science as well as the more instrumental role of criticism to deliver over a continuity between world and mind was a revelation.[21] Defending "Berenice" by a seemingly superfluous reference to Coleridge, then, Poe resituates the terror tale within philosophical stakes and implies that the excesses of "this species of literature" be read through the magnified role aesthetics takes in a Kantian reconstitution of the subject.

"Berenice," composed by Poe at the same time as he was encountering the deep potential of aesthetic philosophy, embeds the stakes of the Kantian critique within an economy of thought and feeling. Taking the Coleridge of the *North American Review* article as a model, Poe equips the narrator, Egaeus, with a mental propensity to convert both outward matter and inward feeling into thought, staging the operation of a self-possessed reason coordinating both fact and feeling. Converting thing to thought, the Coleridge of the *North American Review* article is "of that class of men, 'whose mind is affected by *thoughts* rather than *things*; and only then feels the requisite interest, even for the most important events and accidents, when, by means of meditation, they have passed into thoughts'" ([Cheever] 299). Testifying to the inversion of his "commonest thought," Poe's Egaeus similarly converts real world to conceptual idea, though much less smoothly: "The realities of the world affected me as visions, and as visions only, while the wild ideas of the land of dreams became, in turn, not the material of my every-day existence, but in very deed that existence utterly and solely in itself" (*TS* 1:210). The shared metaphysical habit with regard to objects, in turn, is paired with a bracketing of subjective emotion by mind. In the *North American Review* article, Coleridge thinks to escape from feeling: "'I have sought refuge,' says he [Coleridge] 'from bodily pain and mismanaged sensibility, in abstruse researches, which exercised the strength and subtlety of the understanding, without awakening the feelings of the heart'" ([Cheever] 304). Echoing and amplifying this conceit, Poe's Egaeus diagnoses himself as thinking feelings rather than feeling them: "In the strange anomaly of my existence, feelings, with me, *had never been* of the heart, and my passions *always were* of the mind" (*TS* 1:214). These related conversions of both material things and affective feelings into mental thoughts align Poe's narrator with the conversional processes of Coleridge's idealism. Making everything mental, the conversion of matter and feeling to mind by mind thus levels contrasting modalities, offering a single field of ideas.

Coleridge's tactics of mental conversion, described in the *North American Review* article, lift from the chaos of phenomenal experience firm organizational principles, significantly figured as bones or fossils. Without principles, Coleridge claims, "'the fleeting chaos of facts would no more form experience, than the dust of the grave can of itself make a living man'" ([Cheever] 310). These principles appear later in the essay as explicitly skeletal: "[A]bstract subtleties appear not as mere skeletons, but clad in attractive flesh, living and breathing" (323). Strengthening the connections between these principles and both burial and ossification, the article culminates by suggesting that these principles are fossils to be exhumed: "The ideas, though buried and forgotten, are there, and would be objects of consciousness, were this inner sense once awakened and sharpened by exercise. . . . Amidst all the ruins, moral and intellectual, in which the greater part of mankind are lying, the features of those truths, though mutilated, are yet often to be distinguished. . . . There are such *fossil remains* of godlike intuitions to be found in man" (340). Resonant at multiple points with Poe's horrible tale about extracting the bony essence of Berenice from her buried and mutilated body, the Coleridge article figures the processes of mental conversion as an archaeological and anatomical exploration of the fragmented remains of an ideal reality.

This turn inward, to the bones of the body and even to the bones hidden under the earth, cleverly appropriates a language of material essence to expel materialist understanding. For where the understanding, restricting itself to the material laws of nature, "recognises nothing *but* matter" ([Cheever] 333), it "reduces our intellectual and moral being, with all its operations, to a level with the compulsory movements of blind and dead matter, making the soul, as an independent being, a nonexistence, or nothing better than 'the mere quicksilver plating behind a looking-glass,' whose only office is to throw back images passively received from the world of sensation" (334). Yet if the conversions of matter to mind expose and exhume matter's inner principles, then "[m]atter, informed and enlivened by intellectual power, is as a tablet of wax, on which the soul reads the symbols of its own laws and intuitions" (338). Embodying that shift in aesthetic criticism which M. H. Abrams described in *The Mirror and the Lamp* as the turn from the neo-classical model of art as imitative mirror to the romantic model of art as projective lamp, Cheever adds that what the mind projects upon matter are the hieroglyphical symbols of its own deeper, spiritual nature. Thus, the figurative fossils the mind would find are materializations of its own spiritual processes: converting matter into mind enables the discovery of the mind's own primordial matter, its skeletal laws and principles that lie buried under earth, under flesh.

"Berenice" literalizes the Coleridgean metaphors of burial, skeletal essences, and fossilized ideas, making conversion from matter to mind a gruesome affair. As Dayan points out, though the tale begins as a quest for the "absolute ideal of beauty and purity," it is complicated by remaining "never freed from a highly sensuous though disturbing material contamination and decay" and thus constitutes Poe's "most violent sabotage of the reveries of idealism" (136).[22] Moreover, the tale not only depicts such sabotage but would appear to be caused by it. In an early sentence that Poe would excise from later versions, the tale's telling is explained as a function of feeling: "I have a tale to tell in its own essence rife with horror — I would suppress it were it not a record more of feelings than of facts" (*TS* 1:209n). The sentence is the first in a series of moves that hint at a metafictional tone in the narrative, a scalar hiccup in which the narrator's uncontrollable compulsion to extract Berenice's teeth is paralleled by a similar compulsion to tell the tale. One might explain Egaeus's apology as saying that the inwardness and obscurity of "feelings" anesthetizes the tale's material horror, but such a reading merely reinforces what would seem to be the sentence's other meaning, that the narrator is *unable* to suppress the tale because it is a record of feelings. Facts—Berenice's body, her extracted teeth, or the event of their extraction—can be buried, hidden inside a box, swallowed up in silence. Feelings, however, would exceed their symbolic structures, their conversion into thought that marks the Coleridgean impulse of Egaeus's mind. "Berenice" introduces, through this drama of the excess of feeling, the problem of the aesthetic, that in converting feeling into thought through study, the very formal-material character of the aesthetic effect may be bracketed out.[23] That bit of feeling that reason cannot grip comes back with a vengeance.

Yet, this isn't quite the whole story, for what seems crucially important is not that reason overextends itself into feeling but rather that feeling itself emerges as a production of these mental conversions. In "Berenice," Poe gives us not a single smooth transition between matter and mind but rather two diametrically opposed processes of mental conversion which Egaeus differentiates as the *speculative* and the *attentive* faculties of the mind. The speculative process, which trades object for thought, would endorse a theory of reason as encroachment: thinking speculatively encroaches on the domain of feeling and is punished by the excess that it cannot finally conquer. The attentive, on the other hand, complicates this economy by always returning the same for the same: attentive thinking curtails any conversional process by insisting upon the particularity of the object. Dayan, aligning Poe's attentiveness with Edwards's affectionate perceptibility, describes it as an inverted conversion: "Turning his own mind inside out, he [Egaeus] then attends to his inward thought as it takes on external form" (156). By parsing the conversional process of Coleridgean idealism into two opposing trajectories, Poe's tale raises as a problem not simply emotion but rather the way emotion emerges out of thought's inverted orientation toward the particular.

Early in the tale, Poe distinguishes between the attentive and the speculative to oppose the laser-like focus of attention on unimportant objects with the desultory wandering and "luxury" of speculative deductions:

> The undue, earnest, and morbid attention thus excited by objects in their own nature frivolous, must not be confounded in character with that ruminating propensity common to all mankind, and more especially indulged in by persons of ardent imagination. It was not even, as might first be supposed, an extreme condition, or exaggeration of such propensity, but primarily and essentially distinct and different. In the one instance, the dreamer, or enthusiast, being interested by an object usually *not* frivolous, imperceptibly loses sight of this object in a wilderness of deductions and suggestions issuing therefrom, until, at the conclusion of the day-dream *often replete with luxury*, he finds the *incitamentum*, or first cause of his musings, entirely vanished and forgotten. In my case, the primary object was *invariably frivolous*, although assuming, through the medium of my distempered vision, a refracted and unreal importance. Few deductions, if any, were made; and those few pertinaciously returning in upon the original object as a centre. The meditations were *never* pleasurable; and, at the termination of the revery, the first cause, so far from being out of sight, had attained that supernaturally exaggerated interest which was the prevailing feature of the disease. In a word, the powers of mind more particularly exercised were, with me, as I have said before, the *attentive*, and are, with the day-dreamer, the *speculative*. (*TS* 1:212)

What distinguishes the two powers of mind is not only the way in which they oppose each other as centrifugal (speculative) versus centripetal (attentive) but, moreover, the opposite fates of the object for each. The speculative loses the object of inquiry in a wilderness, while the attentive can never surpass the object, can never put the object "out of sight."

These inverse trajectories of the speculative and attentive powers model the narrator's regard for Berenice herself as the object of mental interest. The first description of Berenice defines her as an object of nature, of the outdoors, of all that is external to the narrator's introspective habits. He says of their childhood: "Yet differently we grew — I, ill of health, and buried in gloom — she agile, graceful, and overflowing with energy; hers, the ramble on the hill-side — mine, the studies of the cloister; I, living within my own heart, and addicted, body and soul, to the most intense and painful meditation — she, roaming carelessly through life, with no thought of the shadows in her path, or the silent flight of the raven-winged hours" (*TS* 1:210). Egaeus's body is hardly a body, buried as it is within a cloister and then within the inner chamber of his own heart. Berenice, on the other hand, roaming as she is with "no thought," is entirely body without mind. The tale would thus begin with a traditional opposition of mind and body, but when that mind is turned toward body—when Egaeus begins thinking *about* Berenice—the consequences of Coleridgean conversion, of thing to thought, rush to the fore.

Egaeus's first conversion of Berenice is speculative, converting her from external object into the *theme* of objecthood: "[S]he had flitted by my eyes, and I had seen her — not as the living and breathing Berenicë, but as the Berenicë of a dream; not as a being of the earth, earthy, but as the abstraction of such a being; not as a thing to admire, but to analyze; not as an object of love, but as the theme of the most abstruse although desultory speculation" (*TS* 1:214). By explicitly abstracting the idea of Berenice from her "earthy" body, Egaeus not only prefigures the excavation of her teeth from her body buried in the earth but also converts the external object, the "living and breathing Berenicë," into an idea within his mind. This conversion process, described through figurations of excavation within the *North American Review* Coleridge article, may also allude to another major contribution to the introduction of German critical theory to the English-speaking world: Thomas Carlyle's "The State of German Literature." Poe's odd adjective, "earthy," points to Paul's first letter to the Corinthians—"the first man *is* of the earth, earthy" (1 Cor. 15:47)—but also recalls the same allusion at a key point in Carlyle's often-reprinted introduction to German aesthetic criticism.

Carlyle's "The State of German Literature," originally published in the *Edinburgh Monthly* and later reprinted in America in *The Zodiac* in 1836, condenses the philosophical potential of aesthetic criticism in presenting, in a parallel fashion to Coleridge, "the science of Criticism," a literary criticism that "springs from the depths of thought, and remotely or immediately connects itself with the subtlest problems of all philosophy" ([Dec. 1836] 92). Like Poe, Carlyle introduces a criticism whose "grand question" is neither the "qualities of diction" of an older tradition nor "psychological . . . delineating the peculiar nature of the poet from his poetry" ([Nov. 1836] 70) of the contemporary British reviews. Rather, it is "inclusively of those two other questions, properly and ultimately a question on the essence and peculiar life of poetry itself" ([Nov. 1836] 70). Carlyle ends his portrayal of the aesthetic dilemma with the same reference to the "earth, earthy" construction of Paul's letter and of Poe's "Berenice":

> Criticism stands like an interpreter between the inspired and the uninspired: between the prophet and those who hear the melody of his words, and catch some glimpse of their material meaning, but understand not their deeper import. She pretends to open for us this deeper import; to clear our sense that it may discern the pure brightness of this eternal beauty, and recognize it as heavenly, under all forms where it looks forth, and reject, as of the earth, earthy, all forms, be their material splendor what it may, where no gleaming of that other shines through.
> ([Nov. 1836] 71)

Though there is good reason to be cautious about assigning Carlyle's essay an influential role with respect to "Berenice," the coincidence suggests that the theme of raising a spiritual essence from the dead body—for this is the context of the original formulation in Paul—might be an influential analogy, a handle by which the new German-inspired criticism could grasp the question of how to think feeling philosophically.[24] Berenice, being of the "earth, earthy," is rendered material, and Egaeus, obeying the new maxims of a new criticism, goes about rendering her as a "theme" rather than a "thing," attempting to raise what Carlyle calls "the deeper import." Just as Carlyle imagines German criticism as raising this theme within the context of spiritual resurrection, grafting the Christian distinction between pure soul and corrupt body onto the distinction between the material reading of literature and the higher spiritual criticism of it, so too does Poe. Yet in Poe the resurrection is a bloody and brutal ordeal. The difference would seem to be the problematic second mental process—speculation may convert thing to theme, but it is the attentive power that returns the fragmentary and resistant material.

The limits of Egaeus's speculative conversion of Berenice are reached when Berenice herself disappears from view, rehearsing what Poe indicates as the speculative's de-objectifying process: the way it "loses sight" of its object in a "wilderness of deductions." Berenice, it would seem, is lost in a mental wilderness of deductions consequent upon Egaeus's speculative dreaming:

> Ah, vividly is her image before me now, as in the early days of her light-heartedness and joy! Oh, gorgeous yet fantastic beauty! Oh, sylph amid the shrubberies of Arnheim! Oh, Naiad among its fountains! And then — then all is mystery and terror, and a tale which should not be told. Disease — a fatal disease, fell like the simoon upon her frame; and, *even while I gazed upon her*, the spirit of change swept over her, pervading her mind, her habits, and her character, and, in a manner the most subtle and terrible, disturbing even the identity of her person! Alas! the destroyer came and went! — and the victim — where is she? I knew her not — or knew her no longer as Berenicë! (*TS* 1:210–211; emphasis added)

In lieu of any explanation, any cause, for her illness, we have this, a description of Berenice's physical change couched in a change of rhetorical register. The abstraction of Berenice into mythological metaphor—the sylph and the naiad—immediately precipitates the mysterious and thoroughgoing change wrought by disease. That the change occurred "even while I gazed upon her" hints that the gaze may itself be complicit. Could it be that the abstraction of Berenice, from her earthy substance to the fantastic totemic creatures of wilderness, under the gaze of Egaeus, is in some way the disease itself? The passage suggests as much when, recalling the earlier definition of speculation as losing sight of the object, it closes with "the victim — where is she?" By raising the earthy Berenice into an allegorical symbol, the sylph or the naiad, in which her essence would be converted from earthly nature grounded in objects to the idea of nature allegorized in mythic symbols, Poe's narrator completes the process of conversion from thing to thought that characterizes Coleridge and distinguishes criticism in Carlyle's account. But whereas Coleridge is praised for such conversions, Poe suggests that there is both an erasure and a remainder—that the conversion cannot account for all of Berenice and that, while she as a person is entirely lost to Egaeus, succumbing to abstraction, there will yet persist a troubling remainder, an essence that is, like a bone, indigestible by the abstracting impulse.

The crucial turn in the tale occurs when Egaeus's monomaniacal disorder of attentiveness affixes itself to Berenice's teeth. Whereas his speculative powers had lost Berenice in a wilderness of deductions and abstractions, it is the "full fury" of the opposing attentive faculty that is incited by the revelation of her teeth. Rather than consider "the *moral* condition of Berenicë," as his previous speculative and desultory daydreaming had, the attentive disorder "revelled in the less important but more startling changes wrought in the *physical* frame of Berenicë—in the singular and most appalling distortion of her personal identity" (*TS* 1:213). Just as Poe describes the attentive faculties as "pertinaciously returning in upon the center," Egaeus's meditations continually return to the irreducible matter and particularity of Berenice's teeth:

> Then came the full fury of my *monomania*, and I struggled in vain against its strange and irresistible influence. In the multiplied objects of the external world I had no thoughts but for the teeth. For these I longed with a frenzied desire. All other matters and all different interests became absorbed in their single contemplation. They — they alone were present to the mental eye, and they, in their sole individuality, become the essence of my mental life. I held them in every light. I turned them in every attitude. I surveyed their characteristics. I dwelt upon their particularities. I pondered upon their conformation. I mused upon the alteration in their nature. I shuddered as I assigned to them, in imagination, a sensitive and sentient power, and, even when unassisted by the lips, a capability of moral expression. (*TS* 1:215–216)

Attentiveness here installs a precious artifact that defies interpretation and possession, or possession *as* interpretation. If the speculative faculties, raising Berenice to a theme, can be read as the hubris of a critical view that bypasses the material and formal aspect of the work as sense, then here the attentive faculties would appear to swerve the other way: giving nothing *but* the material and formal, repeating the punctuated facts of observation like so many teeth ("I held," "I turned," "I surveyed," "I pondered," etc.). No longer a unified theme of beauty or nature, Berenice dissolves into analyzable particles. To be glib, Egaeus misses the forest for the teeth.

Fixing on the possibility of moral expression within the material of the teeth itself, Poe's attentiveness would seem to press Coleridge's metaphor of a priori principle-as-fossil to a literal extension. Rather than be able to reject the earthy material of the object, Egaeus focuses in on the very material-formal quality of the metaphor itself. Returning same for same, attentiveness disallows interpretive claims that would make the object say something beyond itself, yet it is at the same time propelled by the desire for that possibility. If this is criticism, it is not a hermeneutics that abstracts to find a meaning in the aesthetic work; rather, it is an investigation of the grounds of hermeneutics itself. What the teeth end up standing for is the possibility of things "standing for" something else in the first place.

From Cheever's Coleridge article, Poe had received an introduction to Kantian aesthetics and modeled it in his definition of the speculative. For Cheever, the most influential aspect of Kantian aesthetics is the idea of a formal accord between one's sensations of the world and one's cognitive capacities.[25] It is this formal accord, corresponding to Kant's "analytic of the beautiful," that motivates the enfiguration of aesthetic criticism as unearthing the bones and fossils of a priori principles in the soul. Broadly put, through the presumption of a formal accord between the imagination and the understanding, an inquiry into one could lead to reflective conclusions about the other. Complaining of the age's preference for reducing thought to mere understanding, Cheever calls at one point for a return to "speculative meditation" (332), offering Poe the terminology for a mode of thought that converts sensory data into spiritual evidence. Coleridge, as Poe would have read in the article, held that the laws of mind could not be derived from sensory data alone, though that data be the inciting cause of speculation: "'In neither case is our conviction derived, or capable of receiving any addition from outward experience or empirical data, — i. e. matter of fact *given* to us through the medium of our senses, — though these data *may have been the occasion, or may even be an indispensable condition, of our reflecting on the former*'" ([Cheever] 336). Strictly limiting the influence of empirical evidence and necessitating its conversion through a species of speculative reflection, the Coleridge that Poe drew upon would suture the fractured and uncoordinated data of the understanding, enabling the soul "to recognise, among the broken fragments, glimpses of great principles" (339). Such a model, based on the accord between the imagination and the understanding offered by the Kantian analytic of the beautiful, operates behind Poe's own definition of the speculative, a mode of thought that loses the object in a chain of deductions.

For Poe, the attentive opposes itself to the speculative by pressing an incipient difficulty within Kant's scheme of formal accord. This difficulty is that, by insisting on the strict distinction between the imagination and the understanding, formal accord must still explain feeling as sensation, introducing "the presence of a contingent empirical quality . . . to the overall precarious balance of the 'analytic of the beautiful'" (Pfau 37). The contingency of sensation threatens the stable formal accord between mind and world, for if converting world to mind leaves no space for the sensational character of feeling, the feeling of beauty itself slips out of the system it was supposed to positively uphold. Poe's attentiveness challenges the speculative model by insisting on the particularity of the empirical object and refusing the conversional principle by which its sensational data would be refitted into a formal coherence of subject and world. When Egaeus, for instance, regards Berenice's teeth attentively, all other thought is boiled down to bare empirical data: "All other matters and all different interests became absorbed in their single contemplation" (*TS* 1:215). Refusing even the first step toward speculative formalization, attentiveness returns always same for same, any deductions "pertinaciously returning in upon the original object as a centre" (*TS* 1:212). In marking the resistance of the empirical to its formal conceptualization, Poe's attentiveness iterates the distance between thing and thought, between sensation and sign.

This disjunction may at first blush seem to alienate feeling, for if feeling is not wholly conceptual, wholly sensory, or even the smooth connection between the two, then it would seem to have fallen out of the philosophical story altogether. But it is at this juncture that a different line of aesthetic theory emerges. Responding not to the formal accord of Kant's account of beauty but rather to the formal disalignment of Kant's account of the sublime, the Jena critics and, later, poststructuralist theory, notably by way of Derrida, outline a poststructuralist account of emotion that embraces the mismatch of sense and sign.[26] Rather than try to express emotion as sense, concept, or the connection between them, this account asserts that emotion is expressed negatively in the disjunction between them. Rei Terada, unfolding Derrida's reading of Rousseau's account of the savage who calls a strange man a "giant" out of fear, explores how emotion emerges from the inadequacy of mental representation: "It is not the sign's literalness with respect to the idea, then, that represents my fear itself. . . . Nor is it the sign's imprecision regarding the man (its being able to say at most what he is like, not what he is). It is the *difference between* the sign's falseness with respect to its object and its accuracy with respect to its idea that represents the passion. . . . This 'inadequation,' this remainder between 'man' and 'giant,' *measures* my fear of the man" (43). In this account, "[e]motion is not expressive, not subjective: it is the difference between subjective ideality and the external world, appearing within experience" (44).

Thomas Pfau recounts the consequences of inadequation as a signal event in the turn from Kant's a priori continuity of reason to the ironies of Jena criticism and the deconstruction of the individual subject in poststructuralist theory:

> In response, aesthetic, and particularly literary, form forges an (ironically self-qualifying) passage from the dream of the subject as the originator of its own rational constitution to the harsher reality of the subject as the Sisyphus-like producer of symbols. Such a subject no longer "feels" itself cradled by the formal accord of its own faculties but has been consigned to the tenuous realm of simulacra that may "affect" rationality as a necessary, albeit necessarily "inadequate," presentation. (45)

Through these theories of affect as emerging from disjunction, we can understand Poe's two inverse processes of mind as an attempt to install inadequation. This contrasts with a recent reading of "Berenice" in terms of pragmatist aesthetics, a reading that requires recuperating inadequation as a species of adequation on a wider aesthetic level: "Egaeus's disgust—like Poe's bad taste—is a revolt against the aesthetic that also belongs to the aesthetic, in the same sense that the subject's disgusted face withdraws from the disgusting object as the 'signal' of a particular affective disposition toward that object" (McAlister 500). Whereas the pragmatist reading spins misalignment into alignment, revulsion into a signal of affective connection, and finally "idea into deed" (500) (Egaeus's initial thought becomes enacted through his deed), a more particular focus on the radical aspects of inadequation would emphasize and retrench the differences (between discrete objects and between those objects and our ideas of them) that constitute the power of the aesthetic in the first place. Between the speculative and the attentive is measured a remainder, a negative difference, that is analogous to the difference between subjective ideality and external world. This remainder, literalized in Berenice's inassimilable teeth, indexes the tale's emotional content, for here feeling emerges from the limits of both conceptual and empirical conversions of mind. These manic conversions between thought and thing lead Dayan to a reading of the tale in which the dynamic of conversion is ultimately all there is: "As the mind passes continually over itself in reverie, all parts of life—spiritual and physical—exist only in their exchange, in their translation into the other. The seen world becomes the world of seeming, the so-called world of subjectivity, and the mind turns into the very object once external to it" (148). And yet, as the tale dissolves into a continual exchange, then why should there be any feeling of anxiety, terror, or horror? Something, it would seem, must continue to resist conceptualization in order for conversion to be regarded as change in the first place; the flux of difference must be contrasted to position. And herein lies the unique contribution that Poe's terror makes to the philosophical fable. For attentiveness does not merely block speculation by insisting on sense; rather, what it affords is something like an experience of the static baseline demands of the particular in resistance to conceptual conversions. It digs at the mental representations, offering through its process a negative resistance against which their inadequation can be marked and felt as such.

After all, it is not the literal teeth (at least at first) that come to play havoc with Egaeus's mind but rather the idea of literality which the individuality and empirical specificity of the literal teeth provide. For even in the full fury of the attentive disorder, Egaeus would appear to turn the teeth into mental entities, formal ideas which he holds and ponders even in the absence of actual sense data: "I saw them *now* even more unequivocally than I beheld them *then*. . . . They — they alone were present to the mental eye, and they, in their sole individuality, became the essence of my mental life" (*TS* 1:215–216). And then the teeth themselves are likened to ideas, "of Berenicë I more seriously believed *que tous ses dents étaient des idées. Des idées!* — ah, here was the idiotic thought that destroyed me! *Des idées!* — ah, *therefore* it was that I coveted them so madly! I felt that their possession could alone ever restore me to peace, in giving me back to reason" (*TS* 1:216). There are a few reasons for pause at this climactic moment in the tale. For how have the teeth, under the deconceptualizing focus of the attentive, turned into ideas? It would seem that the short-circuited, infinitely recursive quality of attentiveness is necessitated by a desire to avoid the formalization of speculative thought. Yet here, at the limits of the attentive, the object's resistance to conceptualization is itself always on the verge of being conceptualized. In other words, while the Coleridgean and speculative side of the divide is conceptual and involves our own representation of our own ideas to ourselves, the other side of the divide, the "literal" against which our own representation is measured, paradoxically occurs within a mental theater of its own.

The problem that attentiveness opens up is how the mind, how thought, can account for the particular which drives the negative expression of aesthetic effect. Thinking in its common speculative orientation would seek to comprehend, to deliver a positive comprehension of, its object. Yet in the contemplation of the aesthetic, of the meaning of feeling, Poe, the Jena critics, and Derrida all point out that comprehension of feeling paradoxically incurs a loss of object ("Berenicë, where was she?"). Thus Poe posits an opposite orientation, the attentive, which does not function to comprehend but rather to particularize, to insist upon the empirical ground without allowing a single step toward conceptualization. Pulled apart at the seam, the aesthetic object thus produces feeling out of the torsion between the mind's desire to conceptualize and the object's insistent particular demand. Poe, following the Jena critics and anticipating poststructuralist accounts of emotion, complicates this scheme by portraying how the thinking of the particular is also a mental operation. In order to account for aesthetic effect, attentiveness would seek to offer to the mind a nonconceptual representation of the world. Such an entity, though seemingly impossible (how can the mind think mentally the idea of not-mind without converting it to mind?), is also made necessary by the demand of the aesthetic: feeling as inadequation can only inhere if the mind is capable of registering that which it is inadequate to represent. Moreover, the entire conceptual schema, our ability to think at all, without such a paradoxical entity would risk a slide into solipsistic ideality.

It is difficult not to ask, at this point, what's the problem? Why can't we just have the concept of a nonrepresentational concept? To insist on an internal homology between the mental representation and its content, between the sign and its object, would seem to be not only inefficient but perverse. It submits the mind to the rules of a Russellian set paradox, that generic disruption which occurs when we notice that an imaginative entity such as "the set of all sets" must include itself. Yet this insistence, that the mental conception of what lies on the far side of the limits of conception must be itself not a conception, would seem to exert its urgency as fundamental, for what is at stake is precisely the nature of the gap between second-order representation and first-order sensation. Egaeus, in the grip of the attentive, cannot rest in a conceptual distinction between concept and sensation, for that distinction itself becomes a kind of concept, a mental formulation against which the stubborn otherness of the particularity of sense may again assert resistance. The implicit recursion, and the incipient terror, in Poe's attentiveness is like Edwards's challenge of conceptualizing nothing: it cannot rest but must continually return in upon the object, each cycle adding to the object only more "supernaturally exaggerated interest" (*TS* 1:212) that involves mind and object in an infinite feedback loop.

And so what Poe's tale finally does is literalize the conceptualization of literality. Egaeus's attentiveness alights upon teeth because they are remainders (being all that is left of Berenice under the speculative gaze), because they are principles (being allusions to the skeletal, bony, and fossilized principles of the "Coleridge" article), and because they are particular (being material objects, distinctive yet coordinated in their plurality). In these three senses, the teeth become literalizations of literality, the empirical data against which mental concepts as signs can be measured by emotion. Yet the problem is of the set-paradox variety, for in coming to stand for that which is not symbolic, the teeth would symbolize the resistance to symbolization. Thus what Egaeus enacts is yet another literalization, in which the teeth that would stand for ideas are taken to *be* those ideas, and the negative gap that they would represent becomes gruesomely, meaninglessly material. Dramatizing this process, acting it out in the physical exhumation and extraction, thus emphasizes the aesthetic form of the mental process. By making the itinerary of the attentive a story "more of feelings than of facts," Poe writes the underlying mental process of conceptualizing the particular as not just productive of but maintained through the feeling of terror.

Thus we can understand the ending of the tale, which never explicitly portrays the final moment of recollection, as performing its own literalization of Egaeus's desire for conceptual literality. Instead of a final summation, the reader is offered a set of clues to be correlated at a distance. In the person of Egaeus's servant, Poe points out a set of evidence: "He pointed to my garments, they were muddy and clotted with gore. . . . [H]e took me gently by the hand: it was indented with the impress of human nails. He directed my attention to some object against the wall. . . . [I]t was a spade" (*TS* 1:218–219). These evidentiary data culminate in the final clue in the final sentence, the point at which the reader becomes, with Egaeus, apparently aware of the grisly deed. The peculiar box that Egaeus cannot force open (another echo, perhaps, of the futility of one's conscious efforts to uncover essence) is dropped, "and from it, with a rattling sound, there rolled out some instruments of dental surgery, intermingled with thirty-two small, white, and ivory-looking substances that were scattered to and fro about the floor" (*TS* 1:219). In this final scene, the reader encounters a set of particulars and must put together the story (conceptualization) at the very moment that it literally comes apart (scattered on the floor). This, then, is where art seeks to complete criticism through the aesthetic encounter that criticism would comprehend; for the final message of Poe's tale would seem to be that the literalization of the ideas—the making of them into external objects which would exert pressure upon the mind—is itself a tale "more of feelings than of facts." The conception of literalization, not offered through a comprehensible sign, is ultimately communicated by putting the reader in Egaeus's position so that he or she may feel as tone the uncanny pull of inadequation. As Michael Williams argues, Poe's project in these tales is the portrayal of the frustration of an "interpretive desire" that seeks "the ideal sign in which signifier and signified are supposedly one" (82). In the particularization of the final scene of "Berenice," we see how that frustration is passed on to the reader, to the critic. The story itself, a work to be read critically, finally is the particular that encapsulates the particulars, and terror modulates the way the reader puts together, in feeling, the coming apart of literality.

Poe continues, in "Morella" and "Ligeia," to explore the question of thinking feeling by constructing scenes of problematic aesthetic arrangement. In both stories, the male narrators are most distraught not by the loss of their beloveds but rather by their inability to define clearly the strange feelings their beloveds cause. In "Morella," the aesthetic puzzle the narrator describes as the "mystery of my wife's manner" (*TS* 1:231) is linked directly to post-Kantian idealist philosophy. Alluding to philosophies that seek to secure an absolute identity between subject and object (Fichte's pantheism controversy and Schelling's identity philosophy)[27] through a universal formalism, "Morella" revises the literality of body in "Berenice" into a more idealist account of aesthetic form. The mystery of Morella's manner is solved when she returns, for the narrator finally admits that he could *feel* those aspects of her philosophy through her transition into the body of her daughter. Drawing from the formal orientation of "Morella," "Ligeia" likewise portrays a narrator dwelling on the problem of defining feeling, fixating on the expression of Ligeia, yet ending in an exasperated resignation; "'*expression*,'" the narrator ultimately concludes, "[a]h, word of no meaning!" (*TS* 1:313). Examining the particulars of her face, the narrator would seem to reprise Egaeus's attentiveness to the particular, though in "Ligeia" the solution of how to comprehend the expressiveness of the particular is acted out not through tooth extraction but through elaborate interior design (reminding the reader of the "tackle and scene-shifting" of "The Philosophy of Composition"). Appointing a chamber with mechanical devices for the heightening of gloom, the narrator casts through contrived aesthetic construction a reproduction of Ligeia's mysterious affect, establishing the conditions for her return as performed through feeling. Poe uses the search for the origin of feeling in form as the primary quest of his narrators in the dead woman series; yet, rather than discover these origins, the tales themselves turn that search itself into a form capable of being felt, a plot of return that transfers the feeling of thinking over to the reader as a species of terror.[28]

It is in the poem embedded in "Ligeia," "The Conquerer Worm," that Poe elaborates on the relation between the form of the aesthetic work and the production of terror. The conqueror worm is evidently the symbol of death, but the final gruesome curtain call of the poem can overshadow the content of the theatrical work that it describes. "Horror," Poe's poem claims of its embedded tragedy, is "the soul of the plot." This plot puts into aesthetic form the search for interior essence. Two stanzas in particular anticipate how the artificial production of feeling, the role of art as expression, can produce a circular regression of inquiry:

> Mimes, in the form of God on high,
> Mutter and mumble low,
> And hither and thither fly —
> Mere puppets they, who come and go
> At bidding of vast formless things
> That shift the scenery to and fro,
> Flapping from out their Condor wings
> Invisible Wo!
>
> That motley drama! — oh, be sure
> It shall not be forgot!
> With its Phantom chased forevermore,
> By a crowd that seize it not,
> Through a circle that ever returneth in
> To the self-same spot,
> And much of Madness and more of Sin,
> And Horror the soul of the plot. (*TS* 1:318–319)

The "scenery" of "Ligeia," the narrator's furnishings of the chamber and Poe's elaborate furnishing of Ligeia's form, can be read as the formal causes of "invisible Wo." Yet the theatrical display undermines the possession of transcendental aesthetic content, yielding instead a proliferation of representational surfaces. Dramatizing Thomas Pfau's description of the "harsher reality" promised by inadequation, Poe's "mimes" here are like "the Sisyphus-like producer of symbols" that "has been consigned to the tenuous realm of simulacra" (45). Poe's mimetic puppets shift "hither and thither" like the "to and fro" of stage decoration, a dynamic oscillation of representations that yet never yields underlying essence but only more horror, "the soul of the plot." Central to this horror is the ambiguity in the second stanza as to whether the "crowd" that chases the drama's "Phantom" refers to the actors or their audience. The instability underlines the recursive activity it describes: the actors chase a phantom, but that chase is also the chase of the audience, who find in that route the "soul of the plot." If the work of art is to be completed by its auto-production of criticism, in the romantic dream of the Schlegels, Poe here describes such auto-production as a nightmarish cycle. Readers, chasing the phantom of essence, reproduce in that cyclical route the affect they seek to seize. It is at the same time as artificial as it is authentic, the critical impulse to know, to possess, coming to take a part on the stage that it would examine and transcend.

Beginning with "Berenice," and developing through the variations of "Morella" and "Ligeia," Poe presses the philosophical stakes of the Kantian and romantic aesthetic philosophies.[29] Worrying the gap between subject and object by offering fables of the particularizing faculty of mind, Poe attempts to accomplish in practice what the Jena critics had imagined in theory: a work of art that anticipates its own critical reading, producing positive aesthetic feeling out of negative inadequation. The form of the aesthetic work itself comes to be homologous with the form of feeling, and terror is the "soul of the plot" because it continually returns us to the central inadequation; it takes on the form of the infinitely recursive activity of thinking thought. Through inverted arrangements where characters' minds become outward stages and readers' minds become implicated in the dramas portrayed, Poe's tales "act out" the mental drama in order to present, through feeling, the demand of thinking the particular that aesthetic criticism requires. Terror is not, in this sense, a critique or an expressive sign of the limits of aesthetic criticism but rather the inhabitable experience of its attentive, particularizing, but conceptually elusive process. The recursive short-circuiting that terror performs in the plot of return becomes, in Poe's final prose variation of it, an explicit theme played out in multiple registers. If the problem of Kant's aesthetic is finding a structure that can handle both division and inclusion at the same time (speculation seeking to include through static conceptualization, attentiveness discriminating particular difference through ceaseless sensational activity), Poe's solution, made most explicit in "The Fall of the House of Usher," is the derivation of the paradoxical frame which includes itself, a *mise en abyme* architecture that oscillates between static arrangement and dynamic recursion, conceptual frame and affectionate content.

### The Paradoxical Law of Terror: "The Fall of the House of Usher"

Poe's final tale in his dead woman sequence, "The Fall of the House of Usher," further pursues the origin of aesthetic feeling by shifting emphasis from the object itself, the dying and returning woman, to the instability of its external frame. In "Morella" and "Ligeia," the male analysts' attempts to define the origin of affect generate unstable frames of reference, in which their efforts are implicated as entangled with that which they would study. In "The Fall of the House of Usher," Poe adopts a wider frame for the same plot, narrating the drama of death and return not from the perspective of the male lover/scholar but through the external perspective of an observer. "The Fall of the House of Usher" would replay the critical analyst's desire to know from the outside, by taking an outside view of the emblematic drama he had in the earlier tales attempted to write from within. However, such a perspective—an outside view of a plot that destabilizes the concepts of inside and outside—becomes fraught with infinitely recursive reflections, feedback loops, and frames within frames. The abyssal terror is thus not of the aesthetic object precisely but rather of the system of aesthetic criticism applied to it.

"The Fall of the House of Usher" opens, like the earlier tales, with a question of affect. This time, however, the aesthetic object is not the woman but the scene in which she is found, and the culmination of the inquiry is not her death and return but a prefatory recognition of the "paradoxical law of terror" that is responsible for the failure of such aesthetic inquiries. The tale begins with the narrator on horseback, arriving at the Usher estate to aid his suffering friend Roderick. When he first glimpses Usher's manor, he succumbs to a sense of "insufferable gloom . . . unrelieved by any of that half-pleasurable, because poetic, sentiment, with which the mind usually receives even the sternest natural images of the desolate or terrible" (*TS* 1:397). Searching for the origin of such an unredeemable "gloom," the narrator describes the particulars of the scene, "the mere house," "the simple landscape features of the domain," "the bleak walls," "the vacant eye-like windows," "a few rank sedges," "a few white trunks of decayed trees," and is struck "with an utter depression of soul" (*TS* 1:397). In an "unreedemed dreariness of thought which no goading of the imagination could torture into aught of the sublime" (*TS* 1:397) the narrator emphasizes that his gloom and depression, though attendant upon a view of an aesthetic scene, is neither poetic nor sublime; it does not allow for the imagination's transcendent redemption.[30] It refuses the "goading" and "torture" that would appropriate its grim reality for a subjective and second-order pleasure or utility. The affect with which "The Fall of the House of Usher" begins, then, is the baseline terror of reality, a feeling that cannot be recuperated by subjective reframing.

Failing at transforming the feeling by imagination, the narrator turns to the process of rational inquiry. His experiment begins with a question: "What was it — I paused to think — what was it that so unnerved me in the contemplation of the House of Usher? It was a mystery all insoluble; nor could I grapple with the shadowy fancies that crowded upon me as I pondered" (*TS* 1:397–398). This question of terror's cause leads back to the starting point of the post-Kantian aesthetic theory: "I was forced to fall back upon the unsatisfactory conclusion, that while, beyond doubt, there *are* combinations of very simple natural objects which have the power of thus affecting us, still the analysis of this power lies among considerations beyond our depth" (*TS* 1:398). Explicit here, and implicit in the arrangement of the furniture of "Ligeia" or the assumptions of "The Philosophy of Composition," Poe's claim that aesthetic causality cannot be analyzed reopens the gulf between the material-formal nature of the work of art and the particular affect it would produce.

Applying a process of scientific method to the philosophical problem of the aesthetic, the narrator commits himself to a peculiar experiment: "It was possible, I reflected, that a mere different arrangement of the particulars of the scene, of the details of the picture, would be sufficient to modify, or perhaps to annihilate its capacity for sorrowful impression; and, acting upon this idea, I reined my horse to the precipitous brink of a black and lurid tarn that lay in unruffled lustre by the dwelling, and gazed down — but with a shudder even more thrilling than before — upon the remodelled and inverted images of the gray sedge, and the ghastly tree-stems, and the vacant and eye-like windows" (*TS* 1:398). The experiment proves positive: changing the arrangement of the image by looking at its reflection does in fact alter its effect. Instead of removing the terror, though, the reflection in the lake magnifies it. Furthermore, the reflection is not only visual, as Poe's punning insertion "I reflected" implies. Reflecting upon a reflection, the narrator allies his outward experiment with an inward one and compares the tarn's effect to the conversion that outward things undergo when they become objects of consciousness.

It is out of this complex of framed reflections—the unrelenting reality of the scene, its reflection in the lake, and its reflection in the narrator's mind—that Poe derives his "law" of terror:

> I have said that the sole effect of my somewhat childish experiment — that of looking down within the tarn — had been to deepen the first singular impression. There can be no doubt that the consciousness of the rapid increase of my superstition — for why should I not so term it? — served mainly to accelerate the increase itself. Such, I have long known, is the paradoxical law of all sentiments having terror as a basis. (*TS* 1:399)

Here, Poe explicitly defines why terror is special for aesthetic theory. Terror is informed by reflection and magnified exponentially by reflection in consciousness. Its structure is recursive: the knowledge of its rapid increase accelerates the increase itself, which in turn would contribute to the knowledge driving its acceleration. Terror for Poe participates in that same self-recursive pattern that Edwards found during the awakening, in which religious terrors enter into a feedback loop of imagination and affection "till their affection is raised to a vast height, and the person is swallowed up, and loses all possession of himself" (*RA* 157). Poe defines terror as exceeding critical frames by being amplified by the action of its framing.

This "paradoxical law" of terror, the infinite regression of representation, is thematized in several registers of "The Fall of the House of Usher," and in each it is always the first step of reflection, the attempt to observe from an external position, that is responsible for the regression. Poe shows that the problem for philosophy—the problem of shoring up the aesthetic judgment without reducing or denying the content of its affect—becomes itself a kind of pattern; and thus the very process of attempting to solve, by reflection, the aesthetic problem itself determines a figure capable of aesthetic reflection. Poe's terror is the affect of this doubly reflective process, mirroring in its own structure of exponential increase the consequences of logical inquiry into affect.

Poe's paradoxes of reflection, the opening of the abyss of significance, and the final collapse of the house have historically attracted deconstructive readings. John Irwin brings the consideration of *mise en abyme*, the figure of self-inclusion, to bear on Poe's detective fictions, noting that in works which attempt to include themselves, such as "The Purloined Letter," "one confronts a mirror image of the self, a figure of an individual consciousness that is constituted precisely by its mutually reflective relationship to a self-included (mental) representation of its own representational (symbolic/linguistic) status" (*Mystery* 23). The problem of self-inclusion thus encroaches on more expansive metaphysical questions of mind and body, but also on literary problems of form and content: "But in works that circle back to enact the temporally repetitive nature of narrative representation, the problematic character of this spatial imaging of temporal inclusion is structurally evoked as the continual oscillation, in the act of rereading, of the inner/outer relationship between form and content" (21). Riddel similarly senses that Poe "introduces what Schlegel had foreseen as the inevitability for a new literature, a self-critical or self-annihilating textual performance—the poem/story and even the critical essay (as performance) that deconstructs itself" (128). For Riddel, Poe's exposure of a crypt which is "neither a presence nor an absence but a place constructed to install a sign of presence and absence" (134) accomplishes such a narrative self-deconstruction by collapsing the narrative into "an infinitely refracted series of fictions without origin or end, without the sustaining center of the crypt" (135). Irwin's and Riddel's deconstructive readings of Poe focus on reflections and oppositions. Yet without Terada's thesis, that affect underlies poststructuralist methods, these studies may demonstrate the tendency of Poe's tales to auto-deconstruct but leave less accountable the distinctive terror that accompanies them. Considering how we can now see Poe's fiction as responding to the turn from literary appreciation to literary theory, however, we can begin to outline the relation between terror and poststructuralist method. Those deconstructive elements of his fiction—the oscillating binaries of inner and outer, of presence and absence—are prepared for by the very question of aesthetic feeling and, moreover, the installment of terror as the feeling of that question itself. Self-inclusion, then, may gain its metaphysical consequences through an aesthetic operation.

In 1893, André Gide first applied the literary term *mise en abyme* to describe the effect of self-inclusion in art and used as one of his literary examples "The Fall of the House of Usher." Sometimes translated as "falling into the abyss," *mise en abyme* refers to the heraldic device of representing, within a coat of arms, a miniature of the coat of arms itself (and thus a potentially infinite series). In transposing this visual device into literature, Gide states that "[i]n a work of art I rather like to find transposed, on the scale of the characters, the very subject of that work" (29). For most critics, and for Gide himself, the *mise en abyme* in "Usher" is found in the correspondence between the embedded narrative of "The Mad Trist," a medieval romance that the narrator reads aloud to Roderick Usher at the close of the tale, and the main narrative itself. While Ethelred, the hero of "The Mad Trist," bursts through thresholds to enter and conquer forbidden spaces, Madeline bursts through the enclosures of coffin and crypt to re-emerge in the final event. The similarity between the tales, and the apparent coincidental relation between the two, has led some critics to see "The Mad Trist" as a simple if imperfect reflection of the whole.[31] But a closer look at Poe's use of *mise en abyme* reveals a deeper exploration of the way in which reflective structures can generate potentially infinite regressions.

For Poe is not only interested in *mise en abyme*'s simple reduplication, in a single instance of reflection, but rather in the more self-recursive form of the infinite series.[32] In "Philosophy of Furniture" (1840), he maintains that mirrors are an actual evil: "[C]onsidered as a reflector, it [the mirror] is potent in producing a monstrous and odious uniformity: and the evil is here aggravated, not in merely direct proportion with the augmentation of its sources, but in a ratio constantly increasing" (*TS* 1:500). The danger of facing mirrors, Poe continues, is that a room so furnished is "a room of no shape at all" (*TS* 1:500). Poe's description of the evil of mirrors, emphasizing the scalar difference between the merely reflective "direct proportion" and the exponentially exploding "ratio constantly increasing," is the same distinction made at the terror of the tarn. It isn't that mirrors increase the effect, but that they increase the *rate* of increase of the effect. This may explain the reaction of one Poe character, the double-dealing Too-wit in *The Narrative of Arthur Gordon Pym*, caught between two facing mirrors for the first time, who, horrified, throws himself to the floor, "his face buried in his hands" (198). For Poe, the concept of the reflection of a reflection is associated with exponential increase and abject terror; it wreaks havoc upon the boundaries that give shape to space. Thus, in "The Fall of the House of Usher," when the narrator defines the law of terror as belonging to the same figure of exponential and reciprocal increase, he presents terror as itself determined by regressive self-inclusion. According to a logic in which an effect can become its own cause, it is not only that we are terrified by the sight of an infinitely regressive void in reflected reflections, but that our terror continually deepens that void of which we are terrified.

Such affective recursion allows a reconsideration of the depth of *mise en abyme* in the "Mad Trist" episode. Many critics, including Gide, have pointed out how "The Mad Trist" troubles narrative frames.[33] Less attention, however, has been paid to the narrated events of the romance itself, events which give in miniature a drama of destabilized frames themselves. This is due, perhaps, to the narrator's description of "The Mad Trist" as absurdly incongruous to the "lofty and spiritual ideality" of Roderick and his avowed attempt to provide "relief . . . even in the extremeness of the folly which I should read" (*TS* 1:413). Yet considering more closely the narrative he produces as distraction reveals the same structure of self-enclosure, even, or especially within, that which is purported to be radically external.

In the first installment of the embedded tale, the knight Ethelred, caught in the rain, seeks haven in a hermit's dwelling by breaking down its door. "The Fall of the House of Usher" recounts the embedded tale literally, recounting aloud how Ethelred, "'fearing the rising of the tempest, uplifted his mace outright, and, with blows, made quickly room in the plankings of the door for his gauntleted hand; and now pulling therewith sturdily, he so cracked, and ripped, and tore asunder, that the noise of the dry and hollow-sounding wood alarummed and reverberated throughout the forest'" (*TS* 1:413). The embedded narrative pauses at this moment, as the narrator reading "The Mad Trist" aloud hears in the distance what turns out to be Madeline bursting through her coffin. When he resumes reading, we discover that it is not only "The Fall of the House of Usher" that has experienced a radical shift but the narrative of "The Mad Trist" as well:

> "But the good champion Ethelred, now entering within the door, was sore enraged and amazed to perceive no signal of the maliceful hermit; but, in the stead thereof, a dragon of a scaly and prodigious demeanour, and of a fiery tongue, which sate in guard before a palace of gold, with a floor of silver; and upon the wall there hung a shield of shining brass with this legend enwritten –
> 
> Who entereth herein, a conquerer hath bin;
> Who slayeth the dragon, the shield he shall win." (*TS* 1:414)

At the moment when Ethelred crosses the threshold into the hermit's dwelling, he, amazed, discovers himself apparently outside again, facing a palace and confronting a dragon. The "palace of gold" may figuratively evoke a large quantity of gold, but the word "palace" invites a moment of confusion in which the reader must envision Ethelred as again outside in the rain. Even the first words of the legend, "Who entereth herein, a conquerer hath bin," play on Ethelred's uncertain location: Is he already inside, having already conquered? Where exactly is "here" at this moment in the narrative? Is it a hermit's dwelling in a forest, a palace of gold, or a dragon's cave? The shift in spatial proportions enacts in "The Mad Trist" the reversals of exterior and interior that dominate the symbolic economy of its framing tale.

What the structure of self-inclusion does, then, is produce a fearful indeterminacy at the thresholds. Douglas Hofstadter, who has promoted these self-recursive "strange loops" produced by *mise en abyme* figures as structures of consciousness, suggests that the intuitive uneasiness, the taboo-like fear, with which they are regarded "just runs in our human grain" (57).[34] Yet, going deeper into the causes of that fear reveals a structural similarity between the consequences of self-recursion and the ground for Freud's etymological interpretation of the *unheimlich*. By comparing the two, we may understand the uncanny as modeled upon a recursive structure and discover what Poe's architectural poetics asserts: that the problem of feeling as a recursive structure of excess may itself be represented through a feeling, albeit one with exclusive opposition at its core.

Freud's essay on the *unheimlich* uses the term's fundamental doubleness to fit it into a psychoanalytic fable of the primal scene and the Oedipal complex. Freud consults his dictionary and finds two apparently contradictory definitions of *heimlich*, which in turn would promise two corresponding and contrary definitions of its negation, *unheimlich*. *Heimlich* is both (1) "belonging to the house, not strange, familiar, tame, intimate, comfortable, homely, etc." (371) and (2) "[c]oncealed, kept from sight, so that others do not get to know about it, withheld from others" (373). Freud observes the incongruity in these definitions, wonders about a "possible genetic connection between these two sets of meanings" (375), and finds revelatory Schelling's solution that "everything is uncanny that ought to have remained hidden and secret, and yet comes to light" (376). Both accounts explain the *unheimlich* by reference to repression. For Schelling, repression enables freedom by taming the chaotic and Dionysian.[35] For Freud, the uncanny proceeds from repression, especially of primitive beliefs and infantile complexes.[36] Yet neither seems, in his attempt to resolve *unheimlich*'s double meaning, to quite get at the other side of the term: not the repression but the coming-to-light.

This double meaning may be resolved by looking at an aspect of the terms that Freud offers but does not develop: what is *heimlich* for one is *unheimlich* for another. Being familiar, that which is *heimlich* therefore belongs to members of the family, even as it is hidden from those who are not part of the family. It is the central secret that binds and holds together the belonging of a group. *Unheimlich*, on the other hand, reverses the two senses of *heimlich*. It implies both that which is unfamiliar and that which is exposed to view. The difference is not in the object or event, but in perspective. To experience the *unheimlich*, then, is to perceive, to be allowed to view from the outside, another family's secret. Whereas Schelling and Freud concentrate on the *unheimlich* as that which is repressed, understanding it along the lines of perspective (that which is *heimlich* for someone in the know would be *unheimlich* for someone else) helps to emphasize its parallel relation with the paradoxes of self-recursion. The experience of the *unheimlich* is the state of being in-between outside and inside—of knowing oneself as exterior to the group defined by the *unheimlich* event and yet, at the same time, since privy to that event, also feeling its claims of inclusion. It is, that is to say, like going to stay at a friend's family's mansion for the sake of diversion but instead being initiated into their secrets. The narrator of "The Fall of the House of Usher" is figured as external to the house of Usher, an unrelated visitor from elsewhere. Yet he cannot remain outside, because he is exposed to those secrets and thus, being given access to interiors, is implicated within them.

The strange way in which insides become outsides, together with the unique precariousness of the narrator's own external perspective, doubly emphasize the point of aperture, the rupture or threshold, between interior and exterior. Whereas the doorway of the hermit's hut becomes the tenuous threshold of *mise en abyme* qualities that reverberate throughout the tale, and the doorway of the estate through which the narrator will pass becomes the emblem of the narrator's *unheimlich* implication within the closed system, the final rupture comes at the point when the narrator speaks; and thus Poe draws our attention to the way in which speech itself is like a doorway, a passage to an interior, by focusing, in an embedded poem, upon the site of the mouth.

If doorways are the thresholds by which interiors meet exteriors in the architectural framework, then mouths are those thresholds by which the hidden interior of the human consciousness becomes the material of the external world. This sonic quality of speech, the airing of the internal thoughts into material (and textual) exteriors, becomes ultimately responsible for the tale's ultimate catastrophe. The invocatory power of speech in the tale is first hinted at in the detail, noticed by one astute critic, that Madeline only appears in the tale when her name is spoken.[37] In the first instance, Madeline appears coincident with her brother's description of her: "While he spoke, the lady Madeline (for so she was called) passed slowly through a remote portion of the apartment, and, without having noticed my presence, disappeared" (*TS* 1:404). If speech, privileged by its ability to rupture boundaries between interior and exterior spaces of self, has agency in the narrative, then the narrator's reading of "The Mad Trist" aloud may be seen as the direct cause of Madeline's re-emergence. This much, at least, Roderick appears to acknowledge in his final crazed revelation concerning the sounds of "The Mad Trist":

> "Not hear it? — yes, I hear it, and *have* heard it. Long — long — long — many minutes, many hours, many days, have I heard it — yet I dared not — oh, pity me, miserable wretch that I am! — I dared not — I *dared* not speak! *We have put her living in the tomb!*.... [Y]et I dared not — I *dared not speak!* And now — tonight — Ethelred — ha! ha!" (*TS* 1:416)

Roderick emphasizes that he didn't speak in order to emphasize the irony of the narrator's speech, his recitation of "The Mad Trist," as the cause of Madeline's reanimation. Yet it is Usher who performs the final speech act, rendering Madeline present through the conjuration "'*Madman! I tell you that she now stands without the door!*'" Saying she is there, in the uncanny textual logic of the tale, makes it so.

> As if in the superhuman energy of his utterance there had been found the potency of a spell — the huge antique panels to which the speaker pointed, threw slowly back, upon the instant, their ponderous and ebony jaws. It was the work of the rushing gust — but then without those doors there *did* stand the lofty and enshrouded figure of the lady Madeline of Usher. (*TS* 1:417)

Uttering becomes superhuman, doors are opened like jaws, and the final work of the rushing gust, which has been determined as not only wind but the material of speech, is to open the way for a collapsing of boundaries.

As the external and internal categories are released into each other by means of speech, the tale folds in upon itself, much as the mansion ultimately sinks into its reflection in the tarn. The mansion had been characterized as sealed off from the outside, its decay like "old wood-work which has rotted for long years ... with no disturbance from the breath of external air" (*TS* 1:400). It is external air, in the form of the narrator's presence and his speech, that finally precipitates its collapse. The final sentence returns attention to the tarn, the original site of the narrator's aesthetic experiment of viewing the Usher mansion through a different lens:

> While I gazed, this fissure rapidly widened — there came a fierce breath of the whirlwind — the entire orb of the satellite burst at once upon my sight — my brain reeled as I saw the mighty walls rushing asunder — there was a long tumultuous shouting sound like the voice of a thousand waters — and the deep and dank tarn at my feet closed sullenly and silently over the fragments of the "House of Usher." (*TS* 1:417)

The breath of the whirlwind and the shouting sound of the thousand waters mark the destruction of the nested and recursive system of Ushers: the mansion, the family, the man, and the text. The central position of the threshold, of the doors of the Usher mansion, of the uncanny door to the hermit's hut and the exterior of the dragon's palace, of the door through which Madeline finally collapses, of the mouths of both Roderick and the narrator—all of these symbolic apertures are figured within the word "Usher." For not only is an usher someone who escorts others through thresholds, but the word "Usher" is derived from the Latin *ostium*, signifying both a doorway and a river's mouth.

The self-enclosing frames of *mise en abyme* are drawn in "The Fall of the House of Usher" to press the peculiar shape of an auto-critical work. Poe's attempt to write a work that could reframe the perspective of aesthetic criticism without simply replaying its hierarchical mastery yields multiplying figures of self-enclosure. Playing the part of the reader, the narrator approaches the house from an external perspective and struggles, like a critic, to ascertain the origin of its effect. But all of his efforts to deflect that effect, to bring it under control by breathing his own external air into it—by looking into the tarn or by reading the most generically discordant text he can find—in fact aggravate and become complicit in the mounting terror itself. The external perspective is not finally available in this house of mirrors, for wherever the narrator seeks to interpose a level of reflective distance, a fable of hard boundaries between work and audience, he finds that his attempt to frame is itself at the very center of the effect which he would alleviate.[38] What is external becomes internal, and the critical perspective is surprised, in this tale, to find itself in the place where it sought to discover the origin of terror.

Poe's achievement in these tales is to give a literary shape to the new critical perspective informed by German idealism. But this shape, the dizzying arrangement of self-enclosing frames, itself produces a peculiar feeling which cannot be wholly comprehended by the act of aesthetic inquiry. Such interpretive affect helps explain the nature of the resistance Poe's work stages against interpretation, a resistance Riddel identifies as a "feedback of effects" (155).[39] Poe is not criticizing the German critical tradition, using terror in a negative sense to caution readers against reading too closely. Rather, he complicates that critical tradition by forcing it to obey its own rules. For Poe accepts the premise of the idealist argument and the Jena practice: that the study of the aesthetic, the nature of how literature makes us feel, holds out the promise of addressing the metaphysical gap between subject and object. Poe explores this promise, however, within tales that not only depict experiments of feeling but *are* experiments of feeling. In Poe's tales, criticism does not draw the secret of feeling from its literary object, but rather, conversely, the literary object takes as its subject the act of criticism. Terror is the shape of that feeling—the feeling of thinking about feeling.

In other words, Poe both draws and departs from the conventional pattern of romanticism. His insistence upon reversing, unfolding, reflecting, and pairing the relation between criticism and work goes further, perhaps because he is not, as is the tradition of German idealism, initially committed to saving the philosophical subject. In advocating for the centrality of affect, insisting, through his returning women, that the very thing that criticism would claim to love is instead buried, ignored, mutilated under its gaze, Poe initiates a move that we would now call deconstruction. Considering the affective potential of the work, in particular the special case of terror, as reframing yet not dismissing the myth of the external or objective perspective, Poe's work begins to cut a different, more insistent place for the otherness of affect. It is no wonder, perhaps, that poststructuralists have been fascinated by Poe. But it isn't, as I've tried to show here, just a matter of his linguistic play or overdetermined schemes; it isn't just his cold, complicated architecture, that is, but rather that such architecture springs from the pressing question of a moved heart.

# 3

## THE AIR OF ANALYSIS

Resolution and Composition
in Poe's Sublime and Confessional Tales

**THE PREVIOUS CHAPTER CONCLUDED** with the hypothesis that the source of poststructuralism's interest in Poe could be related to his terror. The most conspicuous evidence of that interest, however, Lacan and Derrida's essays on "The Purloined Letter," would appear to center not just on Poe's relatively *un*terrifying detective fiction but on the most austere and nonterrifying version of it, a tale that would appear to foreground reason and method at the expense of feeling. Yet, as Poe explains in a letter to a friend, the "hair-splitting" of his detective Dupin "is all done for effect": "[P]eople think them more ingenious than they are—on account of their method and *air* of method" (*Letters* 2:328). The detective tales' "*air* of method" and their "effect" refer to an affective and aesthetic character of rational method—the atmospheric feeling, either portrayed or received, of thinking. If thinking becomes a special kind of feeling, then the detective tales may have more in common with the aesthetic concerns of the earlier terror tales than would first appear. In this chapter, I want to reconstruct the way in which Poe's seemingly cold mechanism of detection and deferral in the detective tales, the theme of thinking that draws poststructuralist regard, derives from earlier, more affectively charged attempts to dramatize the structure of analysis. These attempts install an originary terror within the analytical project that detective fiction's series of deferrals works to obscure yet also to capitalize upon.

By regaining a sense of the origins and structure of Poe's conception of analysis, we may reassess the terror tales Poe wrote after his detective project, tales in which the terror of thought is no longer closely associated with German idealism or critical accounts of the work of art. The atmospheric mysticism of mind that hung over the early dead woman tales dissipates, revealing, in Poe's later tales of sublime encounters and psychotic confessions, a complex and estranging machinery of mind: giant whirlpools and Piranesian torture engines, meticulously deliberate murders and the cool and rational sound of their compulsive confession. In these later tales, thought becomes an estranged yet crucial component of terror, emerging deliriously at moments of extreme hopelessness or instigating uncontrollable and self-destructive actions. Evoking the same structure of analysis as the austere detective tales do, Poe's confessional and sublime tales explore the affective vectors behind uncanny and poststructuralist paradoxes of mind.

The vexed relation between reason and terror in Poe's tales has often led readers and critics to consider them parodies, essentially ironic and deeply critical of rationalism. Yet recent studies that would re-orient Poe's place in nineteenth-century intellectual history suggest that such a "counter-Enlightenment" version of Poe deserves revision. In something of a meta-ironic moment, Maurice Lee gestures at evidence of this "familiar" Poe, "the marplot of Enlightenment order whose protagonists' insistent claims to logic only highlight the instability of reason (note to self: if you find yourself saying 'mad am I not' or 'how calmly I can tell you the whole story,' you don't sound rational, you sound like a lunatic)" (*Uncertain Chances* 21). Lee's wider study qualifies this conventional anti-rational Poe by restoring the context of probabilistic science to the detective tales. Poe was more attuned to the discourse of science and reason than the traditional romantic view gives him credit for, and Lee and others have sought to restore him from poststructuralist accounts that would sink all of his writing about reason into radical skepticism.[1]

But Lee's joke points toward another avenue of re-evaluating Poe's relation to Enlightenment reason. When Lee's book begins to talk to itself ("note to self"), it exploits and plays upon how one may come to sound like one of Poe's narrators in the very gesture of avowing not to sound like one. In the paradoxical grip of such a logic, in which attesting to one's sanity or not attesting to one's sanity both lead to the same sound of insanity, one may clearly feel the instability of reason. But that instability depends upon an expectation of stability, a desired sound of reason, that always seems to recede in proportion to the attempt to possess it. Lee makes the point that poststructuralist accounts of "The Purloined Letter" crucially overplay the absoluteness of their skepticism: "For all the fissures, instabilities, and paradoxes of language, Dupin's game has material stakes" (*Uncertain Chances* 43). Lee's study presses back against the poststructuralist account of the detective tales, offering a pragmatism-influenced reading that would emphasize those material stakes, the "real-world" outcome and Dupin's manipulation of things "external to the game" that the poststructuralist abstraction too quickly passes over in its skeptical agenda. This chapter offers another alternative to the problem of poststructuralism's seeming dead end. Just as Lee turns to intellectual history to reconsider the detective tales, I want to reconstruct Poe's understanding of analytical method in order to examine the sound of rationality in his later tales of terror. Such a reading finds Poe operating within the Enlightenment tradition, not critiquing reason but extending it, drawing out the terror which is not finally its collapse but its constitution.

In the first section of this chapter, I retrieve the conception of analysis as a double process of resolution and composition, as given in an excised portion of "The Murders in the Rue Morgue" (1841), in order to substantiate the procedural opposition that lies behind the detective tales' poststructuralist effects. This leads to a reading of "The Man of the Crowd" (1840) as coming apart at what I've termed the zero-limit of understanding—the hypothetical state explored by Edwards and similar in nature to what George Levine identifies as the trope of self-sacrifice for objective knowledge.[2] For Poe, this zero-limit is implicated in the balanced zero-sum calculus of the air of method, the weaving and unraveling of resolution and composition working simultaneously to undo one another. In the second section, I show how Poe returns to the processes of analysis in his sublime tales and depicts the perceiver as reduced and resolved in terror to that zero-limit in dramas in which the environment, giant whirlpools and pendulums, comes to enact the force of analytical agon. And in the chapter's final section, I address the strange sound of the confessional tales, the tones of the apparently insane yet hyperrational narrators of Poe's best-known terror tales. Whereas I read the sublime tales as fables of resolution, of being reduced by terror to the bare zero-limit from which reason irrationally emerges, the confessional tales are fables of composition. They begin from the zero-limit of perfectly resolved reason, of a world in which resolution has isolated and erased all outward and material evidence of a crime and all threats that would terrify. But from this space of security comes the elemental force of reason's uncontrollable nature, and against their own wills the narrators compose their crimes into narrative and recognize in the "new terror" inspired by each new "wave of thought" (*TS* 2:1225) the recursive shape of a reason born of terror. Thinking, perversely, would demand the obliteration of the thinking subject. Terror, however, is not, as it might be supposed, felt by the subject as a direct response to this threat but rather becomes the mode by which the subject can feel its way into that requirement.

In short, then, this chapter argues that whereas we find the slippery deferrals of reason in Poe's detective tales, the uncanny poststructuralist readings of those tales depend upon a kind of narrative experiment that Poe began during a period of intense preoccupation with the power of method, and culminate not in the final detective tale but rather in the centripetal and centrifugal forces of his sublime and confessional tales. Attempting to capture the secret of analytical thought, Poe may begin with shows of confident detection and airs of passionless method, but he returns to terror, albeit a new terror constructed within a schematic of analytical structure. In the face of an affective passion, in the terror that empties and fills the contours of thought, Poe seeks to find the feeling of thinking, the affective knot of the "*air* of method" that the ratiocinative tales kept concealed behind cool displays of untying.

## "The Creative and the Resolvent"

To return to a poststructuralist reading of Poe routes us back through the central role Poe's detective fiction plays in the poststructuralist debate following from Lacan's seminar on "The Purloined Letter." This debate could be summed up imperfectly as unfolding the maxim that analysis does not itself admit of analysis. Poe's detective fiction, which stages the activity of analysis in the figure of the detective Dupin, comes to be *about* the structure of reason—and its peculiar tricks, involutions, and doubles thus allow poststructuralist readers to pry open the fissures it models within a myth of reason's smooth and detached mastery over its environment. It would appear, then, that Poe deploys the detective story to shift into irony the lessons that he learned from the dead woman stories. The relation of Poe's terror to his detective fiction remains an incomplete story, however. Telling it requires considering the origins of Poe's analytical detective story and the set of logical terms by means of which Poe would build his narratives of both detection and terror. This section thus rethreads the story of the poststructuralist Poe, leading us to the strange intellectual anxiety of "The Man of the Crowd" as the experimental ground for the maxim that "analysis cannot be analyzed," a claim that formalizes not only the ensuing detective fiction but also, as the concluding sections of this chapter will indicate, his late-career tales of terror.

In the poststructuralist criticism that proliferated following Lacan's seminar on "The Purloined Letter," Poe's detective fiction found itself at the center of increasingly abstract theorization about the nature of analysis. That this theorization, in poststructuralist "down-the-rabbit-hole" fashion, quickly deepened into theorization about the theorization of analysis might have doomed the debate to obscurity if not for two factors, one historical and the other literary. First, because it remains the only sustained encounter in published form between French poststructuralist heavyweights Jacques Lacan and Jacques Derrida, the debate not only had high-profile disciplinary stakes but also provoked philosophically minded American literary scholars, notably Barbara Johnson and John Irwin, to revitalize the study of Poe's literature as theoretically sophisticated. Second, "The Purloined Letter," far from being simply a convenient example, asserted itself, under poststructuralist scrutiny, as an uncanny fable not only of analysis but of the infinitely regressive qualities of poststructuralist analyses themselves. That is, as Poe's tale describes the theft and concealment of an important letter, so too could the critics see their interpretations as attempting to secure the significance of the tale. And, just as the letter in the tale is re-stolen by a detective who employs the same analytical methods as the thief, so too does each poststructuralist interpretation seem particularly vulnerable, not despite but because of the analytical strategies that made the theft possible. At each stage of the debate—from Lacan to Derrida to Johnson to Irwin—analysis, the method of rational thought at the center of Poe's detective fiction, slips from the grasp of the critic and by its own peculiar logic allows each framing conclusion to itself be framed by the next critic in the queue. In this way the later critics, with gestures of self-awareness, came to acknowledge that they were replaying the logic of the tale, that "no analysis—including this one" (Johnson 110) could ever possess and determine the meaning of the letter without leaving itself open to being stolen.[3] The only "conclusion," following this growing awareness of the inevitable interpolation of each critic's own position within the logic of the letter, is that no final word about this tale, or about its subject, is possible: every successive attempt to summarize and interpret the critical legacy will become just another necessarily vulnerable gambit, opening by its attempt to foreclose the next interpretive frame.

Analysis, in its dual function as fictional theme and critical apparatus, appears responsible for the tale's elusiveness. Johnson diagnoses the cause for the critical regression in the self-reflexive procedure of analyzing analysis: "It is the *act of analysis* which seems to occupy the center of the discursive stage, and the *act of analysis of the act of analysis* which in some way disrupts that centrality" (110). Irwin, agreeing in substance with Johnson, points out that the problematic nature of analysis is even more explicit in Poe's first detective story, "The Murders in the Rue Morgue," not just as a theme but as the prophetic first sentence: "That the dizzying, self-dissolving effect of thought about thought—what Johnson calls the 'asymmetrical, abyssal structure' of analyzing the act of analysis—forms the continuing theme of the Dupin stories is announced in the opening sentence of the first tale" (*Mystery* 11). If the sentence Irwin refers to—"The mental features discoursed of as the analytical are, in themselves, but little susceptible of analysis" (*TS* 1:527)—*were* the first sentence of "The Murders in the Rue Morgue," then the critical history would achieve a fitting roundness: Poe begins the drama right where it ends, with the admission that analysis alone cannot be analyzed.

But it wasn't. The often-quoted and prescient line is only the first sentence of the 1845 "Murders in the Rue Morgue." The original publication, in the April 1841 edition of *Graham's Magazine*, contains a long introductory paragraph, after which the "first sentence" appears. Recuperating this introductory paragraph does not invalidate Irwin's argument. But it does reveal that the seductive symmetry of closed systems motivates a rhetorical strategy of ending with a beginning—a strategy, moreover, that informs the structure of the detective story itself.[4] Looking closely at the original beginning that not only the poststructuralist critics but Poe himself will omit reveals an important trace of the compositional problem of analysis that Poe confronted before revising "Murders in the Rue Morgue" for the triptych of Dupin stories published together in the 1845 *Tales*.

To glimpse the early developmental influences upon Poe's detective tales, we must thus recover the sense of the original first paragraph:

> It is not improbable that a few farther steps in phrenological science will lead to a belief in the existence, if not to the actual discovery and location of an organ of *analysis*. If this power (which may be described, although not defined, as the capacity for resolving thought into its elements) be not, in fact, an essential portion of what late philosophers term ideality, then there are indeed many good reasons for supposing it a primitive faculty. That it may be a constituent of ideality is here suggested in opposition to the vulgar dictum (founded upon the assumptions of grave authority however), that the calculat-

ing and discriminating powers (causality and comparison) are at variance with the imaginative—that the three, in short, can hardly coexist. But although thus opposed to received opinion, the idea will not appear ill-founded when we observe that the processes of invention or creation are strictly akin with the processes of resolution—the former being nearly, if not absolutely, the latter conversed. (*TS* 1:527n)

The overriding claim of the original first paragraph is of the mutually constitutive relation, by way of inverse opposition, between the faculties of analytical "resolution" and creative "ideality." The final sentence indicates that Poe is not merely working against the "vulgar dictum" that imagination and reason are discrete and unrelated, antagonistic faculties. Rather, he asserts their interrelation through their opposition. And though the conflation of analytical reason and poetic ideality in the figure of Dupin and the mathematician-poet Minister D—— has long been recognized as critical to Poe's detective tales, the qualification that this paragraph provides is that the opposition between the calculating and the imaginative *constitutes* their mutual identity.[5]

Rather than induction and deduction, separate and distinct roads toward truth for which a later Poe will express contempt, resolution and composition are two stages of the same analytical method.[6] This unity of opposites in resolution and composition significantly shades the narrator's description of Poe's detective as "a double Dupin—the creative and the resolvent" (*TS* 1:533). Furthermore, the adjacency of "composition" as an analytical term to Poe's representation of it as both "creative" and "combining" implies that the narrative performance of analysis, the rhetoric of Dupin's demonstration and of Poe's tale, is part of the analytical process. Thus, whereas Loisa Nygaard finds Poe's loose use of induction and deduction "a *performance* that, to judge from its subsequent effects on readers, has been stunningly successful" (249), I emphasize how his rigorous application of resolution and composition suggests deep connections between the resolvent powers of science and the combining powers of the imagination. Analysis, in Poe's Dupin tales, may end up being read as a mask, but it initially began as a model. For when we consider the narrower definitions of calculation, creativity, and their relation in this excised paragraph, we understand that the claim that analysis cannot be analyzed did not arrive fully formed in "Murders in the Rue Morgue." Instead, it was prepared for by a disquisition on the relationship between resolution and invention—an argument set in phrenological terms but expressly dissatisfied with phrenological distinctions between ideality and causality—that suggests that the reason analysis cannot submit to analysis is bound up in the reciprocal nature of the processes of "creation" and "resolution." For Poe, the use of these terms is both a tilted approximation of the methodological terms "resolution" and "composition" and an appropriation of their historical dynamics.

The methodological senses of resolution and composition derive from the sixteenth-century revision of Aristotelian science in the Padua medical school. John Randall's developmental history of the concept of method traces the genesis of the twin methods of resolution and composition to Pietro d'Abano's application of Galen's rhetorical terms to the doubled form of Aristotelian method.[7] In the reconstruction at the Padua school, these methods taken together become the basis of the generalized method that, in being applicable to all manner of investigation, is fundamental to the definition of modern science. Randall cites Hugo of Siena as an example of this "double process": "[T]he process of discovery in demonstration through causes is resolutive, while that of making known is compositive, and the opposite in demonstration through effects" (Hugo of Siena, *Expositio Tegni Galeni*; qtd. and trans. in Randall 287). The "double process" thus is one of beginning with an observation of an effect, finding the effect's cause through resolution, and finally reversing the expressive direction and being able to explain, by composition, the effect *by way of* the cause.[8]

In the sixteenth century, this doubled methodological process became known as the "regress."[9] And the regress will become definitive of the scientific method, as Randall finds, when Zabarella at the Padua school declares that "[i]t is thus clear that there can be no scientific method except the demonstrative and resolutive" (Jacobi Zabarellae Patavini, *Opera Logica* [c. 1586]; qtd. and trans. in Randall 293). The two terms continue to circulate in methodological concerns throughout the seventeenth century and would have found their way into America most probably through the same primer that was so important to Edwards's development of infinity as a concept of terror: the *Port-Royal Logic*. That work, an older but nevertheless standard philosophy textbook for much of the eighteenth century in America, distinguishes between resolution and composition in figurative terms: "[T]hese two methods differ only as the route one takes in climbing a mountain from a valley differs from the route taken in descending from the mountain into the valley (Arnauld and Nicole, Buroker trans. 238).[10] By Poe's time, however, the terms are rarely found except in astronomical treatises, algebra textbooks, and encyclopedic definitions of analysis.[11]

Regardless of where Poe acquired his specific knowledge of the term "resolution," he would almost certainly have seen it paired with its inverse mode of demonstration, that is, composition. One possible source, Rees's *Cyclopaedia* (1810–1824)—Poe's favorite encyclopedia—contains entries on "analysis," "resolution," and "method," all of which connect resolution and composition with analytical method. We can hear, for example, an echo of Poe's claim for their converse relation in the *Cyclopaedia*'s definition of *resolution* as "the analytic method . . . in direct opposition to composition, or the synthetic method" (Rees, s.v. "resolution"). Another possible source is J. P. Nichol's astronomy primer *Views of the Architecture of the Heavens in a Series of Letters to a Lady* (1840), published in the United States a year before "Murders in the Rue Morgue," in which *resolvable* is defined as "that which may be analyzed, brought together and explained or defined" (155). Poe had read the book—it is mentioned in his *Eureka* (1848)—and it obviously made an impression, as Nichol is referred to by name in "Murders in the Rue Morgue."[12] The confinement of "resolution" and "composition" to sporadic occurrences in algebra textbooks, astronomy treatises, and encyclopedias only makes more remarkable Poe's experimentation with their conceptual possibilities. Poe, in the excised first paragraph, thus draws upon the abstract discourse of analytical methodology as he may have discovered it in Arnauld, Rees, or Nichol and adapts it, through the analogical logic of phrenology, to figure the distinction between compositive writing and resolutive science. The slippage between "composition" as a literary term and "composition" as an analytical one allows Poe to imagine writing as both opposed to science and absolutely necessary to its function; composition is resolution's mirror image, and taken together they comprise analysis proper. According to this model, the reason that analysis cannot submit to analysis, cannot look back at itself, is implicated in the already doubled and internally mirrored nature of its constituent processes.

Given their conspicuous redoubled narrative structure, Poe's detective tales may be considered dramatizations of the regress itself.[13] "Murders in the Rue Morgue," for instance, begins with effects, two dead bodies and a locked room, which Dupin traces back to their causes, an escaped orang-outang, by the processes of resolution. The tale isn't over until this process of resolution is reversed in the process of composition, in which Dupin reconstructs the meaning of the effects, the solution of the crime, by retelling the story of the murders as an effect with a determinate cause. But, for whatever light the model of regress may shine on the model of the narrative structure, it also casts a shadow.

For we may hear a hint of the consideration that would turn the demonstrative regress into its dark cousin, the infinite regress, in the worries of Agostino Nifo, who in 1506 sensed the problem of its tautological potential:

> But on this issue I customarily raise the question whether there are two procedures in natural [sciences], one from an effect to the discovery of the cause, the other from the cause discovered to the effect. It seems not, because then there would be a circle in demonstrations. (Agostino Nifo, *Expositio super Octo Aristotelis Stagiritae Libros de Physico Auditu* [1552]; qtd. and trans. in Jardine 688; brackets in original)

Poe's achievement in the detective tales, then, is not only the dramatization of the demonstrative regress but also the smuggling in of Nifo's skeptical apprehensions about resolution and composition as the unified method of science. It is this potential circularity at the heart of the method of analysis that draws the poststructuralist criticism to Poe and links it with his tales of terror, for by the time of "The Purloined Letter," Poe had not only produced the "*air* of method" but also its most uncanny paradoxes.

But the detective tales should not be considered Poe's only attempt at dramatizing method. During the two-year period before he wrote "The Murders in the Rue Morgue," Poe attempted to portray method as reason several times—culminating in the conclusive futility of "The Man of the Crowd," a tale that ends by admitting an impossibility ("er lasst sich nicht lesen" [*TS* 1:515] / "it does not permit itself to be read" [*TS* 1:506]) with which the "Murders in the Rue Morgue" begins ("The mental features discoursed of as the analytical are, in themselves, but little susceptible of analysis" [*TS* 1:527]). That the focus shifts from the compositional problem of literacy (not able to be read) to the analytical problem (not able to be analyzed) suggests that Poe may have sensed that the narrative impasse confronted in the former story was conceptually rooted in the analytical conundrum of narrating analysis itself. "The Man of the Crowd" may thus be seen as marking a compositional crisis to be overcome in the Dupin tales—a crisis, moreover, brought on by adopting an ambitious narrative strategy, modeled on the doubled nature of resolution and composition, of emplotting both processes of analysis at the same time.

Four pieces Poe published during 1840—"Instinct vs. Reason," "Peter Pendulum, the Business Man," "The Philosophy of Furniture," and "The Man of the Crowd"—display a preoccupation with method. In "Instinct vs. Reason—A Black Cat," Poe expresses amazement over the apparent reasoning ability shown by his cat's elaborate method of unlatching a door. "Peter Pendulum" begins with the mantra "I am a business man. I am a methodical man. Method is *the* thing, after all" (*TS* 1:481). For Peter Pendulum, the con-artist whose name conceals the pendulum-like double motion of analytical method, "it was method—not money—which made the man" (*TS* 1:484). And the earliest version of "The Philosophy of Furniture" sees reason in methods of housekeeping: "There is reason, it is said, in the roasting of eggs, and there is philosophy even in furniture" (*TS* 1:495n). If, as one historian of philosophy has pointed out, "the fundamental principles of a single methodology came to be applied [in the seventeenth century] to mathematics, physics, medicine, and metaphysics" (Schouls 5), then Poe might add to the list feline behavior, conning, and home decoration. For the underlying assumption of each of Poe's pieces is that reason consists of the application of a general method to any and every particular problem, even the problem a closed door might present to a claustrophobic cat. The implication of his pieces is analogous to the universalizing hypotheses of the Padua school—reason and method are synonymous—and this will lead him to attempt in "The Man of the Crowd" an exploration of reason through a dramatization of method.

"The Man of the Crowd" is a tale of two halves. The first half describes the activities of a narrator who is studying the urban crowd through a hotel window. The second half describes the narrator's pursuit, out into the crowd and the night, of one idiosyncratic member of that crowd. The attention to the doubled form of analysis suggests a reading of the tale's two halves as dramatizing the two processes of analysis. However, unlike the detective tale form that Poe will invent months later, "The Man of the Crowd" refuses such steadfast distinctions between the two processes. Instead, resolution and composition occur nearly simultaneously in the first half of the tale, concluding with the discernment of the strange man of the crowd himself. Once found, however, the stranger becomes the problem that the second half of the tale seeks again to resolve and compose. The entanglements of such a narrative structure, with their source in the doubled and reversed methods of analysis, lead not only to the more austere and controlled generic devices Poe adopts in the Dupin cycle but also to the spiraling and self-destructive dilemmas of his later terror tales.[14]

The resolvent nature of the narrator's study fixes on the individual details within the crowd. Taking apart the visual field presented by the hotel window, the narrator resolves the crowd into its component, disconnected parts:

> At first my observations took an abstract and generalizing turn. I looked at the passengers in masses, and thought of them in their aggregate relations. Soon,

however, I descended to details, and regarded with minute interest the innumerable varieties of figure, dress, air, gait, visage, and expression of countenance. (*TS* 1:507)

The narrator begins with generalizations but then descends to details, a methodological move implying that what he finds in the particular might be applicable to the questions raised by their "aggregate relations." That such a move is characterized as a descent intimates the hierarchical relation between abstractions and details: larger ideas are comprised of lower-order, supporting details. The "minute interest" here is thus resolutive; the narrator must lose the relational sense of the passengers in the crowd in order to discover the atomistic minutiae of its texture.

When the daylight that had enabled the resolutive analysis ebbs, the narrator admits a change in the quality of his observation that corresponds to a turn from resolution to composition: "As the night deepened, . . . the general character of the crowd [did] materially alter (its gentler features retiring in the gradual withdrawal of the more orderly portion of the people, and its harsher ones coming out into bolder relief)" (*TS* 1:510). In describing the crowd's "character" as a face changing its expression, the narrator considers the individual countenances he had previously resolved as instances of a single, generalized face. This methodological turn is caused by the deepening night, not only because it brings out the rougher characters but also because it enables the visual effect produced by the gaslights upon the scene. The narrator's recognition of the countenance of the crowd requires the strobe-like effect of the faces of the crowd being presented to him in rapid succession: "The wild effects of the light enchained me to an examination of individual faces; and . . . the rapidity with which the world of light flitted before the window, prevented me from casting more than a glance upon each visage" (*TS* 1:511). The effect of the rapid glances of visages is a pre-cinematic moment of the mind unifying the diversity of static image. The narrator's vision, then, presented with the resolvent instances of multiple faces, blurs their diversity into a single general countenance.

The face that thus presents itself to the narrator, following the resolution of the crowd into individual countenances and their composition by way of the gaslights into a single countenance, is the analyzed face of the general human condition. Such recognition significantly coincides with the introduction of the stranger, the titular man *of* the crowd: "With my brow to the glass, I was thus occupied in scrutinizing the mob, when suddenly there came into view a countenance (that of a decrepid old man, some sixty-five or seventy years of age,)—a countenance which at once arrested and absorbed my whole attention, on account of the absolute idiosyncracy of its expression" (*TS* 1:511). The "absolute idiosyncracy" of the stranger's countenance, its inability to be categorized alongside the other expressions and faces the narrator studies, may depend upon the conditions of its creation. For the catalogue of adjectives used to describe the face recalls the preceding catalogue of character types: "As I endeavored, during the brief minute of my original survey, to form some analysis of the meaning conveyed, there arose confusedly and paradoxically within my mind, the ideas of vast mental power, of caution, of penuriousness, of avarice, of coolness, of malice, of blood-thirstiness, of triumph, of merriment, of excessive terror, of intense—of supreme despair" (*TS* 1:511). What is idiosyncratic about the face doesn't lie in any one feature but in the paradoxical synchronic manifestation of several common yet usually exclusive ones. The narrator cannot classify the man's face because the face itself represents the already-generalized character of the crowd. The stranger's is not just another face in the crowd; it is *all* of them.

If the narrator, in seeing the stranger, is seeing the projected result of his analytical project, then it may not be surprising that critics have recognized the reflection of the narrator in the description of the stranger. Patrick Quinn first made this now widely rehearsed observation, though it is Jonathan Auerbach who first noticed that the window through which the narrator gazes also functions as a mirror, "an instrument of self-reflection as well as vision" (30).[15] The darkness of the night, then, may not only enable the narrator's composition of the generalized stranger, but also allows the hotel window to reflect back to the narrator, "with his brow to the glass," his own expression. But if so, then the mystery of the mental state underlying the strange expression is solved: it is the face of analysis. The narrator's immediate reaction to the face, to attempt "to form some analysis of the meaning conveyed," leads to the list of the particular and resolved ideas. The narrator's employment of resolution upon seeing his reflection, then, makes the stranger, as reflection, the image of resolution itself. As Alexander Howe has noted, "it is when the narrator feels most 'at home' in his method that a specter haunting his system of interpretation emerges" (38). Earlier I suggested that the stranger is a composite figure of the crowd; here, however, it seems that the stranger may be an inherent feature, a ghost in the system, of the narrator's resolutive method. Which is it? Is the stranger a figure of the crowd, composed by the narrator's compositional methods, or is the stranger a figure of the narrator, a reflection of the mind resolving?

My argument is that the double nature of method enables us to see the stranger as both. On one hand, as an aggregate composition, the stranger represents composition. But on the other hand, as a reflection of the narrator in the moment of analysis, the stranger represents resolution. The fact that we are afforded both at the same time underlines the deep, polarized connection between the two functions—if the narrator sees the generalized crowd in the figure of the stranger, then he also sees the reflection of the origin of that generalization, his own analytic method. If we accept this account of the doubled nature of the stranger, then the reasons for the narrator's eventual failure can be seen as correspondingly double. Gerald Kennedy identifies a growing number of delusions on the part of the narrator in the second half of the tale, all of which "occur primarily because the narrator cannot maintain a critical detachment" ("Limits of Reason" 188). This failure, however, must not be seen as an abandonment of the narrator's methodological principles but as an imagined extension of their deployment: an analysis of analysis.

On one hand, when we take the stranger as a composition of the narrator, a kind of stereotypic figure that has been essentialized out of the crowd, then resolution will always fail because the object to be resolved has no fundamental essence itself. If the resolutive process of analysis requires that the object of inquiry be isolated, then the virus-like shifting of the man of the crowd—his circulation through each of the districts of the city, from business thoroughfare to seedy red-light district—derails resolution from the start. Since the man of the crowd, from his genesis in the flashing faces of an aggregate crowd, is the product of a compositive operation in the narrator's mind, the resolution of analysis must fail—what is being sought is not isolatable, not reducible. Instead, as we might predict, to resolve the stranger would be to de-compose him back into the crowd, an intellectual operation that would be analogous to the proliferation of crowds that is the only reward for the narrator's surreptitious pursuit.

On the other hand, when the stranger is taken as the narrator's reflection, as a figure of resolution's search for particularity, then the statement that "he refuses to be alone" may refer not only to the stranger. For it isn't only the stranger who refuses to be alone; in pursuit, the narrator also refuses to be alone, and his attempts to compose, to reconstruct by repetition, the nature of the man fail because he always finds himself in the experiment. As a reflection of resolution, the narrator's pursuit is circular; he must himself lose his aloneness (his situated observational distance) in order to pursue the stranger, yet he cannot himself stand apart, since he is implicated in the subject.[16] That is, just as the resolution of a composition fails because the composition is fundamentally a crowd, the composition of resolution itself also fails because there exists no external point of view from which the narrator could see without also being seen.

This is why the choice to follow the man out into the crowd is a turning point for the story; by leaving behind the comfortable voyeuristic and objective separation that the hotel window affords and searching for the meaning of one's reflection out in the crowd, the narrator's endeavor exposes him to the analytical gaze. For if, as Susan Sweeney argues, abandoning the shelter of the glass leaves the narrator bereft of any corrective lens, blurring his vision of "the crowd as a collective entity rather than an assortment of individuals" (9), it also blurs his own distinction from the crowd itself. In order to see without being seen, he becomes a part of that which he would resolve. The narrator, in this account, pursues the reflection of his own pursuit, now mirrored in action rather than in the image in the glass, the success of which seems to depend on the degree to which he may conceal himself from his analytical reflection. As the narrator follows the stranger, the language of pursuit flirts with the language of evasion: "Still more was I astonished to see him repeat the same walk several times—once nearly detecting me"; however, "[l]uckily I wore a pair of caoutchouc over-shoes, and could move about in perfect silence. At no moment did he see that I watched him" (*TS* 1:513). For the narrator seeking to compose an understanding of the stranger, the task of analysis becomes contingent on how well he can hide his own complicity. The paradoxical activity of hiding while seeking corresponds to the compositional problem of understanding one's own understanding. The narrator can never find what he looks for because, on one hand, the nature of his search requires that he and his motives remain hidden; but on the other hand, the object of his search *is* the nature of his search. Even when he reveals himself to the stranger at the end of the tale, he is only able to restage the initial moment of recognition: "I . . . gazed at him steadfastly in the face" (*TS* 1:515). Revealing himself yields nothing but the recognition that the problem the man represents, the problem of analyzing analysis, cannot be solved directly through literary composition.

The problem of analyzing analysis, dramatized in "The Man of the Crowd," leads directly to the dictum regarding the inseparability of resolution and composition that begins "The Murders in the Rue Morgue." What dooms the narrator's project in "The Man of the Crowd" is that he would attempt to resolve and compose at the same time and, moreover, harness this doubled and reciprocal process to an introspective narrative frame. The achievement of "Murders in the Rue Morgue" is to disengage the doubled process of analysis from the figure of the narrator, to tell the story without having to come out from behind the hotel window. The detachment of the narrative voice from the reasoning mind, an adaptation that would become a major convention for detective fiction, allows Poe to triangulate the object of inquiry, the operation of analysis. Dupin may be a double Dupin—"creative and resolvent"—like the narrator and stranger of "The Man of the Crowd," but significantly he does not command the widest narrative frame. One can speculate that had Dupin narrated "The Purloined Letter," it might have fallen into the same critical illegibility that forecloses "The Man of the Crowd." Instead, the detective tale's unassuming Watson-like narrator may stay behind the glass and observe, may hide his own complicit analysis through a seemingly transparent account of another's. But this move is less a solution than it is a deferral, and while the chiasmic transpositions that undo "The Man of the Crowd" are based in the inseparable functions of analysis, the addition of the outside perspective of the narrator will eventually yield an even more complicated structure of resolutions and compositions—resulting in the inversions, displacements, and deferrals of "The Purloined Letter" and its poststructuralist appendices.

Yet if the deferrals of detective fiction would reframe the problem, enacting the same distancing effect that he had introduced through the external narrator in "The Fall of the House of Usher," in another strain Poe would explore the affective possibilities of the strange pursuit. For "The Man of the Crowd" is tonally dark and obscure; the stranger shows signs of "excessive terror," (*TS* 1:511), "intense agony" (*TS* 1:514), and is finally typified as the "type and genius of deep crime"—a phrase that recalls the opening of the tale, where Poe advances the axiom that some secrets are so dark that they are carried to the grave, "[a]nd thus the essence of all crime is undivulged" (*TS* 1:507). The deferrals of Poe's detective fiction would seem to put this central horror at a distance, trending from grotesque fantasized violence to a more mundane murder to an entirely bloodless theft. An alternate route opens up, however, in the way that "The Man of the Crowd" steeps the mechanics of analysis in anxiety.

The analytical paradox in "The Man of the Crowd" should not be held entirely separate from the horror with which it is regarded.[17] And it can be argued that Poe's ensuing adaptations of the terror tale pursue this affective route, exploring how terror embeds the inexpressible demands of a wholly reflexive analysis. Following this route, the final two sections of this chapter show how, through the peculiar modality of terror, resolution and composition become both less instrumental for and more constitutive of the feeling self. In Poe's sublime tales, terror resolves the subject to a zero-limit in which it becomes merely a particle within the giant and inhuman machinery of an analytical environment. Yet terror is also the way in which an estranged subjectivity composes itself out of that zero-limit in the confessional tales, rewriting the function of analytical composition as a manic and uncontrollable locution. Writing sensational tales that do not frame resolution and composition through an external perspective (as the detective tales do) but rather emplot their internal dynamics, Poe deploys terror as the necessary relation between analysis's structural paradox and a radicalized and inhuman mechanics of both universe and self.

## The Amusement of Relative Velocities: The Sublime Tales

The problem of representing the double processes of analysis, of raising methodical thinking into a narrative topic, appears from "The Man of the Crowd" to be a dilemma of perspective. But if Poe is able to skirt the problem by adding external frames of perspective in the detective tales, it may be possible to consider how the altered character of his later tales of terror may constitute a more direct strategy of coming at the problem of analysis. Whereas the cycle of dead woman tales rendered thought as a mystical and transcendent operation, capable of engendering terror through fantastical conversions, the terror of thinking in his later tales, though at times returning to this program of mystification and abstract reverie, adopts a different attitude. Whereas thinking is still a deep concern for the these later terror tales, the thought depicted is no longer exoticized as "forbidden knowledge" mediated by alien and undead women but rather is domesticated in the plain operations of quantification, resolution and composition. The course of the thoughts depicted—the delirious quantifications of Poe's doomed victims or the disturbingly emphatic rationalizations of Poe's confessing killers—quickly amplify into estranged and monstrous versions of themselves, to be sure, but their models are drawn from Poe's interest in analytical and scientific method.

It may be tempting to conclude that the dysfunction of rational discourse in these tales parodies reason, science, and the Enlightenment order they connote. After all, the early "Sonnet—To Science" (1829) would seem to be Poe's unambiguous romantic manifesto against science. The poem portrays science as a "vulture" that preys upon "the poet's heart" (*CP* 91). The poem also indicts science for dragging "Diana from her car" and driving "the Hamadryad from the wood" (*CP* 91)—crimes that leave poetry bereft of its fantastical materials and inspirations. A closer look at the poem, however, reveals Poe as not, or at least not only, bemoaning the imminent obsolescence of poetry but rather recognizing the increased demands on poetry that modern conceptions of science and truth require.[18]

For despite its tone of lament, "Sonnet—To Science" contains an implicit challenge. Its speaker asks of science:

> How should he love thee? or how deem thee wise,
> Who wouldst not leave him in his wandering
> To seek for treasure in the jewelled skies
> Albeit he soared with an undaunted wing? (*CP* 91)

The challenge for the poet is to wed, to respect, to love a science which now always corrects the poet's vision of the universe. The problem is not that science has banished the mysteries that were once the source of fabulous fancy but rather that such banishment is a function of the new way of seeing that the poet can no longer deny, the alteration performed by the "peering eyes" that will not "leave him in his wandering." As Kent Ljungquist notes, "the poem insinuates the necessity for the poet to develop a more mature and exacting attitude toward his art" (118). Poe's sonnet thus proposes a poetics that must adapt to the austere perspective forced by a scientific worldview that is both universal and detached: universal because its subject is nothing less than *all* things, detached because it analyzes only through penetrating and ocular observation. Yet through this detachment, science still "alterest all things with [its] peering eyes" (*CP* 91), complicating the notion of a wholly transparent objective perspective. Science has transformed the world, Poe's poem indicates, by virtue of its universal detachment from it.

Poe's solution for raising the stakes of literature to the demands of science is to pressure the affective foundations underlying the impulse for such a perfectly universal, perfectly detached perspective. Poe writes three tales that draw immediately upon the issue of objective perspective raised by "Sonnet—To Science." Mediating between detached, transcendent perspectives and immersed, particular ones, these tales figure this scientific perspective as a dynamic of opposing, cyclical processes. Magnified into vast chasms and swinging pendulums, these processes are posited as elemental forces, emerging not from some self-possessed human consciousness but rather from the pre-rational structures of terror which they evoke.[19] Radicalizing the sublime encounter with nature's might, these tales write reason, together with the perspectives and processes that make it possible, as a function of terror.

In a short period following the publication of "The Murders in the Rue Morgue" in March of 1841, Poe published two other pieces, "A Descent into the Maelstrom" in May and "The Island of the Fay" in June. "Descent into the Maelstrom" is a thriller, in which a fishing boat is caught in a deadly whirlpool and its terrified inhabitant deliriously reasons his way to an unlikely escape. "Island of the Fay" is a psychological reverie, beginning with an abstract and scientifically inflected argument about the insignificance of humanity within a cosmos of infinitely great and infinitely miniscule magnitudes.[20] These two tales, sharing the motif of orbital circuit, return to the enfiguration of analysis as an endless cycle begun in "The Man of the Crowd" and inscribe it within wider scales of perspective. This projection of scale developed through "A Descent into the Maelstrom" continues in the later tale, "The Pit and the Pendulum," which shares the sublime plot and develops the origin of analysis from a point of absolute and self-negating terror. In what follows, I find in Poe's more explicit renderings of outward terror, tremendous whirlpools and giant torture engines, a fable of the origins of reason in a blankness of self only accessible through those terrors.

Let me explain why I categorize "A Descent into the Maelstrom" and "The Pit and the Pendulum" (and to a much lesser extent "The Island of the Fay") as sublime tales in light of the distinction between terror and the sublime that I drew in the Introduction. Not only do their materials seem so illustrative of the most influential theories of the sublime,[21] but, moreover, they operate according to the particular scalar misalignment between human comprehension and the infinite world that Kant sees at work in the failure of the senses, in the first stage of the sublime.[22] Yet Poe presses these elements past their sublime aesthetic potential and into what Mark McGurl proposes as the sublime's troubling "third stage":

> [T]he two-stage Kantian sublime—*first* the failure of the senses in the face of the very large, *then* the triumph of reason in the concept of infinity—enters into a third stage, unable now to shake the knowledge that reason, too, is sure to be engulfed in a larger darkness. That time will be the time not only of our death but of the death of death and the concept of infinity, too. ("Posthuman Comedy" 539)

McGurl argues that the horror genre that would imagine this larger darkness in its grossest possible features belongs to the "posthuman comedy." This drama of human conditions continually invokes the utter insignificance of the human in the widest possible scheme of nature, "a turn (and continual return) to naturalism, one in which nature, far from being dominated by technology, *reclaims* technology as a human *secretion*" ("Posthuman Comedy" 550). McGurl points out the double nature of how the posthuman comedy presses the scales of perception to either the massive magnitudes or miniscule ones until what we account as the "human" dissolves or disappears.[23] If the problem for the speaker of "Sonnet—To Science" was to reinvent poetry in the light of a universal and detached scientific worldview, Poe's answer in the sublime tales is not to save the human, along with the elves and hamadryads, but rather to pressure the scalar limits of the poet's perspective to meet the inhuman proportions of the universe.

"A Descent into the Maelstrom," in its description of a whirlpool of immense proportions, foregrounds the problem of gaining an unmediated perspective on an alien and inhuman universe. The quotation from Joseph Glanvill that Poe appends as epigraph to the tale declares the incommensurability between the human scale and nature writ large:

> The ways of God in Nature, as in Providence, are not as *our* ways; nor are the models that we frame any way commensurate to the vastness, profundity, and unsearchableness of His works, *which have a depth in them greater than the well of Democritus.* (*TS* 1:577)

The whirlpool that occupies the center of the action in the tale is thus from the start framed as a problem of modeling, the problem that human models fail to account for inhuman vastness in nature. When the tale comes to describe that whirlpool, Poe expands the discussion of telescopic and microscopic ranges of scale he had begun in "The Island of the Fay," offering both a distant and an inside view of it.

The distant view of the maelstrom is gained through terror. The tale begins with the narrator and his companion, a fisherman, achieving "the summit of the loftiest crag" (*TS* 1:577), overlooking the maelstrom from above. Achieving this view requires first an encounter with fear. The narrator admits that "[i]n truth so deeply was I excited by the perilous position of my companion, that I fell at full length upon the ground, clung to the shrubs around me, and dared not even glance upward at the sky. . . . It was long before I could reason myself into sufficient courage to sit up and look out into the distance" (*TS* 1:578).

The prostration of the narrator before the sublimity of the sight precedes his display of willpower, his ability to "reason myself" into courage. Overcoming fear becomes, according the fisherman, necessary to obtaining perspective: "'You must get over these fancies,' said the guide, 'for I have brought you here that you might have the best possible view of the scene of that event I mentioned—and to tell you the whole story with the spot just under your eye'" (*TS* 1:578). By engaging and overcoming fear by way of reason, the tale would thus reduce the immensity of the maelstrom to a "spot," the best possible view becoming one that seeks, dizzyingly, to enframe the whole of the scene.

Viewing the maelstrom from such a height, the narrator dismisses the conventional descriptions of it for perspectival reasons. Jonas Ramus "cannot impart the faintest conception either of the magnificence, or of the horror of the scene" because his point of view "could neither have been from the summit of Helseggen, nor during a storm" (*TS* 1:581). The Brittanica, on the other hand, would seek to explain the phenomenon through the summary of other forces, making the maelstrom just a wider instance of those whirlpools created in the laboratory, "'the prodigious suction of which is sufficiently known by lesser experiments'" (*TS* 1:582–583). "However conclusive on paper," the narrator allows, "it becomes altogether unintelligible, and even absurd, amid the thunder of the abyss" (*TS* 1:583). The scientific authorities, adopting conclusions based on an assumption of scalar commensurability, are challenged here by the view achieved through, and touched with, terror.[24] The terror of the scene comes to overpower and render absurd the logical quantifications of those measurements taken at sea level.

When the fisherman begins *his* story, Poe offers us the inverse perspective of the maelstrom, now not from such a height as could frame its whole massive complex as a spot, but from within the funnel of the whirlpool itself, the perspective becoming a particle, a spot itself, within the whole. The story he relates, of being pulled into the maelstrom while on a fishing expedition, would give the inside view of the maelstrom. And again this view is accompanied and accomplished by means of passing through abject terror. The fisherman is at first terrified, closing his eyes at the spectacle like the narrator collapsing to the ground at the summit. Yet, echoing the narrator's recovery, the fisherman also regains composure by reasoning through it, apparently mastering bodily terror by an exertion of mind:

> It may appear strange, but now, when we were in the very jaws of the gulf, I felt more composed than when we were only approaching it. Having made up my

mind to hope no more, I got rid of a great deal of that terror which unmanned me at first. (*TS* 1:588)

Though there seems to be a clear relation between reason and fear—conscious reason steps in to interrupt the direct correspondence between world and body—the version of reason that Poe introduces is tonally quite different from any practical account that would fit reason to the problem at hand. It is not the case that the fisherman regains himself, "his self-possession" (*TS* 1:589), in order to apply his reason to the life-threatening crisis he faces. Instead, by getting rid of hope, the narrator detaches his self from self-interest, jettisoning the cumbersome envelope of desires that would make sense of the world "for him." In fact, this detachment plays itself out again within the later drama of the narrative, as the fisherman is able to survive only by abandoning his boat: "I resolved to lash myself securely to the water cask upon which I now held, to cut it loose from the counter, and to throw myself with it into the water" (*TS* 1:593). And though he believes he has communicated his design to his brother, who is also on the boat, the latter "shook his head despairingly, and refused to move from his station" (*TS* 1:593). Throwing himself from the boat, the narrator saves himself by abandoning ship, but his brother, a foil for this action, remains rooted and terrified. Throwing himself into the very sea that threatens him, the narrator's display of reason's mastery over terror would seem to succeed not by bolstering the courage of the self but rather by loosing the self from its individual moorings, resigning oneself to becoming merely an unresistant particle.[25]

Such resolution should recall not only the imperative of Emerson's famous "part and particle of God" transcendental vision, but perhaps the more tonally appropriate wish for annihilation that Edwards seeks through terror. For the narrator gains his escape not through any practical application of his will but rather through the uncanny emergence of reason from his submission to the dynamic forces of the world. In the state of perfect hopelessness, the fisherman is free to attend to the view of nature afforded by his position, rather than worry about the consequences such a position may entail: "I positively felt a *wish* to explore its depths, even at the sacrifice I was going to make" (*TS* 1:588–589). The imperative George Levine calls the epistemological problem of *dying to know* would seem to be literalized at this moment. Yet this desire to know even by means of death, the thought of how "magnificent a thing it was to die in such a manner" (*TS* 1:588), is not prompted by either epistemological or ethical considerations but rather by the whirl itself: "These, no doubt, were singular fancies to occupy a man's mind in such extremity—and I have often thought since, that the revolutions of the boat around the pool might have rendered me a little light-headed" (*TS* 1:589). Considering the detritus surrounding the boat within the vortex of the maelstrom, the fisherman engages in an unprompted calculation: "I *must* have been delirious—for I even sought *amusement* in speculating upon the relative velocities of their several descents toward the foam below" (*TS* 1:591). This consideration, as it turns out, will eventually lead to the discovery that will save the fisherman. He will profess to discover the (specious) Archimedean law that cylindrical objects descend a vortex at a slower rate, abandon ship for barrel, and ride out the storm. Yet this saving calculation is performed from the start as merely a delirious amusement, a wish for knowledge pinned to the dizziness of revolution. Reason would appear to be cast off tangentially from the physical dynamics of nature's unthinking engine and would emerge as what the fisherman calls the "unnatural curiosity which had taken the place of my original terror" (*TS* 1:591).

The original terror thus offers Poe a way to approximate that zero-limit in the face of the manifest demonstration of those outer, incommensurable forces of nature that dip beneath our most cold and calm descriptions of them. It is from this zero-limit that reason emerges, deliriously, as a kind of unselfed effect of the sweeping and inhuman cyclical mechanics of the "black walls" and "inmost recesses of the abyss." Poe materializes, in the figure of the ebony and jet-black whirlpool, an absence determined by a circular force reminiscent of the cyclical pattern of resolution and composition explored in "The Man of the Crowd."[26] Such a figure inspires a terror which empties the self, turning the subject into object and dramatizing how reason, that tool of the mind, in fact precedes it. As Matthew Taylor notes of Poe's environmental fear, "both the fear and its uncanny source cancel the Cartesian distance between (and assuredness of) self and world, such that one's self becomes strangely foreign and the world unsettlingly familiar" (364). Terror, not good intentions or applied study, reduces the human to the zero-limit, and it is through that affective resolution that the elemental forces of nature become indistinguishable from the rational processes they imprint or irradiate. If analysis tends to run in circles, Poe's "sublime" tales suggest that this is because the shape of analysis is itself determined by a spiral curvature of the outer universe.[27]

· · ·

In "The Pit and the Pendulum" (1842), one of Poe's most baldly sensational tales of terror, Poe returns to a portrayal of the genesis of reason in terror. Although the might of nature has been replaced by the dread power of the Inquisition, the torture chamber that the narrator explores, with its gigantic machines and outsized dimensions, comes to play much the same role as the whirlpool of the earlier tale. Indeed, the tropaic inheritance of "The Pit and the Pendulum" is suggested in the opening sentences, as the narrator describes his condemnation to prison as the sound of revolution, of cyclical motion: "[T]he sound of the inquisitorial voices seemed merged in one dreamy indeterminate hum. It conveyed to my soul the idea of *revolution*—perhaps from its association in fancy with the burr of the mill-wheel" (*TS* 1:681). Hearing the sound of revolution calls to mind not only the natural forces of the revolving water in "A Descent into the Maelstrom" but also the conversion of that force, by way of the mill-wheel, toward human ends. Though "The Pit and the Pendulum" would seem to describe a more "human" threat than the maelstrom, Poe frames it as a translation, a mechanical rendering of the dynamics of the universe. The turn from maelstrom to machine in the tale, a modal conversion that maintains the essential pattern of circular revolution, thus parallels the way in which the sublime tales convert terror to reason by means of formal equivalence.

Terror and thought, in "The Pit and the Pendulum," occur simultaneously. The narrator's tale begins with his condemnation, but his swoon leads to an awakening that reboots his consciousness within a space of complete sensory deprivation. As the narrator regains thought, however, it arrives in the same moment as terror:

> Very suddenly there came back to my soul motion and sound.... Then a pause in which all is blank. Then again sound, and motion, and touch—a tingling sensation pervading my frame. Then the mere consciousness of existence, without thought—a condition which lasted long. Then, very suddenly, *thought*, and shuddering terror, and earnest endeavor to comprehend my true state. (*TS* 1:683)

The simultaneous return of thought and terror sets the stage for the laboratory experiment on the relation of fear and thought to follow. Like "A Descent into the Maelstrom," "The Pit and the Pendulum" depicts the emergence of thought from terror, shaped by external forces and detached from motives of self-interest.

Just as the fisherman had deliriously sought amusement in calculating the relative velocities of particles caught within the vortex, the narrator of "The Pit and the Pendulum" sets out in his hopeless condition to calculate the dimensions of his cell, a research program that he admits is prompted by curiosity, not by hope: "I had little object—certainly no hope—in these researches; but a vague curiosity prompted me to continue them" (*TS* 1:686). The narrative continues to proceed along an oscillation of hypothesis and conclusion, making the narrator into a detective of his own mortality: not sleuthing out a criminal, or even calculating a means of escape, but simply measuring the length and width of his fate. The narrator begins by fearing that he has been entombed alive, but exploring the darkness he realizes that his is not "at least, the most hideous of fates" (*TS* 1:685). The narrator then hypothesizes that his cell is irregular in shape, but when it is later lit he discovers, "I had been deceived. . . . The general shape of the prison was square" (*TS* 1:688). Bound later beneath the descending arc of the bladed pendulum, the narrator hopes that the pendulum might cut his bindings but finds that "[t]he surcingle enveloped my limbs in body close in all directions—*save in the path of the destroying crescent*" (*TS* 1:693). Even when the narrator manages to escape the pendulum, the futility of such success is underlined: "Free!—I had but escaped death in one form of agony, to be delivered unto worse death in some other" (*TS* 1:695). The persistent and repeated drama of supposition and correction shows the frail successes of the narrator's reason as accidental and ultimately futile.

This pattern of fits and starts is crucial, however, in revealing how undirected and emergent thought bears the impress of its condition. Finding himself in complete darkness, the narrator contrives a method for ascertaining the cell's circumference: "I tore a part of the hem from the robe and placed the fragment at full length, and at right angles to the wall. In groping my way around the prison, I could not fail to encounter this rag upon completing the circuit" (*TS* 1:685–686). In making his way around the room, the narrator faints midway and thus must add together the fifty-two and forty-eight paces he takes before and after the fit in order to reach the conclusion that the room is a hundred paces in circumference. Yet the project as a whole is beset from the beginning with frustrations. The narrator begins by imagining that he could use a knife to mark his place: "I had thought of forcing the blade in some minute crevice of the masonry, so as to identify my point of departure." But his knife being confiscated, the narrator admits that the "difficulty . . . seemed at first insuperable" (*TS* 1:685). He then appears to have succeeded with the instrument of his torn hem but later discovers that he had unwittingly reversed direction after fainting, thus recounting all the paces he had already counted. The result is that when he eventually sees that the room is smaller than he had figured, he must account for the discrepancy: "For some minutes this fact occasioned me a world of vain trouble; vain indeed—for what could be of less importance, under the terrible circumstances which environed me, than the mere dimensions of my dungeon? But my soul took a wild interest in trifles, and I busied myself in endeavors to account for the error I had committed in my measurement" (*TS* 1:688). From the beginning of the "vain" project, frustrated by his lack of a knife, followed by the success of the hem of the robe, and then reframed by the mistake occasioned by his reversal of orbital trajectory, the achievements of the narrator's reason are always undermined. Even the conclusion that the dimensions are of little importance ultimately turns out to be false when the walls, in the final act of the tale, move on hinges and threaten to push him into the pit.

Yet for all its errors, his procedure has unintended saving consequences. For the narrator's failed measuring instruments do save him from falling into the pit, albeit accidentally. Having assessed its circumference, the narrator attempts to cross the room but trips on the torn hem of his robe just before he would have fallen into the pit. While the torn hem does not serve its designed purpose—it does not ascertain the size of the room—it does save the narrator from death by precipitating his "timely accident" (*TS* 1:687). Thus Poe's tale indexes a rift between the intentions of reason and their practical achievements. The misfit between the actual dimensions of the external environment and their measurement is another example of the Kantian sublime pressed into its uncomfortable third step; the rational attempts to know one's "true state" are constantly circumvented. Yet the curious and uncaused mobilization of reason, emerging within that outer darkness, operates as another elemental force, tearing at the outer edges of a garment to assess limits and finding instead central abysses.

Poe furthers the correlation between environmental terror and reason by building analogies between the torture engines and the modes of thought they induce. Just as the pit would seem to generate a concern for circumference which bears itself out in a method of thinking that circumambulates in reversed circles, the threat of the descending pendulum would seem to imprint the narrator's thought with periodic oscillation, with a giant swing back and forth. The narrator will escape from his binding by spreading his food on his ropes, causing rats to eat through them. But he arrives at this idea through a considerable prolepsis, forming one-half of the idea early, then following another idea, and returning back, like the stroke of the pendulum, to complete the other half. The idea is first broached as "half-formed": "It was, as I say, a half-formed thought—man has many such, which are never completed" (*TS* 1:691). Poe's gallows-humor play on the half-formed thought of a man threatened with being cut in half connects thought itself with the pendulum's motion, a connection that is further borne out by the way Poe introduces a long, contrary motion to the narrative before returning to that idea. Leaving the half-formed idea, the narrator comes to despair and terror, and finally—and seemingly triumphantly—arrives at a state of thought: "For the first time during many hours—or perhaps days—I *thought*" (*TS* 1:693). Thinking clearly, the narrator hypothesizes that the pendulum itself may cut his bindings, offering a split-second means of escape; yet he discovers that the rope has been tied outside of the path of the pendulum. The narrator's clear-headed thinking having failed here, he gives up but then is instantly seized with that other half of the half-formed idea: "Scarcely had I dropped my head back into its original position, when there flashed upon my mind what I cannot better describe than as the unformed half of that idea of deliverance to which I have previously alluded" (*TS* 1:693). Following the back-and-forth pattern of the pendulum rather than a single-minded drive of his clear-headed "thought," the narrator's thinking again bears the metonymic impress of the worldly threat against which it strains.

At the zero-limit of these encounters with the elemental figures of the universe (of the spatial abyss of the pit, the temporal periodicity of the pendulum) the narrators of Poe's "sublime" tales portray the emergence of reason. The shape of reason, starting up again out of the theoretical reset accomplished through terror's reduction and resolution, conforms to the contours of those very elemental and inhuman forces that inspire terror in the first place. But if terror informs thought by resolving it back into the inhuman space of its emergence in these sublime tales, Poe explores, in another set of linked tales, the opposing swing, the opposite revolution, in which composition would reverse course, offering us not the origins of thinking in terror but rather the origins of terror in perfect thought.

## No Reason Can Be More Unreasonable: The Confessional Tales

"True—nervous—very, very dreadfully nervous I had been and am; but why *will* you say that I am mad?" (*TS* 2:792). The first sentence of "The Tell-Tale Heart" (1843) has generally been regarded as an exemplar of manipulated irony.[28] The reader is thrust into the position of imagined interlocutor, and the narrator's repeated and strenuous assertions that he is *not* mad, especially in his careful, deliberate, and rational methods, have the ironic effect of confirming that which they would deny.[29] This reading, which can be extended to the related protestations in "The Black Cat" (1843) and "The Imp of the Perverse" (1845), seems unquestionable: what could be madder than killing one's benefactor without motive, putting out the eye of your beloved cat, or ax-murdering one's wife? Once the crime is committed, it doesn't matter just how "calmly" you can tell the story or how "deliberately" you disposed of the evidence. The narrator's reason turns out to be, in the basic ironic reading, simply veneer, false walls or floors meant to conceal the grisly fruits of a deeply disordered mind.

Yet we may entertain the narrator's question more earnestly for two reasons. First, it is not really the murders that are to be taken as exhibits of madness, but their unprovoked confessions. Second, the question itself anticipates the basic ironic reading and undermines it; to explain the narrator's protestations of sanity as designations of his madness is to open a circular and self-confirming logic. Because we have determined that he is mad, then all of his discourse is mad as well. Yet our determination of his madness depends upon his discourse, and thus we must study where in his discourse the madness is located. This leads us back to those points, like the opening sentence of "The Tell-Tale Heart," in which the narrator seeks to demonstrate his sanity. Why will we say that he is mad? It isn't because he has committed a heinous crime, or that he hears the heartbeat of a dead man, or even that he spontaneously confesses to the crime without external provocation. We say that he is mad because he tells us *not* to.

The simple contradiction implied in such a logic thus weds our interpretive diagnoses to the underlying principle of perversity Poe defines through the tales. The criminal-narrators in the tales are each motivated, in different ways, by what Poe calls the perverse impulse, to "act, for the reason that we should *not*" (*TS* 2:1220). "In theory, no reason could be more unreasonable," one of Poe's narrators explains, "but, in fact, there is none more strong" (*TS* 2:1221). Poe's examples of perversity consistently figure it as action taken against a compelling voice for the reason of its compulsion: "[B]ecause our reason violently deters us from the brink, *therefore*, do we the more impetuously approach it" (*TS* 2:1223). Poe defines perversity as the willful and unanalyzable agent of the desire to disobey the voice of reason. Their confessions testifying to the tyranny of perversity, Poe's narrators rebel against self-interest and are thus incarcerated, punished, and stigmatized as insane because of it.

What, then, can we make of the parallel between the reversal of reason in the criminals' motivations and our own reversal of the criminals' testimony? The narrators act against the projected voice of reason for the very reason that it recommends an action. We call the narrators mad for the very reasons that they tell us not to. But surely these animal-abusing, ax-murdering, corpse-dismembering narrators cannot be considered voices of reason, can they? We may presume, from internal evidence, that the narrator of "The Tell-Tale Heart" is in an institution for the insane, that the narrator of "The Black Cat" awaits his execution upon the gallows, and that the narrator of "The Imp of the Perverse" speaks while fettered in prison. Our reading would have to disregard both the content of their deeds (which seems so obviously heinous) and the institutional marks of their reliability. If Poe really believes in the principle of perversity, why does he expound it through the mouths of the most unreliable characters, destabilizing their testimony in advance by placing them in Bedlam, upon the gallows, or in prison?

But perhaps these institutional marks of societal rejection should not be considered final evidence of their insanity. Elsewhere in Poe's fiction, he raises the possibility that "the question is not yet settled, whether madness is or is not the loftiest intelligence" (*TS* 1:638). And, in a comment in 1849 that would appear to look directly back at the three confessional tales, he makes an a priori argument that true genius would always be considered criminally insane:

> I have sometimes amused myself by endeavoring to fancy what would be the fate of any individual gifted, or rather accursed, with an intellect *very* far superior to that of his race. Of course, he would be conscious of his superiority; nor could he (if otherwise constituted as man is) help manifesting his consciousness. Thus he would make himself enemies at all points. And since his opinions and speculations would widely differ from those of *all* mankind—that he would be considered a madman, is evident. . . . That individuals *have* so soared above the plane of their race, is scarcely to be questioned; but, in looking back through history for traces of their existence, we should pass over all biographies of "the good and the great," while we search carefully the slight records of wretches who died in prison, in Bedlam, or upon the gallows. (*ER* 1459–1460)

These three institutional markers of madness—the prison, the asylum, and the gallows—correspond to the same three markers included within the confessional tales. What if Poe's tales were not about how madness masquerades as reason but rather about how genius could be mistaken for madness?

Adopting such a hypothesis changes the angle of approach. No longer is the irony of the tales exhausted by noticing that the language of reason is a disguise for the madness of insanity.[30] Rather, the irony is deepened to include the reading practices of the reader, and our very evaluation, prepared for by the placement of the speakers in suspicious circumstances, would follow the same compulsive logic of perversity, seizing upon the narrators' protestations of sanity as the damning evidence against it. To escape this compulsion, then, it may be necessary to patronize the convicts for a moment and to consider how reason might not be lacking but rather be too much in abundance. In what follows, I wish to tease out how Poe's complicated formula in these tales returns again to the model of analysis, destabilizing the conventional equation of reason with mental health. As the sublime tales located the origins of reason in the emptied space of terror, these confessional tales press reason back into terror.

One of the most conspicuous features of the confessional tales is the parallel between the method of their narration and the methods of murder and concealment being narrated. How the narrator confesses the crimes verges on coinciding with how the narrator commits the crimes, inviting a comparison between the two and suggesting that confessing is committing, in a subtle sense, or the converse, that committing is confessing. The narrator of "The Tell-Tale Heart" implores his audience to "Hearken! and observe how healthily—how calmly I can tell you the whole story" (*TS* 2:792). And a few lines later, the narrator calmly describes how calm he was in committing the crime: "Madmen know nothing. But you should have seen *me*. You should have seen how wisely I proceeded—with what caution—with what foresight—with what dissimulation I went to work!" (*TS* 2:792). These two implicit arguments against insanity—that his discourse is calm and ordered and that his murder is also calm and ordered—return in the narrator's description of his calm cover-up: "If still you think me mad, you will think so no longer when I describe the wise precautions I took for the concealment of the body" (*TS* 2:796). It is not only the precautions that testify to his sanity, but his description of them.

These parallels between narration and action continue throughout the narratives. When the narrator of "The Black Cat" gouges his cat's eye with a pen-knife, he reports: "I blush, I burn, I shudder, while I pen the damnable atrocity" (*TS* 2:851). The narrator of the "Imp of the Perverse," while attempting to demonstrate the principle of perversity, gives as an example the protractions of "certain involutions and parentheses" through which a speaker may frustrate his audience. Yet, having identified this perverse tendency, he succumbs to it, giving several more apparently nonessential examples of perversity before getting to the tale's proper action.

Jonathan Elmer's sustained reading of the confessional tales notices these and other moments at which the method of narration converges with the narrated, sensing in these moments "the disjunction between description and performance, between offering an example and enacting the example, between, finally, a theoretical text and a narrative text" (*Reading* 135). For Elmer, this convergence generates an uncanny doubling that crosses and volatilizes the social limit: "It is the way in which saying and doing, the theoretical and the narrative, circulation and confinement, double and undo each other that renders the structure of Poe's confessional tales so vertiginous. . . . But this is no simple liberation: rather, like the narrator's furious bounding through the street, it transforms the social space defined by this communicative necessity into another incarceration, which will in turn need to be transgressed" (*Reading* 137). This cyclical doubling and undoing that Elmer relates to the functioning of the social limit recalls the doubled processes of resolution and composition and the show of weaving and unraveling of Poe's "*air* of method." For as the narrators repeat their crimes in their confessions, both the methods of narration and the methods of crime adopt the fantasy of absolute erasure. The narrators' emphasis on method, on how they tell the story rather than what happens in the story, would seem to enact again the resolution of reason into bare process.[31] But rather than argue that there is something outside of process that interrupts their plan, the reduction of reason to process reveals perversity as a ghost hiding in the machine.

We may read these slippery disjunctions and convergences between criminal acts and their confession as being consequences of the internal search for an absolute security that takes as its model the geometry of methodological reason. Earlier in this chapter, we saw how the reversible processes of resolution and composition shaped Poe's understanding of analytical reason as a symmetrical faculty. Here we have narrators, allegedly committed to rational thought, who give as evidence of their reason the rigidly methodical and deliberate commission of a crime and the subsequent, and just as methodical, disposal of the evidence. Perfect, they attest, their crime and concealment would be if not for the imp of the perverse, which compels them to confess. And in their confession, we hear re-echoed the marks of the crime and its justification, how "healthily and calmly" the narrator can recount the tale and explain, through a species of reason, an original cause that would give significance to the effects: "that I may assign to you something that shall have at least the faint aspect of a cause for my wearing these fetters, and for my tenanting this cell of the condemned" (*TS* 2:1223–1224). The problem, it would seem, is that the desire to seek a cause, to resolve backwards in time to some original genesis, seems wholly implicated within the effects themselves. For if the compulsion to confess is responsible for the tale's telling, and if the confession and the crime become uncannily identical, then we may expect to see not only the crime mirrored in the confession, but also the same confessional yet analytical impulse emblematized by the crime.

In this sense, the acts of confession and crime can both be read as analytical acts of composition. Composition, occurring after resolution, leads back up the chain of causes to effect. As the authors of the *Port-Royal Logic* explain, composition is the "method of instruction" and is used "for making the truth understood by others once it is found" (Arnauld and Nicole, Buroker trans. 233). Composition thus reverses the sequential order of one's resolutive discovery in order to deliver an account that conforms to the sequential order of the recovered event. The confessional tales, emphasizing the ordering function of composition, bear everywhere the signs of such chronological reversal. For example, the narrator of "The Tell-Tale Heart" begins his confession by assigning the original cause of what follows: "It is impossible to say how first the idea entered my brain; but, once conceived, it haunted me day and night. Object there was none. Passion there was none. I loved the old man. He had never wronged me. He had never given me insult. For his gold I had no desire. I think it was his eye! yes it was this!" (*TS* 2:792). The eye, then, is the original cause of the murder, concealment, and confession, and as such it seems to belong, as it does, at the very beginning of the tale. Yet the narrator's uncertainty about the fact, followed by an ejaculation of more certainty, indicates that he had just then discovered for himself that the eye was the cause of the murder. His discovery of the cause, then, comes last in the timeline of his crime but first in the timeline of its recounting.[32]

For the narrator of "The Black Cat," the task of composition, of turning a mere sequence of events into a chain of causes and effects, is troubled by the need to assign a cause to the composition itself. The first paragraph of the tale attempts to clarify the narrator's reasons for writing in the first place: "For the most wild, yet most homely narrative which I am about to pen, I neither expect nor solicit belief. . . . But to-morrow I die, and to-day I would unburthen my soul" (*TS* 2:849). The narrator begins by emphasizing that his writing is directed toward no rhetorical purpose; he does not seek to communicate or persuade but rather to "unburthen," as if this confession belongs to the same irrational impulse that prompts his self-incriminating ejaculation at the end of the tale ("In the rabid desire to say something easily, I scarcely knew what I uttered at all" [*TS* 2:858]). It is the performance of writing itself that does the unburdening; merely saying something, even if that thing is not fully or even partially comprehended.[33] The narrator as much as admits that he scarcely knows what he is writing when he, in the next breath, projects the analytical task of finding cause and composing effect onto his audience:

> My immediate purpose is to place before the world, plainly, succinctly, and without comment, a series of mere household events. In their consequences, these events have terrified—have tortured—have destroyed me. Yet I will not attempt to expound them. To me, they have presented little but Horror—to many they will seem less terrible than *barroques*. Hereafter, perhaps, some intellect may be found which will reduce my phantasm to the common-place—some intellect more calm, more logical, and far less excitable than my own, which will perceive, in the circumstances I detail with awe, nothing more than an ordinary succession of very natural causes and effects. (*TS* 2:849–850)

At issue, then, is the purpose to merely recount "without comment" a "series" of events, for which two possible interpretations are left open: the "to me" interpretation, implying some extraordinary agency or awful contingency, which leads to terror; and the "to many" interpretation, which has been reduced by the "logical" into an "ordinary succession" of "causes and effects." By deferring the act of composition, by attempting to simply unburden a series of phenomena without tying them together into cause and effect, the tale does not seek to communicate information but rather merely to perform transparently the semblance of communication, to talk to itself, as it were. It avoids imposing a causal structure, seeking to merely "place" a series of phenomena, as if the representation of those "household events" would simply overlay and become synonymous with the original household events that they represent. The tale, according to the narrator, would reproduce exactly, without subjective interference from either the narrator's self-interest or narratorial "comment," the events. The narrative would, as it were, put everything back just the way it was.

Such an intention coincides with the confessional tales' elaborate displays of concealment, of cleaning up. For what we discover, as a corollary to the already-mentioned resemblances between the act of confession and act of crime, is that the tales' concern for composing reappears as the concern for erasing evidence, of getting the scene of the crime back to the way it was. For the narrators produce, as evidence of their superior reason, the careful methods by which they dispose of bodies and weapons. Dismembering his victim's body and depositing it under the floor, the narrator of "The Tell-Tale Heart" delights in the complete erasure of evidence: "I then replaced the boards so cleverly, so cunningly, that no human eye—not even *his*—could have detected anything wrong. There was nothing to wash out—no stain of any kind—no blood-spot whatever. I had been too wary for that" (*TS* 2:796). In similar fashion, the narrator of "The Black Cat" immediately turns from the accomplished murder of his wife to "set myself forthwith, and with entire deliberation, to the task of concealing the body" (*TS* 2:856). With rational precision and calculation, the narrator walls up the body:

> [W]ith little trouble, I re-laid the whole structure as it originally stood. . . . I prepared a plaster which could not be distinguished from the old, and with this I very carefully went over the new brickwork. . . . The wall did not present the slightest appearance of having been disturbed. The rubbish on the floor was picked up with the minutest care. I looked around triumphantly, and said to myself—"Here, at least, then, my labor has not been in vain." (*TS* 2:857)

The triumphs of the narrators turn out to be labors of cleaning, disposing of, and erasing the "minutest" evidence. They would erase all material trace of the crime, and they do so, in "The Tell-Tale Heart" and "The Black Cat," by carefully taking apart and reconstructing their surroundings. This material taking apart and putting back together echoes the compositional function of the confession, not only because its deliberate method is held up to be evidence of sanity and reason, but also because it becomes a demonstration of analytical process: the corpse's dismemberment can be read as a gory emblem of resolution, and the particular and minute replacement of the floor planks or brickwork can be read as a fantasy of perfect recomposition.

The narrator has committed a crime; he conceals it, then reveals it, but still unable to account for why he has revealed it, he confesses it. In the confession, moreover, the whole sequence of crime, concealment, and revelation are replayed yet again. The conclusion for the narrators is that the ultimate cause for the unfolded and refolded compulsions and processes is a principle of the perverse—not really an "uncaused cause," which would accord with the mistaken verdict of "death by the visitation from God" in "The Imp of the Perverse" but rather a cause that always operates in direct contradiction to one's knowledge. It isn't because we should not do what is perverse that we are compelled to do it—

as Jennifer Fleissner points out, Poe's perversity does not describe anything "as banal as the 'lure of the forbidden fruit'" (19); rather, it is because we "know" we do *not* desire this fruit that we are compelled to take it.[34] Poe thus places this first cause outside of self-interest, or more properly, in the active negation of self-interest. Yet this does not mean that perversity is alien to one's reason but that it lies deeper, in the negation of self-interest implicated within reason's fundamental structures and desires for objective knowledge.

Perversity becomes reason's inverted reflection: "[B]ecause our reason violently deters us from the brink, *therefore*, do we the more impetuously approach it. . . . To indulge for a moment, in any attempt at *thought*, is to be inevitably lost; for reflection but urges us to forbear, and *therefore* it is, I say, that we *cannot*" (*TS* 2:1223). On one hand, the perverse operates against reason, against reason's judgment ("because our reason violently deters"). But on the other hand, the perverse depends upon reason and exerts itself *because* one thinks, not in spite of it. The double emphasis on "therefore" in the maxim underscores the causal relationship between thought and perversity, and does so, moreover, within the habitus of formal logic. The logical sound of "therefore" thus seeks to represent the energies of the perverse within the very logic it would appear to subvert.

Perversity, operating according to a logical structure, would thus decouple the form of reason from its pragmatic intentions. Perversity has been hidden from reason's view because, as Poe argues, "[w]e saw no *need* of the impulse" (*TS* 2:1219). Hamstrung by functionalist preconceptions, our self-directed reason presumes a human-centered coherence, thus "deducing and establishing every thing from the preconceived destiny of man" (*TS* 2:1220). Instead, the narrator of "The Imp of the Perverse" argues, we should adopt a different method of discovery, moving inductively from actual human behavior to determine our general principles: "It would have been wise, it would have been safer to classify, (if classify we must,) upon the basis of what man usually or occasionally did, and was always occasionally doing, rather than upon the basis of what we took it for granted the Deity intended him to do" (*TS* 2:1220). Thus we discover the antagonism of perversity to reason through a method of empirical research: we have missed perversity because reason a priori saw no need of it.

Two off-key notes in the quotation above, however, should give us reason for pause. First, the narrator says that it would have been "safer to classify," indicating that the a priori method was less cautious than the a posteriori method. This is the first occurence of the word "safe," which is re-echoed and amplified throughout the tale until it becomes the autonomous sound of the narrator's perverse confession. As I explored earlier in the Introduction, safety and security become sites of terror in the tale, the narrator repeating to himself, first "in a low, under-tone, the phrase, 'I am safe'" (*TS* 2:1225) but then later "murmuring, half aloud, . . . 'I am safe—I am safe—yes—if I be not fool enough to make open confession!'" (*TS* 2:1225). That the narrator begins the tale by recommending a method of classification that would identify perversity as being "safer" not only foreshadows the problem that trying to be "safe" will become but hints that the discovery of perversity, operating from an assumption that exhaustive and cautious classification is safer, belongs tonally to the narrative of crime and concealment. By being safe, that is, and by proceeding cautiously so that we leave out no "uncounted victim of the Imp of the Perverse," we may keep ourselves from leaving out perversity. But perversely, it is the security that such an exhaustive account provides that inevitably leads to the dangers one would avoid; for it is the "sentiment of satisfaction" in his "absolute security" that grows into the "haunting and harassing thought" (*TS* 2:1224) that will be the narrator's undoing. If, as Fleissner has argued, in these instances "the power of irresistible thoughts [is] neither in pathologized individuals nor in meaningless brain function, but, strangely enough, in the contours of the thoughts themselves" (15), then we might trace the narrator's actions through the shape of absolute security as an idea, derived from the fantasy of exhaustive and classified knowledge. In accounting for everything, safety becomes the site of the perverse, not arbitrarily but because that desire for an a posteriori account of the universe, one that does not take the predetermined destiny of humanity as an assumption, commits itself to an inhuman authority of method.

As for the second off-key note: the parenthetical aside in "it would have been safer to classify (if classify we must)" reinforces the hint that classification shares traits with the perversity it would discover. It would be safer, the parenthetical would seem to suggest, to not classify at all. Yet the obligatory force of "must" determines the spirit of classification as a compulsion not unlike the perverse. Compelled to classify, and going about it as safely as possible (not resting on assumptions), we are brought up short by the "paradoxical something" of perversity, that which is incapable of further resolution: "Nor will this overwhelming tendency to do wrong for the wrong's sake, admit of analysis, or resolution into ulterior elements. It is a radical, a primitive impulse—elementary" (*TS* 2:1221). Even though the narrator insists that the perverse is radical and primitive, irresolvable and elementary, we may notice that it would seem to be activated not simply by the possibility of wrongdoing but rather by its absolute certainty: "I am not more certain that I breathe, than that the assurance of the wrong or error of any action is often the one unconquerable *force* which impels us, and alone impels us to its prosecution" (*TS* 2:1220–1221). Perversity, which operates according to a sort of compelled desire for the kind of radical certainty that can only be found in an absolutely wrong action, is itself discovered through the operation of methods that are "safer" because they are more certain, methods that would discover the irresolvable elemental principle at which analysis must stop. Analysis, as an urge to resolve to an absolute cause in order to render exhaustive certainty, itself brings into being that perversity which it would discover.

The final thing to consider is how this narrative of perverse and spontaneous composition involves terror as an affective dimension. For Poe's hyperrational, frantically methodical narrators are not, as one might expect, portrayed as wholly unfeeling or coldly calculating. The unflinching, mechanistic manner that attends their methodical dismemberment and disposal of the corpses would seem to flaunt their superiority to personal feeling. Yet throughout all three tales, the narrators invoke terror not so much because they are terrified of what they have done or even because they fear the consequences of their capture. The priority of feeling in these tales has led one critic to the claim that Poe's perversity overturns reason by way of sentiment, that behind perversity's show of thought lies a powerful critique of Hegelian rationalism.[35] Such a consideration leads to a further, more particular study of the complicated relation between terror and perversity, as terror emerges in these tales as both provoked and shaped by thought itself.

For when we consider where and how these narrators feel terror, we notice that their terror is proleptic: it anticipates in advance dangers that have not yet materialized. In "The Black Cat," the narrator grows deeply afraid of his cat, afflicted by an "absolute *dread* of the beast," because it carries on its breast a white mark, one that, while it had been "originally very indefinite," yet grows, "by slow degrees—degrees nearly imperceptible, and which for a long time my Reason struggled to reject as fanciful," into "the representation of an object that I shudder to name—and for this, above all, I loathed, and dread, and would have rid myself of the monster *had I dared*—it was now, I say, the image of a hideous—of a ghastly thing—of the GALLOWS!—oh, mournful and terrible engine of Horror and of Crime—of Agony and of Death!" (*TS* 2:855). The gradual crescendo of the narrator's admission here, the way in which it adopts the same "degrees nearly imperceptible" that the murderer in "The Tell-Tale Heart" enacts in his carefully deliberate mode of ingress, emphasizes once again the performative nature of the compositive utterance. As his recognition grows, so too does his volume, and though what he reports is factually history, the urgency of tone collapses together the moment of recognition and the moment of composition into a single utterance: "[N]ow, I say."

This rhetorical performance muddles the chronological linearity of cause and effect within the tale. For we must remember that, at this point in the narrative, the narrator had yet to commit a capital crime. This fear of the mark of the gallows is thus posited as the cause of his dread; his dread the cause of his evil thoughts; his evil thoughts leading, eventually, to the murder of his wife. Thus the terror in the tale would seem to be a self-fulfilling prophecy: his dread of the gallows leads him to the gallows. But we should note that the shape of the dread itself in the gallows is the afterimage of perverse reason, the shadow of the cold and deliberate hanging of his first cat: "One morning, in cool blood, I slipped a noose about its neck and hung it to the limb of a tree;—hung it with the tears streaming from my eyes, and with the bitterest remorse at my heart;—hung it *because* I knew that it had loved me, and *because* I felt it had given me no reason of offence" (*TS* 2:852). The dread that would lead the narrator to the gallows would seem to emerge from this act, an act of perverse reason in direct opposition to emotional appeal.

"The Imp of the Perverse" connects terror's proleptic anticipation more directly to the consciousness, the thought, of its self-fulfilling nature. Reveling in his security, the narrator describes how the feeling of success gives rise to a second order of feeling, to terror: "Every succeeding wave of thought overwhelmed me with new terror, for, alas! I well, too well understood that, to *think*, in my situation, was to be lost" (*TS* 2:1225–1226). The narrator understands, thinks, and feels in this passage, but these individual mental states obtain a complex relation. The new terror arises from a radical degree of understanding ("too well") that the elemental force of thought ("wave of thought") works against any sense of self-preservation. Terror modulates the relation of elemental thought to radical understanding; terrified of the irresistible force of thought, the narrator's terror converts thought into act, transforming the runaway thoughts into a motive for running, turning the safe, secure, and wholly private success of analytical reason into a self-destructive publicity. Terror presides over this reversal, it would seem, because it knows before the confession that such a confession is inevitable. That is, whereas terror seems strangely out of place in "The Black

Cat," seeming to arise before any act is committed, the terror in "The Imp of the Perverse" reveals how that terror instantiates a kind of foreknowledge absolute, arising from and then propelling the thoughts that indict the narrator. The proleptic nature of terror, the way it anticipates and brings about that which it would fear in these two tales, may be best seen in the first of the confessional tales, for it is in "The Tell-Tale Heart" that Poe most explicitly links the nature of terror to the perverse compulsions of analytical reason.

In "The Tell-Tale Heart," terror would seem to cause the murder at the tale's center in two ways. First, the narrator begins, as we have noted, by positing that his victim's eye was the original motive for the crime; in particular, it is the chilling effect the eye has upon the narrator: "Whenever it fell upon me, my blood ran cold; and so by degrees—very gradually—I made up my mind to take the life of the old man, and thus rid myself of the eye forever" (*TS* 2:792). The punning play on cold blood here, indicating the narrator's fear of the eye but also shuttling in a subtle undertone of a deliberate and passionless reason, links the original unsettling fear with the carefully deliberate and very gradual method by which the narrator will dispose of it. Second, the murder is accomplished by projecting terror, by literally scaring the old man to death. By creeping into his victim's room and training a lamp upon his victim's eye, the narrator raises the old man's terror to dangerous levels: "The old man's terror *must* have been extreme!" When the narrator finally throws open the lamp, with a "loud yell," the victim echoes back his demise by "shriek[ing] once— once only" (*TS* 2:795). Fear is not only implicated as the instigating cause but is also the method of the crime.

To consider how the narrator transfers his own fear onto another, projecting it symbolically through the lamp's single ray, draws our attention to a similar projection within the narrator's discourse. For in imagining the terrors of his victim, the narrator admits his own. When the narrator first awakens his victim, fears become a mode of echo between the two: "For a whole hour I did not move a muscle, and in the meantime I did not hear him lie down. He was still sitting up in the bed, listening;—just as I have done, night after night, hearkening to the death-watches in the wall" (*TS* 2:794). The narrator listens to the old man listening and recognizes in it his own former acts of listening. Later, the narrator hears the old man emit the "groan of mortal terror": "I knew the sound well. Many a night, . . . it has welled up from my own bosom, deepening, with its dreadful echo, the terrors that distracted me. I say I knew it well. I knew what the old man felt" (*TS* 2:794). The "dreadful echo" here recalls the recursive amplification that Poe indicated was the paradoxical law of terror in "The Fall of the House of Usher," the ability of knowledge of fear to amplify the fear itself. In this case, the echo chamber of terror is not wholly enclosed within the narrator but projected imaginatively as an economy of sound and terror circulating between the narrator and the old man.

As the projective quality of this terror continues, the narrator ventriloquizes his victim's thoughts:

> His fears had been ever since growing upon him. He had been trying to fancy them causeless, but could not. He had been saying to himself—"It is nothing but the wind in the chimney—it is only a mouse crossing the floor," or "it is merely a cricket which has made a single chirp." Yes, he has been trying to comfort himself with these suppositions: but he had found all in vain. *All in vain*; because Death, in approaching him, had stalked with his black shadow before him, and enveloped the victim. And it was the mournful influence of the unperceived shadow that caused him to feel—although he neither saw nor heard—to *feel* the presence of my head within the room. (*TS* 2:794)

As the narrator projects the character of his own fears onto his victim, instilling a nightmarish psychoanalytical transference, terror becomes not only imaginatively transferable but also anticipatory. Stalking with "his black shadow before him," the personified Death would cast before him a terror that enables knowledge of a thing yet unperceived, still unseen and unheard. The terror projected upon the old man is likewise projected backwards from a future event. Projected, proleptic terror thus mediates the knowledge, the certainty, of the unseen and unheard cause: the "mournful influence of the unperceived shadow." That is, terror itself, like the emanation of shadow in contradistinction to the ray of light from the lamp, leads to the feeling of the narrator's presence, of the head within the room.

To figure out the logic of terror in Poe's tales, the way that they draw from and reflect upon the structure of analytical process and rational thought, we have been led finally to this feeling of "the presence of my head within the room," a strange figure to be sure. Since the narrator earlier describes his brain as a space subject to trespass—"It is impossible to say how first the idea entered my brain; but, once conceived, it haunted me day and night" (*TS* 2:792)—the thrusting of his own head into the old man's room rehearses the scene by which the old man's eye projected into his own darkened mind the inciting idea of murder. Heads and ideas, then, associated with reason, may be felt, through terror, as intrusions from without, projecting the terror that testifies to their presence. But given the proleptic nature of terror in Poe's tales, this idea of the rational mind as the intruder that causes terror can easily be reversed, such that terror in fact forms, like an active imagination in the dark, the shape of the intruder as reason. As priority oscillates through a series of embedded reflections and projections, the tale projects the *feeling* of presence, of some final cause, as a continual and infinitely regressive process, in which one can never be sure whether one is holding the lantern or being blinded by it.

For all its apparently unhinged and excessive displays, Poe's terror, in reversible dynamics of reflection and projection, is one that is everywhere being balanced out. Vast transcendent visions from terrifying heights are balanced against the terrors of the particle caught in a vortex's engulfing suction. Sublime tales that show reason emerging, irrationally, from terror are balanced against confessional tales that show terror emerging, rationally, from reason. Resolving and composing, weaving and unraveling, committing and confessing, Poe's tales stage dialectics of equivalence that cycle and oscillate along the patterns of attraction and repulsion that he would later theorize as the underlying symmetrical principle of the universe.[36] Edwards sought the saving power of terror through infinite subtraction, removing all pieces of security so that divinity could be perceived immediately. Poe gets to a similar place, but through balanced processes of position and negation, modeling his terror within the zero-sum functions of analytical reason. Two dialectics emerge: the internal opposition of resolution and composition, on one hand, and the external dialectic of reason and terror, on the other. But though Poe gets to the external dialectic by way of the internal one, he will not be the one to capitalize on the wider looming consequence that dialectical relation itself presupposes a monological equivalence. For that complication, we must turn to Herman Melville and to the story of his introduction to Hegelian dialectics under the tutelage of a chronically terrified philosopher.

# 4

## THE UNEVEN BALANCE

Dialectical Terror in *Moby-Dick*

**IF YOU WOKE UP** to find yourself a character in a Melville fiction, chances are you would be afraid. Your fears might be rational: you might be afraid that you had fallen in with cannibals who have culinary designs upon your flesh (*Typee*) or that a vengeful slave will slit your throat with the razor he brandishes at your neck ("Benito Cereno"). Your fears might be superstitious: you might find yourself horrified to discover that you have to sleep in the bunk recently vacated by a frenzied suicide (*Redburn*) or wonder at the ghostly grip of an incorporeal hand upon your own (*Moby-Dick*). Or your fears might be abstract: you might be terrified by the slow, meaningful crawl of tortoises ("The Encantadas") or ponder the unidentifiable anxiety provoked by the simple but stubborn preference of an underling ("Bartleby"). The diverse fears in Melville's fiction share one trait: they are almost always touched with epistemological ambiguity. It isn't that you have been captured by cannibals, but that you can't be sure whether or not you have been captured by cannibals. It isn't that you are holding hands with a ghost, but that you're puzzled long afterwards, "to this very hour," by what that horror means. And the most fearsome element in Melville's work, the whale, frightens not by being dangerous and toothy but by being white. Why hue rather than incisor? Because the ambiguity of whiteness cuts a deeper wound. "[B]y its indefiniteness," Melville supposes, "it shadows forth the heartless voids and immensities of the universe" (*MD* 195).

Ambiguity invites interpretation. Critical appraisals find in the catalogue of fears indices of the racial, legal, and economic pressures of the historical period, psychosexual patterns of biographical and national identity, and philosophical arguments about the nature of freedom or the existence of God. What you find in Melville's fears depends upon your approach, and few American authors offer so many possible approaches. On one hand, Melville's metaphysical search for foundational truth and authority appeals to philosophical critics looking past the ephemera of history to the "big questions" of personhood, ethics, and epistemology. On the other hand, the complex wealth of cross-cultural influence upon his work appeals to historicist critics looking to restore the context of the political and cultural issues of Melville's day. Half head and half hands, the balance between the abstract philosophy of an ahistorical order and the real conditions of antebellum America secures Melville's work as opportune to the present literary critical moment that is itself pulled between roughly philosophical and roughly historicist ends.

But in both varieties of interpretation, Melville's thematic fears are usually read as dispositional symptoms, thus allowing commentary to move quickly past the specific fear to the case of its arguable cause. This isn't so much a mistake as it is an expediency, for to attend to the textures of those fears individually, to ponder over the unique problem that fear presents to his narratives, is to begin to sense that our usual interpretive strategies, the task of assessing meaning by fixing cause, may not be well suited for describing the phenomenological structure of Melville's ambiguous fears. In Melville, fear seems to be drawn from the very ambiguity that our interpretive impulse would seek to fix. In *Moby-Dick* (1851) the terror of whiteness eludes causal explanation: "[T]hough without dissent this point be fixed, how is mortal man to account for it? To analyse it, would seem impossible" (*MD* 192). In "The Encantadas" the haunting spectral tortoises emerge in epistemological doubt: "[S]uch is the vividness of my memory, or the magic of my fancy, that I know not whether I am not the occasional victim of optical delusion" (*PT* 129). Considered as effect yet unsure as to cause, Melville's terrors are situated at those moments before interpretive commitment is made and provoke rather than offer explanation. To account for how terror operates in Melville's fiction is thus not to identify either its poetic effect or its "real" referent but rather to describe the unresolved tensions underlying terror's simultaneous demand and resistance to being fit within a causal sequence. This chapter discovers Melville's figurations of those demands and resistances in carefully calibrated yet always uneven balances.

In earlier chapters, we saw Edwards and Poe develop recursive figures out of the logic of infinite quantity and the logic of enclosure. In Melville the primary figure is that of the balance, and the primary mode of apprehending its strange and minute calibrations is in a special state of terror. Moving from explorations of the dialectical figures in *Moby-Dick*, through a discussion of the importance of dialectical antinomy in Kant and Hegel, this chapter initially addresses the stakes of a balanced dialectical method in *Moby-Dick*. The philosophical considerations, however, lead to historical questions, and the second move of the chapter is to recover two important contexts for an understanding of Melville's affective engagement with dialectical metaphysics: Melville's paranoid friend and German professor, George Adler, and the terrifying painting *The Death-Struggle*, of which Melville owned a reproduction. I conclude by addressing the often unasked question "Why fear?" by examining, through the recovered lenses of the philosophical dilemma of antinomy and Melville's historical relation to it, the answer Melville gives in his chapter "The Whiteness of the Whale." By reconstructing the philosophical stakes of balance and recovering the historical story of Melville's engagement with dialectics, this chapter reveals how Melville's terror underlies and disrupts the methodological and interpretive frames by which we would know the world.

## The Uneven Balance

In Melville's oft-cited review of Hawthorne, his claim for the importance of philosophical terror depends upon the way it "strike[s] the uneven balance." Close reading the entire passage reveals Melville's tricky compositional balance—the way a Manichean worldview of balanced opposites comes to be undermined by its own opposite, a Calvinist philosophy of absolute incommensurability and radical disproportion:

> Certain it is, however, that this great power of blackness in him derives its force from its appeals to that Calvinistic sense of Innate Depravity and Original Sin, from whose visitations, in some shape or other, no deeply thinking mind is always and wholly free. For, in certain moods, no man can weigh this world, without throwing in something, somehow like Original Sin, to strike the uneven balance. At all events, perhaps no writer has ever wielded this terrific thought with greater terror than this same harmless Hawthorne. Still more: this black conceit pervades him, through and through. You may be witched by his sunlight,—transported by the bright gildings in the skies he builds over you;—but there is the blackness of darkness beyond; and even his bright gildings but fringe, and play upon the edges of thunder-clouds. (*PT* 243)

This passage is key for understanding how terror and philosophy are, in Melville's mind, connected, but any reading of it immediately raises a host of interpretive problems. That Hawthorne's "power of blackness" derives from an atavistic concept of innate depravity seems clear enough; Hawthorne's writing again and again contemplates the dilemmas caused by the religious commitments of New England's dogmatic Puritan heritage. But the second clause of the first sentence—"from whose visitations, in one shape or another, no deeply thinking mind is always and wholly free"—abstracts innate depravity from its historically specific figuration, suggests its relationship with deep thinking, and echoes, in its description of a mind without freedom, the Calvinist refutation of free will. To paraphrase, the mind is never wholly free of the Calvinist belief that the mind is wholly not free at all.

The slippage between the freedom of the will and freedom from the belief that the will is not free comes to a head in the ambiguous "terrific thought" and "black conceit" that Melville pins to Hawthorne. At first, the "terrific thought" appears to be simply Calvinist innate depravity and original sin, the belief that all people are damned by nature and are constitutionally unable to save themselves. But the continuation of the passage implies that the "terrific thought" might be the more general one expressed by Melville: that the mind in its philosophical pursuits will never be free from the terrors of hell embodied in those Calvinist examples. Thus the passage's question of category—is terror's darkness in contrast with light, or is it the darkness of the wider system that will always conjoin light with dark?—illustrates the dynamics of the oxymoronic "uneven balance." For while light can be balanced against dark, the fact that the balance could never be "always and wholly free" from darkness shrouds the entire balancing act in a terror itself neither of dark nor of light. This terror apprehends the self-confirming nature and virus-like persistence of the "absolute authority" of predestination to the deeply thinking mind. The terror in this case is that thought itself will always lead us back into the grip of innate depravity—that the thought by which we think we are free is the very vehicle of our incarceration.

Robert Milder is close to the paradox when he notices that Melville's blackness is neither "objective outward force" nor "subjective inward feeling" but a "*relationship* . . . that came into being as the perceived nature of reality, neutral in itself, impinged on human demands for order and meaning and called forth an almost visceral response of anger and revulsion" (56). Considering how this relationship continually tips in one direction, however, we should add that the justification for those feelings of revulsion must originate from somewhere in the world, and thus the irony is that whatever adversarial relationship is opened up by feeling, the conflict it would imagine is already decided. So Milder's explanation of the blackness as an expression of "not only how humans *saw* the gap between need and fact but how they *felt* about it" (57) already evokes the sense of capitulation, the feeling coming as a futile backward-looking response to a crisis already decided. Yet we might note that Melville's blackness here seems less a flat reaction than a formative mode of perception. The passage does not say that there is an essential unfairness in the world that we feel badly about but rather defines blackness as a power. As a power, it might comprehend, but it could also contribute to the dimensions of that gap between perceived reality and human need that seems unable to be crossed. It will require a close study of Melville's language to pry out how blackness, as a terror, could be more vital to the epistemological situation than being merely its affective response.

"In certain moods," Melville writes in the second sentence, "no man can weigh this world, without throwing in something, somehow like Original Sin, to strike the uneven balance." This wonderfully suggestive sentence introduces, in three ways, the strategies of *Moby-Dick*. First, Melville frames the act of thinking as an affect: just as *Moby-Dick* will begin with Ishmael in a funk, here Melville qualifies the claim about deep thinking by making it a function of mood. If, as we have seen, the strange mood of blackness is a response to the epistemological situation, Melville here seems to suggest that it could be the origin of the situation as well. Second, the sentence works by way of overdetermined figurative language: Melville uses the idiom "to strike a balance" taken from account keeping and applies it to the balance of a scale. "To strike," here, is both a stroke of the pen and the minute calibration of perfect equipoise. But behind these two senses of finding a zero equilibrium, we also hear the connotations of active violence, the fury of Ahab's roar: "If man will strike, strike through the mask!"; and thus what striking is for Melville—whether it be writing, weighing, or hitting—acquires overtones of deliberate action. Third, besides raising the emotional stakes and playing with the multiple senses of striking, the sentence is simply ambiguous. Original sin must apparently be thrown into the balance of the world, but on which side? On the side of the world? Or on the side of the world's counterweight? Is the world too light without it? Or so heavy it needs sin to balance it out?

But the most stunning feature of this sentence, a feature that figures the multiple ways in which things don't add up, is the description of the "uneven balance." The dominant sense of this figure is that the uneven balance will be made even by the addition of original sin. But the word "uneven" is superfluous to this sense: what is the difference between striking a balance and striking an uneven balance, after all? By overly describing, the word actually generates a grammatical imbalance within the sentence itself and opens a contrary reading: original sin may be necessary to strike the balance *uneven*. In this counterintuitive second reading, the balance is from the start already even and is struck uneven by the thinker who throws in original sin. That both meanings obtain in the same sentence suggests a paradoxical irony that can only be imperfectly formulated at this point: the adversarial figuration of balance against imbalance, in order itself to be balanced, cannot be.

The grammatical openness of the passage—the way Melville's maxim seems balanced in a cursory reading and the way it comes askew in a closer reading—forces the reader to adopt a similar uneven reading. A deep mind, Melville suggests, can never think abstractly and positively about the world without finding itself pulled toward an opposite, a diabolic, negative. Terror may begin as situated within that one dark half of the balance, but it comes to tinge the entire system. Thus, Melville's "uneven balance" may be balanced yet still be uneven. And since the Calvinist tenets "thrown in" are as heavy as a bag of damned souls bound for hell, keeping the balance partially even is out of the question, for in the absolute economy of the Calvinist scales, one side is the infinite God and the other, uneven side is the nothingness of man. As we saw in Chapter 1, Jonathan Edwards defines true terror as incapable of being balanced or mitigated by anything but infinite holiness. If one side of Melville's balance, then, is occupied by a philosophy which believes that the activity of balancing suggests a faulty, even sinful encroachment into God's infinite magnitude, is it any wonder that, as the uneven balance passage continues, what seemed to be a balance of light and dark becomes entirely overwhelmed by the dark—Hawthorne's sunlight becoming ornament, merely "gilding" the immense blackness of darkness?

Deep thinking is figured through the activity of weighing by scales, yet there is a fluid instability between what is required in the scales ("the terrific thought") and what is required for the mind to undertake the balance in the first place ("in certain moods"). The slippery nature of the passage—which teeters between balance and imbalance, literally balancing them but modally unfixing their commensurability—itself requires something besides logical proposition to parse. The prefatory "In certain moods" provides Melville with an affective cover, shifting the delicate task of weighing or judging the world by reason into a mode of feeling. Thus, though the paradoxical recursiveness of trying to strike an (uneven) balance between a philosophy of evenness and a philosophy of uncompromising terror may be difficult to pose as a proposition, it may be felt as mood.

It is in the book Melville was composing at the time he wrote the uneven balance passage—*Moby-Dick*—that he raises the question of thought as a terrifying balance to the level of theme. When approached as a sustained extrapolation of the uneven balance—the literal weights and counterweights, the diametric sets of characters—the doubled yet not quite symmetrical thrusts of plot turn *Moby-Dick* into a dynamic and shifting philosophical scale. Two of the book's prominent features, its philosophical stakes and its figurative trope of balancing doubles, are illuminated by a third: the affect of terror that comprehends balance by adopting an imbalanced perspective. The paradoxical mode in which a balance can be both balanced and imbalanced at the same time—that the balance itself is weighed against imbalance—is not a logically coherent idea, Melville seems to have concluded, but it is inarguably a feeling and, as such, does not itself have to obey logic's strictures.[1]

## Antinomy

Melville evokes the "uneven balance" in "Hawthorne and His Mosses" to instantiate a paradoxical logic. In *Moby-Dick*, he contextualizes that logic within Kantian metaphysical discourse and extends its reach by drawing out its thematic consequences. The demands of the uneven balance, as we will see in this section, are thus turned outward from the axiomatic principle to compositional practice. The impetus for Melville's "deeply thinking mind" to tell the other side of the story betrays his own characteristically verbose equivocation. A reading of Melville across his career, even across his biography, discovers a mind that frequently swerves from one position to its diametric opposite and back again. In his long fiction, he often pairs chapters on speculative topics together, articulating the opposite sides of the same problem. In *Moby-Dick*, for example, after Father Mapple has exhorted being uncompromising in Christian duty and faith, the following chapter shows Ishmael, through a species of argumentative legerdemain, rationalizing the worship of Queequeg's pagan idol as his Christian duty. Though the orthodox Mapple thunders and ecumenical Ishmael soothes, neither enjoys a final upper hand, thus generating in the unresolved friction between their philosophies an affective complex that will carry over into other adversarial tensions in the book. The back-and-forth dynamic of Melville's art, the way he poses the deepest questions within a flux of voices and mutually exclusive positions, enacts a dialectical logic.[2] This logic, as we will see, not only shows a familiarity with Kantian and Hegelian discourse on the dialectic but also poses a radical new approach to the dialectic's most difficult challenges.[3]

Melville was always attracted to philosophical talk, to high-minded debate, especially when alcohol could be obtained. In 1849, during an influential trip to Europe immediately before he began writing *Moby-Dick*, Melville enjoyed whiskey punches while discussing "Hegel, Schlegel, Kant, &c" (*Journals* 8) and organized impromptu debates over political philosophy on board ship, hoping to bait the British passengers to debate "which was best, a monarchy or a republic?" (10). Shortly after this trip, he befriended Nathaniel Hawthorne, with whom, judging by his letters, Melville felt a kinship forged in intellectual debate. In one remarkable letter to Hawthorne, Melville argues with himself over the scope of Goethe's transcendental "Live in the all" (*C* 193). Melville at first ridicules it, asking what good the "all" feeling will do for a man with a toothache. But in a postscript he reverses course, suggesting that there is "some truth in" this feeling. The problem, he summarizes, is that "what plays the mischief with the truth is that men will insist upon the universal application of a temporary feeling" (*C* 194). Things change, Melville insists, even as he rearranges his own position on the matter.[4] The conclusion, then, turns from being an attack on Goethe to being an attack on the Goethe-like propensities of Melville himself: "As with all great genius," Melville concludes, "there is an immense amount of flummery in Goethe, and in proportion to my own contact with him, a monstrous deal of it in me" (*C* 193–194).

This habit of ranging from one position to another, of pursuing abstract questions by pitching both sides of the question, may have led to Hawthorne's exasperation with Melville. In a notebook entry, Hawthorne describes Melville's habit of turning polite talk to the existential:

> It is strange how he persists—and has persisted ever since I knew him, and probably long before—in wandering to-and-fro over these deserts, as dismal and monotonous as the sand hills amid which we were sitting. He can neither believe, nor be comfortable in his unbelief; and he is too honest and courageous not to try to do one or the other. (2:163)

The topic, for Melville, is what happens after death, and though he discusses this with Hawthorne in 1856, it is clear that Hawthorne ascribes such concerns to a long-standing habit. Melville goes back and forth, to and fro, taking one side and then abandoning it for the other. This constant equivocation over deep concerns Hawthorne reads as "dismal and monotonous," giving it an air of futility, because Hawthorne seems more aware than Melville that such questions have no answers, no evidentiary breakthrough that would decide one way or the other. Yet the curious aspect of Hawthorne's description is that, even though futile to the point of madness, Melville's inability to rest in either belief or unbelief is a testament to his honesty and courage. He cannot help, as Melville himself implied of Hawthorne, but adopt the other side of the debate. But why would eternally playing devil's advocate be courageous? Wouldn't honesty and courage suggest that one have a belief to defend? Rather than enjoin static commitment to a single belief, Hawthorne's and Melville's reciprocal comments designate a methodological commitment to the process of dialectical reasoning itself, to the felt mandate to always "try" the other side of the story. Yet, by the end of his experiments with long fiction, Melville had possibly grown to suspect his instruments, as when, in *Pierre*, he implies that the proper home for an evenly pitched and reversible debate is the insane asylum:

> Some were always talking about Hell, Eternity, and God; and some of all things as fixedly decreed; others would say nay to this, and then they would argue, but without much conviction either way. . . . [O]nce, when after a whole day's loud babbling, two of these predestinarian opponents, said each to the other—"Thou has convinced me, friend; but we are quits; for so also have I convinced thee, the other way; now then, let's argue it all over again; for still, though mutually converted, we are still at odds." (*Pierre* 121)

Mutually convertible yet always at odds, the debate over fate and free will is one that is perfectly balanced, but balanced to the point of oddness. When Melville addresses the question of abstract freedom, not only does he come to no resolute conclusion, but he figures that lack of resolution in terms that emphasize the oddity of balance, its unevenness, and the ultimate futility of symmetry.

Although Hawthorne thinks that this has been Melville's habit forever, it first appears most conspicuously in the philosophical rambling of *Mardi*. In this book, a fantasy of a tour through Polynesian islands, Melville experiments with the artistic possibilities of adversarial voice and speculative philosophy. The book is filled with voices. Several interlocutors are swapped in and out of the narrative, seemingly so that Melville can find the right combination of disciplinary advocates for deep talk. In the chapter "Dreams," the narrator seems to find and then become distressed by the "all" feeling generated by incorporating in himself the voices of distant, opposing philosophers:

> In me, many worthies recline, and converse. I list to St. Paul who argues the doubts of Montaigne; Julian the Apostate cross-questions Augustine; and Thomas-a-Kempis unrolls his old black letters for all to decipher. Zeno murmurs maxims beneath the hoarse shout of Democritus; and though Democritus laugh loud and long, and the sneer of Pyrrho be seen; yet, divine Plato, and Proclus, and Verulam are of my counsel; and Zoroaster whispered me before I was born. (*M* 367–368)

The untidy and tangential way in which Melville strings together his list of philosophers does not track their philosophies with any sharpness; at best it describes a collection of empirical doubters (Montaigne, Julian, Democritus, Pyrrho) against rationalist believers (St. Paul, Augustine, Zeno, Plato).[5] But it is not a particular concern for their individual philosophies that this torrent of name-dropping effects. Rather, it imagines them as in conversation, in argument, with one another and suggests that this conversation is in the narrator himself.[6]

Yet merely containing such contrary voices does not indicate a mastery over them. Instead, Taji becomes preoccupied with the idea that his own voice is drowned out in the many, and his tone of transcendent superiority gives way to a desperate loss of control: "My cheek blanches white while I write; I start at the scratch of my pen; my own mad brood of eagles devours me; fain would I unsay this audacity; but an iron-mailed hand clenches mine in a vice, and prints down every letter in my spite" (*M* 368). What has happened? Melville's narrator had been enjoying a dialectical "all" feeling, entertaining the daydream that he could encompass all of the contrary voices. But he realizes that such a position still does not occupy a balanced center, and so he loses his own sense of control: "Yet not I, but another . . . though many satellites revolve around me, I and all mine revolve round the great central Truth, sunlike, fixed and luminous forever in the foundationless firmament" (*M* 368). The change in tone, from dialectical transcendence to a cringing terror of having committed some blasphemy, results from a Copernican shift in Taji's thought. He dreams of being able to hold together, in himself, a unity of the multiple philosophies of the world; but such a dream is itself just another satellite around some fixed yet foundationless truth.

In the very next chapter, Melville seems to arrive at the imbalanced and precarious consequence of the narrator's dialectical musings. In "Media and Babbalanja Discourse," the level-headed and aloof Media points out that the back-and-forth argument, the reversal of ground and figure, that had left the narrator in a murky terror is finally impractical:

> [L]ast thoughts you mortals have none; nor can have. . . . Do you show a tropical calm without? then, be sure a thousand contrary currents whirl and eddy within. The free, airy robe of your philosophy is but a dream, which seems true while it lasts; but waking again into the orthodox world, straightway you resume the old habit. (*M* 370)

Media anticipates Hawthorne's critique of Melville wandering the deserts of belief and unbelief, pointing out that no matter how free a thought may seem in a dream, it can never be the "last" thought, and that the old habit of irresolvable debate must consequently resume. The image that ultimately figures the dialectical tension between the two chapters—the unifying transcendence of "Dreams" posed against the inescapable rejoinder of difference in "Media and Babbalanja Discourse"—is the final one of the interlocutors swaying from one side to the other: "And seated apart, on both sides of the barge, solemnly swaying, in fixed meditation, to the roll of the waves, Babbalanja, Mohi, and Yoomy, drooped lower and lower, like funeral plumes; and our gloomy canoe seemed a hearse" (*M* 370). The contradictory dynamics of the image emblematize the dilemma of the uneven balance; the three men are "swaying" in "fixed" meditation, moving back and forth but not moving at all. Yet they are sinking, "drooping," lower and lower, descending, apparently without limit, as a sign that though the cogitation may come to a standstill, the fall of their affective manner does not. Finally, even though the content of the sentence leads us to believe that the two sides of the debate cannot be bridged—the thinkers are seated "apart, on both sides of the barge"—the picture of balance is uneasy, since Melville names three, an odd number that could not possibly be arranged equally into the two sides of the boat. Balanced on a boat, yet unbalanced in mind, the device of the Mardian canoe is an early version of the figure of balance Melville will extend in the more strained pitches of the *Pequod*.

Although *Moby-Dick* stages its narrative in multiple scenes of doubling and opposition, it is in the two chapters comparing the right whale to the sperm whale that Melville compasses most explicitly the philosophical sides to the dynamic of conviction versus compromise that are the skeletal backbone of the book's concerns. The stage for their comparison is set when the whale heads are hoisted on either side of the boat, making the ship itself an instrument of balance:

> As before, the Pequod steeply leaned over towards the sperm whale's head, now, by the counterpoise of both heads, she regained her even keel; though sorely strained, you may well believe. So, when on one side you hoist in Locke's head, you go over that way; but now, on the other side, hoist in Kant's and you come back again; but in very poor plight. Thus, some minds for ever keep trimming boat. Oh, ye foolish! throw all these thunder-heads overboard, and then you will float light and right. (*MD* 327)

Locke's empiricism, in Melville's image, is counterbalanced by Kant's transcendental idealism. Such a contrast was a conventional distinction, as Kant himself explicitly sought to recuperate the possibility of objective truth from the Humean skeptical abyss he imagined as a consequence of Locke's division between subject and object. However, the dynamic aboard the *Pequod* is not merely lateral, determined by the heads which pull the boat to starboard and port, but also vertical, one of floating versus sinking. The dialectical imperative to "keep trimming boat" is contrasted against throwing both overboard, and thus the choice between Locke and Kant is eclipsed by a greater choice about methodology. Should one maintain balance by counterweight or by cutting weight?[7]

The methodological problem here is analogous to Kant's presentation of the antinomies of pure reason as visual juxtapositions in his *Critique of Pure Reason*. In illustrating the aberrations which the inherent dialectic of pure reason generates, Kant adopts a remarkable form: he displays the two sides of each argument to parallel one another on facing pages of the original codex, the left-hand pages arguing each of the four antinomies from the perspective of "dogmatism" (related to the idealism or rationalism of Descartes and Plato), the right-hand pages arguing each of the four antinomies from the perspective of "empiricism" (related to the empiricism of Locke and Bacon). Kant was clearly dissatisfied with the inherently diachronic mode of prose, which must, through its linear nature, grant the inherent bias, however slight, of temporal priority. To address this inability to say two different things at the same time, the *Critique of Pure Reason* splits down its spine at the moment when pure reason itself is shown to break into mutually exclusive yet perfectly balanced binary consequences.

Of the four antinomies, it is Kant's dilemma of freedom that resonates most directly with Melville's concerns. Just as, in *Mardi*, intellectual freedom leads to a terror of fixity and the chapter ends in despair that neither freedom nor fate could be resolved by thought, Kant conveys a sense of the impossible difference between the two propositions:

| Thesis | Antithesis |
|---|---|
| Causality in accordance with laws of nature is not the only causality from which the appearances of the world can one and all be derived. To explain these appearances it is necessary to assume that there is also another causality, that of freedom. | There is no freedom; everything in the world takes place solely in accordance with the laws of nature. |

(*Critique of Pure Reason* 409 [A 444–445, B 472–473])

Kant's proof of each claim demonstrates how both positions are consequent upon the conditions of reason, and in the ensuing commentary he argues that the contradiction implied in their conflict is imaginary and depends upon a confusion between empirical and transcendental causality. Kant may have tried to explain away the paradox, but it is in his portrayal of it as a carefully balanced system of opposing forces that Kant anticipates the figurative dilemma of the dialectic in *Moby-Dick*. Like Melville, Kant saw the struggle between empiricism and rationalism as an evenly pitched match, visually demarcated across the gutter of the open book, so he might well have been surprised to find his own position, in Melville's weighting of the *Pequod*, on only one side of the ship.

The difficult dialectical problem that slowly emerges from such arrangements—splitting arguments into two and then transcending both, only to find one's position again yoked to only one side of the ship—is clarified when we consider that Melville's sperm whale, merely one half of the balanced whole, is itself figured as internally divided in much the same way as Kant's chapter on the antinomies.[8] Noting that human vision can only see and concentrate attention on a single object at a time, Melville addresses the problem that Kant attempted to solve through page formatting:

> Nevertheless, any one's experience will teach him, that though he can take in an undiscriminating sweep of things at one glance, it is quite impossible for him, attentively, and completely, to examine any two things—however large or however small—at one and the same instant of time; never mind if they lie side by side and touch each other. (*MD* 330–331)

This will become, for Melville, the problem of the dialectic in general, for in swinging from one vision to its opposite, balancing the weight of the world by throwing in the diabolism of sin, he will continually come up against the inaccessibility of some mediate vision that would encompass both sides of every debate. Such mediate vision is no problem, however, for the sperm whale:

> How is it, then, with the whale? True, both his eyes, in themselves, must simultaneously act; but is his brain so much more comprehensive, combining, and subtle than man's, that he can at the same moment of time attentively examine two distinct prospects, one on one side of him, and the other in an exactly opposite direction? (*MD* 331)

The sperm whale, in this description, would be able to read Kant's antinomies as they were intended to be read, in perfect synchronicity. The contradiction between fate and free will, it is implied, would not pose any special challenge for its understanding. This is why, at the conclusion of the comparison, Melville labels the sperm whale "a Platonian" (*MD* 335). The ability to cognize both thesis and antithesis, and to survive, is the province of the floating and skimming Platonist.

Yet this peculiar ability is not itself without shortcomings. Whereas the sperm whale may be able to synthesize opposing prospects of vision, it is by this very capacity rendered subject to fits of terror:

> It may be but an idle whim, but it has always seemed to me, that the extraordinary vacillations of movement displayed by some whales when beset by three or four boats; the timidity and liability to queer frights, so common to such whales; I think that all this indirectly proceeds from the helpless perplexity of volition, in which their divided and diametrically opposite powers of vision must involve them. (*MD* 331)

The careful balance symbolized in the "mathematical symmetry in the Sperm Whale's [head]" (*MD* 329) may be dignified and sublime, but it also generates a peculiar terror, "queer frights," when facing the prospect of death. Unlike the stoic right whale, whose jaw symbolizes for Melville the resolute and firm attitude toward death, the sperm whale, divided and equivocal, can only register the ineluctability of death through an affective field, through a terror that comes to signal the asymmetricality of mortality, when perceived through a symmetrical perceptual habit. In order to understand the role terror plays here and throughout the book's pairing of scenes of balance with affects of fear, it will be useful to point out the resemblance between Melville's recursive dialectics and the major moves of Hegel's critique of this Kantian logic. Such a curious resemblance will then lead us to explore Melville's own peculiar relationship to Hegel and one of the only men in antebellum America who could read Hegel's critique without the mediating interference of Coleridge.

In turning from the content of philosophy to its method, Melville's dialectical passages raise the form of dialectical logic as a thematic concern. The dialectical method of taking opposite points of view on a matter and proceeding through argument and counterargument to a conclusion becomes a consistent logical process. The mechanics of the "uneven balance" passage, however, and the uneven dynamics of the whale heads' comparison complicate this process. Instead of merely subscribing to a dialectical movement through to a conclusion, Melville's images of dialectical balance characteristically fall into metabalances, recursive moves that require symmetry itself to stand on only one side of the equation, making symmetry utterly unfit to transcend an asymmetrical balance.[9] The issues that Melville raises are similar to the interrogation of logic that Hegel performs in his *Science of Logic* (1812–1816). Noting that logic itself is not grounded by phenomenal experience, Hegel seeks in the text to develop a logic that is proven by a species of evidence that logic itself does not determine in advance. Hegel's solution is to consider more carefully Kant's antinomies of reason, the divided and mutually exclusive propositions into which the use of reason falls. By making the antinomies not the failure of logic but logic's deep and dialectical heart, Hegel imagines the possibility of a speculative dialectics more thoroughgoing than anything Aristotle, or even Kant, would envision. Rather than having the way we think, our habitual logic, inform what we find, Hegel encourages us to change the way we think to conform to that which we encounter.

Hegel believed that the old Aristotelian logic had become worn out and suffered from a cart-before-horse problem. In his view, if you decide upon the rules for thinking (the syllogism, etc.) outside of thinking, then those rules of logic have been built upon suppositions that could not themselves be grounded. The distinction between forms (rules for thinking) and matter (thinking in practice), then, leads to "bare forms, as distinct from the content," a determination that "stamps them as finite, and makes them incapable of comprehending the truth, which is in itself infinite" (Hegel 1:46). The result is similar to the merely calculative logic Poe derides through the mouth of Dupin; logic becomes, according to Hegel, "a matter of merely mechanical calculation. The deduction of the so-called rules and laws (especially of Syllogism) is not much better than a manipulation of rods of unequal length in order to sort and arrange them according to size—like the child's game of trying to fit into their right places the various pieces of a picture-puzzle" (1:63). But how could we obtain a better, nonprescriptive method of logic? Hegel finds an escape route through the illogical consequences of Kant's antinomies of reason.

Kant had described the antinomies, the four central paradoxes of reason including Melville's favorite koan, fate or freedom, as an intellectual mirage. Saving, to some degree, the logical axiom that things cannot be what they are not, Kant explained the antinomies as a scalar mistake. We cannot compare, Kant says, the consequences of transcendental deduction with the consequences of empirical deduction. But this conclusion does not satisfy Hegel, and one suspects that it would not satisfy Melville. The basic and most fundamental change that the Hegelian dialectic introduces is the idea that categories, in themselves, contain the sameness with themselves *but also* the difference from their negative. As one Hegel scholar has explained, "Plato affirms that any individual thing can take on a form that is opposed to the one it already has.... But Plato insists that the forms taken on or shed by things cannot themselves change or turn into their opposites" (Houlgate 42). Hegel, conversely, suggests that "this difference [between opposing categories] is not absolute because being *itself* invests things with nonbeing; . . . to be something is *itself* always to be other than something else; and finitude *itself* turns out to constitute true infinity" (Houlgate 43). In Plato, Aristotle, and the strain of Western philosophy before Hegel, dialectic means an external process or procedure applied to categories of thought in which one tests one's theory against opposing views. In Hegel, the nature of that process is grounded in a phenomenon that it itself, from its perspective alone, could not see: that the form of logic as external dialectical movement occurs because it is prepared for by the internal dialectical character of the categories themselves.[10]

Now, when we return to the problem of the "uneven balance," we see that the way in which Melville's doubled sentence turns on itself operates according to a similar logic of internal opposition within the ideas of the world. This distinction itself (concepts are defined by their differences from one another) is nothing new, not even to American literature. Poe had begun "Berenice" with a claim that even joy can become, by virtue of its difference from sorrow, a kind of sorrow. But what makes Melville's unbalanced sentence special is that it aims at a wider insufficiency, tacitly wondering what the concept of balance requires. If everything has its opposite, then what opposes that very principle of the dialectic that everything has its opposite, that everything is balanced? To strike the uneven balance is thus to add the power of the blackness of darkness to sunny accounts of the world. But it is also to add too much, to throw the delicate balance askew, such that one ounce of innate depravity and original sin overpowers the rest. Darkness balances balance by virtue of its imbalance; it swells to overshadow the whole, an approaching thundercloud relegating to mere gildings the sunlight it occludes.

## Adler and "The Death-Struggle"

Elaborate figures of uneven balance, and the deeper metaphysical problem of grounding the dialectic logically, have led me at this point to compare Melville's troping of philosophy as a kind of balance with the Hegelian critique and renovation of dialectical logic. But there is one crucial aspect in which Melville's metadialectical figures do not align with Hegel's dialectical logic. The mood, the feeling, of this philosophical pursuit of a better balance is, in Hegel, one of "passionless calm" (1:51). In Melville, however, the passions themselves are entangled with that which would be balanced, and even as Ishmael may liquify into a Hegelian placidity atop the masthead, the outcome is that one's identity "comes back in horror" (*MD* 159), similar to the "queer frights" of the otherwise Platonic sperm whales. For Hegel, speculative calm is the mode by which abstract thought pursues its utmost ends. For Melville, in *Moby-Dick*, those speculative calms are interrupted, framed, interleaved with terrors and horrors that are no less a part of the modality of abstract thought. To understand how this difference in mood may be one of the most important contributions of *Moby-Dick*'s artistry, we must first look at how that difference may have come about, which leads us to Melville's clinically insane tutor in Hegelian metaphysics.

Melville first mentions Hegel in a journal entry aboard the *Southampton* en route to Europe in 1849:

> Monday Oct 22 Clear & cold; wind not favorable. I forgot to mention that *last night* about 9½ P.M. Adler & Taylor came into my room, & it was proposed to have whiskey punches, which we *did* have, accordingly.... We had an extraordinary time & did not break up till after two in the morning. We talked metaphysics continually, & Hegel, Schlegel, Kant &c were discussed under the influence of the whiskey. (*Journals* 8)

The Adler in this entry is George Adler, an immigrant from Leipzig, valedictorian of one of the first graduating classes of the University of the City of New York (now New York University), and one of that university's first German professors. He would become Melville's close friend and principal traveling companion during the European tour. Adler was going to Europe in the hopes of either escaping the imagined persecutions of a secret cabal aligned against him or treating the insanity that he felt encroaching upon him. That is, Adler told Melville during the trip that writing his German lexicon had driven him "almost crazy" (*Journals* 4), but years later he would revise that account from his new lodging at the Bloomingdale Insane Asylum, suggesting instead that he was escaping a conspiracy of Christian dogmatists intent on disrupting his studies and driving him insane (allegedly by shouting things through his study window such as "'Oh, you are not one of us!' [sung in operatic style]" [*Letters of a Lunatic* 20; brackets in original] and "'I understand that passage so!'" [21]).[11] So, though the journal entry in part substantiates the hypothesis that Melville could have known, at least cursorily, about Hegel's dialectical logic through Adler, the more complicated question is, what version of Hegel did his mentally unstable tutor provide?

Melville criticism has treated the question of Adler's influence as either philosophical or psychological, but it has never broached the question of whether those influences might have been related.[12] Dwight Lee extends Leon Howard's argument that Adler's philosophical interests fired Melville's metaphysical imagination.[13] Sanford Marovitz and Paul McCarthy, however, both grant that philosophical influence but emphasize Adler's deteriorating mental health and the impression it may have made upon Melville's own fears of going insane.[14] Though both points are valid, their disconnection has led critics to miss three important considerations: (1) the specific nature of Adler's philosophical commitments, (2) the connection of Adler's mental decline to those commitments, and (3) an appreciation of his literary criticism. Exploring these concerns reveals all three as related: Adler isn't just philosophical in a general sense but obsessed with Hegel's *Science of Logic*. Then too, Adler isn't just "insane" but specifically paranoid that his commitment to Hegel has led to his persecution by a conspiratorial religious orthodoxy. And finally, Adler doesn't just write lexicons; his Hegel-inspired literary criticism shows a deft appreciation for the philosophical and psychological stakes of aesthetic works. Restoring the specific nature of Adler's interests and fears yields a single unique voice and tone: not a scholar who became a madman, or a lexicographer who also dabbled in philosophy, but a conflicted personality—proud, afraid, yet overwhelmingly committed to the value of intellectual freedom, a personality whose influence on Melville's art might not only be in the ideas he could offer but in the magnified existential and urgent regard in which he held them.

Melville and Adler met through George Duyckinck shortly before going aboard the *Southampton*, bound for London on October 11, 1849. Their friendship was instant, mutual, and intellectual in nature. Melville's first description of Adler notes both his scholarship and his mental health: "[Adler] is author of a formidable lexicon, (German & English); in compiling which he almost ruined his health. He was almost crazy, he tells me, for a time. He is full of the German metaphysics, & discourses of Kant, Swedenborg &c. He has been my principal companion thus far" (*Journals* 4). The fact that Melville already considers Adler a "principal companion thus far" when the trip is only one day old testifies to the almost instantaneous nature of their friendship. A few days later, Melville would note that Adler is "an exceedingly amiable man, & fine scholar whose society is improving in a high degree" (7). Self-conscious about his own lack of a collegiate degree, Melville may have seen the professorial Adler as able to supply the intellectual mentorship he sought. Accordingly, Melville records an almost continual discourse with Adler on German metaphysics:

> [Oct 13] Walked the deck with the German, Mr Adler till a late hour, talking of "Fixed Fate, Free-will, foreknowledge absolute" &c. (4)
>
> [Oct 22] We talked metaphysics continually (8)
>
> [Oct 27] Got—all of us—riding on the German horse again (9)
>
> [Dec 4] [T]alked high German metaphysics till ten o'clock (33)
>
> [Dec 7] Sat up conversing with Adler till pretty late,—(Topic—as usual—metaphysics.) (34)

Melville found in Adler not only a friend and intellectual equal but a mentor who did not tire of late-night metaphysical discussions. Unlike the tone of concern from Hawthorne in his note that "Melville, as he always does, began to reason of Providence and futurity, and everything that lies beyond human ken" (*Notebooks* 163), Melville's similar observation of Adler, that his conversation "as usual" is metaphysics, is positively enthusiastic. What drew Melville to Adler must have been in great part due to what Adler could offer Melville in the way of intellectual stimulation, but Melville's journal also hints at the peculiar affection he has for Adler's idiosyncratic manner.

Adler's personality may be briefly reconstructed from two descriptions in Melville's journal. The first records: "I shall not forget Adler's look when he quoted La Place the French astronomer—'It is not necessary, gentlemen, to account for these worlds by the hypothesis' &c." (*Journals* 8). The hypothesis dismissed here is God, a skeptical dismissal Melville might appreciate. But it is the unforgettable *look* of Adler that Melville admires, the intellectual condescension, the lack of apology, behind the atheist sentiment. The second glimpse of Adler's personality occurs during an evening sojourn through London's Holborn district. Melville writes: "[We] entertained ourselves by vagabonding thro' the courts & lanes, & looking in at the windows. Stopped in at a Penny Theater.—Very comical—Adler afraid" (16). Melville doesn't specify what Adler was afraid of, an abbreviation that suggests the fear was indeterminate, or common, or perhaps both.

Consider now these two facets of Adler's personality, intellectually superior and yet abstractly afraid, as they manifest in one long passage from *Letters of a Lunatic* (1854), Adler's self-published book composed while in the asylum, a paranoid diatribe against his colleagues who had, allegedly, committed him on trumped-up charges because they feared the irreligious threat of his German philosophy. The incidents he depicts are the ones that directly occasioned his trip to Europe and drove him, as it were, into Melville's cabin:

> I distinctly remember the treacherous and inquisitorial anxiousness of a certain (now) president of a prominent University, (with whom I was reading Logic,) to become acquainted with German metaphysics, the mysterious meetings of a certain ecclesiastical committee, the efforts of a certain temperance coterie at a certain hotel, and a dozen other despicable conclaves and combinations, whose machinations were too palpable to be mistaken or forgotten. I also know, that a certain philosophy to which I was known to be particularly partial, is looked upon with jealous suspicion by certain superficial and insignificant pretenders to that science, whose ignorance and malice forges weapons of destruction out of the noblest and sublimest conceptions that have ever emanated from the intellect of man. To all these ambitious and noisy enemies of intellectual freedom, *whose littleness asperses, calumniates and levels whatever is gigantic and sublime*, I would here say, once for all, that if they could but rationally comprehend this Goethe, this Jean Paul, this Fichte, Kant and Hegel, whom they regard with so much horror, their *moral regeneration* would almost be beyond a doubt. (*Letters of a Lunatic* 18)

Adler believed that he had been set up, that the president of the university, Isaac Ferris, had pretended an interest in metaphysics in order to get Adler to out himself as an atheist by opening up Hegel's *Logic*. Could Adler have pulled the *Logic* out again while sipping whiskey punches in the cabin of a young writer who was genuinely interested in metaphysics? Such a conjecture is reasonable, especially since, when Adler returned to New York, his descent into insanity was coupled with an intense return to that same work: "[I]t was painful and disgusting for me to be awake," he writes, "that all I read for several successive months was 'Hegel's Logic' for two or three hours a day" (*Letters of a Lunatic* 14).

What Melville may have gotten from Adler, then, isn't an inchoate German transcendentalist stew but, more specifically, an introduction to Hegel's antinomy-dependent grounding of dialectic in the *Logic*. This may help explain why *Moby-Dick* consistently portrays philosophy in recursive balancing acts and agonistic struggles—atop the masthead, amid the whaleboat line, behind the try-works. But more importantly, we sense how these logical forms are infused with affect. A tone of fear and condescension colors Adler's philosophy—the power of which is closely associated, even validated, by its relentless persecution. From these fears, then, may come the unique terror of those philosophical moments in *Moby-Dick*: the terrifying "all-color of atheism from which we shrink" (*MD* 195), the "queer frights" of the diametrically organized sperm whales. Adler not only acquaints Melville with German metaphysics but does so in a way that couples the Ahab-like pride of intellectual independence with Ishmael's disoriented paranoia behind the try-works.

In addition to his dramatic regard for metaphysics, Adler may also have impressed Melville as a careful reader of literature. In 1851 Adler sent to Melville an inscribed copy of his translation of Goethe's *Iphigenia in Tauris*. Reading not only that translation but also Adler's long later critical introduction to it reveals a deep investment in the mythic narrative of escape from madness. *Iphigenia* is a redemption story of the fateful house of Tantalus, the final chapter of the long saga beginning with Agamemnon, his murder by Clytemnestra, and Clytemnestra's death at the hand of her son Orestes under the influence of his sister Electra. Orestes, seeking to escape the furies that haunt him following his matricide, travels to Tauris, discovers his older sister Iphigenia, still alive, and is cured by her sisterly influence. Goethe, Adler notes, citing the literary historian Georg Gervinus, wrote *Iphigenia* during his remove to Italy, mirroring the actions of Orestes in seeking recuperation of mind through travel: "'The Iphigenia is a symbolical poem, in which the poet . . . celebrates in the redemption of the ancient house of Tantalos, his own reconciliation, his own newly acquired clearness and serenity of mind'" (*Handbook* 222). When Adler writes that "[i]t was by his absentment from the Court of Weimar, that Goethe brought about this change of mind . . . to put himself at a distance from some of his earlier friends, whose influences on his mode of thinking and on his productivity he felt to be pernicious" (222), we can hear a projection of Adler's own hoped-for change of mind at a distance from "earlier friends" such as Isaac Ferris. Adler, fleeing to Europe from his own furies, could see himself as both Goethe, fleeing the court of Weimar, and Orestes, searching for sanity. Melville, then, himself searching in many ways for a change of mind, may have listened all the more attentively to Adler's version of the Iphigenia story—perhaps even had it in mind when beginning *Moby-Dick* with a narrator taking to sea to cure the "damp, drizzly November" in his soul.

Yet it isn't just the play's psychological myth but its Hegelian ending as well that draws Adler's attention. Adler ends his description of the play by noting Hegel's observation that, though the ancients wrote dramas that would occasionally end with the two parties resolving their conflict, the sources of such resolution are usually "'accomplished *ab extra* by the interposition of the gods, &c.'" (*Handbook* 239). But in Goethe's adaptation of *Iphigenia*, the contending parties themselves "'by the course of their own actions find themselves gradually brought . . . to a mutual reconciliation of their separate aims and characters'" (239). The victory of sanity, then, that Adler reads into the play is joined with a Hegelian plot—a dialectic that requires nothing supererogatory to bring about sublation. Read against Melville's criticism of Goethe to Hawthorne, who in many ways seems to have become the ambivalent recipient of the philosophical discourse Melville could no longer have with the asylum-bound Adler, Adler's *Iphigenia* promises a dream of that "all" feeling as mental equilibrium, a dream that Melville can appreciate but also criticize. The greater melancholic irony, that the contending parties in the play resolve their differences by agreeing to let one another go, leads to Adler's final, heart-wrenching sentence: "This reconciliation is so complete in the piece before us, that its close is invested with an evening-sky of calm serenity and godlike repose; and the reader cannot suppress the wish, that favorable breezes may gently swell the sails of the departing ones, and that the gods may smile on all their future purposes!" (240). If we read this final reconciliation through the irony of Adler's failure to regain his own mental health, it seems less a reconciliation than a capitulation—a capitulation hauntingly echoed in Adler's farewell wishes to Melville, described in a letter to their mutual friend Evert Duyckinck:

> Our friend Mr. Melville has, I hope, long ago reached his home again safely. . . . I regretted his departure very much; but all that I could do to check and [indecipherable] his restless mind for awhile at least was of no avail. This loyalty to his friends at home and the instinctive impulse of his imagination to assimilate and perhaps to work up into some beautiful chimeras (which according to our eloquent lectures on Plato here, constitute the essence of poetry and fiction) the materials he had already gathered in his travels, would not allow him to prolong his stay. (Letter to Evert Duyckinck)

Adler could not convince Melville to stay with him, and he was not finally successful at attaining his own serenity of mind; but in his reconciliation, his wish that the gods smile on Melville's future purpose, his beautiful chimera in *Moby-Dick*, he may have had more influence than he and we have realized.

The George Adler story helps answer the question concerning the affect behind Melville's portrayal of dialectic. For Adler, Hegelian reconciliation is raised to the level of a myth, a potential haven from the paranoia and madness coming upon him. But raising Hegel to this position at the same time activates Adler's paranoia about being persecuted for those same commitments. Melville, or even Adler in one of his more clear-headed moments, could have recognized the irony—that in the same gesture by which Adler sought to save himself, he also condemned himself by taking the first step toward the superiority that fueled his paranoid conspiracy theories. In any case, Melville's deep yet finally abortive friendship with Adler helps explain and contextualize both the Hegelian dialectical paradoxes of *Moby-Dick* and the idiosyncratic affiliation with fear those portrayals work to evince.

Adler is not the only patient at the Bloomingdale Asylum to have had an influence on *Moby-Dick*. There is no way to tell whether or not Melville ever visited his old friend during his intermittent internments there, or whether Melville was one of the five people[15] (among whom were probably Melville's friends Evert and George Duyckinck) who supported his expensive residence there. Yet Melville may have recognized the name of the asylum as the institution that had treated an American painter whose own art bore the impress of an encroaching insanity: Charles Deas. Melville owned a print of Deas's nightmarish painting *The Death-Struggle*, which Deas had painted shortly before entering Bloomingdale Asylum. Though there is no evidence that Deas and Adler crossed paths at Bloomingdale and no evidence to prove that Melville connected the two in his mind, their proximity and their shared story—promising careers cut short by the deterioration of their mental health—enables a speculative reading of *The Death-Struggle* (fig. 1) against the entangled dialectics and fears of Adler and *Moby-Dick*.

*The Death-Struggle* illustrates the conflict between adversity and reconciliation through a tangled array of balanced and imbalanced forces. Deas painted *The Death-Struggle* in 1844, four years before he would be admitted to the Bloomingdale Asylum to be treated for religious anxiety and monomania.[16] Initially exhibited in 1845 at the American Art-Union, *The Death-Struggle* was considered a highlight of the exhibition. It was reproduced by W. G. Jackman as a print in the same 1846 issue of the *New York Illustrated Magazine* that reviewed Melville's *Typee*. At some point, Melville purchased the Jackman print and added it to his print collection. Melville may have first seen the painting at either the American Art-Union or the National Academy of Design, the two venues through which Deas exhibited his work.[17]

Deas, whose reputation had been built on realistic portraits of American Indian and western American subjects, turned toward more chaotic and frightening subjects during the deterioration of his mental health in the late 1840s. The relation between his mental struggles and his work is explicitly noted in a review of one of his works in Duyckinck's periodical, *The Literary World*, in 1848:

> Of Mr. Deas' picture of *The Savior* (229), we forbear to speak. The late melancholy circumstances of his derangement may somewhat account for the exhibition of the picture, and shield it from the shafts of criticism. We have heard of the unfortunate occurrence with much pain, but we trust that the evil may in time be remedied, and the talented artist restored to his friends and to the Art of which he is so much an ornament. ("National Academy Exhibition" 350)

Evert Duyckinck was aware of Deas's mental decline and the relation of it to his work, and most likely of Deas's commitment to the Bloomingdale Insane Asylum, the same asylum in which his brother George would help secure Adler's treatment.[18] Duyckinck's awareness may have influenced Melville's interest in Deas, since Melville's proximity to mental illness throughout his life was an enduring concern.[19] Such overlap permits a speculative possibility at this point, for Melville would thus have been in a position to view Deas's final exhibition effort, the nightmarish and now-lost oil painting titled *A Vision*, which Deas painted

**FIGURE 1.** Charles Deas, *The Death-Struggle*, 1840–1845, oil on canvas. © Shelburne Museum, Shelburne, VT. Reprinted with permission.

while in treatment at Bloomingdale and which both horrified and enthralled viewers when it was exhibited at the National Academy of Design in 1849.[20] A review of it in *The Knickerbocker* describes it as a chaos of entanglement, a kind of watery madness that it is hard to imagine Melville would not appreciate:

> No. 145. A *Vision*: C. DEAS. What have we here? How disentangle the human sufferers from those winding serpents, and release them from those fangs, so wild, so horrible, of shapeless, unknown monsters? Until we *do* disentangle, we can make nothing of this extraordinary effort of paint. You must separate the beings that struggle and die in the blue waves of the mystic sea, and then when you have done so, you will be astonished at the beauty and delicacy of the handling, and the correctness of the drawing. A 'vision,' is it? Yes, and a horrid one! Despair and Death are together, and Frenzy glares from the blood-red sockets of the victims, and haunting and weird thoughts arise, as we reflect over this singular effort of talent. ("Exhibition at the National Academy of Design" 470)

If Melville had seen this painting, or even just this description of it, he might have had it in mind when describing the chaotic wildness of the singular painting Ishmael encounters at the Spouter-Inn, the "unaccountable masses of shades and shadows" that endeavor "to delineate chaos bewitched."[21] A picture abstract enough to "drive a nervous man distracted," the painting Melville describes requires, like *A Vision*, disentanglement and interpretation:

> Yet was there a sort of indefinite, half-attained, unimaginable sublimity about it that fairly froze you to it, till you involuntarily took an oath with yourself to find out what that marvellous painting meant. Ever and anon a bright, but, alas, deceptive idea would dart you through.—It's the Black Sea in a midnight gale.—It's the unnatural combat of the four primal elements.—It's a blasted heath.—It's a Hyperborean winter scene.—It's the breaking-up of the ice-bound stream of Time." (*MD* 12–13)

The interpretive ambiguity Melville describes here accords with the chaos, the "half-revealed shapes of horror which afflict the feverish minds of the insane," that one reviewer saw in Deas's notable painting ("Topics of the Month" 315). Yet, though a direct influence of the indescribable horrors of *A Vision* upon the Spouter-Inn's "portentous, black mass of something" is certainly possible, it must remain conjectural. Perhaps all that can be said with certainty is that Melville had multiple opportunities to view Deas's more terrifying paintings and that his art-viewing companionship with Duyckinck meant he would have had someone to tell him about Deas's insanity if, during one of their exhibition outings, he had inquired about the artist.[22]

We do not have to recover *A Vision* to recognize those same entanglements and terrors in *The Death-Struggle*. Melville owned a reproduction of *The Death-Struggle*, a print from William Jackman's engraving that appeared in 1846 in the *New York Illustrated Magazine of Literature and Art*. Reading its precarious imbalance against the Hegel-inspired fears of George Adler suggests not only Melville's continued fascination with madness but, more importantly, his interest in the complicated schemes of balance that Deas portrayed and Adler theorized. That is, the fact that Deas and Adler were treated at the same asylum is not as important as the fact that they seem to have alighted upon the same paradoxical theme of dialectical adversity. And even that coincidence would mean very little if not for the fact that Melville recognized and valued that theme in both of them and raised it to a controlling motif in his own writing.

*The Death-Struggle* depicts two adversaries—one a white trapper, the other a Native American warrior—just as their mounts have carried them over the edge of a chasm. In existential peril, the gestures of the riders, locked in combat a moment earlier, signify a more desperate mood. For though both riders still maintain a grip on their knives, the blades are not pointed toward their respective assailants but have instead become obstructions to their embrace, their futile attempt at self-preservation. At the center of the canvas, the beaver held by the white trapper bites and claws at the warrior. The warrior embraces the white trapper with both arms, looking up, not with an "expression of tiger-like ferocity" that a contemporary reviewer saw ("Paintings at the American Art-Union" 155), but in desperate hope. The trapper, in turn, clutches with his fingertips at a dead overhanging branch. Gestures of ferocity are changed by the extremity of context to gestures of hope.

Even though "Deas put the Indian in a more vulnerable position," Carol Clark notes, "he intertwined their fates" (101). The painting's doubled yet linked gestures perform this asymmetrical entanglement on several levels. The skewed nature of the struggle asks the viewer to align with the dominant figure of the white trapper clad in bright red or with the dusky and muscular Native American warrior, subordinate yet more expressive in his searching gaze at the trapper's face. In their interlocked grasps, each element's hold on another that itself holds something else, the painting may seem to suggest reciprocity in mode (an embrace, for example, would suggest two people embracing one another), yet it circumvents such balance by denying any return or reflection in kind (the figures do not embrace each other). Even the light/dark composition of the painting, in which the dark man rides the black horse and the pale man rides the white horse, suggests a chiaroscuro blank assertion of equal difference. Yet as the horses' heads strain away from one another, seeking to separate themselves, their legs are tangled together in a vine that binds them to each other. In a similar complication, just as the clothed trapper may seem the dominant figure, the color of his red shirt tonally blends with the reddish-brown skin of the arm that clutches it in the triangular knot of grasps at the painting's center. Deas's painting portrays the reconciliation of stark, even violent difference into a single form, but this reconciliation is darker than the epiphanic one hoped for in Adler's *Iphigenia*. The native onlooker in the background views the scene with concern, but his raised eyebrows and averted face also connote a more conservative apprehension: the two men have sacrificed their mutual enmity and will travel to their death in a posture of love.

The array of forces in *The Death-Struggle* are dynamic. They oscillate from antagonism to reconciliation to antagonism as the eye follows the chain of gestures, grasps, and embraces. Horses' heads strain away from one another but are locked at their knees. The riders carry weapons in their hands, but their arms are directed toward their preservation. Yet these reconciliations are not perfectly balanced; the beaver, whose body spans and joins the two figures, strikes out at the wrong hand, mistaking the warrior for the trapper. The expressions of the two men, one desperately searching and hoping, the other vacant and looking neither down at his fate nor at his companion but out through the canvas at something absent, lead the viewer off a cliff as well. Just as we follow the interlocked chain of grasps, from beaver to warrior to trapper to the dead branch that is the last point of contact with the earth, the chain of gazes move unilaterally as well, from the curious and concerned onlooker to the warrior looking up searchingly at the trapper's face to the trapper's vacant stare off the canvas. The painting's composition at first seems to be a battle between frontier antagonists, a balanced antagonism. One degree closer and we see that they have given up their battle, that they are less different than they are the same, that their struggle is really an embrace, a balanced reconciliation. Yet an even closer analysis of the gazes and grips shows that this reconciliation is not one based in a mutual reflexivity but rather is composed of minute imbalances, one-sided directional gestures, that lead the eye back to the deadened branch and the emptiness of the space outside the canvas.

This dynamic movement is an example of the paradoxical recursiveness of Melville's figure of "uneven balance." The riders' pitched struggle against one another may not have tipped one way or the other, but both of them are tipped off the edge of a cliff, forced to finally struggle with a different and infinitely more powerful opponent. In the extremity of the moment, in the terror of certain death, the dynamic structure of carefully balanced antagonisms is itself balanced against the absolute authority of the unknown that is death. The horror that leads the eye up the chain of grasps to the tree that cannot possibly support them gives way to the terror in the blank vision of the trapper's face. We know by their expressions that what lies ahead is a precipitous drop, but it is in the tangled balances and imbalances, the way each gesture and each grasp seeks to trim the balance and regain control, that the terror of the unpictured void takes shape. In other words, we are given a reaction, not a cause. But the viewer is asked to infer the cause, the threat, through the expressive gestures and the multiple layers of balance come askew. Terror reflects the uneven balance; it expresses in feeling the disproportions of the painting's deliberately off-balance composition.

*The Death-Struggle* resonates throughout multiple scenes in *Moby-Dick*. The embrace between the white and his dark-skinned antagonist is reminiscent of Queequeg's locked "bridegroom clasp" (*MD* 26) of Ishmael in bed at the Spouter-Inn: "[H]e still hugged me tightly, as though naught but death should part us twain" (*MD* 26). The entanglement of the adversaries in the painting and their shared fate also recall the discourse on shared fate and free will that Ishmael relates in the "Monkey-Rope" chapter. Tied by a rope to Queequeg, who dangles over the side of the ship, Ishmael "metaphysically" considers their mutual entanglement as an "interregnum in Providence; for its even-handed equity never could have sanctioned so gross an injustice" (*MD* 320). A contrivance, as Melville admits in a footnote ("it was only in the Pequod that the monkey and his holder were ever tied together" [*MD* 320n]), affixing a line between Ishmael and Queequeg allows Melville to explore the moral unevenness of symmetrical union through a mechanism of opposing forces. But the passage perhaps most evocative of *The Death-Struggle* is the book's climax. The deep red of the trapper's jacket in Deas's painting, the Native American's flexed arm, the beaver's ferocious but futile defense, and the overarching representation of struggle in the face of certain death: all of these visual elements are echoed in the tableaux of the *Pequod*'s sinking. Tashtego, whose "red arm and a hammer hovered backwardly uplifted in the open air," is nailing to the mast the red flag of Ahab, when he catches, in the final moment, a sky-hawk that has "chanced to intercept its broad fluttering wing between the hammer and the wood" (*MD* 572). Caught in the "death-grasp" of the "submerged savage" and enfolded in the "flag of Ahab," the bird sounds the beaver's plight in Deas's painting, struggling with "archangelic shrieks" (*MD* 572) against its captivity. Melville's final image thus draws from *The Death-Struggle* not only its tangled schematic of red against white and its figuration of the innocent animal victim caught in a violent human conflict, but also and finally the radical unevenness of the outcome.

These two influences on *Moby-Dick*, George Adler and Deas's *The Death-Struggle*, may both have been associated with the Bloomingdale Asylum, but it is their overlapping concerns with the tones and feelings, the fears and terrors, of asymmetrical dialectical struggle that help reveal the structural troping of terror and balance in *Moby-Dick*. If Deas's painting of the terrified unity of opposing forces and Adler's terrified diatribes about the truth of Hegelian dialectic both appealed to Melville during the years before he composed his most famous book, it may be because Melville himself was formulating his own portrayal of the "uneven balance."

## The Rocking Life

*Moby-Dick* is both a balanced and an imbalanced book. The whale heads, strung up on either side of the deck, emblematize a broad array of doubles, opposites, and asymmetrical pairings that readers have long seen as the book's controlling structure.[23] Following the tradition of parsing the binary relation between Starbuck and Ahab philosophically, K. L. Evans argues that it models a dilemma between pragmatic pluralism (Starbuck) and a commitment to conviction (Ahab). If the book has two philosophies, then the usual next question is which philosophy is dominant. Evans, for instance, advocates for Ahab, citing the usually overlooked public and communal consequences of his conviction.[24] Yet between balance and imbalance, in the margin before philosophical commitment, *Moby-Dick* stages scenes that oscillate between oscillation and fixity, recursive balancing acts that recall *The Death-Struggle*'s entanglements and Adler's metaphysical angst. Rather than resolve the dilemma, then, we might describe its aesthetics. Unfolding along the crease between Starbuck's liberal pragmatism and Ahab's one-sided conviction, three chapters—"The Mast-Head," "The Line," and "The Try-Works"—offer an affective account of the philosophical dilemma, finding in terror the tone of being caught between asymmetrical dangers: the threat of being balanced out and the threat of not being balanced at all.

The first of these encounters with philosophical antinomy, the "Mast-Head" chapter, is usually read as Melville's critique of transcendentalism.[25] Ishmael's description of the dreamy philosopher, rocked to a sensation of transcendental oneness atop the masthead and subsequently dropped to his death, is explicitly a warning to "Heed it well, ye Pantheists!" (*MD* 159). But the fall into the infinite is symbolized not only in the literal fall but also in the sway of Melville's prose. For what begins as a simple dialectical either/or statement—were there whales or not?—sets in motion a grander dialectic that sweeps the practicality of a single answer into an oratory of universal motion. An impatient harpooner insists to the philosopher-lookout that "[w]hales are scarce as hen's teeth whenever thou art up here" (*MD* 159). Ishamel's rejoinder is a masterful piece of misdirection:

> Perhaps they were; or perhaps there might have been shoals of them in the far horizon; but lulled into such an opium-like listlessness of vacant, unconscious reverie is this absent-minded youth by the blending cadence of waves with thoughts, that at last he loses his identity; takes the mystic ocean at his feet for the visible image of that deep, blue, bottomless soul, pervading mankind and nature; and every strange, half-seen, gliding, beautiful thing that eludes him; every dimly-discovered, uprising fin of some undiscernable form, seems to him the embodiment of those elusive thoughts that only people the soul by continually flitting through it. (*MD* 159)

The original concern over an objectively known existence—perhaps there were no whales, or perhaps there were shoals of them—is siphoned off into the cadence of Melville's rhythmic prose, rhetorically answering the problem by either transcending or abandoning it. We can imagine the harpooner's bafflement at such an illogical response. Parsed, it reads: "Perhaps there were no whales, or perhaps there were many whales, but the youth loses his identity so that everything seems himself." In his reverie, he takes every "uprising fin" as one of his own thoughts, lapsing into a solipsism in which whales become symbols of his mind. Such logic supplants empirical positivism with transcendental idealism, and it does so by raising the oscillating dynamic inherent in the question to a controlling yet abstract thesis; the logic of the question becomes the form of the self.

This movement is, I believe, what Melville has in mind when he claims that at such moments of transcendence, no self is left except a vacillating movement: "There is no life in thee, now, except that rocking life imparted by a gently rolling ship; by her, borrowed from the sea; by the sea, from the inscrutable tides of God" (*MD* 159). The "rocking life" here is the life of the dialectician, swaying from one position to the other in an attempt to see mutually exclusive propositions at the same time. But keeping one's balance theoretically means losing one's grip: "But while this sleep, this dream is on ye, move your foot or hand an inch, slip your hold at all; and your identity comes back in horror" (*MD* 159). The fear here, at first glance, may be seen as of merely losing balance: in maintaining a perfect equilibrium with God's inscrutable tides in one's mind, one may lose equilibrium in one's body. But the trigger for the horror of the fall is taking a single action, moving foot or hand. Identity comes back in horror not only when one loses balance, but when one takes an action that would disturb the paralyzing placidity of transcendental union. Melville's critique of transcendentalism is not that it raises, then throws you from vertiginous heights, but more sharply that the dream of swaying and rocking, of gaining that Hegelian or Goethean "all" feeling in which contraries unite, precludes action or volition. To take action in that sleep is to regain one's identity, the horror of individuality in the dream of transcendence. If the philosopher sinks, "no more to rise for ever" (*MD* 159), it is because attaining that transcendental union cannot be achieved without sacrificing the individual identity that seeks it.

Fear attends the philosophical overreach not because the dream is false but because it has come true. The sleepy philosopher does, after all, obtain that selfless merger with the sea, but in the horror of his fall he registers the self-dissolution such success incurs. Melville's critique of transcendentalism, just like his critique of Goethe's "all" feeling, contains a caveat. It is not that the "all" feeling is wrong or misleading, but rather that, applied to its fullest consequences, the dictum to become absorbed into the rocking, swaying, dialectical movement of the universe is self-destructive. The terror that attends its success is not so much the fear of imminent death as the mood of that tipping point at which both transcendent merger and individual self can be grasped at the halfway point. For it is at "mid-day," and with one "half-throttled shriek," that "your identity comes back in horror" (*MD* 159). It is not *because* your identity comes back that you feel horror but rather that horror ushers in identity's return. Unlike Hegel's assertion that philosophical abstraction requires the "passionless calm of purely speculative knowledge" (1:51), Melville's illustration suggests that calmness takes thought only up to a certain point of abstraction. Terror provides the final step, delivering in a single passion simultaneously one's individual identity and its loss in a transcendent unity. Thus the final goal of transcendental philosophy—some dreamy unity of self and world—is shown to abrogate its own method; it would attain the merger by leaving out half of the equation. Terror restores balance by tipping it the other way, returning identity and offering an affective glimpse of that untenable position midway between sublimity and submergence.

When Melville reprises the problem of balance, terror, and philosophy in "The Line," however, the terror of losing one's self by rocking too much is replaced by the terror of losing one's self by not rocking at all. In the whaleboat, the swiftly unraveling whaling line presents a unique danger:

> For, when the line is darting out, to be seated then in the boat, is like being seated in the midst of the manifold whizzings of a steam-engine in full play, when every flying beam, and shaft, and wheel, is grazing you. It is worse; for you cannot sit motionless in the heart of these perils, because the boat is rocking like a cradle, and you are pitched one way and the other, without the slightest warning; and only by a certain self-adjusting buoyancy and simultaneousness of volition and action, can you escape being made a Mazeppa of, and run away with where the all-seeing sun himself could never pierce you out. (*MD* 280–281)

In the whaleboat, the danger is of remaining motionless, of failing to adapt to the pitch of the boat. The "self-adjusting buoyancy and simultaneousness of volition and action" required for escaping the line, then, seems to echo the unique skill set of the sperm whale on its best days, of being able, say, to demonstrate two distinct problems in Euclid simultaneously.

But Melville focuses on the terror of the line in its calmness, apparently joining the terror of the midday masthead to the terror of the relaxed whale line: "[S]o the graceful repose of the line, as it silently serpentines about the oarsmen before being brought into actual play—this is a thing which carries more of true terror than any other aspect of this dangerous affair" (*MD* 281). Why would a calm, reposed rope have more "true terror" than the "actual play" of the whizzing line? Melville seems to clarify that true terror is not in the actual threat but in the universality of the threat. Like Jonathan Edwards's scriptural exhortation that "[t]he arrows of death fly unseen at noonday; the sharpest sight can't discern them" (*Sinners* 407), the terror of the line is a reminder of imminent mortality. That terror, as we saw in Chapter 1, is both internalized and universal; it is one that attends to every moment, such that daily life itself can be eclipsed by a constant and ambiguous terror. This is why, at the end of his description of the line, Melville reveals that the terror of the line is the same as the terror of the philosopher: "And if you be a philosopher, though seated in the whale-boat, you would not at heart feel one whit more of terror, than though seated before your evening fire with a poker, and not a harpoon, by your side" (*MD* 281). Again, with characteristic balance, Melville's sentence runs two ways at once. One can read it as saying that philosophers, convinced of their mortality, are inured and desensitized to the terror of the line. But the other sense is that, for philosophers, every moment is filled with terror, whaleboat and evening parlor included.

If, atop the masthead, horror shows us that evenness is unbalanced, and if, in the whaleboat in the line, terror becomes the wider mood of a self-adjusting and balanced philosophy, the scales would seem to tip again to the other side in the "Try-Works" chapter. There Ishmael, working the tiller, is lulled to drowsiness while watching the demoniac shadows and silhouettes cast by the fires of the try-works and listening to the "tales of terror" that fork out of them. When he wakes, he finds that he has become disoriented, literally turned around, and his attempts to steer backwards, as it were, throw the whole boat into jeopardy:

> Starting from a brief standing sleep, I was horribly conscious of something fatally wrong. The jaw-bone tiller smote my side, which leaned against it; in my ears was the low hum of sails, just beginning to shake in the wind; I thought my eyes were open; I was half conscious of putting my fingers to the lids and mechanically stretching them still further apart. But, spite of all this, I could see no compass before me to steer by. . . . Nothing seemed before me but a jet gloom, now and then made ghastly by flashes of redness. Uppermost was the impression, that whatever swift, rushing thing I stood on was not so much bound to any haven ahead as rushing from all havens astern. A stark, bewildered feeling, as of death, came over me. (*MD* 423–424)

Ishmael is able to right himself "just in time to prevent the vessel from flying up into the wind, and very probably capsizing her" (*MD* 424). The moral of this story—"Look not too long in the face of the fire, O man! Never dream with thy hand on the helm!" (*MD* 424)—recalls and reverses the moral of the masthead. Similar to the masthead, the imperative is to avoid dreaming, but here the nature of the dream is the "face of the fire," the "tales of terror told in words of mirth" that are patently diabolical (*MD* 423). The boat, itself "plunging into that blackness of darkness," recalls the power of blackness Melville praises in Hawthorne, and "[w]rapped, for that interval, in darkness myself," Ishmael claims he "but the better saw the redness, the madness, the ghastliness of others" (*MD* 423). Just as too much transcendental and wishy-washy "all" feeling could overload the balance by forgetting the stubborn individual identity, here too much diabolical darkness inverts one's position and leads not to being thrown overboard but rather to throwing the boards themselves over, capsizing the entire vessel. Such danger would seem to suggest, according to the affective economy I've been sketching through the examples of the masthead and the line, that there is a limit to the quantity and effect of terror as a mode of philosophical insight. Terror may be a way of apprehending and correcting the tendency of philosophical dialecticism to set up evenly pitched and zero-sum equations, but too much terror can upset those distinctions, leaving one in a uniform blackness of darkness.

But Melville is quick to qualify this claim. After claiming that one must not dwell upon darkness, Ishmael considers how the "natural sun" itself illuminates that darkness: "Nevertheless the sun hides not Virginia's Dismal Swamp, nor Rome's accursed Campagna, nor wide Sahara, nor all the millions of miles of deserts and of griefs beneath the moon. The sun hides not the ocean, which is the dark side of this earth, and which is two thirds of this earth" (*MD* 424). In reasserting the importance of darkness, Melville does not point to the side of the earth facing away from the sun, the actual dark side of the earth, but rather to those darkened places shining in the light of the natural sun. Had Melville simply pointed out that every light side has a dark side as well, he would have merely reiterated that essentialist dichotomy against which Hegel rebelled.[26] It isn't that there is a dark and a light that require each other by way of contrast, Melville and Hegel alike argue, but rather that the light is—in a different, less balanced schematic which privileges enclosure rather than stark difference—conspiratorial with darkness. The sun, by shining on the darkness of the sea, is thus not only part of that darkness but out of proportion with it—the darkness of the sea "two-thirds" of the earth, a significantly odd proportion for the uneven weight of the world.

Thus, when Melville continues the chapter, we hear reverberations of that uneven balance he defined in "Hawthorne and His Mosses." When he writes "mortal man who hath more of joy than sorrow in him, that mortal man cannot be true" (*MD* 424), Melville seems to suggest that the recipe for truth is equal parts joy and sorrow. Yet his illustration of this point, from the book of Solomon, emphasizes the overwhelming nature of sorrow: "'All is vanity.' ALL. This wilful world hath not got hold of unchristian Solomon's wisdom yet" (*MD* 424). Since they seem to set up a quantification of equal parts, what makes Melville's illustrations so surprising is how out of proportion they turn out to be. The dark half, which is really two-thirds, Melville says, is necessary for truth, which is the elusive truth that *all* is vanity and thus total darkness.

Moving through these quantified measures, Melville's final image and reconciliation of balance is a complicated one. An eagle, he suggests, is able to be paradoxically both deep in darkness and high in the light at the same time: "[T]here is a Catskill eagle in some souls that can alike dive down into the blackest gorges, and soar out of them again and become invisible in the sunny spaces. And even if he for ever flies within the gorge, that gorge is in the mountains; so that even in his lowest swoop the mountain eagle is still higher than other birds upon the plain, even though they soar" (*MD* 425). Again, a figure of balance is immediately disturbed, then redrawn as a balanced figure of imbalance. Melville's chapter would appear to perform what it preaches: it flaps down into diabolical fires, then up to the natural and sole true sun, then back down to the dark two-thirds of the earth, down further to the truth of Solomon, then back up again to what at first seems the conclusive point: "Give not thyself up, then, to fire, lest it invert thee" (*MD* 425). But this isn't where the image ends. The passage concludes, not with the Catskill eagle shuttling back and forth, spending equal time in darkness and light, but with the bird "for ever" in the gorge, always in darkness, suggesting that it soars high by sinking low. Here, as throughout Melville's affective staging of balances, the impulse for equilibrium paradoxically demands an ecliptic, imbalanced eternity of the power of blackness which is equality's counterweight.

Terror is the tone by which what I've been calling the uneven balance—the disproportion between the opposing principles of dialectical balance and monolithic imbalance—becomes apprehensible in *Moby-Dick*. But why terror? Why should this arrangement, this metaskeptical flux, produce, much less be enabled by, an affect of existential fear? It is a difficult question to answer–which may be why Melville undertakes it himself in one of the most crucial chapters of the book.

## Whiteness

We have seen, by this point, how terror modulates scenes of balance and philosophy in *Moby-Dick*. We moved from Melville's paradoxical logic of the "uneven balance" through an exploration of its thematic extension in *Moby-Dick* and its metaphysical context through Kant's antinomies and Hegel's critique of logic. We then recovered Melville's relation to Hegel through Adler and drew out how the tone of terror comes to motivate and operate the multiple dramas of balance in *Moby-Dick*. But what has escaped an explicit formulation is why terror is the crucial feeling of thinking the uneven balance. In an argumentative yet searching central chapter, "The Whiteness of the Whale," Melville recognizes and seeks to describe that deeper relation between the feeling of terror and modes of idealized abstraction symbolized by the color white. Rather than force his readers to speculate blindly about the ubiquitous role of terror in his book, he leads the way by joining them; and though he ends in a portrait of blindness, his argument itself sketches a prospective answer to the question "Why terror?"

The first task of the chapter, though, is to explain the what, before the why. Ishmael marshals a catalogue of examples of terrifying whiteness to support his claim that whiteness *is* terrifying. To do so, he initially distinguishes between the mystical and ineffable sources of the terror of whiteness and the real and substantial sources of common alarm. He offers the example of the mariner who sees his ship "sailing through a midnight sea of milky whiteness" and feels a "silent, superstitious dread; the shrouded phantom of the whitened waters is horrible to him as a real ghost" (*MD* 193). The mariner's dread in this case is terror; it is directed at the "real ghost" of white waters. However, when that terror is explained, Ishmael's subsequent question implies, it is usually translated from abstract terror into common alarm, explained as a fear of rocks, not of the white waters that are their index: "Yet where is the mariner who will tell thee, 'Sir, it was not so much the fear of striking hidden rocks, as the fear of that hideous whiteness that so stirred me?'" (*MD* 194). The conventional response implied negatively here models the general interpretive strategy when explaining fear: what terrifies is not actually the phenomenon in itself but an underlying and substantial reality that such phenomena express. So when Ishmael resists the mariner's response and continues to insist that it is the whiteness itself that causes fear, he is also rejecting the common interpretive logic that would explain effect by way of cause. No wonder Ishmael despairs of "putting it [the terror of whiteness] into comprehensible form," for "it" defies the methods and assumptions that enable comprehension in the first place. Effects are not explainable by causes, and appearances swim free of underlying substance; what remains is a "real ghost," a spectral appearance that is effective in its phenomenal being, not in its antecedent cause.[27]

Obviously, Ishmael is facing an uphill battle, then, since our usual mode of comprehending fear is to assess its real cause. He consequently adopts a searching, unorganized method of inquiry—a "dim, random way" (*MD* 188)—which accords with the deft disorganization of his anatomical narrative itself, since the nature of the problem eludes rational analysis:

> To analyse it, would seem impossible. Can we, then, by the citation of some of those instances wherein this thing of whiteness—though for the time either wholly or in great part stripped of all direct associations calculated to impart to it aught fearful, but nevertheless, is found to exert over us the same sorcery, however modified;—can we thus hope to light upon some chance clue to conduct us to the hidden cause we seek? (*MD* 192)

Ishmael is trying to get at the terror of whiteness as a category abstracted from "all direct associations" but can do no better than to simply cite objective instances in an uncalculated way. There just is no other way in, Melville seems to suggest, to a nonsymptomatic analysis of an abstraction than to essay its concretization in examples. At the same time, the adoption of a "random" method that hopes only for a "chance clue" places the project in the field of chance, a field which offers a crucial third alternative to those exclusive paradigms of fate and free will. The chance of the chapter, its troubling caveats and largely speculative conclusions, means for Maurice Lee that "what most coherently links the color of Moby Dick to atheism is not race, language, theodicy, or perception so much as the absence of causal logic connecting whiteness to the feelings it brings" (*Uncertain Chances* 52). The vicissitudes of chance circumvent the causal logic of interpretation; it comes to displace those methods of analysis that would retrench the hierarchy of cause over effect, substance over appearance. By this method, then, we get not a systematized argument but rather a "chance clue," a pun slipped into the very language of the problem; for if the chapter proceeds from "dim" prospects to "light upon" the answer, what it eventually lights upon is the "great principle of light" itself.

In the final paragraphs of the chapter, Melville links the terror of whiteness with light's perceptual instrumentality. Yet this whiteness is radically uneven, based upon a paradoxical ontology caught between total presence and total absence. If perception, like interpretation, requires an assumption of causal relations between things-in-themselves and their appearances, between events and their psychological effects, then our perceptual faculties predispose us to linear narratives of explanation, to seek meaning by looking "behind" or "beneath" appearances for hard realities. On the contrary, as Melville explores in the final considerations of the chapter, light, as a mode without which nothing is seen, does not itself obey the same causal logic; it isn't a thing that makes perception possible but rather a mood, comprehensible itself only as a color or a terror.

The uneven balance of whiteness becomes apparent in Melville's consideration of its ontological instability. Melville describes the mystery of whiteness in its double character: it is both "the most meaning symbol of spiritual things" and yet "the intensifying agent in things the most appalling to mankind" (*MD* 195). The doubleness of its symbolic valence is met, in Melville's final paragraph, by the doubleness of its physical properties. Whiteness is "not so much a color as the visible absence of color, and at the same time the concrete of all colors," and thus it is both "a dumb blankness" yet still "full of meaning" (*MD* 195). Whiteness is divine and diabolical, presence and absence, all colors and no color at all. Thus, the terror of Melville's whiteness can draw affective consequences from a Hegelian dialectic of being and nothingness, but it cannot be sublated. If evil becomes worse by whiteness, and good becomes better by whiteness as well, then whiteness itself exceeds both categories and testifies to an underlying unity of mode behind even the most diametrically opposed concepts. Thus the double character of whiteness would at first seem to be perfectly balanced, a joining together of the ultimate oppositions of good and evil, being and nothingness.[28] But in Melville's take, this is never quite an even balance, for it manifests not placid equipoise but rather a weighty and disproportionate terror.

What would finally tip whiteness into terror is that "other theory of the natural philosophers," that color is not "actually inherent in substances, but only laid on from without; so that all deified Nature absolutely paints like the harlot, whose allurements cover nothing but the charnel-house within" (*MD* 195). Melville's angst-ridden point here recalls the perceptual problem of the whiteness of breakers over hidden rocks. Alluding to Locke's theory of secondary qualities, Melville reminds us that vision is mediated and distorted through light. Color is not "real" in the sense of inhering in substances, but is rather a quality painted on by light's interaction with substance's surface, a deceit in its differences of tone. Thus, "when we proceed further, and consider that the mystical cosmetic which produces every one of her hues, the great principle of light, for ever remains white or colorless in itself, and if operating without medium upon matter, would touch all objects, even tulips and roses, with its own blank tinge," we are led to Melville's final horrific image: "[P]ondering all this, the palsied universe lies before us a leper; and like wilful travellers in Lapland, who refuse to wear colored and coloring glasses upon their eyes, so the wretched infidel gazes himself blind at the monumental white shroud that wraps all the prospect around him" (*MD* 195). This passage links whiteness's categorical shiftiness with light's perceptual instrumentality in order to undermine all sensuous knowledge, all understanding. It isn't simply that whiteness comes to transcend and encompass all other colors, but that its capability for this transcendence is bound up with its own blankness. From no meaning we get meaning. From no color we get all the colors. No immediate perception of whiteness is possible because whiteness itself underlies perception. Yet, for this chapter, that which we cannot see by means of our eyes may nevertheless be apprehended through other means.

The final conclusion of "The Whiteness of the Whale," that whiteness is terrifying because it is the "color" of light, is prepared for by the earlier claim that terror is a special perceptual faculty of its own. Ishmael, defending his stance from an objection that his claims for a universal terror of whiteness might simply be a personality disorder, a surrender to "a hypo" (*MD* 194), appeals to the example of a colt in Vermont, with no experience of the wild, becoming terrified by the scent of a buffalo robe. Since the fearful instinct of the colt cannot be explained by experience, Melville offers a deeper causal explanation: "[T]hou beholdest even in a dumb brute, the instinct of the knowledge of the demonism in the world" (*MD* 194). This instinctual knowledge of that which cannot be verified by sense experience becomes the defense for the irrational mode of Ishmael's terror. Whiteness, to Ishmael, is like the buffalo robe to the colt, yet "[t]hough neither knows where lie the nameless things of which the mystic sign gives forth such hints; yet with me, as with the colt, somewhere those things must exist. Though in many of its aspects this visible world seems formed in love, the invisible spheres were formed in fright" (*MD* 194–195). This is not usually taken for iron-clad logic: that one is scared of ghosts does not logically entail that ghosts must exist. But Ishmael proposes this mode of flawed reasoning as a faculty of intuition that operates outside of the strictures of syllogistic logic. What enables this instinct to make an impression upon the rational mind, which would otherwise scoff at it, is that it models itself upon the paradoxical structure of light. Terror ultimately registers the uneven demands of whiteness, both its doubleness and its lack of balance, because it not only perceives but it also creates, it "forms," even as it likewise eludes, the categories that enable its availability for perception.[29]

The visible world, after all, *seems* formed in love. But the invisible spheres *were* formed in fright. Both the unevenness and the analogy with visibility and sense perception prepare for Melville's subsequent explanation of light's doubled ontology as an explanation for the terror. By comparing visibility's seeming love to the mood of invisibility's actual fright, the chapter shows how terror, like light, may invisibly project our phenomenal world. Paul Brodtkorb puts it another way: "[T]he emotion that constitutes white makes vibrantly visible as a presence the nothingness with which all existence is secretly sickened" (119). Terror takes on not just a receptive ability to apprehend the paradox and antinomies of light but also a formative role. It isn't, then, that abstractions, the blankness of meaning, terrify because of their consequences for the feeling subject, but rather that the blankness of meaning that is also the source of all meaning is integral to the terror that forms it. This isn't a complete reversal of priority. For the terror that informs the blankness is not wholly accounted for in it; just as light is both no color and all-color, terror inheres in and measures out the aporia between no meaning and all meaning. It is half in, half out, but the discomfiture and urgency of its tone reveal the insufficiency of a figure of balanced halves. One term comes to master the other, and terror becomes the feeling of those categories pursued to their most abstract ends, the feeling of that tipping point between the carelessness of a completely blank world of meaninglessness and the deep care of that meaning world promised by our affective capacities.

Through the turns and overturns of dialectical procedure, Melville has followed the deceptively simple question "What am I scared of?" round to the much more distressing question "How can we know anything in a world of appearance?" If terror is affixed to phenomena rather than to substance, its urgency would be paradoxically raised from the consideration that it isn't *about* anything; there is literally nothing to fear. From the beginning of this chapter we have seen that Melville figures terror not by presenting the object of fear but rather by portraying the entangled and uneven relations between comprehensive yet opposed dialectical categories. The "hidden cause" of terror is not easily found in such schemes, because the very notion of cause answers the problem of phenomenal affect by dismissing it as secondary, as an effect of underlying substance. The question of Ishmael's terror is an important preliminary one for *Moby-Dick* because, as it searches for an alternative mode of explanation outside the logic of cause and effect, it discovers its origins in the Hegelian dialectical relations between being and nothingness, substance and appearance. It suggests that terror returns us to the metaphysical moments of imbalance that precede the stabilizing and dismissing effects of either empirical or transcendental philosophies. On this level, then, Melville discovers that terror is central not simply because it reacts to the flux of opposing forces that underlie experience, but also because, as a perceptual principle like light, terror *forms* that which it perceives. Terror may react to the prospect of annihilation, but it also produces those categories that allow us to think annihilation in the first place.

Melville's terror is thus generative, though in a way importantly different from the proliferation of experience offered by pragmatism's theory of distortion, adaptation, and balance. For whereas pragmatism's "search for a momentary resting-place, a perch, specious, 'a fiction,' to catch onto" provides "an organism with the temporary homeostatic balance essential to its being able to go on, to continue" (Richardson 22), Melville's terrifying uneven balance produces without, in a sense, being productive. Its variation of infinite recursion—akin to Edwards's figure of "swallowing up" and the self-containing frames of Poe's "The Fall of the House of Usher"—is neither balanced out by God's infinite mercy nor erased in a final cataclysm of unification. Rather, it is confirmed in the physics of light, a paradox that nevertheless informs the world with tone, hue, and even substance.[30] What holds together the perceptual world is something yet estranged from it, and this disproportion is itself phenomenologically arranged through terror. At first this may simply be a matter of tone, for pragmatism as well acknowledges an always fluctuating disproportion and advocates for thought as a responsive continual adjustment, what Melville might call "trimming boat." To emphasize the disproportion rather than the adjustment, the terror rather than the hope, might seem merely the prerogative of those acolytes of the half-empty. But Melville's terror of the uneven balance threatens to eclipse those binaries, turning back on itself the dialectical method that parses them out and offering a mood wherein the act of balancing comes to seem, at core, unbalanced itself.

In *Moby-Dick*, Melville portrays these moments of imbalance through acute and punctual terrors, focusing on the moments in which one loses one's grip, tips over, falls off. Yet, as he hints in "The Line," those immediate terrors are not wholly contained in these moments of thought or threat, for they are only visible eruptions of a more unsettling and universal terror. In following the relation of terror to perceptual knowledge, Melville's later short fiction diffuses and blunts these acute terrors into a more omnipresent, less volatile, and yet more disturbing dread. For if in *Moby-Dick* Melville came to figure in flashes the tremendous disruptions that terror indexes in our systems of knowledge, in *The Piazza Tales* he explores the aftereffects, variations on a world in which dread continues to determine the organizing principles of experience.

# 5

## DREAD

Space, Time, and Automata in *The Piazza Tales*

**ALTHOUGH THE MAGAZINE STORIES** Melville collected as *The Piazza Tales* in 1856 were written as independent pieces, and even though the collection itself has been seen as a hasty effort to secure income during a period of financial turmoil for Melville, there exist for the careful reader patterns of linked motifs within and between the disparate tales. Like the polymorphous and multiple identities of the title character of *The Confidence-Man* (1857), these motifs resist static classification. A literal lightning strike in one tale will become a figurative one in others. The primitive timepiece made by notches on a tropical reed in one tale will resemble the elaborate clock tower in the next and the clock-like daily behavior of office workers in the one previous. Characters and narrators alike become obsessed with the deformative effects of gazing at objects in the distance, even when those objects are as varied as a house on a mountaintop, the drowning of one's loved ones in the ocean, and the sentry watchman atop a tower. When reading *The Piazza Tales* as a whole, these imperfect resemblances suggest an underlying thematics to Melville's magazine work, regardless of its diverse genres.

I will argue in this chapter that the shared motifs of *The Piazza Tales*, for all their individual differences, constellate around two fundamental axes: that of space and that of time. The ground of these motifs, the dark and uncanny tone of the narratives themselves, suggests that what is at stake in the magazine tales is not only the relation of space to time but the relation of both with terror. Figured in atmospheric mood rather than passionate crisis, the tales' fears are perhaps less horrifying, less immediate threats than the ones of *Moby-Dick*, but what seems like mellowing is actually a deepening. Rather than bracketed episodes of terror, *The Piazza Tales* offers a panoply of variations on the same bleak theme. Drawing on the centrality of dread to the phenomenological and existential critiques of metaphysics in Kierkegaard and Heidegger, and considering recent theorization of this same dread as spatialized thrownness by Sianne Ngai, I consider in this chapter how Melville's repeated touches of spatial deformation and temporal miscalibration revise the philosophical significance of terror. What is revealed is not so much a better understanding of terror in time and space but rather the more difficult to conceive understanding of time and space as a function of terror.

Such a reading of *The Piazza Tales* thus takes a philosophically abstract approach to the often-perceived "darkness" in them. For Marvin Fisher, one of the first to consider the tales as a whole, the darkness is shot through with disillusionment with certain categories of American idealism: "They [the tales] suggest apocalyptically that the social and political ideas of American life and the uniqueness and optimism of the American dream—rather than Melville's talent or intellect—were going under" (xi). In another reading of *The Piazza Tales* as a whole, Scott Donaldson links the tales by their limited perspective, Melville's sustained and manufactured ironies that "[t]hings are not what they seem, and only the wise can perceive the true nature of the world" (1082). Across the span of these two not mutually exclusive propositions—one about the historical context of their subjects, the other about the obscurity of their ironies—exists a wide range of approaches to the individual stories. In the case of "Bartleby, the Scrivener" (1853), scholars offered so many different interpretations of the tale that even in 1989, eons ago in its literary critical history, Dan McCall could name them "the Bartleby Industry" and group them into several categories—"source study, psychoanalytic interpretation, Marxist analysis, and so on" (x)—only to discover that Bartleby is shockingly silent in the face of any of his interpretive appropriations.[1] The dread that I define through my reading of the tales may, I hope, help describe this stubborn silence, this encounter with the absolutely inhuman—not to explain it away, but to consider it within the post-Hegelian turn to fear in metaphysical philosophy. This is not to say that "Bartleby" or "Benito Cereno" or any of the other tales is really about philosophy, to the exclusion of their historical and intertextual contexts and meanings, but rather that the mood that pervades each of these narratives in their excursions among and through such localized and historical discourse, the predominant pessimism or anxiety, may not be only a reaction to the world but an organizing phenomenological methodology by which that world comes to be.

This chapter's structure—generalizing from a distance the major motifs of the collection and then bringing those motifs close in the close reading of a single tale—parallels the methods of the tales themselves. The first section finds in "The Lightning-Rod Man" (1854) the clearest example of the encounter and struggle with the prospect of fear in the collection. I argue that the strange demands and structure of the fear at stake in that tale can best be understood in relation to the phenomenal place of dread in Kierkegaard's philosophy of freedom. The second section compares Melville's portrayal of these fears through spatial and temporal manipulations to the definition of dread undergirding Heidegger's phenomenological philosophy. With an understanding of fear in its spatial and temporal modulations in place, I turn in the final part of this chapter to the last tale in *The Piazza Tales* more particularly. Showing how "The Bell-Tower" (1855) draws upon these motifs of space and time, I conclude that the tale mobilizes the fear of the automaton, a stock gothic horror, to rearrange the subjective and objective positions within philosophical terror. The terror that Melville works with and upon, ultimately, is not a fear of the objectivity of the human but rather the fear of its idealized subjectivity.

## The Dread of Freedom: "The Lightning-Rod Man"

The six works that comprise Melville's *The Piazza Tales* have received uneven critical appraisal. Two of them, "Bartleby, the Scrivener" and "Benito Cereno" (1855), are among the most popular works in Melville's canon. Three others, "The Piazza" (1856), "The Encantadas" (1854), and "The Bell-Tower," are less well known yet have enjoyed renewed interest in Melville scholarship. The only other tale, "The Lightning-Rod Man," despite being one of the most immediately reprinted of the collection, is generally considered to be a failure, or at best a success only in its wholesale subscription to the generic conventions of magazine satire. The uneven appraisals and the relatively few attempts to take the collection as a whole have as one of their main causes the motley nature of the tales themselves. From domestic sketch to overwrought gothic, from metaphysical fable to comedic satire, the tales range over genres and styles. When considering the recurring motifs and faintly echoic resemblances that flicker through the otherwise discrete works, however, one discovers a general affective concern returned to again and again: the encounter with fear.

But even when recognized as a recurring concern, the fears in *The Piazza Tales* seem vague and disconnected. The anxieties of responsibility plaguing the narrator of "Bartleby" seem a far cry from the gory horror of mechanistic murder in "The Bell-Tower." The nervous compulsion of the dissatisfied narrator in "The Piazza," wandering the countryside in an attempt to escape an eerie malaise, seems incommensurable with the stark terror of slave-ship captain Benito Cereno or the genial misgivings of his companion, Captain Delano. And just as the degrees of fear differ from tale to tale, so too do their ostensible objects. The fears of slave rebellion in "Benito Cereno" seem to point toward the anxious political situation of the antebellum United States. The fears along Wall Street in "Bartleby" gesture instead to an economic referent or to the changing conditions of labor in New York. The fear peddled by the salesman in "The Lightning-Rod Man" has unmistakably religious overtones and may indict the midcentury evangelism of upstate New York. In each case, Melville's uses of fear may be severally interpreted as discrete political, religious, or economic claims. Yet such discrete readings of fear tend to further obscure possible connections between them.

Ironically, the problem of fear central to *The Piazza Tales* is made most explicit in the collection's most traditionally estranged and relatively unfrightening tale, "The Lightning-Rod Man." Within the tale's apparent critique of both religious evangelism and commercial marketing, Melville offers a subtle choreography of the encounter with fear; yet, unlike the other tales, "The Lightning-Rod Man" does not inspire fear in the reader. A narrative confined to a single conversation between a traveling lightning-rod salesman and his unwilling client, "The Lightning-Rod Man" portrays the narrator as a consumer hero. Despite the salesman's best efforts to frighten the narrator into purchasing a lightning rod, the hero rebukes him and, in the surreal scene of violence that ends the tale, breaks the rod and throws its salesman out of his house. Despite this victory, however, the final sentence admits that "the Lightning-rod man still dwells in the land; still travels in storm-time, and drives a brave trade with the fears of man" (*PT* 124). The figure of the lightning-rod man becomes that of the fearmonger in general, the salesman, politician, or religious evangelist who would frighten others for personal gain. Thus the narrator's victory champions the intransigence of the self-determined individual against forces of social persuasion.[2] Taken in such a way, the tale delivers a neat moral, but only by virtue of its divorce from the melancholy and skeptical darkness of the other tales in the collection.

But there is a way to understand the theme of "The Lightning-Rod Man" within the scope of the other tales. Its theme may seem to be an outward complaint, directed against social forces, but it can also be read as an inward struggle, an argument between the willful self and the fears that afflict it. For the real question of the story is not so much whether the narrator will buy the rod as whether he will allow himself to become afraid. His victory, in this more abstract sense, then, is not necessarily over persuasive social forces but, more specifically, over his own body's tendency to react to them. When the stranger attempts to frighten the narrator off the hearth by exclaiming that "'the most dangerous part of a house during such a terrific tempest as this, is the fireplace,'" the narrator's body reacts without will, "involuntarily stepping upon the first board next to the stone" (*PT* 119). As the narrative proceeds, the salesman continually asks that the narrator leave the hearth and join him in the center of the room. The argument over lightning rods thus assumes spatial dimensions; the salesman at the center of the room, unmoving—"the stranger eyed me . . . but did not move a foot" (*PT* 119)—and the narrator on the hearth. The space between the two measures out the fear the narrator is enjoined to feel. When the narrator "involuntarily" steps off the hearth in response to the imposition of fear, it would suggest a momentary lapse of steadfast will. When the narrator retakes his place on the hearth, however, the language of the text is no less insistent on the absence of will: "The stranger now assumed such an unpleasant air of successful admonition, that—quite involuntarily again—I stepped back upon the hearth" (*PT* 119). The narrator's intransigence is thus no more voluntary than his initial flinch.

Seen in this light, the narrator, not the salesman, would seem more in line with a Calvinist determinism. Ultimately, the narrator's reasoning does not champion individual human subjectivity in freedom but rather its futility: "'The hairs of our heads are numbered, and the days of our lives. In thunder as in sunshine, I stand at ease in the hands of my God'" (*PT* 124). The narrator's freedom to decline the lightning rod depends on a greater lack of freedom— for what the rod stands for, in the narrator's gloss, is the attempt to divert the "divine ordinations" (*PT* 124) of a predestined universe. As several critics have noted in regard to this tale, the lightning rod in nineteenth-century America carried the connotations of science's challenge to Calvinist orthodoxy.[3] Though it initially appears as if the narrator's refusal of the lightning rod corresponds to a rejection of fear, the symbolism of the rod as humanity's protection against divine providence leads us to see that what the narrator is actually rejecting is any attempt to mitigate the fearful threat. The narrator stands "at ease" not because there is nothing to fear but rather because what is feared is certain and immitigable.

In light of these observations, it becomes less clear whether the reader's sympathies can rest easily with the triumphant narrator. Fisher, for instance, raises the concern that "[t]he mood of positive optimism marking the end of 'The Lightning-Rod Man' . . . is a mood that Melville more often treats with irony rather than advocacy" (123). Could the optimistic success of the narrator be ironic? For, while the "stranger" is clearly marked as a villain by the narrator, the claims of the salesman are by no means entirely irrational. Indeed, each of the stranger's arguments about lightning—that it would more frequently strike a hearth, for example—are drawn directly from recently published scientific discoveries about lightning.[4] Meanwhile, the philosophical investments underpinning the lightning-rod man's sales pitches are much closer to a liberal notion of free will than those in the narrator's refusal. From the narrator's spitefulness to his inflated lexicon (for example, he greets the salesman with absurd hyperbole: "Sir . . . have I the honor of a visit from that illustrious god, Jupiter Tonans?" [*PT* 119]) to his problematic fatalism, the narrator's stalwart yet flat character obstructs readerly identification. The irony, then, is that what seems like a victory for the free subject over the coercive and self-serving fearmonger comes at the cost of the reader's ability to share in such a victory: refusing to feel, the narrator vindicates subjectivity, but at the cost of the emotional contact by which such subjectivity could be available for the reader. This may account for the reversal of roles in the tale's conclusion, in which the narrator now, not the lightning-rod man, is the one on a campaign of coercion, publishing warnings against the salesman and deploying "dissuasive talk" (*PT* 124) of him to his neighbors.

The importance of contact between persons as both the promise and threat of subjectivity is invited by Melville's deliberate blocking of the tale's cramped stage. The difference between the two men, the stranger and the narrator, is written into the distance between them, a distance that each enjoins the other to cross. When the narrator asks the stranger to sit with him on the hearth, the stranger replies: "'Sir . . . excuse me, but instead of my accepting your invitation to be seated on the hearth there, I solemnly warn *you*, that you had best accept *mine*, and stand with me in the middle of the room'" (*PT* 119). The drama over where to stand plays out over the course of the dialogue, the stranger entreating the narrator four times to "'come hither to me'" (*PT* 122). To obey would be to capitulate to fear, but it would also bring them together, offering the possibility of contact between them. Thus the irony is that, although it is the narrator who consistently and spitefully refuses the salesman's invitations to join him, he is also the one who seems incredulous at the misanthropy inherent in the salesman's admission that he avoids tall men in thunderstorms: "'Do I dream? Man avoid man? and in danger-time too?'" (*PT* 123). The distance between the salesman and the narrator becomes a figure of a more demanding gap between persons—each invites the other to join him, but also each refuses the other's offer.

Since Melville depicts the encounter with fear as a spatial negotiation between bodies, the conductive nature of lightning's physics comes to signify Melville's concern for the possibility of meaningful interpersonal connection. Melville had, a few years before, imagined himself as part of a brotherhood of writers who, hand in hand, would feel the "shock of recognition" (*PT* 249) received by any one of them. In "The Lightning-Rod Man," he again calls upon the conductive nature of electricity to conceive the relations between persons, but now the laws of conductivity arrange such connection as a threat. Because the threat of lightning operates according to contiguity, the salesman continually warns the narrator against touching anything conductive. What makes lightning so dangerous, the salesman explains, is that it turns the human body into a piece of furniture: "'The current will sometimes run down a wall, and—a man being a better conductor than a wall—it would leave the wall and run into him'" (*PT* 122). If the danger of lightning lies in the human's contiguity in the world, then to preserve self would be to isolate and disconnect from the stuff of the world. Sharon Cameron observes that Melville's conception of character treats persons as if they "were not different from a stone or a manifestation of light" (182) and that such elemental description "opens" character "to what lies outside of it—an openness manifested by the fact that character does not seem to be an autonomous or independent entity" (181). The dangers of lightning's connection, its elemental regard for the openness of the human to what it touches, would thus similarly recast meaningful connection between persons as a danger to the individual personhood.

But there is another way conductivity resonates with the wider themes of the tale. For in choosing the path of least resistance, lightning brings a physical dimension to the tale's psychological issues of choice and freedom. Lightning's route selects the best conductors, giving the appearance of choice: "'Nay, if the six-footer stand by running water, the cloud will sometimes *select* him as its conductor to that running water'" (*PT* 123). Coercion, like a lightning rod, impinges upon freedom by influencing and thus determining choice. Exercise of subjective freedom could then be written, in the tale's vocabulary, as resistance against powers of coercion figured by both the salesman's rhetoric and the physics of the lightning rod. The narrator is a nonconductor, a resistant figure standing in "the erectest, proudest posture" (*PT* 120). But in such a posture, the narrator's desire for autonomy can be cleverly recast as actually a more profound captivity and capitulation to nature's determined forces.

Such reversal is what the salesman performs in his final plea: "'Think of being a heap of charred offal, like a haltered horse burnt in his stall;—and all in one flash!'" (*PT* 124). The figure at the center of the passage—the "haltered horse burnt in his stall"—projects the state of redoubled lack of freedom upon the consequences of the narrator's refusal. Here, the individual freedom as resistance that the narrator would seem to champion, resistance to the coercive forces of religion and capitalism, comes to seem like a halter and a paradoxical lack of resistance to the thunderbolt. Intransigence, the refusal to allow oneself to be persuaded, is not freedom but rather its confinement.[5] Thus, fear in "The Lightning-Rod Man" both impinges on free will (the fear of being struck by lightning compels and coerces the individual to give up his freedom) and facilitates it (the fear of being struck by lightning enables the choice to divert natural necessity from its predetermined path). How can fear be used to play both roles? To help formulate an answer, I turn to Søren Kierkegaard, a writer who, like Melville, would propose affective descriptions of philosophical dilemmas.

Kierkegaard, in *The Concept of Dread* (1844), confronts the problem implicit in "The Lightning-Rod Man" and offers a similar solution.[6] In developing an account of how individual freedom can emerge from natural necessity, Kierkegaard introduces an affective term, *angest*. This term will continue to influence one strain of continental philosophy, notably the existentialism of Sartre and the phenomenology of Heidegger, by placing at the heart of human experience a feeling that is much like, but importantly distinct from, ordinary fear. Kierkegaard's term is today most commonly translated as "anxiety" but was originally translated into English as "dread." My own preference for the earlier translation, "dread," owes itself to the connotations of determinism in that term rather than the post-Freudian connotations of nervous disorder now sedimented in "anxiety." Dread, for Kierkegaard, is more functional than pathological; it plays an essential role in preparing for and ushering in individual freedom and responsibility from a deterministic field of necessary innocence.

Kierkegaard analyzes dread as a phenomenological experience in accordance with the fall of humanity through the sin of Adam. The basic problem for Kierkegaard is how to account for the origination of free will in a world of necessity. As one commentator summarizes: "Kierkegaard's penetrating analysis of the phenomenon of anxiety is generally thought to bridge the gap between innocence and guilt and to explain—insofar as this is possible—the paradoxical appearance of evil from an original goodness" (Cope 554). Evil and sin, the blameworthiness that is their essence, depend upon free will and a subject who would choose them. But between an original ignorant innocence and a later enlightened sinfulness, there is a qualitative gap that threatens an infinite regress to any explanation. Sin, as Kierkegaard points out, cannot come into the world through anything other than sin, and it cannot be committed by anything that isn't completely human:

> If one would say that Adam's sin brought the sin of the race into the world, one either means this fantastically, and thereby every concept is annulled, or one can with the same justification say it of every man who by his first sin brings in sinfulness. Getting an individual who has to stand outside the race to begin the race is a myth of the understanding, like that of letting sinfulness begin in any other way but by sin. What one attains is merely to retard the problem, which naturally turns then to man No. 2 for an explanation, or rather now it is man No. 1, since the first man No. 1 has become in effect No. 0. (31)

The echoes of regressive paradox reverberate strongly through Kierkegaard's description of the problem. Sin must be committed by someone capable of sinning. But if Adam is posited as the figure that makes it possible to sin, then he himself cannot at the same time be capable of sinning. What Kierkegaard has set out for himself, then, is the problem of explaining how free will and its consequent sin can come about if they are neither inherent in the original innocence of humanity nor brought about through any external influence or factor. In both "The Lightning-Rod Man" and *The Concept of Dread*, the problem of getting freedom from nature is described as a problem of contiguity—the "leap" of Kierkegaard spanning the gap like lightning crossing a nonconductive material—and is resolved through fear.

For just as Melville stages the drama of freedom and coercion within an economy of fear, Kierkegaard posits that the secret of freedom's emergence in nature is only experienced phenomenologically as a special kind of fear, namely, dread. Out of innocence and ignorance comes knowledge and freedom, Kierkegaard writes, but the initial self, innocent and whole, must contain an element of difference that would open up the possibility of freedom:

> In this state [innocence] there is peace and repose; but at the same time there is something different, which is not dissension and strife, for there is nothing to strive with. What is it then? Nothing. But what effect does nothing produce? It begets dread. This is the profound secret of innocence, that at the same time it is dread. Dreamingly the spirit projects its own reality, but this reality is nothing, but this nothing constantly sees innocence outside of it. (38)

In order to get to individual freedom, one must have a choice. And in order to have a choice, one must be able to imagine at least two possible futures for the self. But in order for the self to have the difference of two possible futures, it itself must have some characteristic of difference within itself—the self must be self-divided. In innocence, the self is differentiated only from nothing. So the origin of the self-difference underlying freedom must be in the difference of self from nothingness. Kierkegaard, at this point, claims that this initial self-difference, beginning from the self's difference from nothing, is experienced as affect rather than understood by logic. And that affect is dread.

One may wonder here, why dread? Indeed, Kierkegaard's philosophical critics who notice that the turn to affect can hardly be said to "solve" the inherent problem, leave open why dread is chosen as the special affect from which freedom emerges out of self-difference.[7] A psychological reading may explain that Kierkegaard simply "found," in his own experience, dread at the heart of freedom and the beginning of conscious thought. A biographical interpretation might point to Kierkegaard's Lutheran pietism and tie the importance of fear to religious experience in that theology to his later turn to it when presented with an apparently irrational paradox. But I would like to focus on how Kierkegaard defines the structure of dread—if it is the key to unlocking freedom, then perhaps Kierkegaard chose it because its shape fit the peculiar lock he imagined.

When Kierkegaard sets out to describe dread's field of self-difference, he writes that difference into a metaphor of sleeping and waking: "When awake, the difference between myself and my other is posited; sleeping, it is suspended; dreaming, it is a nothing vaguely hinted at" (38). But this "other," which is really the nothing of the self-differentiated self, may only be glimpsed in the aftereffect of the fear it inspires: "The reality of the spirit constantly shows itself in a form which entices its possibility, but it is away as soon as one grasps after it, and it is a nothing which is able only to alarm" (38). Drawing a distinction that will inspire Freud and Heidegger, Kierkegaard defines this particular feeling of the self as a kind of fear that is not fear: "I must therefore call attention to the fact that it is different from fear and similar concepts which refer to something definite, whereas dread is freedom's reality as possibility for possibility" (38). This is not to say that dread is entirely unlike fear, but rather it is fear without the definite object. Dread's structure, therefore, borrows from fear the orientation of being directed outward, but removes anything external for that orientation to grasp; Kierkegaard answers the problem of freedom's paradoxical emergence with a paradoxical feeling, one that estranges the internal self by looking out at external nothingness. As in Poe's description of perversity, such experience is like being on a precipice, threatened not by the height of it but by the subject's self-regard: "One may liken dread to dizziness. He whose eye chances to look down into the yawning abyss becomes dizzy. But the reason for it is just as much his eye as it is the precipice. For suppose he had not looked down. Thus dread is the dizziness of freedom" (55). Posing mood as possessing a unique logic of its own, Kierkegaard's dread critiques dialectical metaphysics as missing the affective insistence of the problem of freedom, the alarm that is not assuaged by dialectical explanation.[8]

The structure of dread prefigures freedom because it opens up self-difference and generates possibility. But to do so, it works negatively, as the encroaching feeling of being determined projects the category of being not-determined. Thus our ability to feel the dread of necessity guarantees our freedom: "[I]n dread there is the egoistic infinity of possibility, which does not tempt like a definite choice, but alarms (*aengster*) and fascinates with its sweet anxiety (*Beaengstelse*)" (55). Kierkegaard chooses dread precisely because, in his definition, it reflects the paralyzing paradox of nothingness with the urgency of fear. The acceptance of fear by the narrator in "The Lightning-Rod Man" may thus appear to gain freedom through its exercise, but the hollowness of his victory would seem to be due to the way he has released himself from the dread that would make such freedom apparent. There is no struggle on the narrator's part; he is from the start self-determined, a completely free subject. What becomes strange, then, is the way complete subjectivity looks more and more like determinism in the absence of dread.

Turning back to the way that fear is the site of central antagonism in "The Lightning-Rod Man," we discover that the tale's ironies anticipate the problem from which Kierkegaardian dread emerges. Through the narrator and the salesman, Melville opposes two equally dogmatic responses to fear, staging the problem fear poses for subjectivity through a manifestly dialectical engagement. It would seem that the narrator triumphs, becoming a perfectly autonomous subject according to a Cartesian model; he rejects fear as coercive of individual freedom just as he rejects the lightning rod as coercive of providential destiny. But in such a rejection, the narrator also seems to distance himself, not just from the salesman but from the reader's capacity for sympathy. In opening himself up to the environment, dispelling fear by becoming an object contiguous with the world, his subjectivity comes to look less like human freedom and more like elemental physics. The salesman, on the other hand, advocates restricting conductivity, insulating the self from the environment, and thus getting rid of fear by actively catering to it. Both positions undertake an inoculation of fear to free the subject, fleeing a second-order Kierkegaardian subjectivity (characterized by dread) in their advocacy and pursuit of a first-order Cartesian subjectivity (characterized by autonomy).

"The Lightning-Rod Man" imagines perfect freedom in the absolute banishment of fear, either by removing the threat or submitting to it entirely. Yet this freedom is finally troubled by the sense that it is too perfect, that in getting rid of fear entirely, freedom slides into an even more tyrannical determinism. Yet the spatialized difference between the two characters projects negatively the self-difference that dread installs within the Kierkegaardian subject, the self-difference that prevents a subject from being so wholly self-determined that its perfected freedom becomes null. Between their static positions, Melville plots the coordinates for another kind of relation to fear, the more reflexive one described by Kierkegaardian dread, in which subjective freedom comes forward only through its deep fear of that dream (or nightmare) of the idealized, fearless, autonomous, and undifferentiated subject. It is in the other *Piazza Tales* that the spatial rift of "The Lightning-Rod Man" becomes a central affective complex, a disalignment felt by both character and reader.

## Thrownness

The central dilemma of "The Lightning-Rod Man" opens up the space between two versions of freedom that equally fall back into similar kinds of determinism. The question then seems to be, is there a way to think freedom with fear, to describe more closely the phenomenological mood of dread that Kierkegaard situates as the origin of individualized subjectivity? And what complications might be imposed upon a Cartesian-inflected conception of free subjectivity by the implication that subjectivity itself comes out of a fear of subjectivity?

We may find the beginning of an answer in deep undercurrents of melancholy, anxiety, and unease that run in the other, more explicitly dread-filled tales of the collection. These ugly feelings, more pervasive moods than passionate eruptions, are difficult to pin down to specific objective causes. Indeed, they come to be associated not so much with this or that experience within the world but rather with experience itself taken generally. We feel this centrifugal pull in moments like the telescopic extrapolation from "Ah Bartleby!" to "Ah humanity!" (*PT* 45) and in the abstract shadow of "'[t]he negro'" (*PT* 116) that haunts Don Benito even after the immediate threat of slave insurrection has been quelled. Delano, in trying to cheer his companion, might as well have been responding to the author of *The Piazza Tales*: "'You generalize, Don Benito; and mournfully enough'" (*PT* 116). This atmospheric drift, in which the immediate fears of the tales generalize outward toward the human condition, should not be taken, however, as a loss of focus or willful obscurantism. For, when regarded across the collection, Melville's moods consistently take shape through two motifs—as an impelled movement through space (such as the narrator's quest in "The Piazza" or the lawyer's flight from his office in "Bartleby") or as a concern with the indexical markers of time (such as the calendar of the Cholla widow in "The Encantadas" or the "'tall man and time-piece'" [*PT* 93] of Atufal in "Benito Cereno"). Melville's fears may feel abstract in *The Piazza Tales* because they orient themselves along the abstract conditions and modes of phenomenal experience itself: space and time.

By turning to these fundamental categories of experience, Melville anticipates the spatial and temporal extension of Kierkegaardian dread that Martin Heidegger performs in *Being and Time* (1927). Heidegger, analyzing further the dimensions of the Kierkegaardian "gap," takes Kierkegaard's dread as fundamental in the definition of *Dasein* (roughly translated as "the being of the human"): "the basic state-of-mind of anxiety [dread] as a distinctive way in which Dasein is disclosed" (228).[9] Dread, in *Being and Time*, becomes the modal feeling through which Dasein individuates itself, feels its own self-difference from the world as an experience of both spatial displacement and temporal immanence. Dread individuates the subject spatially through a kind of ungrounded sky-hook maneuver, casting the subject out through an incessant movement that Heidegger calls *thrownness*. Dread likewise attends to the temporalization of Dasein by offering an experience of authentic, primordial time, one that is always obscured and "leveled off"[10] by the inauthentic mechanized time promised by the clock or the calendar. In opening up both a space and a time outside of our conventional or worldly sense, dread signals a confrontation with the insignificance of the world-at-hand, fearing not things in the world nor events that await in the future but rather the deeper alienness behind our capacities to regard the world in the first place. Even though the concepts of space and time cannot finally be either distinguished or collapsed together—as Heidegger notes, "the demonstration that this spatiality is existentially possible only through temporality, cannot aim either at deducing space from time or at dissolving it into pure time" (418)—they may be treated separately (as Heidegger does in parts 1 and 2 of his treatise). While we should keep in mind that Melville often plays upon the translations and miscalibrations between space and time—most literally in the way the lightning-rod salesman uses the time between lightning and thunder to measure distance—it will therefore be clearer to treat Melville's invocations of dread's spatial and temporal aspects sequentially at first.

In the first part of *Being and Time*, Heideigger figures dread through a series of spatial metaphors, a rhetorical drama of moving toward and away from, turning, throwing, falling, and sinking:

> Our Interpretation of fear as a state-of-mind has shown that in each case that in the face of which we fear is a detrimental entity within-the-world which comes from some definite region but is close by and is bringing itself close, and yet might stay away. In falling, Dasein turns away from itself. . . . Thus the turning-away of falling is not a fleeing that is founded upon a fear of entities within-the-world. . . . [W]hat this turning-away does is precisely to *turn thither* towards entities within-the-world by absorbing itself in them. *The turning-away of falling is grounded rather in anxiety [dread], which in turn is what first makes fear possible.* (230)

By relating dread to fear first, as an orientation that is affected by movement and proximity, Heidegger's removal of any specific site of fear generates the paradoxical recursiveness of Dasein revealing itself to itself. What Dasein dreads is an entity that "is Dasein itself." And thus the threat itself implies that nothing in the world is significant at all—the world "falls" or "sinks" away in the contemplation of Dasein by Dasein in dread:

> That in the face of which one is anxious [feels dread] is completely indefinite. Not only does this indefiniteness leave factically undecided which entity within-the-world is threatening us, but it also tells us that entities within-the-world are not "relevant" at all. . . . Here the totality of involvements of the ready-to-hand

and the present-at-hand discovered within-the-world, is, as such, of no consequence; it collapses into itself; the world has the character of completely lacking significance. (231)

Dread thus is not caused by anything particular in the world but rather "the world as such" (231). By describing Dasein and dread in spatial terms of falling or turning away, despite not occurring within worldly space, Heidegger implies that dread offers a kind of self-propelled movement by which Dasein can distinguish itself from the insignificance of the world and in such a movement make that world available as such for thought.

Put in this way, dread is conceptualized in movement, not as something which impels movement. The in-motion quality of dread discloses the "there" of Dasein (literally, "being-there"), its spatiality within the world,[11] through what Heidegger terms "thrownness": "An entity of the character of Dasein is its 'there' in such a way that . . . it finds itself [*sich befindet*] in its thrownness" (174; brackets in original). The curious way in which subjectivity is routed through a kind of anxiety movement, a dread voyage, is the emphasis of Sianne Ngai's retheorization of thrownness as the last resort of the intellectual facing the epistemological chasm of blank skepticism and unending nondifference. Ngai theorizes that, for the tradition in Western philosophy associated with Kierkegaard and Heidegger, dread is revealed by the structure of thrownness, of ejection and movement through space, that characterizes intellectual pursuit: "[T]he externalizing aspect of 'projection' which the image of thrownness hyperbolizes can be perceived not just as a strategy for displacing anxiety [dread], but as the means by which the affect assumes its particular form" (212). That is, dread is not originally interior and then projectively exterior but is from the start engaged in the concept of spatialization in general. For Ngai, the thrownness that she identifies in knowledge-seeking subjects is what ultimately "rescu[es] the intellectual from his potential absorption in sites of asignificance or negativity" (246). Ngai's study reveals the paradoxical self-levitation enabled by dread, the way in which dread's particular logic, made conceptually available through spatial figuration, generates distance without admitting position: "[T]he fantasy of thrownness . . . enables the intellectual to achieve a strategic form of *distance* without the fixed or constant positions on which our concept of distance ordinarily depends" (246–247).

Melville emplots the narrative arc of Ngai's intellectual in flight in the first tale of his collection, "The Piazza." The tale begins as a type of romantic quest, the narrator venturing forth from his house and mundane domestic life in pursuit of an enchanted "fairy-land" capable of redeeming a richer significance to the world: "No more; I'll launch my yawl—ho, cheerly, heart! and push away for fairy-land—for rainbow's end, in fairy-land" (*PT* 6). Yet, when he meets an insurmountable obstacle, the depressing reality of a woman, Marianna, toiling in her wasp-infested wreck of a house, he retreats back to his house: "—Enough. Launching my yawl no more for fairy-land, I stick to the piazza" (*PT* 12). In the aftermath of this failure, what linger are ghostly presences of dread radiating from a now-constant movement and displacement.[12] For though the narrator seemingly resigns himself to a stationary perspective, it is at night, "when the curtain falls," that "truth comes in with darkness" (*PT* 12), that he is again thrown into incessant movement, restaging his intellectual search as a now-delimited pacing: "To and fro I walk the piazza deck, haunted by Marianna's face, and many as real a story" (*PT* 12). Like the chiasmus that bookends his journey—"No more; I'll launch my yawl"; "Launching my yawl no more"—the dynamics of the narrator's journey become reversible, capable of endless oscillation without arrival. Back and forth, the narrator is thrown into the choreography of dread as an engagement with the darkness of truth and the insignificance of the world.

The narrator's apparent failure directs attention back to the initial moment of his "launching," for if his journey corresponds to the thrownness of the intellectual, as Ngai describes, then we might consider more closely how the original impetus of the voyage aligns with the sites of nonsignificance and negativity that, in theory, promote thrownness as a strategy of individuation. The narrator's initial launch is an act of being repelled, specifically by the sight of a vermin infestation. It is in the description of the vermin, and their relation to the narrator's efforts to cultivate a Chinese creeper vine, that we find Melville's construction of nonsignificance and negativity:

> I could not bear to look upon a Chinese creeper of my adoption, and which, to my delight, climbing a post of the piazza, had burst out in starry bloom, but now, if you removed the leaves a little, showed millions of strange, cankerous worms, which, feeding upon those blossoms, so shared their blessed hue, as to make it unblessed evermore—worms, whose germs had doubtless lurked in the very bulb which, so hopefully, I had planted: in this ingrate peevishness of my weary convalescence, was I sitting there. (*PT* 6)

Melville's Chinese creeper scene suggests that beneath fair surfaces lie foul creatures. But it also emphasizes that what makes the worms repellent is their pestilential contamination of color. It is not that the worms are destroying the blossoms but that they are absorbing their color, eroding distinction, so that the blossoms and worms become, to the eye at least, the same. The unblessedness of this spread of color is a revelation of nondifference underlying the tonal variation of color.[13] Reminiscent of Ishmael's terror of the "colorless, all-color" which "would touch all objects, even tulips and roses, with its own blank tinge" (*MD* 195), the Chinese creeper scene launches the narrator into his thrownness by revealing to him a negativity based in contamination. The spread of color belies the attempt to cultivate difference (a difference emphasized in the exotic foreignness of the plant), suggesting the threat of absorption from which the subject must flee.

Since the infestation that "had lurked in the very bulb" from the start begets the narrator's romantic quest, then the entire voyage that follows may be seen as a desperate attempt to recover the original assumption of difference. Such search for otherness fails when he discovers in Marianna merely a reflection of his own distressed melancholy. The narrator's more restricted thrownness—the pacing on the piazza—thus inhabits the search itself and acknowledges the ultimate failure to discriminate (in the adoption of the exotic, in the discovery of a fairyland) any difference that would recuperate the significance of the world. That is, dread, manifest as incessant movement, operates to install an individuating subjectivity in the face of negativity as sameness.

A spatial repulsion from the nondifference that would be brought close is also the organization of the next tale in the collection, "Bartleby, the Scrivener." What perspective "The Piazza" sheds on "Bartleby" may be seen in the moments of attraction and repulsion between the narrator and his obscure copyist. It may be easy to simply assert that Bartleby, in his confounding refusals, comes to embody a site of negation. But the story uses an organization of space, the narrator's movement in relation to Bartleby's stationary omnipresence—"he was always there"—to figure in dread not only the subject's relation to negation as sameness, but also the more alien sense that such a site of negativity corresponds to a fantasy of perfected and idealized subjectivity.

The narrator is expelled several times in "Bartleby," and, as in "The Piazza," these expulsions are figured as repulsions by sights of sameness, though here the sameness resides in Bartleby's implacable consistency. Finding Bartleby in the office on a Sunday, the narrator finds himself directed to "walk round the block two or three times"(*PT* 26), a dictate to which he accedes, citing the "strange effect" of Bartleby's "cadaverously gentlemanly *nonchalance*, yet withal firm and self-possessed" that evicts him: "[I]ncontinently I slunk away from my own door, and did as desired" (*PT* 27). Incontinent, the narrator registers the absence of self-integrity in the face of Bartleby's firm self-possession. In the following pages, the narrator's feeling of self-differentiation manifests in habitual walking: "I walked homeward, thinking what I would do with Bartleby" (*PT* 29); "As I walked home in a pensive mood, my vanity got the better of my pity" (*PT* 33); "After breakfast, I walked down town, arguing the probabilities *pro* and *con*" (*PT* 34); "And so I kept veering about" (*PT* 34). This wandering about contrasts starkly with Bartleby's motionlessness, his admitted preference: "'I like to be stationary'" (*PT* 41). In what seems the final confrontation, the narrator stages his own displacement as an effect of Bartleby's stationary presence:

> "Stationary you shall be then," I cried, now losing all patience, and for the first time in all my exasperating connection with him fairly flying into a passion. "If you do not go away from these premises before night, I shall feel bound—indeed I *am* bound—to—to—to quit the premises myself!" I rather absurdly concluded, knowing not with what possible threat to try to frighten his immobility into compliance. (*PT* 41)

Succumbing to the motionless specter of Bartleby, the narrator, "flying into a passion" and away from his office, renders affect and spatial distance analogous to one another. Even in the figuration of the narrator's inability "to frighten his immobility," we sense the connection between fear and mobility; within what seems a frustrated capitulation is the tighter wire of terror. Thus propelled, the narrator's final separation from Bartleby takes the shape of a manic and thoroughgoing spatial displacement: "[F]or a few days I drove about the upper part of the town and through the suburbs, in my rockaway. . . . In fact I almost lived in my rockaway for the time" (*PT* 42). Thrown into flight, the narrator manifests in motion the dread that he feels at the limit of sympathy, feeling his "melancholy merge into fear" and "pity into repulsion" (*PT* 29). Bartleby is a site of stubborn negativity, outside the reach of the narrator's sympathy and generative of the narrator's self-differential dread through his presentation of a completely unmitigated and wholly self-possessed subjectivity.

In the character of Bartleby's self-possession, marked as undivided preference in will and a "freedom from all dissipation" (*PT* 25), negativity is conceived not only as a uniform sameness but also as the inaccessibility of a perfect, autonomous, and insular freedom. That is, the lack of difference in Bartleby results in the peculiar shape of freedom by resistance that Melville explores in "The Lightning-Rod Man." Just as the narrator of the latter tale exerts a freedom from coercion by adopting a more wholesale fatalism, Bartleby's passive resistance to all coercion makes his relation to "humanity" more and more problematic. Although it may be tempting to read Bartleby as an object, as a piece of stubborn furniture without any preference, it is perhaps just as enlightening to read Bartleby as the ideal Cartesian subject, as the one truly willed and self-determined character. Nothing sways Bartleby. As Branka Arsić notes, Bartleby is "the monolithic activity of the will: a self inhabited exclusively by itself, incapable of any receptivity, a windowless room with a locked door" (*Passive Constitutions* 20). Thus his initial refusal to compare his copy with the original, to "verify the accuracy of his copy" (*PT* 20), can be read as denying the possibility of error (the self-difference that inheres in Kierkegaard's concept of sin). And his later refusal to copy at all then becomes the only possible willed action—because it *isn't* action—in the world of coercion and duplication that encroaches on the freedom of originality. The estrangement the reader, and the narrator, feel when approaching Bartleby again and again, the quality that leads McCall to find the tale "truly haunting" in its double claims upon a narrator who "understands, because he can't, quite" (*PT* 152), may be understood through the ambiguous darkness of dread—the feeling that attends and opens the phenomenological subject's recognition of a perfected subjective freedom, even as it measures in fear the distance between that subject and that freedom.[14]

To recast Bartleby as the ideal of a perfect Cartesian subject, transparent and perfectly self-consistent (opaque only to those who cannot fathom such consistency), reframes Giorgio Agamben's and Gilles Deleuze's related readings of Bartleby as a messianic figure, a "new Christ" (Deleuze 90) who "comes not, like Jesus, to redeem what was, but to save what was not" (Agamben 270). Agamben reads Bartleby as pure potentiality or contingency, an "experiment without truth" that appears so strange to us because it is "by definition withdrawn from both truth conditions and ... the principle of contradiction" (261). Similarly, Deleuze reads the attorney as recoiling from the threat of a new community of Bartlebys, one in which the "hero of pragmatism is not the successful businessman, it is Bartleby" (88). Beyond the binary logic of positive and negative in Agamben's account, and outside the bounds of paternalistic relation in Deleuze's, Bartleby hovers over a separate and new ontology, one that is freed from reason's enstructuring principle: "Emancipating itself from Being and non-Being alike, potentiality thus creates its own ontology" (Agamben 259). Agreeing with their claim that Bartleby represents some new and strange ontology that exceeds binary categories (by exhibiting a radical freedom of which reason only dreams), my reading above would yet return attention to the ugly feelings of repulsion, alienation, and even terror that this display engenders in the attorney. There is something new in Bartleby, what Arsić has captured as the interruption of the Original, an "atmosphere of different thinking" (10) that disables the "familiar" modes of interpretation that would comprehend him. To glimpse Bartleby's newness is to be repelled by it, feelingly.

And thus the attorney's anxiety can be seen as a response to the prospect of this new, pragmatist messiah of contingency. But these feelings determine Bartleby's originality through differentiation, by measuring out the distance between our internally divided selves and this specter of potentiality, of raw and unconditioned freedom. By shifting attention from Bartleby's prospect to the attorney's trial of affective disaffiliation, what is opened up for experience is not quite the possibility of following Bartleby's lead into a nonbinary, nonlogical formlessness of thought but rather the constitution of our phenomenological subjectivity out of the projective repulsion that such a prospect induces. Like the dead letters that Bartleby handles, "[o]n errands of life . . . speed[ing] to death" (*PT* 45), what may finally be most significant is neither the good intention nor the failed outcome but rather how the misalignments in space and time (the letters arrive too late, doomed to be lost in their thrown transit) produce the difference of the feeling subject from the free one.

### Now-Time

In Heidegger's treatment of dread across the two parts of *Being and Time*, dread is rigged not only to spatialization but to temporalization. In space, dread becomes feeling through thrownness. In time, as we will see, dread becomes the orientation of "being-toward-death," a primal orientation that underlies our conceptualization of time itself. Bringing Heidegger's temporalization of dread to bear on *The Piazza Tales* opens a correlative vantage to its spatial formulation of Dasein in flight from its own idealization. For Melville's collection not only portrays protagonists in flight, experiencing dread through movement, but also returns again and again to a peculiar motif of time's measurement. The multiple mechanisms of time telling—clocks and calendars, pocket watches and sundials—manifest a concern with the projective and supplementary character of chronometry. Affixing time becomes, in Melville's fiction as well as in Heidegger's philosophy, the dreadful correlative to the flight of thrownness.

Of the moments in Melville's collection which signal an awareness of the existential boundedness of space and time, the most pronounced occurs in the account of Hunilla, in "The Encantadas," watching from shore as her husband and brother drown in the ocean. In this passage, Melville collapses time into an instant while opening space into a wide gulf, a literary version of the cinematic track-out/forward-zoom effect that destabilizes the relationship between figure and ground:

> So instant was the scene, so trance-like its mild pictorial effect, so distant from her blasted bower and her common sense of things, that Hunilla gazed and gazed, nor raised a finger or a wail. But as good to sit thus dumb, in stupor staring on that dumb show, for all that otherwise might be done. With half a mile of sea between, how could her two enchanted arms aid those four fated ones? The distance long, the time one sand. After the lightning is beheld, what fool shall stay the thunderbolt? (*PT* 154)

Here time and space are both conjoined and miscalibrated—"the distance long, the time one sand." The event for which she should have extreme affective involvement is perceived as one of insignificance; it falls away before her as a kind of sinking: "Before Hunilla's eyes they sank. The real woe of this event passed before her sight as a sham tragedy on the stage" (*PT* 154). The sinking of her brother and husband is echoed as a sinking of "real woe" into "sham tragedy," and the incited passion is thus not woe but the second-order dread that modulates such sinking of significance: "In anxiety [dread] what is environmentally ready-at-hand sinks away, and so, in general, do entities within-the-world" (Heidegger 232). In Melville's formulation, the loss of the beloved companions is juxtaposed with the loss of the significance of that loss. Thus, if Hunilla's perception here is touched with dread, then it would seem to play upon the interrelation of space and time, her thrownness now not merely spatial individuation but also temporal dislocation rendered as the hiatus between lightning flash and thunderbolt. To better understand how space and time work together as dreadful elements in Melville's fiction, it will be helpful to retrieve the basic steps of Heidegger's temporal theory. For just as Heidegger's spatialization of dread through thrownness explains the significance of movement as affect in Melville's fiction, his temporalization through dread reveals the deep affective underpinning of Melville's clocks and calendars.

Heidegger's theorization of the temporality of dread may be summarized by three points. Heidegger claims that dread is the temporality of authentic being-toward-death: "Being-towards-death is essentially anxiety [dread]" (310). Subsequently, being-toward-death corresponds with an authentic conception of time, that of "primordial time," as distinguished from the ordinary conception of time which Heidegger terms "now-time" or the "world-time" presented by clocks. And last, even though primordial time is held distinct from now-time, the "leveling-off" that now-time performs still contains traces of the primordial time that it levels, and thus the dread of being-toward-death can still be incited by aspects of now-time.

The distinction between these two temporalities (now-time and primordial time) can be understood as following from a distinction in our way of thinking about death. Heidegger claims that death has two senses, the commonplace understanding of death which he locates in the bromide "Death is certain," and the authentic understanding of death as pure possibility: "[I]t must be understood *as a possibility*, it must be cultivated *as a possibility*, and we must *put up with* it *as a possibility*, in the way we comport ourselves towards it" (306). The first understanding is a way of sanitizing death's dreadful power; we think that death is something which is certain to happen but has not happened yet ("One says, 'Death certainly comes, but not right away.' With this 'but . . . ,' the 'they' denies that death is certain" [302]). The second understanding is more radically aware that death is not something that is experienced later but is experienced immediately as possibility: "*Death is*, as *Dasein's* end, in the Being of this entity *towards* its end" (303). Thus the authentic being-toward-death acknowledges death as in the present, as operating prior to that commonplace consideration of death that would cast it into some future state.

Authentic being-toward-death would thus seem to have the character of dwelling on death as it intrudes upon everyday life, an orientation that Melville approximates in the strange vision of the tortoise's memento mori in "The Encantadas": "For often in scenes of social merriment . . . I have drawn the attention of my comrades by my fixed gaze and sudden change of air, as I have seemed to see, slowly emerging from those imagined solitudes, and heavily crawling along the floor, the ghost of a gigantic tortoise, with 'Memento ****' burning in live letters upon his back" (*PT* 129). Authentic being-toward-death is obviously not a practical attitude, and Heidegger does not load into "authenticity" a prescriptive or evaluative sense; since being-toward-death is "essentially anxiety [dread]," it is thus a state in which the world-at-hand falls away into insignificance, detaching one from social engagement through a recognition of death's constant and ubiquitous claim. Not just upon the desolate islands do we feel this authentic dread of death, as Melville's tortoise-in-the-parlor scene implies, but everywhere and always.

The unique temporal character of being-toward-death corresponds, for Heidegger, with an authentic category of time, which he calls "primordial time." Since being-toward-death is unceasing and ever-present, it opens a different sense of the future than the "'now' which has *not yet* become 'actual'" (373). Thus this primordial time is not a linear sequence but rather a phenomenological category that arises out of the anticipation of being-toward-death: "Anticipation makes Dasein *authentically* futural, and in such a way that the anticipation itself is possible only in so far as Dasein, *as being*, is always coming towards itself—that is to say, in so far as it is futural in its Being in general" (373). Primordial time is distinguished from the linear sequence of now-time or world-time. Now-time is the ordinary way of thinking about time as an endless succession of nows, a way of thinking that has become associated, for Heidegger, with the mechanism of the clock: "Thus when *time* is *measured*, it is *made public* in such a way that it is encountered on each occasion and at any time for everyone as 'now and now and now.' This time which is 'universally' accessible in clocks is something that we come across as a *present-at-hand multiplicity of 'nows,'* so to speak, though the measuring of time is not directed thematically towards time as such" (470). This temporality grounded in clocks ends up "leveling off" the significance of primordial time, making time a public entity in the world, removing time from Dasein and covering over the essential finitude of primordial time.[15] The leveling off here is the same kind of evasion that the everyday conception of death undertakes, and both are habits of covering up, by falling into the world or into the "now," the fundamental character of Dasein that is grasped in dread.

It is this difference between primordial time as an authentic and dreadful being-toward-death and now-time as an inauthentic leveling off of significance that explains the affective valence of Melville's concern with time's measurement. In "The Encantadas," following the drowning scene analyzed earlier, Melville depicts Hunilla as negotiating between now-time and primordial time. After her companions' deaths, she falls out of now-time, forced into a "labyrinth" of undifferentiated primordial time: "Little accurate note of time had Hunilla taken under such emotions as were hers, and little, outside herself, served for calendar or dial" (*PT* 155); "Time was her labyrinth, in which Hunilla was entirely lost" (*PT* 156). The timelessness of this state is related to her contemplation of death, not only precipitated by the deaths of others but in its now-constant draw that renders now-time insignificant: "[T]o those whom earth's sure indraft draws, patience or impatience is still the same" (*PT* 156). Lifting herself from the timelessness of death's contemplation requires projecting an arbitrary measurement, reasserting a "now" in the world. But such a move involves a sacrifice, a leveling off, an exchange that trades "sane despair" for a "hope which is but mad":

> "The ship sails this day, to-day," at last said Hunilla to herself; "this gives me certain time to stand on; without certainty I go mad. In loose ignorance I have hoped and hoped; now in firm knowledge I will but wait. Now I live and no longer perish in bewilderings. . . . Oh, past length of weary weeks—all to be dragged over—to buy the certainty of to-day, I freely give ye, though I tear ye from me!" (*PT* 156)

Marking days as notches upon a reed from that point forward, Hunilla launches herself from the being-toward-death ("perish in bewilderings") into now-time, a resurrection linked to the momentous present ("*Now* I live"). Time's measurement becomes the route out of dread, out of the bewildering labyrinth of primordial time.

Yet leveling off by way of time's measurement does not, according to Heidegger, entirely displace the being-toward-death of primordial time or the dread which is its essence. Primordial time can still be seen in now-time, but through distortion: "[J]ust as he who flees in the face of death is pursued by it even as he evades it . . . even the innocuous infinite sequence of 'nows' which simply runs its course, imposes itself 'on' Dasein in a remarkably enigmatical way" (477).[16] Now-time, characterized here as analogous to fleeing in the face of death, would seem to bear, even in the marks that level off primordial time, a trace of the dread which it suppresses. This helps to explain why, in *The Piazza Tales*, the clocks and calendars, the notches in the reed and the chimes of the bell tower, would seem to be occasions for dread; all that is skimmed off primordial time by the leveling function of now-time is displaced into the indexical marks of the latter.

In "Benito Cereno," a story over which looms a pall of dread from its very first pages, Melville imposes a rigid and seemingly superfluous gridwork of now-time. A forecastle bell marks time, intruding into the narrative at several auspicious moments, and is joined in its temporal function by the presence of Atufal, the seemingly captive slave who performs his punishment with periodic regularity every two hours. The punctuality of Atufal gives him the character of a clock and is explicitly referred to as such: "your tall man and time-piece, Atufal" (*PT* 93). These emblems of now-time, punctuating the narrative, set up the scene where Delano glimpses, for a moment and in the dread of an instant, a sense of his deception:

> He was hardly midway in the narrow corridor, dim as a tunnel, leading from the cabin to the stairs, when a sound, as of the tolling for execution in some jail-yard, fell on his ears. It was the echo of the ship's flawed bell, striking the hour, drearily reverberated in this subterranean vault. Instantly, by a fatality not to be withstood, his mind, responsive to the portent, swarmed with superstitious suspicions. He paused. In images far swifter than these sentences, the minutest details of all his former distrusts swept through him. (*PT* 95–96)

Why should the bell's tolling have such an effect? When considered against Heidegger's understanding of the trace of dread in now-time, Delano's instantaneous and fatal dread can be read as residing in the mark of now, in that slice of nothingness which is all that remains of primordial time's being-toward-death. Thus, the images must run "far swifter than these sentences" because the sentences, read in time, would overrun the signal hiatus of the tolling itself. Struck from the continuum of now-time, this moment offers a pause in which the deceit can be seen, not only on the level of the duplicitous crew but in the concept of now-time itself, hinted at by the flaw in the bell.[17] Significantly, it is only by moving past Atufal that the narrator is able to quiet his distress. The narrow, tunnel-like corridor, the darkness of that transition, is accompanied by the tolling of a bell that would make the experience of that passage, the terror it engenders, an imaginative point between times and places. A hiatus in time, a thrownness in space, a terror in darkness: the event of Delano's passage is the nonsite and nontime of the dread that laces the narrative.

Unlike the case of Hunilla, who, alone and lost, comes to dread naturally and must wrest herself into the "now-time" that characterizes life with others, Delano habitually suppresses his dread by appealing to the imagined domesticity, the "benign aspect of nature" (*PT* 96), of the scene around him. In this respect they approach the mark of time from different directions. Hunilla imposes the artificiality of now-time in order to level off the dread of her temporal labyrinth. Delano is only able to feel behind that artificiality, to get outside the everyday world, in the estrangement that the slivered mark of time provides.[18]

In this respect, Melville's "Benito Cereno" draws from the more explicit rendering of the dread and being-toward-death of now-time in Poe's "The Masque of the Red Death." The tolling of the bell of the *San Dominick* functions in the same way as the tolling of the clock in Poe's story of the doomed masquerade; it uses the mark of time as the memento mori that reveals the fundamental dread of death that is covered over by chronometrical quantification:

> [W]hile the chimes of the clock yet rang, it was observed that the giddiest grew pale, and the more aged and sedate passed their hands over their brows. . . . But when the echoes had fully ceased, a light laughter at once pervaded the assembly . . . and then, after the lapse of sixty minutes, (which embrace three thousand and six hundred seconds of the Time that flies,) there came yet another chiming of the clock, and then were the same disconcert and tremulousness and meditation as before. (*TS* 1:672–673)

Poe's story of the dread of time's measurement locates it in the alienated state that exists outside of now-time's busy numbering, that emerges from the fractures in now-time and generates an affective dread from within the necessary distinctions (the tolling of the bell, the chiming of the clock) that allow for its measurement. Poe here and Melville more generally are drawn to the mechanism of the clock for the very reason that they would seek to portray what it works to conceal, the dread of being-toward-death that remains as a trace in its projected marks. Versions of clocks in *The Piazza Tales*—from the lightning-rod salesman's pulse to Nippers's face in "Bartleby" to Hunilla's reed to Atufal's presence—make time present and measurable. As kinds of fiction, though— Hunilla's arbitrary decision to begin time "now," for instance, or Atufal's dissimulation of servitude—these points of connection with the temporal world of others are from the start flimsy and convenient, saying "infinity" in the face of death's finitude. As space is made accessible through the flight of dread, so too does dread manifest itself in time. We can thus restage Ngai's spatial claim that thrownness not only displaces anxiety but is "the means by which the affect assumes its particular form" (212) in a temporal register: the leveling off of now-time not only suppresses the dread of being-toward-death but is also the means by which dread assumes its particular form.

We may come back, then, to the question that opened the investigation of dread's spatial and temporal character, about the relation between fear and subjective freedom. For in my reading of "The Lightning-Rod Man" I had suggested that autonomous subjectivity came to seem like freedom's impingement. Kierkegaard's concept of dread, picked up by Heidegger, assumes more perceptual contours and is embedded within the concepts of space and time that organize experience. Thus, to confront and vanquish fear, as the narrator of "The Lightning-Rod Man" would do, would be to tear down with it fundamental categories of phenomenal experience; an absolute subjectivity would come at significant cost. The intertwined motifs of spatial movement and temporal measurement in Melville's collection thus show how mood—dread, in particular—manifests individuation without subjectivity. Or, to put it more strongly, Melville shows how dread, emerging as the character of repulsion from sites of negativity and as the temporal orientation toward death, determines the individual by way of its difference from either undifferentiated space or universalized time.

The physical space opened up between the two characters of "The Lightning-Rod Man," and the conceptual distance between the threat of and desire for contact that those characters represent, thus offers in negative the miscalibration that dread will come to express positively. What the linked motifs of space and time do for Melville is to develop dread as an "in-between" orientation that inheres in detached movement rather than the positive coordinates of space, and in the stitches rather than the spans of time. Taking this model of dread and returning to the problem of fear in the final tale, "The Bell-Tower," Melville again stages the desire to abolish fear and thus to perfect, apparently, the absolute subject. In this final tale, presided over by a giant clock atop a tower raised to unprecedented heights, Melville brings together the motifs of distance over space and the mark in time, as means by which to accomplish the dream of being free from all fear. The solution, as we will see, which feels no dread, all the more inspires it.

### The Monster of Method: "The Bell-Tower"

In this final section, I analyze how the gothic tale "The Bell-Tower" employs the two dread-inscribed motifs, spatial dislocation and temporal marking, to address the problem of "The Lightning-Rod Man": the ambition to perfect the autonomous subject by wholly eliminating fear. "The Bell-Tower" casts as its solution a robotic automaton, a physical mechanism that terrifies not because it is an object but rather because it comes to play, through its relation to space and time, the indifferent and wholly undivided pure Cartesian subject. Subjectivity in this sense is being at once perfectly free and perfectly enslaved, inspiring human dread through the asymmetry it demands between subject and object. To perfectly balance the system, to defeat dread in all its stages, to conquer distance's estrangement, to precisely and for the last time admeasure time in perfect iteration—these all are the goals of the automaton's doomed engineer, Bannadonna. His method, that of the automatic supplement, displaces the searches and retreats in the other tales. Free from fear itself, Bannadonna's automaton fulfills the promise of perfect, undivided subjectivity. Yet the dread it inspires in us shapes a more contingent, limited affective phenomenological subjectivity, characterized by internal difference and capable of thought.

"The Bell-Tower" is at first glance an allegory of the dangers of pride. The tale, set in Renaissance Italy, depicts the design and construction of a gigantic bell tower by the eccentric genius Bannadonna. Contracted to construct it by the town's nobles, Bannadonna builds not only the tallest tower but also the biggest bell for it. His final piece, however, an automaton concealed under a domino veil, is an object of apprehension and dread for the townspeople. On the day of its revealing, Bannadonna is found dead, having been killed by the automaton he designed specifically for striking the bell on each hour. The clichéd moral that ends the tale, "Pride goeth before the fall," would seem to evacuate any deeper meaning from the gothic fable. But having prepared for this tale by noting the conceptual significance of struggles with fear (the fear of the nobles and others), distances in space (the height of the tower), and markings of time (the striking of the bell), we are in a position to assess the philosophical stakes of the phenomenological dread in both the project and its failure.

Critics have most often been drawn to "The Bell-Tower" because of its oblique relation to slavery. The reference to slavery in the epigram—"Like negroes, these powers own man sullenly; mindful of their higher master; while serving, plot revenge" (*PT* 174)—echoes the plot of "Benito Cereno" and thus enables Carolyn Karcher to read the automaton as a figure for the black slave and Bannadonna as the morally bankrupt slave owner whom the state nevertheless tacitly supports.[19] Russ Castronovo likewise reads the tale as a critique of slavery, focusing on how the tale's broken temporality enables the nobles and their republic to place "the sins of their own history in the parenthesis of forgetfulness to deny a temporal continuity that would indict their state" (537). Reading the tale as an allegory for slavery, though indispensable for an understanding of how race and slavery influence Melville's work, can risk leveling out the tale's strange particulars in pursuit of an ideologically coherent message. Considering another of the epigrams, for instance, opens up alternate possibilities: "[S]eeking to conquer a larger liberty, man but extends the empire of necessity" (*PT* 174). Whereas the first epigram clearly marks the tale in the context of black slavery, the last epigram stages the idea of power in explicitly metaphysical terms. Are the metaphysical questions about freedom and necessity to be seen as figurations of slavery, or is the reference to slavery meant to exemplify a deeper metaphysical problem? Such a division may already be an illusion, as Maurice Lee has shown that slavery itself was for Melville a philosophical problem.[20] What we may discover, then, by applying the analysis of phenomenological dread to the tale is not an evasion of the question of slavery that has prompted recent interest in the tale but rather an exploration of how deep slavery's fundamental principle—a difference in self-determination—runs in the fundamental principle of metaphysics exposed by dread—a difference in self-identity.

In the fearless figure of Bannadonna, "The Bell-Tower" reprises the transcendence over fear championed in "The Lightning-Rod Man." Just as the narrator in that tale gains leverage upon the fearmongering salesman through a steadfast refusal of fear's propelling impulses, Bannadonna's artistic and mechanical genius is grounded in his exceptional resolve: "In firm resolve, no man in Europe at that period went beyond Bannadonna" (*PT* 174). Bannadonna's transcendence of fear, in the opening of the tale, literally raises him above the people of his state, enabling him to stand "erect, alone, with folded arms" (*PT* 175), high above them on the tower he has constructed. The people celebrate not only the tower's grand scale but also Bannadonna's seemingly superhuman mastery over instinctual fears: "That which stirred them so was, seeing with what serenity the builder stood three hundred feet in air, upon an unrailed perch. This none but he durst do" (*PT* 175). Bannadonna's achievement is double: he has built the tower; he has conquered his fear. The coincidence of the two links them, such that the mechanical and artistic feats of which a man is capable are indexes of the degree to which he has freed himself from the base emotion of fear, a degree that can be quantified by measuring the distance from fearless man to admiring public.

Melville marks the tower as parallel to the tower of Babel in its blasphemous ambition, but also to the myth of the Enlightenment, that humanity's self-mastery could rise over its brute nature: "Like Babel's, its base was laid in a high hour of renovated earth, following the second deluge, when the waters of the Dark Ages had dried up, and once more the green appeared. No wonder that, after so long and deep submersion, the jubilant expectation of the race should, as with Noah's sons, soar into Shinar aspiration" (*PT* 174). Melville equates the Enlightenment, "when the Dark Ages had dried up," with the Biblical period following the flood in Genesis. Bannadonna's transcendence of fear is thus a visible synecdoche of the rise of humanity in general from the morass of nature. The Shinar aspirations, to build a tower to heaven and have a unified language, are replayed in the Enlightenment. It would seem, then, that Melville's tale is a rehearsal of the biblical tale, a reminder that the pride of humankind will bring destruction from God. Babel's power, the source of God's jealousy, was in its single language: "And the Lord said, Behold, the people is one, and they have all one language; and this they begin to do; and now nothing will be restrained from them, which they have imagined to do" (Gen. 11:6). Bannadonna's power, I would speculate, also comes from the new single language of the Enlightenment: the language of method.

For Bannadonna's singular achievement of standing fearless and erect atop the tower is itself a victory of method rather than of the human. As the tower rises, month by month, Bannadonna "standing alone upon its ever-ascending summit, at close of every day saw that he overtopped still higher walls and trees" (*PT* 175). Even though he is raising the tower, the scene describes the tower as raising him. Ascending recursively, Bannadonna and the tower equally propel each other. Bannadonna's fearlessness is the eventual outcome of the method: "His periodic standing upon the pile, in each stage of its growth—such discipline had its last result" (*PT* 175). Habituated by periodic and gradual increments to the height of the tower, Bannadonna's victory over fear and "the race's" victory over its historical submergence owe themselves to the discipline of method.

But even as Bannadonna is raised by method, his estrangement and individualization threaten to turn him into a terror. His next project, the gigantic and stylized bell to be housed in the tower, is, like the tower, closely associated with Bannadonna's mastery over fear. However, when his workmen become afraid in the inferno of the bell's casting, Bannadonna's victory over them is not as laudable:

> The unleashed metals bayed like hounds. The workmen shrunk. Through their fright, fatal harm to the bell was dreaded. Fearless as Shadrach, Bannadonna, rushing through the glow, smote the chief culprit with his ponderous ladle. From the smitten part, a splinter was dashed into the seething mass, and at once was melted in. (*PT* 176)

Somewhat obscured by Melville's passive constructions, the paragraph describes Bannadonna murdering the workman whose fear threatens the completion of the bell. Thus Bannadonna's fearlessness enables him to dispatch the fear of another. Rather than flee from fear, Bannadonna confronts it. But this confrontation with fear may be a reconstitution of it, for though Bannadonna is explicitly "fearless" of the flames and heat, his act is motivated by a more general and second-order dread, a fear of fright. Reprising this fear of fear later in the tale, the nobles shoot and kill a spaniel that "stood shivering as before some unknown monster in a brake: or, rather, as if it snuffed footsteps leading to some other world" (*PT* 182). The violent dispatch of the fearful workman and the shivering spaniel come to emblematize how the mastery of instinctual fear may be prompted by some other, more general and dreadful fear. The Enlightenment, in seeking to remove all traces of instinctual fear, betrays its own fear of fear. In the indication that what frightens is an "other world," such victory, symbolic of the Enlightenment, yields a wholly different, perhaps dreadful, prospect, an "unknown monster."

The transcendence of the human over the brute nature of mere fear becomes complicit in the murder of the workman, and precipitates, as a flaw, the fall to come. Bannadonna seeks to eradicate fear, presumably for the sake of freedom, but in exerting his own freedom to abolish fear he becomes complicit in dread's ambiguity. Bannadonna attempts to look down without dizziness, to habituate himself and wield the methods of incremental gradation to inoculate himself against vertigo. To become free from fear, he and the admiring public think, is to be free in will. But what he seeks to be free from is that which is the determinant affect of freedom itself:

> Thus dread is the dizziness of freedom which occurs when the spirit would posit the synthesis, and freedom then gazes down into its own possibility, grasping at finiteness to sustain itself. In this dizziness freedom succumbs. . . . That very instant everything is changed, and when freedom rises again it sees that it is guilty. (Kierkegaard 55)

If in the earlier tales of the collection Melville approximates a Kierkegaardian model for developing in dread the forms of individuation from the world, then in "The Bell-Tower" he uses Bannadonna to explore what it might mean to try to get at freedom by transcending fear rather than fleeing from it, to get freedom to rise without guilt. Bannadonna's limit, however, like the spaniel's instinctive shudder, is still his vital body. Bannadonna will need to get outside his body, as it were, which is precisely his crowning, and fatal, final achievement.

The passing encounters with fear in the tale pale somewhat in comparison with the principal object of terror: the automaton Bannadonna constructs. The introduction of the automaton beneath a domino, a veil, brings together two stock gothic conventions in a single article of horror. But it not only plays upon the shared logics of veil and automaton in the abstraction of essence; it is conceived in the dread of spatial gaps and temporal continuity. By repurposing dread's features, not for analysis but for plain work, Bannadonna would adopt a method that presupposes superiority in order to subjugate the ideal subject. "The Bell-Tower" may be read as completing, or at least centralizing, Melville's preoccupation with terror and method by making a monster out of method itself. Perfection comes in the shape of a mechanical human, a totalized subject, constructed from the basic principles of abstraction.

The automaton commands the most conspicuous fears in the tale. It appears first as merely an object hoisted up to the top of the tower, shrouded in the cloaking veil of a domino and displaying vaguely human characteristics to the onlooking audience. When two magistrates climb the tower to investigate, they discover more signs of life; the object, still covered by the domino, appears seated, and near the top the weave has been plucked out of the domino to suggest what might be an outlet for breathing. The magistrates are struck by dread at the sight of this uncanny object:

> Again, and again, they gazed at the domino, as at some suspicious incognito—at a Venetian mask. All sorts of vague apprehensions stirred in them. They even dreaded lest, when they should descend, the mechanician, though without a flesh and blood companion, for all that, would not be left alone. (*PT* 177)

The nobles "again and again" gaze at the domino, drawn to it even as they fear it. Such fear accords with the feeling of the uncanny in the face of animated objects such as dolls or wax figures that Ernst Jentsch originally noted in his seminal essay on the subject.[21] Here the automaton would cast the dichotomy of human/object into doubt, generating an uncanny ontological instability that can be read through the prism of US slavery (indeed, the automaton is referred to as an "iron slave" later in the narrative, suggesting the route by which one could trace an affiliation between these abstract fears and the historical institution of slavery).[22] Yet there is more here than just the appearance of a human-like object, for what causes this uncanny fear in the magistrates is not exactly the automaton but rather the veil, the "domino," that substitutes for the thing it covers.

Eve Sedgwick's study of the veil convention in gothic literature argues that the veil, in covering a certain kind of content, does not render that content unavailable or buried but instead comes to embody that content and register it as surface rather than depth.[23] The transference works both ways: as the veil comes to take on the properties of flesh (whiteness, etc.) the flesh comes to take on the properties of the veil. Abstracted into surface, the deep "contents" of character or essence are released into a circulating milieu, floating free of direct referentiality and capable of being spread or exchanged as mere attributes written as visible character. Applied to the magistrates' apprehensions, Sedgwick's point means that their fears cannot be wholly summed in the object they cannot see. If the function of the veil is to rewrite essence as surface, then the domino writes as surface the fears of the automaton, and the automaton, conversely, will take on the essential attributes of the veil.

The metonymy between veil and veiled most explicitly occurs when the domino is removed to reveal the automaton at last. This moment of revelation should mark the difference between the two, yet Melville's nomenclature blurs the distinction between surface and depth. Discovering Bannadonna's corpse, the magistrates also see for the first time the automaton that has been concealed by the domino up to that point in the narrative: "With downcast face impending over him, like Jael over nailed Sisera in the tent, was the domino; now no more becloaked" (*PT* 182). The "domino" no longer refers to the domino that covers the object but metonymically also refers to the automaton that had been cloaked by it. The automaton has become, through the contagious logic of transference noted by Sedgwick, the domino. And thus the problem of the uncanny, that indeterminacy between human and object, is rewritten as an indeterminacy between surface and content. The implications of this homology are twofold and reciprocal.

First, the automaton itself may be seen as a kind of veil. The mechanical reproduction of the human form, designed to "appear" to have the qualities of a living being, is manifestly all surface: "Bannadonna had resolved that his invention should likewise possess the power of locomotion, and, along with that, the appearance, at least, of intelligence and will" (*PT* 183). Like a veil, the automaton draws attention to the surface of the human, evacuating content by rendering the essences of human identity—intelligence and will—as mere appearances. But by claiming that such investment is "at least" simply appearance leaves open the possibility that the automaton might possess more than just appearance, or rather that the distinction between mere appearance and actual possession might be tenuous. To a philosopher of consciousness, Bannadonna's project raises the problem of consciousness as physicalism—is the "appearance" of intelligence and will, conceived of as "locomotion," actually the content of those mental phenomena? Is there any difference between the bodily mechanism operating according to consciousness, the human, and the bodily mechanism operating without consciousness, the zombie?[24]

That a consideration of the automaton as a veil, as all surface, may lead to the philosophical problem of zombies reveals the second implication of Melville's veil/automaton symbol. Just as the automaton may be seen as catching the surface aspects of the veil, becoming itself a sign of surface, the veil becomes infused with the fear associated with the automaton: the possibilities and threats of the living dead thing. If the automaton opens up a space between life and death, an uncanny slippage in which each can appear the other, then the domino's two-dimensional liminality, its metonymic convergence of surface and depth, registers the thin skim between life and death, human and inhuman, subject and object. Transformed into an uncanny object, the veil leads to a reversal of the conventional way of understanding the uncanny as the threat that the human may be no different from an object. The uncanny fear here is not of our repressed objectivity somehow returning, but of the aspect of repression itself as it becomes constitutive of that which it conceals. In other words, if the veil becomes indistinguishable from what it hides, it thus consolidates the uncanny instability between subject and object. Here, repression brings into being the thing repressed. Interposing between subject and object and rewriting the instability of that distinction as surface, the veil casts our dread as the uncanny.

In the conclusion to her book on the central role of affect in poststructuralist theory, Rei Terada uses the figure of the zombie to rethink the difference between subject and object. The urge, she asserts, is to see the zombie as the poststructuralist monster of total objectivity; bereft of emotion, all machine and no "heart," the zombie, the living dead, is made to "emblematize postmodern subjectivity" because "everyone knows that if there's one thing dead subjects don't have, it's emotion" (156). Terada quickly reverses such assumptions:

> Actually things are the other way around. Romero's living dead are notably undivided about their desires, or rather, because their desires are undivided, they are mere needs and compulsions. . . . They don't think twice about anything; they are pure intentionality, directional in one direction at a time. A living system is self-differential; only self-differential entities—"texts"—feel. Romero's zombies have no feelings *because they* are *subjects*. (156)

Terada's reversal here—zombies are subjects rather than objects—would distinguish the fear that the automaton inspires as fear of the radical, undifferentiated subject. This special fear, for her, is the mark of self-difference and the difference between the felt self and the projected subject:

> Perhaps Rousseau's primitive man is panicked most of all by the idea that the stranger coming over the horizon may be, finally, a human subject—as he knows himself, being frightened, not to be. A real subject would be really frightening; if I thought I saw one coming, I too would run away. (157)

The flight Terada imagines here, the flight of the self-differentiated and objective self from the specter of subjectivity, helps us to understand the magistrates' fear and regard of the domino. Melville's automaton, veiled and "at least" appearing to have mental faculties, is a version of Terada's zombie subject; it may be an "object," a lifeless mechanism, but the fear it inspires originates in its evocation of radical subjectivity, a being that is determined and constructed out of the very axes of space and time central to dread and thrownness. Its lack of internal differentiation—it is all surface, through and through[25]—is a projection of Dasein without dread. For Melville's automaton is no basic robot but rather a giant designed by distortions of space to fix unerringly perfect time; it is, as it were, a monster of method.

The second half of the tale, after Bannadonna is found dead, expostulates on his possible motives and methods and speculates about the way in which spatial displacement and temporal marking account for its final shape. According to the suppositions, Bannadonna first conceived of the mechanical creature while gazing up at conventional bell towers and their sentry-watchmen who strike the bells on the hour:

> It was from observing these exposed bells, with their watchmen, that the foundling, as was opined, derived the first suggestion of his scheme. Perched on a great mast or spire, the human figure, viewed from below, undergoes such a reduction in its apparent size, as to obliterate its intelligent features. It evinces no personality. Instead of bespeaking volition, its gestures rather resemble the automatic ones of the arms of a telegraph. (*PT* 183)

The distance between Bannadonna and the watchmen here becomes an abstracting agent capable of effacing the intelligence and personality of the human. Like the veil, vision over distance releases formal human features from their idiosyncratic differences. The "thrownness" of space in dread may be seen to inform, at a base level, the fundamental design of the automaton. Human form, beheld at a distance, can be abstracted from the watchmen and replicated up close in the automaton itself. The dread, then, that the automaton inspires is not related simply to its difference from the human but to its up-close representation of the faraway human.

This distorted and formalized abstraction of the human that distance provides is crystallized in the anachronistic invocation of the optical telegraph. Melville is clearly referring to the Chappe optical telegraph, a type of semaphore telegraph (fig. 2), which he may have come across as he toured France before writing *Moby-Dick*. A precursor of electrical telegraphs, the Chappe telegraphs were giant structures, vaguely anthropomorphic, that communicated over large distances by means of an arrangement of their arms. The telegraph's form, taken from the human figure, is a supplement to it and an extension of its bounds. It is a means for collapsing space in time (the first optical telegraph required the use of synchronized clocks). For messages to travel across space was, until the telegraph's invention, limited by the speed of the messenger. But with the optical telegraph, the transfer of information is limited only by the speed of light; and thus space, felt as time, contracts as well as expands. The optical telegraph abstracts the human form into a sign, which then magnified transcends the felt natural limits of space and time. What the telegraph represents to Melville may thus be what the automaton eventually becomes, the reduction of human to signifier through the promise of instantaneous transmission—a silent glide through time that would sidestep personality and human emotion to connect immediately with the automatic.

What Bannadonna aspires to build, then, is a vision of the human proffered by the distance of space, an automaton that would manifest in its design the distance by which the telegraph is perceived. If the form of dread is determined by the spatialization it incurs, then the automaton would seem to incorporate the spatialization of the telegraph into the shape of its own dreadful proportions. Rising through space vertically, the telegraph collapses space on the horizon, its long reach enabled by the abstraction of the human form. Space, through the telegraph, is mastered by anthropomorphic abstraction, a human projection that extends the reach of the human by effacing its idiosyncrasies. The automaton, gigantic in its proportions and modeled upon the spatially effaced watchmen, consolidates the abstraction of the telegraph and draws out its dreadful contours: a grotesque of the human form reflected through its abstracting instruments. The telegraph reforms the human to cross great dis-

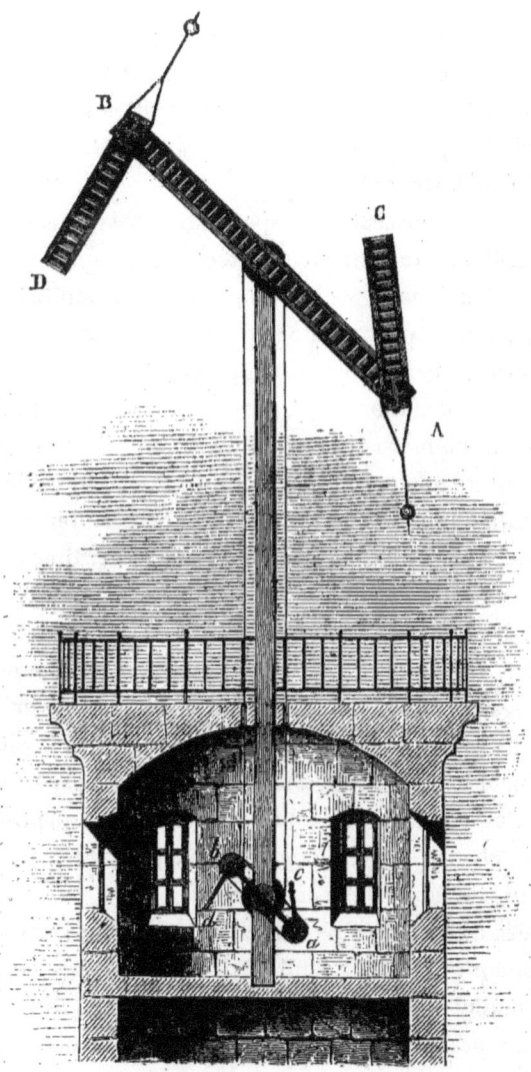

Fig. 19. — Télégraphe de Chappe.

**FIGURE 2.** Chappe telegraph. Illustration from Louis Figuier, *Les merveilles de la science*, 1868. Source: Wikimedia Commons (commons.wikimedia.org/wiki/File:Télégraphe_Chappe_1.jpg).

tances in no time. Bannadonna's automaton remediates that transmission into both physical form and dreadful affect; the automaton becomes a symbol not of the human's use of the telegraph, but of the dream of a new, limitless, subjectivity installed by the telegraphic medium. If Bannadonna is limited by his humanity, he nevertheless can, through an act of creation that is also a throwing, perfect this subject as projection, itself not subject to the vicissitudes of bodily emotion and animal instinct.[26]

And what does this projection of spatial distance into a human form do? It permits Bannadonna to generate a better timekeeper: it would "strike the hour with its mechanic hand, with even greater precision than the vital one" (*PT* 183). And, not only will the automaton strike the bell with inhuman precision, but its strike is designed to land upon the clasped hands of the twelve engraved girls, representations of the joined hours, encircling the bell. The implication is that the mechanical would sever and parcel the continuum of time, breaking it into measurable and flat quantities—in other words, breaking primordial time into leveled-off now-time. The automaton's function of striking with precision a mark in time that would sever time's flow is, like the distance manifest in its telegraph-like form, the vision of a perfect subject in the face of which we feel dread. It has no features of emotion because it has been designed at a distance. And in striking perfect now-time, it establishes another world against which humans may measure the difference of their own (at one point, the townspeople compare their own watches with the clock in the tower). It enables the fiction of the clock by breaking apart the continuum implied in the clasped hands of the twelve hours. And it deposits *in the mark* the negativity of change and difference which allows the span between numbered instants to have uniformity and content.

From the idea of the telegraph comes the dreadful dream of precision, of making the human body into a kind of clockwork which would correct the tremblings of vitality. In this way, time becomes estranged from the human; it becomes, like space, the nature of the world of difference, its measurement requiring new devices to mediate between the ideal and the fallen vital. But even if vision allows a kind of connection across space, the abstract quality of its distance and its illusion of instantaneousness combine to reveal the visible as sign rather than essence. And here we come back to terror, for the feeling of this mediated experience, the sinking or falling within the world, is delivered as our terror of the subject. It is the view of the subject on the horizon, perfected as machine, abstract as arms, moving through space at the speed of light.

Recalling the alien hiatus of time in Hunilla's wait and Delano's portentous regard of the ship's hourly bell, the climactic moment in "The Bell-Tower" is preoccupied with, as a kind of zero-limit, the genesis of now-time. Waiting for the bell to strike the hour of 1 o'clock, the townspeople consult their watches, emphasizing the invention whose etymology carries along with it an association of space with time:

> Watches were held in hands of feverish men, who stood, now scrutinizing their small dial-plates, and then, with neck thrown back, gazing toward the belfry. . . . The hour-hands of a thousand watches now verged within a hair's breadth of the figure 1. A silence, as of the expectation of some Shiloh, pervaded the swarming plain. Suddenly a dull, mangled sound—naught ringing in it; scarcely audible, indeed, to the outer circles of the people—that dull sound dropped heavily from the belfry. At the same moment, each man stared at his neighbor blankly. All watches were upheld. All hour-hands were at—had passed—the figure 1. (*PT* 181)

This passage shows the remarkable complexity of the tale's linked symbols. The "watches" here, conspicuous by their anachronism, prefigure the "stalwart watchmen" that are Bannadonna's inspiration. What perhaps condones such anachronism is the implied etymology—the timepiece called the watch would appear to get its name by reference to those same watchmen, whose title has to do with their other function, not to mark time but to "watch" from their high vantage—that is, the watch is a timepiece with sight over distance built into its origins.

But the watch here not only connects the telling of time with space but also recalls an earlier moment in the narrative and figures the problem of telling perfect time as connected with the problem of human personality. When the "hour-hands of a thousand watches now verged within a hair's breadth of the figure 1," the reader hears the faintest echo of what Bannadonna explains as the law of art: the "hair's breadth" that accounts for entirely different effects in the representation of the human face. As Bannadonna explains to the magistrates,

> there is a law in art, which bars the possibility of duplicates. Some years ago, you may remember, I graved a small seal for your republic, bearing, for its chief device, the head of your own ancestor, its illustrious founder. . . . I graved an entire plate, containing one hundred of the seals. . . . Gravity is the air of all; but, diversified in all. In some, benevolent; in some, ambiguous; in two or three, to a close scrutiny, all but incipiently malign, the variation of less than a *hair's breadth* in the linear shadings round the mouth sufficing to all this. (*PT* 179–180; emphasis added)

The problem of perfect now-time is thus associated, subtly, with the law in art that forbids perfect iteration. The hair's breadth of difference between primordial time and now-time is analogized to the slivers of affective difference that persist in the imperfections of representation. Perfecting a clock or perfecting mimesis through mechanical means is always a hair's breadth away, and it is in that gap of difference that emotion, character, and humanity reveal themselves. Once seen through that hair's breadth, the connections between now-time and personality appear to proliferate throughout the narrative. Bannadonna, in relating the story of the hundred heads, is merely trying to explain why, of the personified hours—"twelve figures of gay girls, garlanded, hand-in-hand, danced in a choral ring—the embodied hours"—the face of Una alone wears a "fatal" air. And it is his last-minute attempts to correct that imperfection that place Bannadonna in the path of the automaton's strike. Although Bannadonna can get time just about perfect, he can't get the personifications of the hours perfectly alike. Personality, written as an analog, not-quantized quality deviating by hair's breadths from one "air" to the next, is thus closely related to the analog conception of time as a continuum. The attempt to perfect time through the automaton, accordingly, is thus an attempt to stamp out personality, to mark perfect sameness through perfect iterability. What makes the automaton so dreadful is not so much its uncanny resemblance to the human but rather its apotheosis of the human and our uncanny resemblance to it. Like Bartleby, that machine-like character whose perfectly undivided will inspires dread without feeling it, the automaton, conceived in the thrownness of space and meant to mark perfect time, is Terada's giant subject coming over the horizon; it is not an imperfect copy of a human but the perfect original against which we must view ourselves as imperfect copies.

The final achievement of Bannadonna's automaton is to produce the terrifying specter of human subjectivity: "the more terrible to behold, the better" (*PT* 185). Conceived in the distorting effects of space and time as the fundamental modes of dread, the automaton becomes a symbol for dread, that terrifying affect that determines and complicates the relations between self and subject, human and inhuman. Constructed according to a mechanical method as a supplement to nature, "a supplement to the Six Days' Work" (*PT* 184), the automaton in its servitude stands as the mute and terrifying prospect of a self-projected inhuman subjectivity, the abstracted emblem of the dread underlying method's fundamental premise. To use method in such a way is to correct the variability of the human, to erase personality, and to manifest dread in order to perceive, if only in rearward glances in our flight, the visage of truth outside condition.

To fit the findings of this chapter within the longer story of American terror is to notice that *The Piazza Tales* provides nightmares of evenness within gaps and hiatuses. The fundamental and infinite disproportion between God and the human, felt through terror in Edwards, figured terror as an affective calculation. The reciprocal and opposing operations of analysis, moving from and to terror in Poe, showed how what was felt as disproportion was, uncannily, the structure of thought. In *Moby-Dick*, Melville tipped the scales again, showing how dialectical balances were disrupted and always made uneven through terror. In *The Piazza Tales*, terror becomes even once again, but this evenness is gained through the inhuman and projected supplementarity of the very instruments that level off our phenomenal world. In the alienated flights through space and the hiatuses in marks of time, the characters of Melville's moody short fictions build up their own fictions of perfect time, of differentiated space, and watch in terror and dread as those fictions come to usurp and estrange the dream of intellectual subjectivity they were meant to realize.

The fallen ruin of the tower with which "The Bell-Tower" begins is the tale's ultimate timepiece, one that gives not the exact time of the world, but the dreadful, affect-laden time of the human:

> As all along where the pine tree falls, its dissolution leaves a mossy mound—last-flung shadow of the perished trunk; never lengthening, never lessening; unsubject to the fleet falsities of the sun; shade immutable and true gauge that cometh by prostration—so westward from what seems the stump, one steadfast spear of lichened ruin veins the plain. (*PT* 174)

The ruin of the tower, described as a kind of organic sundial, marks not the time of the world but rather, in shadow and shade, the long moment of the human's failure to master it. The fall of the human project to attain perfect subjectivity ultimately becomes humanity's defining characteristic. Such may explain how the passage combines the image of humility ("prostration") with the resolution of resistance ("unsubject," "steadfast"), to end with a figure of vital organic life ("lichened," "veins"). The true gauge of time, the one that marks absolute and unchanging time in the face of the sun's now-time, is the resolute ruin of the attempt to perfect now-time's measurement. That which persists, in the end, is not really the subject or the world but rather only the attitude of prostration. But wouldn't prostration be like those methods of abstraction and pursuit, the attempts to reduce and efface our subjective interference in order to more accurately know the objective world? The resolute quality of Melville's prostration, then, signals something darker and more complex: we may not know the world fully nor become perfect subjects, but the darkness of those failures is itself a kind of living resolve. Endless prostration is finally true for Melville because it alone is unchanging; it determines our relation to the world and requires an intellectual methodology of continual self-effacement. Thus, those methods of thought, built to know the world by effacing the self, are most true not really in their success for the world but in their failure for us, a failure that we do not seek to redeem but rather to deepen.

# AFTERWORD
## "Some Dim, Random Way"

**IT IS CUSTOMARY AND GOOD MANNERS** for an author to conclude a critical study with a summary statement of what the book has set out to do, how it has done it, and what difference it makes. I am aware that this book is no exception. Both the length and the method of my argument exact from the reader a patience for which I am grateful. The reward for such patience should be clarity, put briefly, and directed toward the future. However, I would be a poor reader of my own work were I not to suspect that trying to say a final word might send me, like one of Poe's victims of the perverse, into a spiraling terror of thought, a self-propelling and self-defeating urge to keep talking senselessly in circles. How can one bring to closure a book that has focused throughout on how the dream of absolute closure is not only impossible but also a function of the terror it has set out to contain? Ishmael despairs at the outset of his explanation of his terror: "[H]ow can I hope to explain myself here; and yet, in some dim, random way, explain myself I must, else all these chapters might be naught" (*MD* 188). But perhaps at these moments one should, like Hume treating his "philosophical melancholy" (Hume 179) by turning to a backgammon table or Melville raising a sherry toast with Adler, postpone the terrifying skeptical descent and talk as one does among friends.

This book began by asking again one of the most enduring questions about American literature: Why are so many of its founding works so thematically *dark*? I was dissatisfied with the two conventional ways of explaining its terrors. On one hand, the aesthetic approach of the earlier scholars—Leslie Fiedler,

Harry Levin, Perry Miller—has the tendency to regard terror tautologically: literature was terrifying because its authors had pierced through to some real and abstract truth, the "terror of modern man" as Miller put it. On the other hand, the turn toward ideological interpretation and historicist methodology of the past two decades of scholarship questioned the sweeping assumptions of terror's inherent and existential truth, but it also tended to diminish the significance of terror by reading it pathologically. In taking literature as tracing political and cultural currents of their age, that trend reduces terror to an index of historical moment, a merely negative disposition toward one or another concealed cultural context: democracy, slavery, industrialization, urbanization, and so on.

This trend was poorly equipped to analyze the case of American literary terror, I thought, for two reasons. First, indexical interpretation would reduce the aesthetic and affective particularity of terror to a fungible disposition—not clearly differentiated from horror, dread, anxiety, or a host of other fearful feelings which each have their own unique logic—and thus read all affect as embryonic political belief imperfectly formulated. Second, when I paid close attention to the logic of terror in American literature, I discovered that the special tone of American terror is intricately associated with the problem of explaining affect by assigning an empirical cause. What makes terror so tricky for rational explanation is that it seems to be *about* the compulsion to explain in the first place.

What I set out to do in this book, then, was to correct the tendencies of both interpretive traditions by providing an account of terror that was at once historically situated in the intellectual discourse of the period and at the same time drawn from and attentive to the aesthetic claims of the literary work. This means that half the time my book has attempted to recover context—the changing practice of hellfire preaching, Edwards's debates with Charles Chauncy over the place of terror, the influence of the Jena critics on Poe's literary criticism, the rise of analytical terminology from the Padua medical school, Melville's friend George Adler and his print of Charles Deas's *The Death-Struggle*. But I have tried throughout to show how these historical contexts do not ultimately explain literary terror away but rather help to illustrate the conditions within which aesthetic terror operates. Thus, the other half of the time my book has worked, through close readings of the literary texts themselves, to reveal the unique and specific aesthetic powers of American literary terror: the infinite subtractions of Edwards, the dramas of absolute equation in Poe, the disproportional imbalance of dialectical thought in Melville.

Through this two-handed approach, the book has sought to define terror in American literature as the special literary affect informed by the historical emergence of the ahistorical pretensions of universal systems of knowledge. That is, the writers in this study were uniquely attuned to the way in which the concept of thinking had become, in the wake of Enlightenment empiricism, more and more coterminous with a set of austere mechanical processes, such as the scientific method or the denuded functions of analytical logic. Yet, rather than broadly adopting a romantic rejection on the basis of feeling, these American writers innovated a particular tone of uncompromising terror to give it feeling. The scientific demand to efface subjectivity is registered as the terror of an infinite reduction of self. The deductive and inductive dynamics of analysis as the skeletal essence of thinking are convertible into terrors of mental mechanics gone haywire.

So, what difference does this make today?

First, it recovers the affective texture of American literature's engagement with philosophy. The troubling and excessive romantic passions—which Enlightenment philosophy would seek to explain away in valiant displays, like so many of Poe's perverse narrators obsessively erasing the traces of their crime—come to reframe the scene of that concealment. By developing in terror the feeling of these explanatory impulses, the feeling of the operation of reason, American literature addresses the questions of philosophy not by turning away but by recursively deepening, pressing, extending the fundamental assumptions embedded within the new ways of thinking about thinking. Feeling matters in these works, not as a symptom of some more real or concrete cause but as underlying our very idea of cause in the first place. In the long story of the "ancient quarrel" between philosophy and literature, the episode this book tells—the invention and development of American terror—reasserts the primacy of aesthetic affect, not as separate from the claims of truth but as fundamental to its ratification in the rules and forms of method.[1]

A second, corollary outcome of this book is that it outlines how important American literature is to the *other side* of the schism of philosophy in the twentieth century. In the past decade, studies delineating the connections between American literature and American pragmatism have proliferated. The general effect of this is a reclamation of American literature for a quintessentially American philosophy back from the mystifying and skeptical pessimisms of the poststructuralist 1980s and 1990s—back, that is, from the French. What the study of terror may give us, however, is a way of understanding how the rise of poststructuralist theory in US English departments was less an invasion than a homecoming. As I see it, one important contribution this book makes is to recover the genealogy of poststructuralist feeling as from the first an aesthetics that refuses explanatory compartmentalization. To take this idea further would be to trace terror's route from Poe to Baudelaire, Mallarmé, and the other French symbolists and then to the explosion of deconstruction (especially through Barthes, Lacan, and Derrida, each of whom read Poe closely) as a form of thinking unrecognizable and baffling to the analytical and pragmatic traditions of philosophy. It may turn out that the initial moment of schism between philosophy and theory did not occur in the late-twentieth-century *écoles* but rather in the parlor of Reverend Noyes and the debates between Edwards and Chauncy over the meaning of the new, feverish desire of their parishes to be terrified.

So, have we finally understood terror? At times in this book's composition I have been aware of that troubling irony attaching to the task of trying to explain something as being resistant to explanation. Fear is, like humor or even irony itself, the kind of thing that disappears in the face of its explanation, and so I have been reminded all too often of the lesson of a fairy tale the Grimm brothers transcribed in the nineteenth century—"The Boy Who Left Home to Find Out about the Shivers" (1819). In that tale, a not-too-bright young man decides that the one thing he wants to learn is how to be afraid. He confronts fear in its usual guises—ghosts and zombies and giants—but is constitutionally unable to be afraid (because, the story suggests, he is too dull and stupid to know fear). Finally his wife, tired of his complaining, dumps a bucket of cold water and squirming minnows on him while he's sleeping. To this he finally, triumphantly exclaims: "I've got the shivers at last!" (Pullman 26). In trying to get at the terror of American literature, I hope to have preserved the unique and rich character of the terror of the literature itself and not to have, finally, reduced it all to a bunch of cold minnows.

But I take solace in the fact that the young man's understanding of fear in that tale is the kind of flat, empirical understanding of terror that I have tried to complicate. And in doing so, I hope this book reinvigorates readings that would pay attention to, linger over, what to me seems the most important contribution of literature—its evocation of specific feelings and states of mind that could not be put otherwise. To know terror rationally would be to wrestle it away, to be like the fool who leaves the horror movie proudly proclaiming, "It didn't scare me one bit!" This, according to the authors of my study, is not the sign of a stable, ascendant mind but rather of its penury and short-sightedness. In Edwards's hellfire sermons as much as in Poe's and Melville's fictions, we read terror not for the embarrassed laugh that comes after the chill but for the chill itself. To take this terror seriously would seem to necessitate a cool, rational, objective approach. But such an approach would not ultimately frame terror to understand it but rather, in its attempt, restage terror's ground. It would willingly spring the trapdoor in the otherwise secure room of reason, revealing the yawning darkness under its foundation. And it would do so not really for a reason, but because of reason, because the Enlightenment dream of universal knowledge cannot tolerate a vacancy, even when it is its own. For the affective economies of these authors, being thus drawn to terror is not the sign of a deeply disordered mind. Or, if it is, then the disorder is rather a common one, inherent in all minds that think and different only in degree.

# NOTES

### Introduction: Reopening Darkness

1. Matthiessen, acknowledging the "optimistic strain from Emerson to Whitman" (179) and "the reaffirmation of tragedy by Hawthorne and Melville" (179), cautions that a "white and black contrast . . . would tend to obscure the interrelations between the two groups, and it would make it sound as though the last word in this age lay with tragedy" (179). Nevertheless, his generalized categories have proved convenient, albeit provisional.

2. See Eric Savoy's discussion of the gothic in America as distinguished by a need to give voice to "the underside, the Otherness, of the narratives of national self-construction" (18).

3. For essays following from Morrison's thesis, see Kennedy and Weissberg's *Romancing The Shadow*. See also Justin Edwards's *Gothic Passages* for an argument about how "[d]isruptions in the stable categories of race . . . result in a dread that is often represented by gothic discourse, contributing to the development of American gothic discourse" (xxx).

4. See also Lawrence Buell's reading of "gothic fiction as a historical symptom expressive of the limits of human order and rationality at the very moment when these were being most aggressively promoted as values" (352).

5. For the call for an aesthetic criticism that could accommodate historicist modes of ideological interpretation, see Otter and Sanborn (2), as well as Weinstein and Looby (10). For a skeptical stance toward the possibility of such a merger, see Altieri's claim that the only way aesthetics may engage "history and politics is to build predicates for social use into the definition of *aesthetic* from the start" ("Are Aesthetic Models" 393). The present study demonstrates how terror uniquely precludes explanations through "social use" yet at the same time derives its power from the historical models of thought that would compel such explanations.

6. For a summary of the development of affect theory, see Gregg and Seigworth. For influential recastings of affect philosophy and psychology for the humanities, see Sedgwick's *Touching Feeling*, especially her essay written with Adam Frank, "Shame in the Cybernetic Fold," and Brian Massumi's *Parables for the Virtual*, especially the chapter "The Autonomy of Affect."

7. Antonio Damasio has popularized the case that "feelings are poised at the very threshold that separates being from knowing and thus have a privileged connection to

consciousness" (43). One of his key examples, a patient who suffered from brain damage to her amygdala and thus appeared to be incapable of feeling fear, exhibited an "inability to make sound social judgments," which suggests to Damasio that emotion, and fear specifically, plays a key role in human behavior and judgment (62–67). Ruth Leys has recently leveled a critique at what she sees as affect theory's primary axiom: "the belief that affect is independent of signification and meaning" (443). She attacks the appropriation and misreading of the neurosciences in the work of cultural affect theory.

My own interest in affect is concerned less with the high cultural theory which Leys criticizes, and more with the attention to the literary-aesthetic which affect as a philosophical concern can bring about. I would not disagree with Leys's perception of an implicit paradox within the cultural theory of affect: "A related question is why anti-intentionalism exerts such a fascination over the cultural critics and theorists . . . especially since one price their views exact is to imply such a radical separation between affect and reason as to make disagreement about meaning, or ideological dispute, irrelevant to cultural analysis" (472). But where this may be a disabling paradox for cultural critics engaged in political and moral evaluation, it is a rich source of aesthetic potential for the writers of my study, who seek to envision the feeling tones of various anti-intentionalisms.

8. See Steven Shapin's *The Scientific Revolution*; George Levine's *Dying to Know: Scientific Epistemology and Narrative in Victorian England*; and Lorraine Daston and Peter Galison's *Objectivity*.

9. See Aristotle's *Poetics* 1449b23. For a full discussion of how Aristotle's use of *catharsis* is associated with physical health within a classical and homeopathic system of humors, see Lucas.

10. See Lucas 285.

11. Nussbaum 4; italics in the original. Henceforward, all italics in quotations are in the original unless otherwise indicated.

12. Two influential psychoanalytical recastings of the sublime alter its inherent structure of recuperation. Thomas Weiskel shows how the cause of Kant's "negative" sublime is "the aggrandizement of reason at the expense of reality and the imaginative apprehension of reality" (41) and offers an alternate "positive" (49) egotistical mode in which sublimation occurs within the imagination, a "drastic" example of which is Emerson (50). But in both modes, the ultimate phase of the sublime is recuperation, albeit of a precarious "balance of outer and inner" in which indeterminacy "is taken as symbolizing the mind's relation to a transcendent order" (24). Neil Hertz, expanding on the psychoanalytical mapping of the sublime, argues that the sublime is an Oedipal wish for a confirmation of the "unitary status of self" through the prospect of "utter self-loss" (53), thus serving a kind of saving function (60).

13. Weiskel describes this version of the sublime as "a permanent attitude of alienation from nature" (44) that leads us, ethically at least, to a "transcendent dead end" (48).

14. For a general account of how gothic horrors symbolize hidden "secrets from the past" in both cultural and psychological valences, see Hogle 2–6. See also Anne Williams's argument that what joins the gothic is an interest in the "other" modeled upon family structures (19–22).

15. My distinction between terror and horror is expedient for the present purposes. For an inverse version of this distinction, see Heller 19. For other definitions see Anne Radcliffe's "On the Supernatural in Poetry" and King 25.

16. See Matthew Taylor's elegant formulation in an ecocritical context: "The object of our fear . . . becomes indistinguishable from ourselves, which is not to say that we become the world but rather that we become afraid of the shadows that we sense we are, scared as much by our inanimation as by the animation of the world" (364–365).

17. For a psychological account of this tendency, see Heller's description of how the uncanny disrupts aesthetic categorizations of horror and terror (41–42).

18. Betsy Erkkila also links Poe's perversity with the Frankfurt School but reads it as a critique, "a more critical tool for brushing democratic history against the grain than Hegelian dialectics" ("Perverting the American Renaissance 88).

19. Horkheimer and Adorno describe "explanation" as the expression of a mythic human fear: "The dualization of nature as appearance and sequence, effort and power, which first makes possible both myth and science, originates in human fear, the expression of which becomes explanation" (15).

20. See Thomas Nagel's *The View from Nowhere*. For a history of objectivity's negotiation of the distance between knower and knowledge, see Daston and Galison's *Objectivity*.

21. Thacker's claim that "'horror' is a non-philosophical attempt to think about the world-without-us philosophically" (9) is an approximation of this study's definition of terror.

22. "[C]an philosophy become literature and still know itself?" (Cavell, *Claim* 496).

23. "Poe's view . . . is a materialization, no doubt ironic, of . . . the view, roughly, that skepticism's repudiation of knowledge is merely a function of having set the sights of knowledge too high" (Cavell, *In Quest of the Ordinary* 139).

24. These studies update and extend the thesis of Richard Poirier's *Poetry and Pragmatism* that in Emerson and "the pragmatist-poetic line" deriving from him, "it is possible to reveal, in the words and phrases we use, linguistic resources that point to something beyond skepticism, to possibilities of personal and cultural renewal" (11). In addition to Richardson's book, see Russell B. Goodman's *American Philosophy and the Romantic Tradition*; James Albrecht's *Reconstructing Individualism*; Kristin Case's *American Pragmatism and Poetic Practice*; Andrea Knutson's *American Spaces of Conversion*; and Paul Grimstad's *Experience and Experimental Writing*. For an account of how these studies might respond to Cavell's resistance to calling Emerson a pragmatist, see Grimstad 3–14.

25. Pragmatism, Cornel West notes, is less a descriptive philosophy than an active one. Rather than use thought to better sense the world around us, pragmatism enjoins us to "deploy thought as a weapon to enable more effective action" (5).

26. Another prospect is offered by Douglas Robinson, who links Poe and Emerson as pragmatic ironists, who look forward to "an apocalyptic future not as Being but as Doing" (122), even if what is done will probably fail. For Poe and pragmatism, see also Sean McAlister's "Revolution of Thought / Revulsion of Feeling."

27. For an extended discussion of these competing philosophical outlooks, see K. L. Evans's study of Starbuck's pragmatic pluralism in contrast to Ahab's "cetological philosophy" (62–109).

28. Riddel's essay on Emerson critiques how Emerson's "alleged authority" tends to polarize American thought into "yea-sayers" or "nay-sayers": "[e]ither of the party of Hope or the party of . . ." (42; ellipsis in original). Riddel's ellipsis signals a significant lack, the refusal or inability to articulate positively what Emerson's other is. In that hiatus, I find both the opportunity and the necessity for the current study. To understand terror as a feeling of thinking may offer an alternative economy for which the thought of something besides hope may entail more than only stubborn despair.

29. See Terada's *Feeling in Theory: Emotion after the "Death of the Subject."*

## Chapter 1: Awakening Terror

1. Perry Miller first suggested the proposition that the Awakening was a precursor to democratic revolution (*Errand into the Wilderness* 166). See also Alan Heimert's claim that "[w]hat was awakened in 1740 was the spirit of American democracy" (lxi). Eugene White concurs: "Among the most important influences of the Great Awakening, in a wide variety of ways it encouraged a development of the democratic sentiment" (57). For Great Awakening millennialism and revolutionary politics, see Marty 111–154. Sacvan Berkovitch deepens the connection by noting the ironies in how the putatively orthodox Awakening spurred an ideology of progressive liberalism (*Rites of Assent* 156–157). See also Lovejoy 222–230. For an account of the Great Awakening that de-emphasizes class-based distinctions, see Gaustad 42–60.

2. In *Philosophical Theology*, Sang Hyun Lee distinguishes Edwards's philosophy as more dynamic than classical theism but less radical than a pragmatism-influenced process theology that tends to diminish the "perfect actuality" of God "upon which all being and creative process are ultimately dependent" (5).

3. See Colacurcio 77–98.

4. For more on how a positive sense of Puritan theology explains Puritan violence, see Breitwieser 26–29.

5. Assessing the prevalence and evolution of hellfire preaching in the colonies raises methodological challenges. Emory Elliot, for example, charts a decline in hellfire preaching in the late seventeenth century by differentiating between whether sermons were preached on Old or New Testament texts (14n). Yet this statistical shortcut may be misleading, since many hellfire sermons take New Testament texts. As Wilson Kimnach notes in regard to Edwards's sermon corpus, "If you want a jeremiad, look under Luke as well as Jeremiah" ("General Introduction" 132).

6. Another colorful example is John Webb, who caters his extended and violent depictions of hell's punishments to the crime. See his *A Seasonable Warning against Bad Company Keeping* and *Practical Discourses.*

7. For more on the relation of will to action, see Knutson 15–53.

8. Andrew Delbanco shows how Thomas Shepard reconceptualized the new "invasive and chameleon nature of sin" through a revision of his inside-outside metaphors:

"The plant-root metaphor—sin offers boughs for excision while its roots remain concealed—joins the imagery of invasive disease, and with it a corresponding interdependence of the violated sectors of the soul" ("Thomas Shepard's America" 173). Delbanco's Shepard may thus anticipate the inner turmoil occasioned by the recognition that external evil flowered, paradoxically, from within.

9. See Warner's *Letters of the Republic*. Warner locates 1720 as an approximate turning point in the new conception of the public sphere shaped by print discourse (36–38).

10. On the effect of the half-way covenant on the changing church membership and its relation to hellfire preaching, see Eugene White 27–28. Harry Stout points out that the relatively safe borders of New England in the 1730s and 1740s coincided with an increased attention to internal discord ("The Puritans and Edwards" 279).

11. For a link between the universal scope and subtractive logic of the sermon, see Kimnach's "The Sermons" 255.

12. For a fuller account of Edwards's early sermons and their heterogeneous yet densely imagistic attention to the invisible world, see Kimnach, "Jonathan Edwards' Early Sermons" 255–266.

13. On the internal thematic diversity of Edwards's sermons, see Kimnach, "General Introduction" 133–134.

14. In *The Value of Salvation*, Edwards figures hell's punishments as fitted to the crime. Those used to "gorgeous apparel" will find only "scorching and tormenting flames which will wrap themselves about their otherwise naked bodies forever" (320). "[B]eds of down" are replaced by "a sea of liquid fire" (320). And drinkers "shall have nothing but the cup of God's wrath and fiery indignation which they shall be compelled forever to drink" (321).

15. This and similar citations follow the preferred style of The Works of Jonathan Edwards Online: "L." means "leaf"; the following number indicates which leaf; and "r." means recto, "v." verso. The sermon's number may be found in "Works Cited."

16. The self-recursive structure of this hellfire rhetoric may be seen as the ultimate culmination of what Patricia Roberts-Miller has characterized as the thoroughgoing monologism of Puritan rhetoric (6). Rather than posit a dialogical other voice, the hellfire sermon turns back on itself, raising feeling not from tension but from uniform submission.

17. See also Sarah Rivett's reading of how Edwards's *A History of the Work of Redemption* works to transform "the mental conception of the infinite" into "the indwelling feeling of Christ within the souls of Edwards's audience" (316).

18. "Some have had such a sense of the displeasure of God, and the great danger they were in of damnation, that they could not sleep at nights; and many have said that when they have laid down, the thoughts of sleeping in such a condition have been frightful to them" (*Faithful Narrative* 161).

19. See Mark Longaker's helpful genealogy of the conversion morphology as it develops from Hooker to Stoddard to Edwards.

20. For another view on how Edwards's affections become deeply implicated within his epistemology, see Leon Chai's reading that, because emotional response reflects the externality of sense experience, "[t]hus knowledge becomes something more than a

mere assimilation of data: what it reflects, in some measure, is the way we represent to ourselves the very conditions of our existence" (34).

21. The aesthetic character of Edwards's perception of God is closely related to both his relational ontology of being (in which entities are constituted through relations) and his theory of beauty (in which this network of relations is realized as a harmony). See Sang Hyun Lee 78–79 and 82–85. See also Delattre's claim that "[u]ltimately, being-in-general and beauty are essentially one in Edwards' ontology" (44).

22. See Delattre's discussion of how Edwards's beauty relates to a "boundary concept" of nothing (44–47).

23. See Knight 211.

24. See Rivett 288–332.

25. Nagel articulates the problem for objectivity: "how to combine the perspective of a particular person inside the world with an objective view of that same world, the person and his viewpoint included" (3).

26. For a description of how the *Port-Royal Logic* fits into Edwards's intellectual development, see Thuesen 16–19.

27. The manuscript transcript is archived at the Beinecke Library under the heading "Downame."

28. Edwards distinguishes between the two in "Notes on the Mind": "One reason why at first, before I knew other logic, I used to be mightily pleased with the study of the old logic, was because it was very pleasant to see my thoughts . . . ranged into order and distributed into classes and divisions" (*SP* 345). Edwards's adoption of the *Port-Royal Logic* thus represents a significant departure from Puritanism's conventional allegiance to Ramist method. For the relation between Puritanism and Ramist logic, see Morgan 105–112. For more on Edwards's logic manuscripts, see Wallace Anderson 21n.

29. Edwards was influenced by the *Port-Royal Logic*'s inculcations of methodical logic and its hypothetical thought experiments with infinite calculations. But he may also have been drawn to it for the strained religious politics attending its composition. Its authors, Antoine Arnauld and Pierre Nicole, wrote from religious exile at Port-Royal, having been accused by the church of holding heretical notions regarding the nonexistence of free will. The Jansenist controversy, as this ongoing debate between church officials and French intellectuals would come to be known, is not at the center of the *Port-Royal Logic*, yet it is mentioned in ambiguous terms in the introduction. That Edwards may have paid attention to the religious politics of the logic book's inception is speculative, but it nevertheless opens up an intriguing question: What is the relation between the methodization of logic and the growing assault on the notion of free will that will fire the Calvinist reformation and the Jansenist controversy?

30. Edwards, in his early philosophical writing, invents his own thought experiments concerning infinity, as the *Port-Royal Logic* recommends. See "The Mind" (*SP* 332–393).

31. Niebuhr's reading of Edwards's aesthetics enables us to "discern that the existence of this displeasing deformity may be indispensable to the widening of our intellectual view upon a greater and more intense harmony than our unassisted imaginations could ever open to us" (40).

## Chapter 2: Critical Terrors

1. See Jerome McGann's "Poe, Decentered Culture, and Critical Method" for how the historicizing turn in Poe studies has been exceptionally fruitful, given Poe's embeddedness within popular and print culture. For Poe and race, see Toni Morrison's *Playing in the Dark* and Gerald Kennedy and Liliane Weissberg's *Romancing the Shadow*. For Poe's engagement with political economy, see Terence Whalen's *Edgar Allan Poe and the Masses* and Teresa Goddu's "Poe, Sensationalism, and Slavery." For Poe, race, and sexuality, see Leland Person's "Cruising (Perversely) for Context"; Person suggests that historicized readings of Poe are validated by Poe's theory of perversity. For biographically informed psychological explanations of Poe's themes, see Marie Bonaparte's *The Life and Works of Edgar Allan Poe* and Kenneth Silverman's *Edgar A. Poe: Mournful and Never-Ending Remembrance*.

2. Poe, letter to Thomas W. White, Apr. 30, 1835 (*Letters* 1:57–58).

3. The critic referred to here is almost certainly White, who had not only publicly complained of the "Germanism" in "Berenice" but, in the same fashion, had qualified Poe's very next tale, "Morella," with a similar editorial remark at the end of the issue in which the story first appeared: "[W]e cannot help but lament that he [Poe] has drank so deep at some enchanted fountain, which seems to blend in his fancy the shadows of the tomb with the clouds and sunshine of life" ("Editorial Remarks" [Apr. 1835] 460).

4. For Poe and German literature, language, and culture, see Thomas S. Hansen and Burton R. Pollin's *The German Face of Edgar Allan Poe: A Study of Literary References in His Works*.

5. Such a turn to aesthetics was possibly influenced by his literary and political milieux. William Carlos Williams characterizes Poe's criticism as a rejection of the "gluey imagination of his day" (221). Betsy Erkkila, however, sees in Poe's defense of pure poetry "a defense of whiteness, slavery, and a whole way of Southern life" ("Poetics of Whiteness" 60).

6. For Poe's close reading of the post-Kantian critics, especially A. W. Schlegel, see Thompson 19–38. See also Moreland and Shaw's "'As Urged by Schelling': Coleridge, Poe, and the Schellingian Refrain"; and Voloshin 280–281. For Poe's knowledge (and occasional plagiarism) of Schlegel, see Alterton 30–45, 68–79.

7. T. S. Eliot was perhaps the first to voice this opinion: "Poe in analyzing his poem was practising either a hoax, or a piece of self-deception.... Hence the essay has not been taken as seriously as it deserves" (333). More recently, Adam Gordon's essay "'A Condition to be Criticised'" (2012) argues that "The Philosophy of Composition" should be taken as a serious burlesque in which Poe "turned the famed tomahawk on himself" (15).

8. See Gerald Kennedy's discussion of how the bird becomes "the sign of an irrevocable absence" (*Poe, Death, and the Life of Writing* 69) in the culture's preoccupations with death and the afterlife.

9. See Hoffman 78–93. Paul Grimstad, recognizing the trick but taking it seriously, shows how it evolves out of Poe's distinction between reasoning and machine-like algorithms (55–64).

10. See also Debra Fried's discussion of the echoic relation between "The Raven"

and "The Philosophy of Composition" according to a "poetics of refrain" that oscillates between voice and epitaph (624–629). Fried's study shows how the essay amplifies, rather than supplants, the "majestic silence" (629) of the poem and its raven.

11. Though similar, this analogy differs from Donald Pease's alignment of the essayist with the raven, not the speaker: "The analyst, like the raven, has reduced potentially dangerous repressed material to the level of mere sounds" (183). The result for Pease is that both poem and essay strive to disconnect grief and object as part of a broader destructive agenda against a collective cultural past.

12. See Pease 184: "[T]he poem interprets the essay, for the poem provides the only context in which the purely mechanical, 'ravening' activity . . . of the essay can *seem* to make sense."

13. For the way in which the poem structurally requires the reader's complicity, see Richards 206.

14. For tunneling structures and Poe's "power of a negative that is not simply nothing," see Riddel 155.

15. The feeling projected might be speculatively related to Eliza Richards's study of the poem as structured by a "reception-based poetics" (221) of never-ending recirculation: "'The Raven' is made to be re-made; it is turned in a way that enables its return, over and over again, in the most unlikely places" (207).

16. For a related view of how Poe's aesthetic theory is incorporated into his horror, see Joseph Moldenhauer's reading of Poe's criminals as artists attempting to propel the work toward aesthetic unity through violence (291–293).

17. For Poe's awareness of the market and political economy in this letter, see Whalen 8–11.

18. The chronology of the three pieces—"Berenice," "Coleridge," and Poe's review of "Coleridge"—may at first seem to disqualify my hypothesis that the "Coleridge" piece influenced "Berenice." "Coleridge" was published in the April 1835 issue of the *North American Review*; "Berenice" was published in the March 1835 issue of the *Southern Literary Messenger*. However, the fact that Poe reviews the April issue of the *North American Review* in the April issue of the *Southern Literary Messenger* shows that the publication schedule of the *Southern Literary Messenger* was behind that of the *North American Review*. The *Southern Literary Messenger* often fell behind schedule, and it is still possible, given the wide latitude between expressed publication dates and their actual appearance, that Poe read "Coleridge" prior to composing "Berenice." Even if he had not, "Coleridge" is still clearly an influence on Poe's defense of "Berenice," so that, even if he didn't have Coleridge in mind when writing it, he recognized its Coleridgean character afterwards and defended it accordingly.

19. For Coleridge and Poe, see Edward Davidson 57–67; Polonsky 42–56; Voloshin 280; and Alterton 103–112. For a general account of Poe's early *Southern Literary Messenger* reviews, see Hutchisson 298–299.

20. *Critique of Judgment* 29–30: "[W]e refer the presentation not to the object but solely to the subject; and the pleasure cannot express anything other than the object's being commensurate with the cognitive powers that are . . . brought into play when we

judge reflectively, and hence [expresses] merely a subjective formal purposiveness of the object" (brackets in original).

21. In his review of the article, Poe applauds that "justice so ample should have been done to that extraordinary mind" and defends Coleridge from the charge of mysticism by writing that "no man who ever lived thought *more distinctly even when thinking wrong*, or more intimately felt and comprehended *the niceties of words*" ("Critical Notices" 457). Poe's enthusiasm for Coleridge cools, though only marginally, by the time he writes "Exordium upon Critical Notices" in 1842.

22. In addition to Dayan's chapter, see Kennedy's similar discussion of the "impotence of language" (*Poe, Death, and the Life of Writing* 76) to recover textually a sense of presence: "[F]or writing as a play of signs merely substitutes one absence for another."

23. Jonathan Elmer points to the surplus, the remainder, of affect that cannot be incorporated into symbolization:

> When that basis of enjoyment is revealed as constitutively in excess of such symbolization—its leftover, or slag—and when, moreover, that excess is shown to be the very substance of our reading desire, then we recoil from this impossible embodiment of sociality. And here we touch on the possibility that the most obscure pleasure of sensationalism—obscure because it is indistinguishable from its greatest threat—resides in this very irrecuperability of affect." (*Reading* 125)

Elmer locates the pleasure of horror in a double move of desire and fear, promise and threat.

24. Other internal evidence suggests that Poe may have read the Carlyle article prior to its appearance in *The Zodiac* in late 1836. Among several similarities are the charges, which Carlyle refutes, of both "bad taste" and "mysticism" in German literature—vocabulary Poe rehearses in his defense of "Morella."

25. For the formal accord in Kantian aesthetics, see Pfau 34–35.

26. See Pfau 44–45.

27. Fichte's pantheism controversy emerges from his "On the Basis of Our Belief in a Divine Governance of the World" (1798). Schelling's identity philosophy is found in his *System of Transcendental Idealism* (1856–1861). Fichte and Schelling both consider form—in order or in action—to close the epistemological gap between subject and object.

28. See Michael Williams's argument that the narrators' quests are ultimately failed attempts to recuperate or access ultimate meaning through the romantic symbolization of Berenice and Ligeia (80–104). Williams attributes this failure to the way in which writing and language entangle the interpretive approach, such that the narrators end up imposing, rather than discovering, significance—finally offering us as readers a better view not of the infinite beyond but of the "inexpressible madness" of the "interpreting mind" (104).

29. For "Ligeia" as staging a conflict between German and English transcendentalism, see Clark Griffith's "'Ligeia' and the English Romantics."

30. See Jack Voller's argument that Poe's terror rejects the "canonical optimism" (33) of Burkean and Kantian sublimity, as well as Sean Moreland's qualification that "The Fall of the House of Usher" is nevertheless influenced by accounts of the sublime (62).

31. See Dällenbach 13–14, 44–45; and Jefferson 205. Dällenbach distinguishes between types of *mise en abyme*, finding in the "Mad Trist" episode only the first category of simple reflexion. For how *mise en abyme* does not actually disable the tale's narrative, see Jefferson 197.

32. For the distinction between simple, infinite, and paradoxical varieties of *mise en abyme*, see Dällenbach 24–25.

33. See Riddel 133–135; see also Johansen on the failure of the narrator's framing attempts (3–6). Scott Peeples revises the common *mise en abyme* reading by arguing that the enframed story reflects not the framing story but the framing story's genre (185).

34. See Hofstadter 57: "Feedback — making a system turn back or twist back on itself, thus forming some kind of mystically taboo loop — seems to be dangerous, seems to be tempting fate, perhaps even to be intrinsically *wrong*, whatever that might mean. . . . This suspicion of loops just runs in our human grain, it would seem. However, as with many daring activities such as hang-gliding or parachute jumping, some of us are powerfully drawn to it, while others are frightened to death by the mere thought of it."

35. Schelling, in particular, imagines that pure poetry emerges in Homer because classical Greece had succeeded in subduing an exotic and Dionysian "uncanny principle which dominated earlier religions" by "pushing it back into the interior, that is, into secrecy, into the Mystery" (Schelling, *Philosophie der Mythologie*; qtd. and trans. in Vidler 26–27). The uncanny is, for Schelling, that which should remain repressed in order to enable the mind's "outward freedom."

36. See Freud 403.

37. See Johansen 5.

38. For a similar reading of the narrator's projective centrality, see Griffith, "Poe and the Gothic" 130.

39. Riddel drafts the lines of connection between Poe's "tunneling structure" (155) in "The Fall of the House of Usher" and its deconstruction of interpretive strategies: "Poe's staging of the hermeneutical circle renders both scenes and effects that represent performance and resist that interpretative act" (155).

## Chapter 3: The Air of Analysis

1. See also Shawn Rosenheim's *The Cryptographic Imagination* for an argument about the influence of Poe's cryptographic interests upon Lacan (53–57).

2. See Levine 1–15. Levine acknowledges his concern for recuperating "a kind of greatness in the willingness to sacrifice even to death in order to find things out" (14). Poe's version of this zero-limit seeks to imagine what such a perceptual state, deemed "impossible" by Levine and other defenders of objectivity, would really look like. That is, whereas Levine cedes the point that perfect objectivity is "an 'aspiration' rather than a possible achievement" (14), Poe's tales continue to pursue this radical objectivity in fiction without a priori assumptions.

3. The thread of poststructuralist criticism described here is partially anthologized in *The Purloined Poe: Lacan, Derrida, and Psychoanalytic Reading*, edited by John P. Muller and William J. Richardson (Baltimore: Johns Hopkins University Press, 1988),

which contains the criticisms of Lacan, Derrida, and Johnson, among others. For their first translations into English, see Lacan's "Seminar on 'The Purloined Letter'"; Derrida's *The Post-Card: From Freud to Socrates and Beyond*; and Johnson's *The Critical Difference*. Irwin's later study, *The Mystery to a Solution: Poe, Borges, and the Analytic Detective Story* (1994), revisits these three critics and defines the critical story even as it participates in it. A more recent return to Lacan's seminar is Lydia Liu's "The Cybernetic Unconscious: Rethinking Lacan, Poe, and French Theory" (2010).

4. Franco Moretti's study of the structure of detective fiction notes that "weight gravitates towards the ending." This emphasis on the ending comes, in his reading, as a function of detective fiction's pretensions to scientific knowledge—"It is science become myth" (149)—which render the literary digressions of the story itself only waste and error, a delay between the proper beginning and proper ending. In bookending the narrative, then, the figure of science and certainty can contain and control the more anarchic, properly literary forces.

5. Richard Kopley characterizes this first paragraph as celebrating "the double process of creation and resolution, of imagining and unimagining, of writing and the 'kindred art' of reading" (41). See David Halliburton's comment that the doubling systems in "Murders in the Rue Morgue" are not "contraries" but "coequal partners" working in "a reciprocity in which each member works with and for its complement" (238). See also David Ketterer's discussion of the identification of "Dupin the analyst" with "Dupin the artist" (242). In these and other cases, the critics are correct in emphasizing Poe's attempt to square math with poetry; but the present study recovers Poe's model for such attempts in the already-doubled form of analysis. What is misunderstood, in regard to Poe, in traditional distinctions between poet and mathematician is not only that they need one another but, moreover, that the force of that necessity comes from their mutual participation in the more comprehensive functions of analysis.

6. The narrator of Poe's "Mellona Tauta" criticizes the exclusivity of inductive and deductive modes of investigation and argument; however, after "Mellona Tauta" appears in *Eureka*, Poe immediately espouses the very proposition that "Mellona Tauta" ridicules, namely, that there can be only two modes of demonstration or explanation: "This thesis admits a choice between two modes of discussion:—We may *ascend* or *descend*" (*Eureka* 16). Since *Eureka* finally adopts both methods, descending and then ascending again, the problem with induction and deduction may be not only their preclusion of alternate forms of inquiry but their exclusion of one another, at least in Poe's cagey representation. For further discussion of Poe's sometimes contradictory claims about and practices of deductive and inductive method, see Limon 96–99.

7. See Randall 288–300.

8. The medical application of such a method was a way to make distinctions between the symptoms of a disease and the disease itself. For a longer history of how this movement from effects back to causes comes to influence not only the detective genre but the nineteenth-century epistemology in which it comes to fruition, see Carlo Ginzburg's "Clues: Morelli, Freud, and Sherlock Holmes."

9. For more on the development of resolution and composition and the demon-

strative regress, see Jardine's "Problems of Knowledge and Action: Epistemology of the Sciences."

10. The *Port-Royal Logic* uses the terms "resolution" and "analysis" synonymously: "[T]here are two kinds of method, one for discovering the truth, which is known as *analysis*, or the *method of resolution*, and which can also be called the *method of discovery*. The other is for making the truth understood by others once it is found. This is known as *synthesis*, or the *method of composition*, and can also be called the *method of instruction*" (Arnauld and Nicole, Buroker trans. 233).

11. For examples, see the *Encyclopaedia Americana*'s (1829–1833) definition of *algebra* (1:168–169): "In the application of algebra to the resolution of problems, we must first translate the problem out of common into algebraic language; . . . this forms the composition. Then the resolution, or analytic part, is the disentangling the unknown quantity from the several others with which it is connected, so as to retain it alone on one side of the equation, while all the known quantities are collected on the other side, thus obtaining the value of the unknown. This process is called *analysis*, or *resolution*; and hence algebra is a species of the analytic art." See also the description of Laplace's *Traité de mécanique céleste* in the *American Quarterly Review* (June 1, 1829), which attributes to Laplace's astronomy text the idea of resolution and composition of forces, a geometric adaptation of the analytical operations (Rev. of *Traité de mecanique celeste* [sic] 5, 10). The two terms also take on a related use in algebra textbooks such as Yale professor Jeremiah Day's *A Course of Mathematics* (1814–1817), though one reviewer appreciates Day's reluctance to go further into the "thorough knowledge of analysis" of the resolution and composition of equations and suggests that resolution and composition belong to the theoretical and analytical nature of algebra, not to its practical application (Rev. of *A Course of Mathematics* 461).

12. "'The larger links of the chain run thus — Chantilly, Orion, Dr. Nichol, Epicurus, Stereotomy, the street stones, the fruiterer'" (*TS* 1:535). What draws attention in particular to Dupin's inclusion of Nichol in this chain is that Nichol never appears in his elaboration of the chain. What's more, Poe's original misspelling of Nichol ("Nichols" in 1841) is corrected in 1845, suggesting that his inclusion is not the remnant of a later-abandoned idea. See Irwin's discussion in "Reading Poe's Mind: Politics, Mathematics, and the Association of Ideas in 'The Murders in the Rue Morgue.'"

13. See Kopley 7–26 for an instructive archive and extension of the discoveries of formal symmetry in Poe's detective tales. Kopley ends his structural observations by noting that Poe's tales may be seen as ring structures, in which the ending of the story is linked to the beginning, making it seem continuous.

14. For an early modern source for Poe's affinity for chiastic structures, see William Engel's *Early Modern Poetics in Melville and Poe: Memory, Melancholy, and the Emblematic Tradition*.

15. See Quinn, *The French Face of Edgar Poe* 230. See also Patricia Merivale's distinction between critics who read the stranger as a double of the narrator and critics who do not (105).

16. This outsider position is inimical to what Walter Benjamin identifies as the *flâ-*

*neur* in Poe's tale. The *flâneur*, the character type of the aimless urban observer, seeks to hide himself within the new crowd of the early-nineteenth-century city, "an enormous crowd in which no one is either quite transparent or quite opaque to all others" (Benjamin 49). Individuality, in such a crowd, is subsumed by the machine-like uniformity of the urban mass: "If the crowd is jammed up, it is not because it is being impeded by vehicular traffic . . . but because it is being blocked by other crowds" (53). Alexander Howe reiterates the point, emphasizing that the narrator's individuality disrupts his aim, and that "[w]ere the aporia of this unknown man allowed its full repercussions, his [the narrator's] entire system of categorization would be in ruins" (39–40). The angle that the current study affords reads the problem of the individual versus the mass as not only sociological but also epistemological, a paradox embedded within the methods of knowing.

17. See also Shawn Rosenheim's discussion of the gothic consequences of the "analytical sublime" of Poe's detective fiction (74–83).

18. For the scientific context of Poe's poem, see Limon, *The Place of Fiction in the Time of Science* 70–75. Limon shows how the poem should be read as a critique not of science broadly construed but rather of a pedestrian American Baconianism that was already becoming obsolete by 1829.

19. Edward Davidson describes the objectification of the mind within the world of Poe's stories as being a unique solution, neither transcendentalist nor solipsistic, to the Cartesian fracture between self and world. As he points out, Poe's journeys are not finally conquests, but varieties of submission without a final saving reassertion of the subject: "The material world was too often unyielding; instead of the mind's willing comprehension, the mind lost itself and became the object" (55).

20. See Matthew Taylor's reading of "The Island of the Fay" (367–369).

21. See Kent Ljungquist on the Kantian sublime in "A Descent into the Maelstrom" (72–79) and the Burkean sublime in "Pit and the Pendulum" (195–203).

22. Kant (108–109) uses the examples of the Egyptian pyramids and St. Peter's Basilica to illustrate how objects that outscale the immediate human vision generate the sublime.

23. See also Matthew Taylor's ecocritical account of Poe's terror: "Poe repeatedly makes the nonhuman environment the field against which discrete selves disappear" (364). His account emphasizes the destructiveness of Poe's posthuman vision against more popular, self-affirming, and positive alternatives and concludes with a kind of ecocritical and posthuman version of Kantian inadequation: "Poe's texts foreclose both the idea that human selves are inherently distinct from or superior to their nonhuman environments and the seemingly antithetical (but actually coextensive) notion that we can self-constructively lose ourselves to the world" (369).

24. See Leland Person's argument that the tale's epistemology is relative and experiential rather than abstract and transferable: "In this unprecedented realm action must be grounded not in knowledge of law or precedent or in appeals to external authority, but in perceptions of the moment" ("Trusting the Tellers" 52).

25. See also Kenneth Egan's argument that, in the final part of the tale, revelation occurs in an "impersonal attitude" according to which "body serves mind" (161).

26. For the physics of the whirlpool as reflecting a pattern of philosophical thinking, see Murphy 25–26. For the mathematical infinite of the vortex and its aesthetic function, see Justin 131–132.

27. This idea may be influenced by Poe's engagement with Schelling's *Naturphilosophie* and will come to fruition in the later tract *Eureka*. For more, see Limon's study of Poe's eventual embrace of the post-Kantian, idealist conflation of mind with nature (82–96).

28. Daniel Hoffman perhaps sums up this reading best: "When a narrator commences in *this* vein, we know him to be mad already" (222). See also Benjamin Fisher: "Setting out to prove his sanity, this narrator, well before his story ends, convinces us that he is indeed mad" (87).

29. "[T]he narrator succeeds in convincing us not of his rationality but of his irrationality" (Thompson 174). See also Michael Hoffman, more generally: "Reason is often a mere shield for madness, and at virtually no time, except in the almost playful tales of ratiocination, does Poe ever view the highly rational with anything but mistrust" (162). The perverse tales, for Charles Feidelson, are evidence of Poe's "extreme hostility to reason," which sought to "destroy the rational mind and world" (37).

30. The major study of Poe and irony, G. R. Thompson's *Poe's Fiction* (1973), finds Poe's voice as consistently ironic throughout his gothic tales, such that there emerges a "double perception" in which the ironic perspective undercuts the gothic or terrifying one. The result for Thompson is "a kind of ambivalent mockery" (14) that offers a vision of the universe as "not so much malevolent as mocking or 'perverse'" (165). Stressing irony rather than terror, Thompson's version of Poe is cynical or indifferent; yet if ironic reading itself becomes the source of terror, then Poe's irony becomes, paradoxically, a way of being earnest.

31. Jonathan Auerbach also notes the resolvent structure of the confessional tale and links it to the qualities of Poe's first-person narration: "[T]his compulsive plotting most often follows the pattern of a regression or decomposition, as the first person moves backward to search for a first cause that would make sense of his current confusion" (27).

32. Poe's display of discovering cause *after* effect, throughout these tales, echoes Nietzsche's deconstruction of causality: "The fragment of the outside world of which we become conscious comes after the effect that has been produced on us and is projected *a posteriori* as its 'cause.' In the phenomenalism of the 'inner world' we invent the chronology of cause and effect. The basic fact of 'inner experience' is that the cause gets imagined after the effect has occurred." (*Werke* [1966] 3:804; qtd. in Culler 86). See Culler's description of how such a move is not "skeptical detachment" but rather "unwarrantable involvement," a distinction that pithily describes the problem of Poe's perverse narrators (88).

33. See Jonathan Elmer's productive comparison between Poe's confessing narrators and Ted Bundy's final televised confession. Elmer draws out how these confessions evade juridical purpose and circumvent communicative purpose. Instead, the confession exceeds "what Foucault would call its disciplinary function, and veers toward a primitive address to the big Other, like the babbling children Lacan invokes in *The Four*

*Fundamental Concepts of Psycho-Analysis*, who talk volubly to no one in particular, *à la cantonade*" (*Reading* 129).

34. This qualifies Slavoj Žižek's interpretation of Poe's perversity as "a purely negative grounding of an act accomplished only because it is prohibited . . . in which the very *absence* of a feature functions as a *positive feature*" (99). But Poe's construction complicates the idea of perversity as a nonpathological desire, for it isn't simply that, as Žižek paraphrases, "I accomplish an act 'only because it is prohibited'" (99) but rather that I accomplish the act only because I know that I do not desire it. This is a very fine hair to split, but the possible consequence is that Poe's perversity doesn't just negate objective compulsion as cause but negates the logic of compulsion entirely, in both objective and symbolic registers.

35. See Sbriglia 19–26.

36. See Poe's *Eureka*. For a discussion of Poe's philosophy as Hegelian and dialectical, see Carton 15–16. See also Milton Stern's note regarding the closed reciprocity of Poe's universal forces as a political stance against a rhetoric of openness (16–18).

## Chapter 4: The Uneven Balance

1. See also Paul Brodtkorb's phenomenological study of *Moby-Dick*, in which "[t]he power of moods is so great that it can determine how we experience ultimates" (16).

2. Melville's late poem "Art" appears to recognize this habit. The poem, which lists categorical opposites—"Humility—yet pride and scorn; / Instinct and study; love and hate; / Audacity—reverence"—would seem to privilege transcending their differences: "These must mate, / And fuse with Jacob's mystic heart." Yet the final line—"To wrestle with the angel—Art" (*Published Poems* 280) suggests that the unifying potential of mating and fusing is trumped by a wider antagonism, the wrestling that joins Jacob with the angel even as it describes their struggle against one another.

3. In emphasizing the Kantian and Hegelian strain in Melville's philosophical interests, I only intend to pursue one angle of Melville's much broader philosophical interests. For a recent description of the challenges of Melville's philosophy, see Mark Anderson's "Melville in the Shallows." For an assessment of Melville's eclectic philosophical influences, see John Wenke's "Ontological Heroics: Melville's Philosophical Art"; and Merton Sealts's "Melville and the Philosophers." For an argument for Melville's awareness of Kant, see Brodtkorb 11–18.

4. For a longer study of Melville's sometimes contradictory stances on transcendentalism, see Sealts's "Melville and Emerson's Rainbow."

5. For a summary of philosophical influences and their generative appropriation in *Mardi*, see Wenke, *Melville's Muse* 13–26. See also Wenke's claim that in *Mardi*, conflicting voices help Melville "to extend the possibilities of fictional form, especially as the genialist or the solipsist come to suggest metaphysical qualities of consciousness" (36).

6. See Nina Baym's reading that Taji's internal dialecticism becomes the motive power of *Moby-Dick*'s Ishmael through the contrast between its heterogeneous plentitude against the monochromatic fullness of the whale (918).

7. Elizabeth Duquette's answer is to cut weight: "[L]oosening oneself from the

'thunderheads' of institutional philosophy . . . frees the American thinker from the baggage of dead European doctrine" ("Speculative Cetology" 45). Yet that stance might itself be balanced against the unspoken consequence: in cutting both heads away, the *Pequod* would come away empty-handed, losing the blubber with the bathwater. In terms of method, then, flexibility would seem to be purchased at the cost of point, an arrangement that underscores the pervasive asymmetry in philosophy's possible methods.

8. For a longer discussion of the philosophical consequences of the difference between duality and nonduality in *Moby-Dick*, see Rachela Permenter's "Pythagoras and Nonduality: Melville among the Pre-Socratics."

9. See Edwin S. Shneidman's study of Melville's "non-summative deductive logic," wherein "one thought can actually be a half, or two, and . . . the two can even be contradictory while embraced in the same thought" (554). The recursive sway of Melville's method in *Moby-Dick* may thus be related to what Elizabeth Duquette has argued is its "sidling philosophical methodology that presupposes the nature of truth to be fundamentally antithetical to any process emphasizing intellectual ownership or conceptual mastery" ("Speculative Cetology" 37).

10. At stake for Hegel's reinvention of logic is the place of freedom. The way Hegel conceives of the threat to reason posed by conventional logic depends upon a remarkable analogy to the tyranny of emotion. In one passage, Hegel suggests that his entire project is to save reason from becoming like emotion, from becoming impulses that entangle our freedom with the particulars in the world (see Hegel 44).

11. For more of the imagined insults, see Adler's list of grievances in *Letters of a Lunatic* (20–21).

12. Walter E. Bezanson characterizes Adler's influence on Melville as that of "an informed and eloquent teacher" upon "an excited undergraduate," but concludes that "[i]t was to writers, however, not philosophers, that Melville turned once the course with Adler was over" (174). See also Sanford Marovitz's two articles on Melville and Adler, "More Chartless Voyaging" and "Correspondences: Paranoiac Lexicographers and Melvillean Heroes," as well as Wenke, *Melville's Muse* 95–96.

13. For Adler's philosophical influence on Melville's works after *Mardi*, see Maurice Lee, *Uncertain Chances* 140–141.

14. "[T]he German philologist simultaneously reflected an image of Melville's present psychological state and represented to him as well a portentous confrontation with his own fears and intellectual aspirations" (Marovitz, "More Chartless Voyaging" 377). See also Marovitz, "Correspondences," for how Adler's intellectual paranoia may have been an influence for the tragic metaphysical questing of Ahab and Pierre.

15. Adler's support, recorded in the *Medical Registrar of Bloomingdale Asylum, 1821–1866*, is referenced with permission of the Medical Center Archives of New York–Presbyterian Hospital, Weill Cornell Medical Center.

16. See Clark 36–38.

17. Deas exhibited his work in New York almost exclusively through the National Academy of Design and the American Art-Union. These were two of the most prominent art institutions in New York City, and evidence shows that Melville visited both at

least once: the American Art-Union exhibition with Duyckinck in 1847 (Leyda 261), and the National Academy of Design in 1865 (Leyda 674).

18. See George Duyckinck's September 1854 letter to the Council of the University of the City of New York. In it, Duyckinck and F. W. Downes propose that the university pay for Adler's continued treatment at Bloomingdale's and suggest that the university's reputation is at stake.

19. See Paul McCarthy's study of Melville's biographical proximity to mental illness, *"The Twisted Mind": Madness in Herman Melville's Fiction*.

20. Another possible route between Melville and *A Vision* can be charted through his friendship with poet and art critic Henry Tuckerman, dated as beginning in 1849 (Parker 59–60). Tuckerman apparently saw *A Vision*, which was only on display at the Art-Union from September 1849 to March 1850 (Clark 214), as he gives a description of a Deas painting much later, in 1867, that accords with the description in *The Knickerbocker*: "[O]ne of his wild pictures, representing a black sea, over which a figure hung, suspended by a ring, while from the waves a monster was springing, was so horrible, that a sensitive artist fainted at the sight" (Tuckerman 429). Evidence thus suggests that Melville and Tuckerman became friends during the same year that Tuckerman saw the strange watery horror, a painting that made such an impression that he would recall it nearly two decades later.

21. For a discussion of other potential sources for Melville's Spouter-Inn painting, see Wallace 318–330.

22. For the centrality of painting and visual art to Melville and Duyckinck's friendship, see Wallace 117–128.

23. See Harrison Hayford's "Unnecessary Duplicates: A Key to the Writing of *Moby-Dick*."

24. According to Evans, Starbuck's balanced pragmatism slides into pluralism and ends in "an administrative and disconsolate relativism" (70), while Ahab's conviction is "not to reject or abandon the world but to save it" (17). For an opposing reading, see John Williams's criticism of Ahab and advocacy of Starbuck's implicit transcendentalism (147–151); and Elizabeth Duquette's reading of the book as criticizing all canonical and institutionalized philosophical dogma ("Speculative Cetology" 45). For other philosophical parsings, see Merton Sealts's "Melville and the Platonic Tradition" 300–317.

25. See John Williams 145–146.

26. Melville will later reprise this unified dichotomy in his image of the two-tone tortoise in "The Encantadas": "The tortoise is both black and bright" (*PT* 130).

27. For an extended discussion of how "fright . . . is abstracted from any specific cause in order to wander in a void" (117), see Brodtkorb's reading of the chapter (115–119).

28. Wenke, noticing with others the abyssal "inhuman ideality" of whiteness in the chapter, further points out that it connects Ahab's and Ishmael's metaphysical quests: "Ishmael saves his book—his chapter—from the vortex of 'naught' by dramatizing a version of what drives Ahab *and* himself" (158).

29. The perceptible and projective qualities of light here help contextualize the way that the passage, as Dennis Williams points out from a Lacanian perspective, uses

"semantic indeterminacy, and even possible semantic evacuation," to "become the screen upon which fantasy projections appear and thus create the space for empirical 'meanings'" (75).

30. Edwards, in one of the many passages where his ideas rhyme with Melville's, surmises that, if it were not for color, we would not presume external substance: "For what idea is that which we call by the name of body? I find color has the chief share in it. 'Tis nothing but color, and figure which is the termination of color" (*SP* 351).

## Chapter 5: Dread

1. Nancy Ruttenburg's recent appraisal of Bartleby criticism similarly finds it caught between the cultural studies approach favored by American scholars and the theoretical approach favored by continental philosophers. According to Ruttenburg, these approaches remedy "the nullification of choice" in the story by "choosing anyway," as if "the tale of Bartleby had formally mandated an exclusivity of interpretive choice that, in opening one avenue of approach, closes others off" ("'The Silhouette of a Content'" 138).

2. Early critical interpretations of the tale focus on the religious allegory. Ben Kimpel and Marvin Fisher see the salesman as an allegorical figure of the orthodox minister. See Kimpel 30–32; and Fisher 118–124. Joshua Matthews suggests an economic allegory (57). More recently, Sean Silver has argued that the tale critiques allegorical modes in general (3).

3. For Steven Frye, the satiric thrust of the story is mainly against "applied science that has become complicit with capitalism" (120). For Sean Silver, the rod is an allegorical idol, a kind of inoculation against providence (19). Eric Wertheimer adds that for Melville, the rod "is an emblem of a thoroughgoing skepticism, of all that cannot be satisfactorily secured and underwritten" (178).

4. Allan Emery finds the sources for Melville's lightning in Benjamin Franklin's *Letters and Papers on Electricity* (1836–1840) and Lucius Lyon's *Treatise on Electrical Conductors* (1853). See Emery's "Melville on Science: 'The Lightning-Rod Man.'"

5. D. H. Lawrence links this dialectical paradox of freedom to American culture and literature. Allergic to any infringement upon individual liberty, Lawrence's American is truly mastered. "'Henceforth be masterless,'" Lawrence concludes; "[h]enceforth be mastered" (14).

6. Kierkegaard's theology, attentive both to aesthetic conditions and to the power of distressed affect, is particularly suited for the lyrical anxiety of American literature's darker strain. As Elisa New has argued, Kierkegaard "reattaches to Emerson's self-reliance its due quotient of solitary terror," repelling transcendental synthesis to "give form to a species of faith inexpressible in discursive philosophy" (*The Regenerate Lyric* 159). For Melville and Kierkegaardian dread, see also Brodtkorb 112.

7. Gordon Marino summarizes the philosophical consensus that, for Kierkegaard, "anxiety is a manifestation of the fact that we are free. Anxiety is a shining forth of our spiritual nature. It reflects our relationship to possibility and the future" (320). But this does little to explain why anxiety, and not some other affect, performs this role. In fact, Marino expresses bafflement that Kierkegaard would assert that one loves one's anxiety:

"For anyone who has suffered from anxiety, the suggestion that he or she loves their anxiety will seem callous. After all anxiety in all its variegated forms is today listed as a 'mental disorder' and no one loves having a mental disorder" (322–323). Such confusion may arise from the semantics, previously discussed, regarding the translation of "anxiety." Vincent McCarthy asserts that Kierkegaard "takes moods and the emotional life with the utmost seriousness" (2), but leaves somewhat obscure why Kierkegaard defines anxiety in the terms that he does. One exception is James Giles's answer: "Anxiety [dread] is thus a reaction to feeling oneself pulled towards making a choice that one fears: one shudders at the idea that one is attracted towards that which is frightening, that one might actually freely choose the frightening option" (80). Such an explanation runs into difficulty because it explains the fear of dread by positing a prior fear ("the frightening option") to define it. I do not think that dread, for Kierkegaard, can be attributed to the fear of making the wrong choice but must be attributed, rather, to the fear of being able to make a choice at all.

8. See Kierkegaard's prefatory argument about how dialectical method is the wrong mood for engaging with the problem of sin (14). See also Charlotte Cope's description of how the turn to affect ultimately fails in traditional philosophical logic, relying finally upon mere "inscrutability" (559).

9. Heidegger's translators have chosen to adopt "anxiety" as the translation for his *angst*. I have incorporated, in the quotations from Heidegger, my preferred translation of "dread" in order to emphasize both its difference from Freudian anxiety and its indebtedness to Kierkegaard.

10. Heidegger uses "leveling off" (*nivellieren*) to express how mental formalizations of phenomena may lose phenomenal content as a consequence. Leveling off phenomena is to turn sensations into concepts that fit into a formal system, and Heidegger's use of the term emphasizes how that process has both a positive gain (phenomena can be categorized, definitively thought) and a negative loss (the phenomenal specifics of the particular must be discarded): "in such formalizations the phenomena get levelled off so much that their real phenomenal content may be lost" (121).

11. For Heidegger, "the 'there'" (*das Da*) is the existential spatial character of Dasein: "'Here' and 'yonder' are possible only in a 'there'—that is to say, only if there is an entity which has made a disclosure of spatiality as the Being of the 'there'" (171). Loosely, "the 'there'" is Dasein in the space of the world, a body and the world which it perceives and which it perceives itself in.

12. Edgar Dryden shows how the narrator's allusive language tropes another kind of displacement, a ubiquitous and slippery intertextual one, that both drives and ultimately disenchants the narrator's pursuit. See *Form of the American Romance* 63–75.

13. For Dryden, the creeper vine represents the irreducible persistence of difference (*Form of the American Romance* 71). I would add that this difference is perceived as a contagion of sameness, perhaps indicating the dialectical double bind in which the desire to overcome difference is obviated by the disenchanting realization that there was no difference in the first place.

14. For a longer discussion of how Bartleby's will becomes a "loose existence" (27)

that interrupts a smooth and unbroken chain of necessity, see Arsić, *Passive Constitutions* 12–32.

15. See Heidegger 474.

16. Heidegger points out two ways in which now-time still bears the marks of the primordial time that it levels off: now-time regards time as "*passing away*" (478) and defines time as an "*irreversible* succession" (478), neither of which is necessitated by the concept of time as a sequence of "nows."

17. The relation between the deceit of the slaves and the inauthenticity of now-time may open a possible chronopolitical reading of the tale. For more on how race and slavery are linked to unstable conceptions of time, see Cindy Weinstein's "When Is Now?: Poe's Aesthetics of Temporality."

18. Delano's temporary falls into fractures in time thus accord with what Jonathan Elmer has found to be the tale's tension between normalizing Nature and eruptive History. Delano's commitment to naturalization would normalize the discrete and historical event, smooth it out into uninterrupted clock-time, but is continually disturbed by the "evental site" that poses "a great danger for forces of normalization, for what is thereby exposed is the void itself, as that from which the world of presentation emerges" ("Babo's Razor" 77).

19. Karcher shows how Melville's focus is not on slavery but on its state-sanctioned violence: "[I]n 'The Bell-Tower' [Melville] confronts us directly with a slave society's naked contempt for human values" (208). Karcher thus expands on Marvin Fisher's claim that the tale is "not only a rejection of technological progress but also a fearful response to that other contemporary phenomenon—the institution of Negro slavery" (96–97). For a reading that links the tale's critique of slavery with industrial capitalism, see Ivy Wilson's "'No Soul Above': Labor and the 'Law in Art' in Melville's 'The Bell-Tower.'"

20. See Maurice Lee, *Slavery, Philosophy, and American Literature* 147–164. Lee finds that Melville's treatment of slavery in "Benito Cereno" is an excursion of political philosophy, one which always has the potential to devolve into "a more metaphysical quest" (156) yet can still be understood according to "the historically available lenses of Machiavelli and Hobbes that focus less on unknowability and more on the uses and abuses of power in an ambiguous world" (157).

21. See Jentsch 11–15. Jentsch theorizes uncanny fear as caused by a lack of certainty regarding the boundaries between the human and natural worlds.

22. See Bill Brown's essay "Reification, Reanimation, and the American Uncanny" for the centrality of the uncanny to America's history of slavery. Brown also finds that the fear associated with the uncanny is bound up not with the threat that the uncanny object poses to our humanity but rather with the "apprehension that within things we will discover the human precisely because our history is one in which humans were reduced to things" (207).

23. "Those critics who have been the most intent on grasping the essence of the Gothic novel whole have also been the most impatient with its surfaces—'claptrap,' 'decor,' 'stage-set'—and the quickest to find 'true depths.' But their plunge to the themat-

ics of depth and then to a psychology of depth has left unexplored the most characteristic and daring areas of Gothic convention, those that point the reader's attention back to surface" ("The Character in the Veil" 255).

24. The "zombie problem" in the philosophy of consciousness is a wide and vibrant debate. For an introduction to the problem, see Kirk 71–72.

25. As a figure of surface, all the way down, the automaton may be read as an inverse variation on what Samuel Otter has found as Melville's "quest for depth through overwrought surface" (2). Otter's study shows how Melville, from *Typee* (1846) through *Pierre* (1852), generates excess from the pursuit of depth through the anatomization of embodied surfaces, from skin to skull to skeleton (145–158). Yet Otter notes that Melville ends this experiment in *Pierre*, finding that under the "surface stratified on surface" (Melville, *Pierre* 285) lies only more surface, "an eloquent, layered emptiness" (Otter 250). If Melville turns away from "inside critique" (258) after *Pierre*, as Otter suggests, then the automaton may be read as a projection from the outside, derived at a distance, of the endless emptiness of the stratified surfaces of subjectivity.

26. See Klaus Benesch's related point that Bannadonna's automaton is not "another 'Prometheus unbound,' taking revenge on its inventor's sacrilegious effort," nor an "emblem of technology out of control" (139). Rather, the automaton is merely clockwork, oblivious to human aims or ends and representative, for Benesch, of the discrepancy between modern technologies of reproduction and human artistic originality (139).

### Afterword: "Some Dim, Random Way"

1. See Colin Davis's chapter on "The Ancient Quarrel" in *Critical Excess* (1–25).

# WORKS CITED

Abrams, M. H. *The Mirror and the Lamp: Romantic Theory and the Critical Tradition.* 1953. New York: W. W. Norton, 1958.
Adler, George. *Handbook of German Literature.* New York: D. Appleton and Co., 1854.
———. Letter to Evert Duyckinck. February 16, 1850. MS. Duyckinck Papers. New York Public Library, New York.
———. *Letters of a Lunatic, or A Brief Exposition of My University Life, during the Years 1853–54.* New York, 1854.
Agamben, Giorgio. "Bartleby, or On Contingency." 1993. *Potentialities: Collected Essays in Philosophy.* Ed. and trans. Daniel Heller-Roazen. Stanford, CA: Stanford UP, 1999.
Albrecht, James M. *Reconstructing Individualism: A Pragmatic Tradition from Emerson to Ellison.* New York: Fordham UP, 2012.
"Algebra." *The Encyclopaedia Americana: A Popular Dictionary of Arts, Sciences, Literature, History, Politics, and Biography, Brought Down to the Present Time . . .* Ed. Francis Lieber. 13 vols. Philadelphia: Carey and Lea, 1829–1833.
Alterton, Margaret. *Origins of Poe's Critical Theory.* Iowa City: University of Iowa, 1925.
Altieri, Charles. "Are Aesthetic Models the Best Way to Talk about the Artfulness of Literary Texts?" *American Literature's Aesthetic Dimensions.* Ed. Cindy Weinstein and Christopher Looby. New York: Columbia UP, 2012. 393–404.
———. *The Particulars of Rapture: An Aesthetics of the Affects.* Ithaca, NY: Cornell UP, 2003.
Anderson, Amanda. *The Powers of Distance: Cosmopolitanism and the Cultivation of Detachment.* Princeton, NJ: Princeton UP, 2001.
Anderson, Mark. "Melville in the Shallows." *Literature and Philosophy* 36.2 (Oct. 2012): 496–503.
Anderson, Wallace. Editor's Introduction. *Scientific and Philosophical Writings.* By Jonathan Edwards. Ed. Wallace Anderson. New Haven, CT: Yale UP, 1980.
Aristotle. *The Poetics.* Trans. W. Hamilton Fyfe. 1927. *Aristotle, The Poetics; "Longinus," On the Sublime; Demetrius, On Style.* Cambridge, MA: Harvard UP; London: William Heinemann, 1965. 4–118.
Arnauld, Antoine, and Pierre Nicole. *Logic or the Art of Thinking.* 1662. Ed. and trans. Jill Vance Buroker. Cambridge: Cambridge UP, 1996.

———. *Logic or the Art of Thinking.* 1662. Trans. [John] Ozell. London, 1717.
Arsić, Branka. *On Leaving: A Reading in Emerson.* Cambridge, MA: Harvard UP, 2010.
———. *Passive Constitutions, or 7½ Times Bartleby.* Stanford, CA: Stanford UP, 2007.
Auerbach, Jonathan. *The Romance of Failure: First-Person Fictions of Poe, Hawthorne, and James.* New York: Oxford UP, 1989.
Baym, Nina. "Melville's Quarrel with Fiction." *PMLA* 94.5 (1979): 909–923.
Benesch, Klaus. *Romantic Cyborgs: Authorship and Technology in the American Renaissance.* Amherst: U of Massachusetts P, 2002.
Benjamin, Walter. *Charles Baudelaire: A Lyric Poet in the Era of High Capitalism.* Trans. Harry Zohn. London: NLB, 1973.
Berkovitch, Sacvan. *The American Jeremiad.* Madison: University of Wisconsin Press, 1978.
———. *The Rites of Assent: Transformations in the Symbolic Construction of America.* New York: Routledge, 1993.
Bezanson, Walter E. "*Moby-Dick*: Document, Drama, Dream." *A Companion to Melville Studies.* Ed. John Bryant. New York: Greenwood Press, 1986. 169–210.
Bonaparte, Marie. *The Life and Works of Edgar Allan Poe, A Psycho-Analytic Interpretation.* Trans. John Rodker. London: Imago, 1949.
Breitwieser, Mitchell Robert. *American Puritanism and the Defense of Mourning: Religion, Grief, and Ethnology in Mary White Rowlandson's Captivity Narrative.* Madison: U of Wisconsin P, 1990.
Brodtkorb, Paul, Jr. *Ishmael's White World: A Phenomenological Reading of Moby Dick.* New Haven, CT: Yale UP, 1965.
Brown, Bill. "Reification, Reanimation, and the American Uncanny." *Critical Inquiry* 32.2 (Winter 2006): 175–207.
Buell, Lawrence. *New England Literary Culture: From Revolution through Renaissance.* Cambridge: Cambridge UP, 1986.
Cameron, Sharon. *Impersonality: Seven Essays.* Chicago: U of Chicago P, 2007.
Carlyle, Thomas. "State of German Literature." *The Zodiac* 2.5 (Nov. 1836): 69–71; 2.6 (Dec. 1836): 91–92.
Carton, Evan. *The Rhetoric of American Romance: Dialectic and Identity in Emerson, Dickinson, Poe, and Hawthorne.* Baltimore: Johns Hopkins UP, 1985.
Case, Kristin. *American Pragmatism and Poetic Practice: Crosscurrents from Emerson to Susan Howe.* Rochester, NY: Camden House, 2011.
Castronovo, Russ. "Radical Configurations of History in the Era of American Slavery." *American Literature* 65.3 (Sept. 1993): 523–547.
Cavell, Stanley. *The Claim of Reason: Wittgenstein, Skepticism, Morality, and Tragedy.* Oxford: Clarendon Press–Oxford UP, 1979.
———. *In Quest of the Ordinary: Lines of Skepticism and Romanticism.* Chicago: U of Chicago P, 1988.
———. *The Senses of Walden.* 1972. Chicago: U of Chicago P, 1992.
———. "Thinking of Emerson." 1979. *The Senses of Walden: An Expanded Edition.* Chicago: U of Chicago P, 1992. 123–138.

Chai, Leon. *Jonathan Edwards and the Limits of Enlightenment Philosophy*. New York: Oxford UP, 1998.
Chauncy, Charles. *Enthusiasm Described and Cautioned Against*. Boston: Draper for Eliot and Blanchard, 1742. Early American Imprints 1, 4912.
———. *Seasonable Thoughts on the State of Religion in New England*. 1743. New York: Regina Press, 1975.
[Cheever, George]. "Coleridge." *North American Review* 40.87 (Apr. 1835): 299–351.
Clap, Thomas, John Punderson, John Munson, Theoph. Munson, Andrew Tuttle, and Samuel Mix. Letter. *The Boston Weekly Post-Boy* Oct. 5, 1741: 2–3.
Clark, Carol. *Charles Deas and 1840s America*. Norman: U of Oklahoma P, 2009.
Colacurcio, Michael. *Doctrine and Difference: Essays in the Literature of New England*. New York: Routledge, 1997.
Cooper, William. *Three Discourses Concerning the Reality, the Extremity, and the Absolute Eternity of Hell Punishments*. Boston: S. Kneeland and T. Green for Joseph Edwards, 1732. Early American Imprints 1, 3526.
Cope, Charlotte. "Freedom, Responsibility, and the Concept of Anxiety." *International Philosophical Quarterly* 44.4 (Dec. 2004): 549–566.
Rev. of *A Course of Mathematics, Adapted to the Method of Instruction in the American Colleges*, by Jeremiah Day. *Analectic Magazine* June 1817: 441–467.
Culler, Jonathan. *On Deconstruction: Theory and Criticism after Structuralism*. 1982. Ithaca, NY: Cornell UP, 2007.
Dällenbach, Lucien. *The Mirror in the Text*. 1977. Trans. Jeremy Whiteley with Emma Hughes. Chicago: U of Chicago P, 1989.
Damasio, Antonio. *The Feeling of What Happens: Body and Emotion in the Making of Consciousness*. Orlando, FL: Harcourt, 1999.
Daston, Lorraine, and Peter Galison. *Objectivity*. New York: Zone Books, 2007.
Davidson, Cathy. *Revolution and the Word: The Rise of the Novel in America*. 2nd ed. Oxford: Oxford UP, 2004.
Davidson, Edward H. *Poe: A Critical Study*. Cambridge, MA: Belknap Press–Harvard UP, 1966.
Davis, Colin. *Critical Excess: Overreading in Derrida, Deleuze, Levinas, Žižek and Cavell*. Stanford, CA: Stanford UP, 2010.
Dayan, Joan [Colin]. *Fables of Mind: An Inquiry into Poe's Fiction*. New York: Oxford UP, 1987.
Delattre, Roland André. *Beauty and Sensibility in the Thought of Jonathan Edwards: An Essay in Aesthetics and Theological Ethics*. New Haven, CT: Yale UP, 1968.
Delbanco, Andrew. *The Puritan Ordeal*. Cambridge, MA: Harvard UP, 1989.
———. "Thomas Shepard's America: The Biography of an Idea." *Studies in Biography*. Ed. Daniel Aaron. Cambridge, MA: Harvard UP, 1978. Harvard English Studies 8. 159–182.
Deleuze, Gilles. "Bartleby; or, The Formula." 1993. *Essays: Critical and Clinical*. Trans. Daniel W. Smith and Michael A. Greco. Minneapolis: U of Minnesota P, 1997. 68–90.

Derrida, Jacques. *Of Grammatology*. 1967. Trans. Gayatri Chakravorty Spivak. Baltimore: Johns Hopkins UP, 1976.

———. *The Post-Card: From Freud to Socrates and Beyond*. Trans. Alan Bass. Chicago: U of Chicago P, 1987.

Donaldson, Scott. "The Dark Truth of 'The Piazza Tales.'" *PMLA* 85.4 (Oct. 1970): 1082–1086.

Dryden, Edgar. *The Form of American Romance*. Baltimore: Johns Hopkins UP, 1988.

———. *Monumental Melville: The Formation of a Literary Career*. Stanford, CA: Stanford UP, 2004.

Duquette, Elizabeth. "Making an Example: American Literature as Philosophy." *The Oxford Handbook of Nineteenth-Century American Literature*. Ed. Russ Castronovo. Oxford: Oxford UP, 2012. 343–357.

———. "Speculative Cetology: Figuring Philosophy in *Moby-Dick*." *ESQ: A Journal of the American Renaissance* 47.1 (2001): 33–57.

Duyckinck, George, and F. W. Downes. Letter to the Council of the University of the City of New York. September 19, 1854. MS. Duyckinck Papers. New York Public Library, New York.

Edwards, Jonathan. "Benjamin Colman's Abridgment, November 1736." 1736. *The Great Awakening*. Ed. C. C. Goen. New Haven, CT: Yale UP, 1972. The Works of Jonathan Edwards 4. 112–127.

———. *The Distinguishing Marks of a Work of the Spirit of God*. 1741. *The Great Awakening*. Ed. C. C. Goen. New Haven: Yale UP, 1972. The Works of Jonathan Edwards 4. 213–288.

———. Downame Manuscript. Notes to *Expositionis Georgii Dounami, in petri rami dialecticam catechismus*, by George Downame. MS. GEN MSS, vol. 159. Jonathan Edwards Collection. General Collection, Beinecke Rare Book and Manuscript Library, Yale University University, New Haven, CT.

———. *A Faithful Narrative*. 1737. *The Great Awakening*. Ed. C. C. Goen. New Haven, CT: Yale UP, 1972. The Works of Jonathan Edwards 4. 97–212.

———. Fragment: From an Application on Seeking God. [1721–1722]. *Sermons and Discourses, 1720–1723*. Ed. Wilson H. Kimnach. New Haven, CT: Yale UP, 1992. The Works of Jonathan Edwards 10. 377–387.

———. ["God sometimes defers the punishment for sinners till they are fully ripe for destruction"]. 35. Sermon on Rev. 14: 18–19 [1726]. *Sermons, Series II, 1723–1727*. Jonathan Edwards Center, Yale University, 2008. Works of Jonathan Edwards Online 42. Accessed June 9, 2014.

———. ["God sometimes punishes sin by giving men up to sin"]. 28. Sermon on Rom. 1:24 [1722–1723]. *Sermons, Series II, 1723–1727*. Jonathan Edwards Center, Yale University, 2008. Works of Jonathan Edwards Online 42. Accessed June 9, 2014.

———. *God's Excellencies*. [1722–1723]. *Sermons and Discourses, 1720–1723*. Ed. Wilson H. Kimnach. New Haven, CT: Yale UP, 1992. The Works of Jonathan Edwards 10. 413–436.

———. ["It is a strange punishment that God has assigned to the workers of iniquity"]. 110. Sermon on Job 31:3 [1729]. *Sermons, Series II, 1729*. Jonathan Edwards Center, Yale University, 2008. Works of Jonathan Edwards Online 44. Accessed June 9, 2014.

———. *Letters and Personal Writings*. Ed. George S. Claghorn. New Haven, CT: Yale UP, 1998. The Works of Jonathan Edwards 16.

———. "The Mind." *Scientific and Philosophical Writings*. Ed. Wallace E. Anderson. New Haven, CT: Yale UP, 1980. The Works of Jonathan Edwards 6. 332–393.

———. *The "Miscellanies": Entry Nos. 1153–1360*. Ed. Douglas A. Sweeney. New Haven, CT: Yale UP, 2004. The Works of Jonathan Edwards 23.

———. ["The miseries of the wicked in hell will be absolutely eternal"]. 509. Sermon on Matt. 25:46 (Apr. 1739). *Sermons, Series II, 1739*. Jonathan Edwards Center, Yale University, 2008. Works of Jonathan Edwards Online 54. Accessed June 9, 2014.

———. "Of the Prejudices of the Imagination." *Scientific and Philosophical Writings*. Ed. Wallace E. Anderson. New Haven, CT: Yale UP, 1980. The Works of Jonathan Edwards 6. 196–201.

———. *Personal Narrative: Letters and Personal Writings*. Ed. George S. Claghorn. New Haven, CT: Yale UP, 1998. The Works of Jonathan Edwards 16. 790–804.

———. *Religious Affections*. 1746. Ed. John E. Smith. New Haven, CT: Yale UP, 1959. The Works of Jonathan Edwards 2.

———. *Scientific and Philosophical Writings*. Ed. Wallace E. Anderson. New Haven: Yale UP, 1980. The Works of Jonathan Edwards 6.

———. *Sinners in the Hands of an Angry God*. 1741. *Sermons and Discourses, 1739–1742*. Ed. Harry S. Stout and Nathan O. Hatch with Kyle P. Farley. New Haven, CT: Yale UP, 2003. The Works of Jonathan Edwards 22. 400–435.

———. *Some Thoughts Concerning the Revival*. 1743. *The Great Awakening*. Ed. C. C. Goen. New Haven, CT: Yale UP, 1972. The Works of Jonathan Edwards 4. 289–530.

———. ["The torments of hell will be eternal"]. 152. Sermon on Mark 9:44 [1729]. *Sermons, Series II, 1729–1731*. Jonathan Edwards Center, Yale University, 2008. Works of Jonathan Edwards Online 45. Accessed June 9, 2014.

———. "Unpublished Letter of May 30, 1735." 1735. *The Great Awakening*. Ed. C. C. Goen. New Haven, CT: Yale UP, 1972. The Works of Jonathan Edwards 4. 99–110.

———. *The Value of Salvation*. [1722]. *Sermons and Discourses, 1720–1723*. Ed. Wilson H. Kimnach. New Haven, CT: Yale UP, 1992. The Works of Jonathan Edwards 10. 308–336.

———. *Warnings of Future Punishment Don't Seem Real to the Wicked*. [1727]. *Sermons and Discourses: 1723–1729*. The Works of Jonathan Edwards 14. 198–213.

Edwards, Justin D. *Gothic Passages: Racial Ambiguity and the American Gothic*. Iowa City: U of Iowa P, 2003.

Egan, Kenneth V., Jr. "Descent to an Ascent: Poe's Use of Perspective in 'A Descent into the Maelström.'" *Studies in Short Fiction* 19.2 (Spring 1982): 157–162.

Eliot, T. S. "From Poe to Valéry." *Hudson Review* 2.3 (Autumn 1949): 327–342.

Elliot, Emory. *Power and the Pulpit in Puritan New England*. Princeton, NJ: Princeton UP, 1975.

Elmer, Jonathan. "Babo's Razor, or, Discerning the Event in an Age of Differences." *Differences: A Journal of Feminist Cultural Studies* 19.2 (Summer 2008): 54–81.

———. *Reading at the Social Limit: Affect, Mass Culture, and Edgar Allan Poe*. Stanford, CA: Stanford UP, 1995.
Emery, Allan. "Melville on Science: 'The Lightning-Rod Man.'" *New England Quarterly: A Historical Review of New England Life and Letters* 56.4 (Dec. 1983): 555–568.
Engel, William E. *Early Modern Poetics in Melville and Poe: Memory, Melancholy, and the Emblematic Tradition*. Farnham, UK: Ashgate, 2012.
Erkkila, Betsy. "Perverting the American Renaissance: Poe, Democracy, Critical Theory." *Poe and the Remapping of Antebellum Print Culture*. Ed. J. Gerald Kennedy and Jerome McGann. Baton Rouge: Louisiana State UP, 2012. 65–100.
———. "The Poetics of Whiteness: Poe and the Racial Imaginary." *Romancing the Shadow: Poe and Race*. Ed. J. Gerald Kennedy and Liliane Weissberg. New York: Oxford UP, 2001. 41–74.
Evans, K. L. *Whale!* Minneapolis: U of Minnesota P, 2003.
"Exhibition at the National Academy of Design." *The Knickerbocker; or New York Monthly Magazine* May 1849: 468–470.
Feidelson, Charles, Jr. *Symbolism and American Literature*. 1953. Chicago: U of Chicago P, 1966.
Fichte, J. G. "On the Basis of Our Belief in a Divine Governance of the World." 1798. *Introductions to the Wissenschaftslehre and Other Writings (1797–1800)*. Ed. and trans. Daniel Breazeale. Indianapolis: Hackett, 1994. 141–154.
Fiedler, Leslie A. *Love and Death in the American Novel*. 1960. Dalkey Archive, 2008.
Fiering, Norman. *Jonathan Edwards's Moral Thought and Its British Context*. Chapel Hill: U of North Carolina P, 1981.
Fisher, Benjamin Franklin. "Poe and the Gothic Tradition." *The Cambridge Companion to Edgar Allan Poe*. Ed. Kevin J. Hayes. Cambridge: Cambridge UP, 2002. 72–91.
Fisher, Marvin. *Going Under: Melville's Short Fiction and the American 1850s*. Baton Rouge: Louisiana State UP, 1977.
Fisher, Philip. *The Vehement Passions*. Princeton, NJ: Princeton UP, 2002.
Fleissner, Jennifer. "Poe's Imp, Melville's Formula." *Fictions* 4 (2005): 13–27.
Foucault, Michel. *Discipline and Punish*. 1975. Trans. Alan Sheridan. 2nd ed. New York: Vintage Books, 1995.
Freud, Sigmund. "The Uncanny." 1919. *Collected Papers*. Vol. 4. Trans. Joan Riviere. New York: Basic Books, 1959. 368–407.
Fried, Debra. "Repetition, Refrain, and Epitaph." *ELH* 53.3 (Autumn 1986): 615–632.
Frye, Steven. "Melvillean Skepticism and Alternative Modernity in 'The Lightning-Rod Man.'" Special issue in honor of G. R. Thompson of *Poe Studies / Dark Romanticism: History, Theory, Interpretation*. Ed. Steven Frye and Eric Carl Link. Vols. 39–40 (2006–2007): 115–125.
Gaustad, Edwin Scott. *The Great Awakening in New England*. Gloucester, MA: Peter Smith, 1965.
Gide, André. *The Journals of André Gide*. Trans. J. O'Brien. New York: Alfred Knopf, 1947.
Giles, James. "Kierkegaard's Leap: Anxiety and Freedom." *Kierkegaard and Freedom*. Ed. James Giles. New York: Palgrave, 2000. 69–92.

Ginzburg, Carlo. "Clues: Morelli, Freud, and Sherlock Holmes." *The Sign of Three: Dupin, Holmes, Peirce*. Ed. Umberto Eco and Thomas A. Sebeok. Bloomington: Indiana UP, 1983. 179–197.

Goddu, Teresa A. *Gothic America: Narrative, History, and Nation*. New York: Columbia UP, 1997.

———. "Poe, Sensationalism, and Slavery." *The Cambridge Companion to Edgar Allan Poe*. Ed. Kevin J. Hayes. Cambridge: Cambridge UP, 2002. 92–112.

Goodman, Russell B. *American Philosophy and the Romantic Tradition*. Cambridge: Cambridge UP, 1990.

Gordon, Adam. "'A Condition to be Criticised': Edgar Allan Poe and the Vocation of Antebellum Criticism." *Arizona Quarterly* 68.2 (Summer 2012): 1–31.

Gregg, Melissa, and Seigworth, Gregory J. "An Inventory of Shimmers." *The Affect Theory Reader*. Durham, NC: Duke UP, 2010. 1–25.

Griffith, Clark. "'Ligeia' and the English Romantics." *University of Toronto Quarterly* 24.1 (Oct. 1954): 8–25.

———. "Poe and the Gothic." *Critical Essays on Edgar Allan Poe*. Boston, MA: G. K. Hall, 1987. 127–132.

Grimstad, Paul. *Experience and Experimental Writing: Literary Pragmatism from Emerson to the Jameses*. Oxford: Oxford UP, 2013.

Gura, Philip. "Lost and Found: Recovering Edwards for American Literature." *Jonathan Edwards at 300: Essays on the Tercentenary of His Birth*. Ed. Harry S. Stout, Kenneth P. Minkema, and Caleb J. D. Maskell. Lanham, MD: University Press of America, 2005. 86–97.

Halliburton, David. *Edgar Allan Poe: A Phenomenological View*. Princeton, NJ: Princeton UP, 1973.

Halttunen, Karen. "Early American Murder Narratives: The Birth of Horror." *The Power of Culture: Critical Essays in American History*. Ed. Richard Wightman Fox and T. J. Jackson Lears. Chicago: U of Chicago P, 1993. 67–101.

Hansen, Thomas S., and Burton R. Pollin. *The German Face of Edgar Allan Poe: A Study of Literary References in His Works*. Columbia, SC: Camden House, 1995.

Hawthorne, Nathaniel. *The English Notebooks: 1856–1860*. 2 vols. Ed. Thomas Woodson and Bill Ellis. Columbus: Ohio State UP, 1997.

Hayford, Harrison. "Unnecessary Duplicates: A Key to the Writing of *Moby-Dick*." *New Perspectives on Melville*. Ed. Faith Pullen. Edinburgh: Edinburgh UP, 1978. 128–161.

Hegel, [Georg Wilhelm Friedrich]. *Science of Logic*. 1812–1816. 2 vols. Trans. W. H. Johnston and L. G. Struthers. London: George Allen & Unwin, 1929.

Heidegger, Martin. *Being and Time*. 1927. Trans. John Macquarrie and Edward Robinson. New York: Harper Perennial Modern Thought, 1962.

Heimert, Alan. Introduction. *The Great Awakening: Documents Illustrating the Crisis and Its Consequences*. Ed. Alan Heimert and Perry Miller. Indianapolis: Bobbs-Merrill, 1967.

Heller, Terry. *The Delights of Terror: An Aesthetics of the Tale of Terror*. Urbana: U of Illinois P, 1987.

Hertz, Neil. *The End of the Line: Essays on Psychoanalysis and the Sublime.* New York: Columbia UP, 1985.

Hoeveler, Diane. *Gothic Riffs: Secularizing the Uncanny in the European Imaginary, 1780–1820.* Columbus: Ohio State UP, 2010.

Hoffman, Daniel. *Poe Poe Poe Poe Poe Poe Poe.* 1972. New York: Paragon House, 1990.

Hoffman, Michael J. "The House of Usher and Negative Romanticism." *Studies in Romanticism* 4.3 (1965): 158–168.

Hofstadter, Douglas. *I Am a Strange Loop.* New York: Basic Books, 2007.

Hogle, Jerrold E. Introduction. *The Cambridge Companion to Gothic Fiction.* Ed. Jerrold E. Hogle. Cambridge: Cambridge UP, 2002. 1–20.

*The Holy Bible, King James Version.* Cambridge Edition. 1769. *King James Bible Online,* 2014. http://www.kingjamesbibleonline.org/.

Horkheimer, Max, and Theodor W. Adorno. *Dialectic of Enlightenment.* 1944. Trans. John Cumming. New York: Continuum, 2002.

Houlgate, Stephen. *The Opening of Hegel's Logic: From Being to Infinity.* West Layfayette, IN: Purdue UP, 2006.

Howe, Alexander. *It Didn't Mean Anything: A Psychoanalytic Reading of American Detective Fiction.* Jefferson, NC: McFarland, 2008.

Hume, David. *A Treatise of Human Nature.* Ed. John P. Wright, Robert Stecker, and Gary Fuller. London: Everyman, 2003.

Hutchisson, James M. "The Reviews: Evolution of a Critic." *A Companion to Poe Studies.* Ed. Eric W. Carlson. Westport, CT: Greenwood Press, 1996. 296–322.

Irwin, John T. *The Mystery to a Solution: Poe, Borges, and the Analytic Detective Story.* Baltimore: Johns Hopkins UP, 1994.

———. "Reading Poe's Mind: Politics, Mathematics, and the Association of Ideas in 'The Murders in the Rue Morgue.'" *American Literary History* 4.2 (1992): 187–206.

Jardine, Nicholas. "Problems of Knowledge and Action: Epistemology of the Sciences." *Cambridge History of Renaissance Philosophy.* Ed. Quentin Skinner and Eckhard Kessler. Cambridge: Cambridge UP, 1988. 685–711.

Jefferson, Ann. "*Mise en abyme* and the Prophetic in Narrative." *Style* 17.2 (1983): 196–208.

Jentsch, Ernst. "On the Psychology of the Uncanny." 1906. Trans. Roy Sellars. *Angelaki: A New Journal in Philosophy, Literature, and the Social Sciences* 2.1 (1996): 7–21.

Johansen, Ib. "The Madness of the Text: Deconstruction of Narrative Logic in 'Usher,' 'Berenice,' and 'Doctor Tarr and Professor Fether.'" *Poe Studies / Dark Romanticism: History, Theory, Interpretation* 22.1 (1989): 1–9.

Johnson, Barbara. *The Critical Difference: Essays in the Contemporary Rhetoric of Reading.* Baltimore: Johns Hopkins UP, 1980.

Justin, Henri. "An Impossible Aesthetics or an Aesthetics of the Impossible?" *Poe Writing / Writing Poe.* Ed. Richard Kopley and Jana Argersinger. New York: AMS Press, 2013. 127–142.

Kant, Immanuel. *Critique of Judgment.* 1790. Trans. Werner S. Pluhar. Indianapolis: Hackett, 1987.

———. *Critique of Pure Reason.* 1787. Trans. Norman Kemp Smith. New York: St. Martin's Press, 1965.
Karcher, Carolyn. *Shadow over the Promised Land: Slavery, Race, and Violence in Melville's America.* Diss. U of Maryland, 1980. Ann Arbor, MI: UMI, 1994.
Kennedy, J. Gerald. "The Limits of Reason: Poe's Deluded Detectives." *American Literature* 47.2 (May 1975): 184–196.
———. *Poe, Death, and the Life of Writing.* New Haven, CT: Yale UP, 1987.
Kennedy, J. Gerald, and Liliane Weissberg, eds. *Romancing the Shadow: Poe and Race.* Oxford: Oxford UP, 2001.
Ketterer, David. *The Rationale of Deception in Poe.* Baton Rouge: Louisiana State UP, 1979.
Kierkegaard, Søren. *The Concept of Dread.* 1844. Trans. Walter Lowrie. 2nd ed. Princeton, NJ: Princeton UP, 1957.
Kimnach, Wilson H. "General Introduction to the Sermons: Jonathan Edwards' Art of Prophesying." *Sermons and Discourses, 1720–1723.* Ed. Wilson H. Kimnach. New Haven, CT: Yale UP, 1992.
———. "Jonathan Edwards' Early Sermons: New York, 1722–1723." *Journal of Presbyterian History* 55 (Fall 1977): 255–256.
———. "The Sermons: Concept and Execution." *The Princeton Companion to Jonathan Edwards.* Ed. Sang Hyun Lee. Princeton, NJ: Princeton UP, 2005. 243–257.
Kimpel, Ben D. "Two Notes on Herman Melville." *American Literature* 16 (1944): 29–32.
King, Stephen. *Danse Macabre.* 1981. New York: Berkley Books, 1983.
Kirk, Robert. *Raw Feeling: A Philosophical Account of the Essence of Consciousness.* Oxford: Clarendon Press, 1994.
Knight, Janice. *Orthodoxies in Massachusetts: Rereading American Puritanism.* Cambridge, MA: Harvard UP, 1994.
Knutson, Andrea. *American Spaces of Conversion: The Conducive Imaginaries of Edwards, Emerson, and James.* Oxford: Oxford UP, 2011.
Kopley, Richard. *Edgar Allan Poe and the Dupin Mysteries.* New York: Palgrave Macmillan, 2008.
Lacan, Jacques. "Seminar on 'The Purloined Letter.'" Trans. Jeffrey Mehlman. *Yale French Studies* 48 (1972): 39–72.
Lacoue-Labarthe, Philippe, and Jean-Luc Nancy. *The Literary Absolute: The Theory of Literature in German Romanticism.* 1978. Trans. Philip Barnard and Cheryl Lester. Albany: State University of New York Press, 1988.
Lawrence, D. H. *Studies in Classic American Literature.* 1923. London: Penguin, 1977.
"Lecture of Mr. Combe." *Atkinson's Saturday Evening Post* Feb. 2, 1839: 2.
Lee, Dwight. "Melville and George J. Adler." *American Notes and Queries* 12 (1974): 138–141.
Lee, Maurice. "Skepticism in Nineteenth-Century American Literature and Philosophy." *The Oxford Handbook of Nineteenth-Century American Literature.* Ed. Russ Castronovo. Oxford: Oxford UP, 2012. 252–268.

———. *Slavery, Philosophy, and American Literature, 1830–1860*. Cambridge: Cambridge UP, 2005.
———. *Uncertain Chances: Science, Skepticism, and Belief in Nineteenth-Century American Literature*. Oxford: Oxford UP, 2012.
Lee, Sang Hyun. *The Philosophical Theology of Jonathan Edwards*. Princeton, NJ: Princeton UP, 1988.
Levin, Harry. *The Power of Blackness: Hawthorne, Poe, Melville*. New York: Vintage, 1960.
Levine, George. *Dying to Know: Scientific Epistemology and Narrative in Victorian England*. Chicago: U of Chicago P, 2002.
Leyda, Jay. *The Melville Log: A Documentary Life of Herman Melville 1819–1891*. 2 vols. New York: Gordian Press, 1969.
Leys, Ruth. "The Turn to Affect: A Critique." *Critical Inquiry* 3.37 (Spring 2011): 434–472.
Limon, John. *The Place of Fiction in the Time of Science: A Disciplinary History of American Writing*. Cambridge: Cambridge UP, 1990.
Liu, Lydia. "The Cybernetic Unconscious: Rethinking Lacan, Poe, and French Theory." *Critical Inquiry* 36.2 (Winter 2010): 288–320.
Ljungquist, Kent. *The Grand and the Fair: Poe's Landscape Aesthetics and Pictorial Techniques*. Potomac, MD: Scripta Humanistica, 1984.
Longaker, Mark Garrett. "Puritan Sermon Method and Church Government: Solomon Stoddard's Rhetorical Legacy." *New England Quarterly* 79.3 (Sept. 2006): 439–460.
Loring, Israel. *Serious Thoughts on the Miseries of Hell*. Boston: J. Phillips, 1732. Early American Imprints 1, 3559.
Lovejoy, David S. *Religious Enthusiasm in the New World: Heresy to Revolution*. Cambridge, MA: Harvard UP, 1985.
Lucas, D. W. "Pity, Fear, and *Katharsis*." *Poetics*. Oxford: Clarendon Press, 1968. 273–290.
Lyon, Lucius. *A Treatise on Lightning Conductors*. New York: George Putnam, 1853.
Marino, Gordon. "Anxiety in *The Concept of Anxiety*." *The Cambridge Companion to Kierkegaard*. Ed. Alastair Hannay and Gordon D. Marino. Cambridge: Cambridge UP, 1998. 308–328.
Marovitz, Sanford. "Correspondences: Paranoiac Lexicographers and Melvillean Heroes." *"Ungraspable Phantom": Essays on "Moby-Dick."* Ed. John Bryant, Mary K. Bercaw Edwards, and Timothy Marr. Kent, OH: Kent State UP, 2006.
———. "More Chartless Voyaging: Melville and Adler at Sea." *Studies in the American Renaissance* (1986): 373–384.
Marty, Martin E. *Religion, Awakening and Revolution*. [Wilmington, NC]: Consortium, 1977. Faith of our Fathers 4.
Massumi, Brian. *Parables for the Virtual: Movement, Affect, Sensation*. Durham, NC: Duke UP, 2002.
Mather, Cotton. *Perswasions from the Terror of the Lord*. Boston: Timothy Gre[en], 1711. Early American Imprints 1, 1511.
———. *The Valley of Hinnom*. Boston: J. Allen for Robert Starke, 1717. Early American Imprints 1, 1910.
Mather, Increase. *The Greatest Sinners Exhorted and Encouraged to Come to Christ and*

*That Now without Delaying*. Boston: R. P. for Joseph Brunning, 1686. Early American Imprints 1, 415.
———. *Heaven's Alarm to the World*. Boston: Samuel Sewall, 1682. Early American Imprints 1, 320.
———. *The Wicked Mans Portion*. 1675. *Sermons for Days of Fast, Prayer, and Humiliation and Execution Sermons*. Ed. Ronald A. Bosco. Delmar, NY: Scholars' Facsimiles & Reprints, 1978. 191–217. The Puritan Sermon in America, 1630–1750 1.
———. *Wo to Drunkards*. Cambridge, MA: Printed by Marmaduke Johnson, 1673. Early American Imprints 1, 179.
Matthews, Joshua. "Peddlers of the Rod: Melville's 'The Lightning-Rod Man' and the Antebellum Periodical Market." *Leviathan: A Journal of Melville Studies* 12.3 (Oct. 2010): 55–70.
Matthiessen, F. O. *American Renaissance: Art and Expression in the Age of Emerson and Whitman*. 1941. Oxford: Oxford UP, 1968.
McAlister, Sean. "Revolution of Thought / Revulsion of Feeling: Edgar Allan Poe and the Interest Concept." *Criticism* 55.3 (Summer 2013): 471–506.
McCall, Dan. *The Silence of Bartleby*. Ithaca, NY: Cornell UP, 1989.
McCarthy, Paul. *"The Twisted Mind": Madness in Herman Melville's Fiction*. Iowa City: U of Iowa P, 1990.
McCarthy, Vincent A. *The Phenomenology of Moods in Kierkegaard*. The Hague: Martinus Nijhoff, 1978.
McGann, Jerome. "Poe, Decentered Culture, and Critical Method." *Poe and the Remapping of Antebellum Print Culture*. Ed. J. Gerald Kennedy and Jerome McGann. Baton Rouge: Louisiana State UP, 2012. 245–259.
McGurl, Mark. "Dark Times: On the 21st Century Gothic." *Los Angeles Review of Books* Sept. 22, 2012.
———. "The Posthuman Comedy." *Critical Inquiry* 38.3 (Spring 2012): 533–553.
Melville, Herman. *Correspondence*. Ed. Lynn Horth. Evanston, IL: Northwestern UP; Chicago: Newberry Library, 1993. The Writings of Herman Melville 14.
———. *Journals*. Ed. Howard C. Horsford and Lynn Horth. Evanston, IL: Northwestern UP; Chicago: Newberry Library, 1989. The Writings of Herman Melville 15.
———. *Mardi: And a Voyage Thither*. 1849. Ed. Harrison Hayford, Hershel Parker, and G. Thomas Tanselle. Evanston, IL: Northwestern UP; Chicago: Newberry Library, 1998. The Writings of Herman Melville 3.
———. *Moby-Dick*. Ed. Harrison Hayford, Hershel Parker, and G. Thomas Tanselle. Evanston, IL: Northwestern UP; Chicago: Newberry Library, 1988. The Writings of Herman Melville 6.
———. *Pierre; or The Ambiguities*. 1852. Ed. Harrison Hayford, Hershel Parker, and G. Thomas Tanselle. Evanston, IL: Northwestern UP; Chicago: Newberry Library, 1971. The Writings of Herman Melville 7.
———. *The Piazza Tales and Other Prose Pieces, 1839–1860*. Ed. Harrison Hayford, Hershel Parker, and G. Thomas Tanselle. Evanston, IL: Northwestern UP; Chicago: Newberry Library, 1987. The Writings of Herman Melville 9.

———. *Published Poems*. Ed. Robert C. Ryan, Harrison Hayford, Alma MacDougall Reising, and G. Thomas Tanselle. Evanston, IL: Northwestern UP; Chicago: Newberry Library, 2009. The Writings of Herman Melville 11.
Merivale, Patricia. "Gumshoe Gothics: Poe's 'The Man of the Crowd' and His Followers." *Detecting Texts: The Metaphysical Detective Story from Poe to Postmodernism*. Ed. Patricia Merivale and Susan Elizabeth Sweeney. Philadelphia: U of Pennsylvania P, 1999. 101–116.
Milder, Robert. *Exiled Royalties: Melville and the Life We Imagine*. Oxford: Oxford UP, 2006.
Miller, Perry. *Errand into the Wilderness*. 1956. Cambridge, MA: Belknap Press–Harvard UP, 1984.
———. *Jonathan Edwards*. N.p.: William Sloane Associates, 1949.
———. *The New England Mind: From Colony to Province*. 1953. Cambridge, MA: Belknap Press–Harvard UP, 1983.
———. *The New England Mind: The Seventeenth Century*. 1939. Cambridge, MA: Belknap Press–Harvard UP, 1982.
Moldenhauer, Joseph J. "Murder as a Fine Art: Basic Connections between Poe's Aesthetics, Psychology, and Moral Vision." *PMLA* 83.2 (May 1968): 284–297.
Moreland, Sean. "'Torture[d] into aught of the sublime': Poe's Fall of the House of Burke, Ussher, and Kant." *Deciphering Poe: Subtexts, Contexts, Subversive Meanings*. Bethlehem, PA: Lehigh UP, 2013. 53–65.
Moreland, Sean, and Devin Zane Shaw. "'As Urged by Schelling': Coleridge, Poe, and the Schellingian Refrain." *Edgar Allan Poe Review* 13.2 (Fall 2012): 50–80.
Moretti, Franco. *Signs Taken for Wonders: Essays in the Sociology of Literary Forms*. Trans. Susan Fischer, David Forgacs, and David Miller. London: Verso, 1988.
Morgan, John. *Godly Learning: Puritan Attitudes towards Reason, Learning, and Education, 1560–1640*. Cambridge: Cambridge UP, 1986.
Morrison, Toni. *Playing in the Dark: Whiteness and the Literary Imagination*. Cambridge, MA: Harvard UP, 1992.
Muller, John P., and William J. Richardson. *The Purloined Poe: Lacan, Derrida and Psychoanalytic Reading*. Baltimore: Johns Hopkins University Press, 1988.
Murison, Justine. *The Politics of Anxiety in Nineteenth-Century American Literature*. Cambridge: Cambridge UP, 2011.
Murphy, Christina. "The Philosophical Pattern of 'A Descent into the Maelström.'" *Poe Studies* 6.1 (June 1973): 25–30.
Nagel, Thomas. *The View from Nowhere*. New York: Oxford UP, 1986.
"National Academy Exhibition." Review. *The Literary World* June 3, 1848: 350–351.
Nelson, Victoria. *Gothicka: Vampire Heroes, Human Gods, and the New Supernatural*. Cambridge, MA: Harvard UP, 2012.
———. *The Secret Life of Puppets*. Cambridge, MA: Harvard UP, 2001.
New, Elisa. *The Line's Eye: Poetic Experience, American Sight*. Cambridge, MA: Harvard UP, 1998.

———. *The Regenerate Lyric: Theology and Innovation in American Poetry*. Cambridge: Cambridge UP, 1993.
Ngai, Sianne. *Ugly Feelings*. Cambridge, MA: Harvard UP, 2005.
Nichol, John Pringle. *Views of the Architecture of the Heavens in a Series of Letters to a Lady*. 3rd ed. New York: H. A. Chapin, 1840.
Niebuhr, Richard R. "Being and Consent." *The Princeton Companion to Jonathan Edwards*. Ed. Sang Hyun Lee. Princeton, NJ: Princeton UP, 2005. 34–43.
Novak, Frank G., Jr. "'Warmest Climes but Nurse the Cruellest Fangs'": The Metaphysics of Beauty and Terror in *Moby-Dick*." *Studies in the Novel* 15.4 (1983): 332–343.
Nussbaum, Martha C. *Upheavals of Thought: The Intelligence of Emotions*. Cambridge: Cambridge UP, 2001.
Nygaard, Loisa. "Winning the Game: Inductive Reasoning in Poe's 'Murders in the Rue Morgue.'" *Studies in Romanticism* 33.2 (1994): 233–254.
Oakes, Urian. Introduction. *The Day of Trouble Is Near*. By Increase Mather. Cambridge: Printed by Marmaduke Johnson, 1674. Early American Imprints 1, 192.
Otter, Samuel. *Melville's Anatomies*. Berkeley: U of California P, 1999.
Otter, Samuel, and Geoffrey Sanborn. "Introduction: Aesthetics and Melville." *Melville and Aesthetics*. New York: Palgrave Macmillan, 2011. 1–10.
"The Paintings at the American Art-Union." *Broadway Journal* Sept. 13, 1845: 154–155.
Parker, Hershel. *Melville: The Making of the Poet*. Evanston, IL: Northwestern UP, 2008.
Pease, Donald. *Visionary Compacts: American Renaissance Writings in Cultural Context*. Madison: U of Wisconsin P, 1987.
Peeples, Scott. "Poe's 'Constructiveness' and 'The Fall of the House of Usher.'" *The Cambridge Companion to Edgar Allan Poe*. Ed. Kevin J. Hayes. Cambridge: Cambridge UP, 2002. 178–190.
Permenter, Rachela. "Pythagoras and Nonduality: Melville among the Pre-Socratics." *Melville "Among the Nations."* Ed. Sanford E. Marovitz and A. C. Christodoulou. Kent, OH: Kent State UP, 2001. 140–158.
Person, Leland S., Jr. "Cruising (Perversely) for Context: Poe and Murder, Women and Apes." *Poe and the Remapping of Antebellum Print Culture*. Ed. J. Gerald Kennedy and Jerome McGann. Baton Rouge: Louisiana State UP, 2012. 143–169.
———. "Poe's Composition of Philosophy: Reading and Writing 'The Raven.'" *Arizona Quarterly: A Journal of American Literature, Culture, and Theory* 46.3 (Autumn 1990): 1–15.
———. "Trusting the Tellers: Paradoxes of Narrative Authority in Poe's 'A Descent into the Maelström.'" *Journal of Narrative Technique* 23.1 (Winter 1993): 46–56.
Pfau, Thomas. *Romantic Moods: Paranoia, Trauma, and Melancholy, 1790–1840*. Baltimore: Johns Hopkins UP, 2005.
Poe, Edgar Allan. *Complete Poems*. 1969. Ed. Thomas Ollive Mabbott. Urbana: U of Illinois P, 2000.
———. "Conti." *Southern Literary Messenger* 2.3 (Feb. 1836): 195.
———. "Critical Notices." *Southern Literary Messenger* 1.8 (Apr. 1835): 456.

———. *Edgar Allan Poe: Tales and Sketches*. 2 vols. 1978. Ed. Thomas Ollive Mabbott. Urbana: U of Illinois P, 2000.
———. *Essays and Reviews*. Ed. G. R. Thompson. New York: Library of America, 1984.
———. *Eureka*. Ed. Stuart Levine and Susan F. Levine. Urbana: U of Illinois P, 2004.
———. *The Letters of Edgar Allan Poe*. 2 vols. Ed. John Ward Ostrom. Cambridge, MA: Harvard UP, 1948.
———. *The Narrative of Arthur Gordon Pym*. 1838. Ed. Frederick S. Frank and Diane Long Hoeveler. Petersborough, ON: Broadview, 2010.
Poirier, Richard. *Poetry and Pragmatism*. Cambridge, MA: Harvard UP, 1992.
Polonsky, Rachel. "Poe's Aesthetic Theory." *The Cambridge Companion to Edgar Allan Poe*. Ed. Kevin J. Hayes. Cambridge: Cambridge UP, 2002. 42–56.
Pullman, Philip. *Fairy Tales from the Brothers Grimm: A New English Version*. New York: Viking, 2012.
Quinn, Patrick. *Edgar Allan Poe: A Critical Biography*. New York: D. Appleton-Century, 1941.
———. *The French Face of Edgar Poe*. Carbondale: Southern Illinois UP, 1957.
Radcliffe, Anne. "On the Supernatural in Poetry." *New Monthly Magazine* Jan. 1826.
Randall, John. *The Career of Philosophy: From the Middle Ages to the Enlightenment*. New York: Columbia UP, 1962.
Rees, Abraham, ed. *The Cyclopaedia; or, Universal Dictionary of Arts, Sciences and Literature*. Philadelphia: S. F. Bradford, 1810–1824.
Richards, Eliza. "Poe's Lyrical Media: The Raven's Returns." *Poe and the Remapping of Antebellum Print Culture*. Ed. J. Gerald Kennedy and Jerome McGann. Baton Rouge: Louisiana State UP, 2012. 200–224.
Richardson, Joan. *A Natural History of Pragmatism: The Fact of Feeling from Jonathan Edwards to Gertrude Stein*. Cambridge: Cambridge UP, 2007.
Riddel, Joseph N. *Purloined Letters: Originality and Repetition in American Literature*. Ed. Mark Bauerlein. Baton Rouge: Louisiana State UP, 1995.
Rivett, Sarah. *The Science of the Soul in Colonial New England*. Chapel Hill: U of North Carolina P, 2011.
Roberts-Miller, Patricia. *Voices in the Wilderness: Public Discourse and the Paradox of Puritan Rhetoric*. Tuscaloosa: U of Alabama P, 1999.
Robinson, Douglas. *American Apocalypses: The Image of the End of the World in American Literature*. Baltimore: Johns Hopkins UP, 1985.
Robinson, Marilynne. "On Influence and Appropriation." Interview by Tace Hedrick. *Iowa Review* 2.1 (Winter 1992): 1–7.
Rosenheim, Shawn James. *The Cryptographic Imagination: Secret Writing from Edgar Poe to the Internet*. Baltimore: Johns Hopkins UP, 1997.
Ruttenburg, Nancy. *Democratic Personality: Popular Voice and the Trial of American Authorship*. Stanford, CA: Stanford UP, 1998.
———. "'The Silhouette of a Content': 'Bartleby' and American Literary Specificity." *Melville and Aesthetics*. Ed. Samuel Otter and Geoffrey Sanborn. New York: Palgrave Macmillan, 2011. 137–155.

Savoy, Eric. "The Face of the Tenant: A Theory of American Gothic." *American Gothic: New Interventions in a National Narrative*. Ed. Robert K. Martin and Eric Savoy. Iowa City: U of Iowa P, 1998. 3–19.

Sbriglia, Russell. "Feeling Right, Doing Wrong: Poe, Perversity, and the Cunning of Unreason." *Poe Studies: History, Theory, Interpretation* 46 (2013): 4–31.

Schelling, Friedrich Wilhelm Joseph. *System of Transcendental Idealism*. 1856–1861. Trans. Peter Heath. Charlottesville: UP of Virginia, 1978.

Schouls, Peter. *The Imposition of Method: A Study of Descartes and Locke*. Oxford: Clarendon Press, 1980.

Sealts, Merton. "Melville and Emerson's Rainbow." 1980. *Pursuing Melville, 1940–1980*. Madison: U of Wisconsin P, 1982. 250–277.

———. "Melville and the Philosophers." 1942. *Pursuing Melville, 1940–1980*. Madison: U of Wisconsin P, 1982. 23–30.

———. "Melville and the Platonic Tradition." *Pursuing Melville, 1940–1980*. Madison: U of Wisconsin P, 1982. 278–336.

Sedgwick, Eve Kofosky. "The Character in the Veil: Imagery of the Surface in the Gothic Novel." *PMLA* 96.2 (Mar. 1981): 255–270.

———. *Touching Feeling: Affect, Pedagogy, Performativity*. Durham, NC: Duke UP, 2003.

Shapin, Steven. *The Scientific Revolution*. Chicago: U of Chicago P, 1996.

Shelley, Mary. *Frankenstein*. 1818. Ed. J. Paul Hunter. New York: Norton, 1996.

Shneidman, Edwin S. "Melville's Cognitive Style: The Logic of *Moby-Dick*." *A Companion to Melville Studies*. Ed. John Bryant. New York: Greenwood Press, 1986.

Silver, Sean. "The Temporality of Allegory: Melville's 'The Lightning-Rod Man.'" *Arizona Quarterly: A Journal of American Literature, Culture, and Theory* 62.1 (Spring 2006): 1–33.

Silverman, Kenneth. *Edgar A. Poe: Mournful and Never-Ending Remembrance*. 1991. New York: Harper Perennial, 1992.

Stern, Milton R. *Contexts for Hawthorne: "The Marble Faun" and the Politics of Openness and Closure in American Literature*. Urbana: U of Illinois P, 1991.

Stoddard, Solomon. *The Efficacy of the Fear of Hell to Restrain Men from Sin*. Boston: Thomas Fleet for Samuel Phillips, 1713. Early American Imprints 1, 1651.

Stout, Harry S. "The Puritans and Edwards." *The Princeton Companion to Jonathan Edwards*. Ed. Sang Hyun Lee. Princeton, NJ: Princeton UP, 2005. 274–291.

Sweeney, Susan. "Spectacular Distance in Poe's 'Man of the Crowd.'" *Poe Studies / Dark Romanticism: History, Theory, Interpretation* 36 (2003): 3–17.

Taylor, Matthew. "The Nature of Fear: Edgar Allan Poe and Posthuman Ecology." *American Literature: A Journal of Literary History, Criticism, and Bibliography* 84.2 (June 2012): 353–379.

Terada, Rei. *Feeling in Theory: Emotion after the "Death of the Subject."* Cambridge, MA: Harvard UP, 2001.

Thacker, Eugene. *In the Dust of This Planet*. Winchester, UK: Zero Books, 2011.

Thompson, G. R. *Poe's Fiction: Romantic Irony in the Gothic Tales*. Madison: U of Wisconsin P, 1973.

Thuesen, Peter J. "Edwards' Intellectual Background." *The Princeton Companion to Jonathan Edwards*. Ed. Sang Hyun Lee. Princeton, NJ: Princeton UP, 2005. 16–33.

"Topics of the Month." *Holden's Dollar Magazine* May 1849: 313–320.

Rev. of *Traité de mecanique celeste* [sic], by M. Le Marquis de Laplace. *The American Quarterly Review* 1 (June 1829).

Tuckerman, Henry. *Book of the Artists: American Artist Life*. New York: G. P. Putnam and Son, 1867.

Vidler, Anthony. *The Architectural Uncanny: Essays in the Modern Unhomely*. Boston: MIT Press, 1992.

Voller, Jack. "The Power of Terror: Burke and Kant in the House of Usher." *Poe Studies / Dark Romanticism: History, Theory, Interpretation* 21.2 (1988): 27–35.

Voloshin, Beverly R. "The Essays and 'Marginalia': Poe's Literary Theory." *A Companion to Poe Studies*. Ed. Eric W. Carlson. Westport, CT: Greenwood Press, 1996. 276–295.

Wallace, Robert K. *Melville and Turner: Spheres of Love and Fright*. Athens: U of Georgia P, 1992.

Warner, Michael. *The Letters of the Republic: Publication and the Public Sphere in Eighteenth-Century America*. Cambridge, MA: Harvard UP, 1990.

Webb, John. *Practical Discourses on Death, Judgment, Heaven & Hell in Twenty-Four Sermons*. Boston: Printed by J. Draper for D. Henchman, 1726. Early American Imprints 1, 2823.

———. *A Seasonable Warning against Bad Company-Keeping: In a Discourse from Prov. XIII. 20*. 2nd ed. Boston: Printed for Samuel Gerrish in Cornhill. 1726. Early American Imprints 1, 2825.

Weinstein, Cindy. "When Is Now?: Poe's Aesthetics of Temporality." *American Literature's Aesthetic Dimensions*. Ed. Cindy Weinstein and Christopher Looby. New York: Columbia UP, 2012. 197–218.

Weinstein, Cindy, and Christopher Looby. Introduction. *American Literature's Aesthetic Dimensions*. Ed. Cindy Weinstein and Christopher Looby. New York: Columbia UP, 2012. 1–36.

Weiskel, Thomas. *The Romantic Sublime: Studies in the Structure and Psychology of Transcendence*. Baltimore: Johns Hopkins UP, 1976.

Wenke, John. *Melville's Muse: Literary Creation and the Forms of Philosophical Fiction*. Kent, OH: Kent State UP, 1995.

———. "Ontological Heroics: Melville's Philosophical Art." *A Companion to Melville Studies*. Ed. John Bryant. Westport, CT: Greenwood Press, 1986. 467–601.

Wertheimer, Eric. "Jupiter Underwritten: Melville's Unsafe Home." *Nineteenth-Century Literature* 58.2 (Sept. 2003): 176–201.

West, Cornel. *The American Evasion of Philosophy: A Genealogy of Pragmatism*. Madison: U of Wisconsin P, 1989.

Whalen, Terence. *Edgar Allan Poe and the Masses: The Political Economy of Literature in Antebellum America*. Princeton, NJ: Princeton UP, 1999.

White, Eugene. *Puritan Rhetoric: The Issue of Emotion in Religion*. Carbondale: Southern Illinois UP, 1972.

White, Thomas. "Editorial Remarks." *Southern Literary Messenger* 1.7 (Mar. 1835): 387.
——. "Editorial Remarks." *Southern Literary Messenger* 1.8 (Apr. 1835): 460.
Williams, Anne. *The Art of Darkness: A Poetics of Gothic*. Chicago: U of Chicago P, 1995.
Williams, Dennis. "Filling the Void: A Lacanian Angle of Vision on *Moby-Dick*." *"Ungraspable Phantom": Essays on "Moby-Dick."* Ed. John Bryant, Mary K. Bercaw Edwards, and Timothy Marr. Kent, OH: Kent State UP, 2006. 61–80.
Williams, John B. *White Fire: The Influence of Emerson on Melville*. Long Beach: California State University, Long Beach, 1991.
Williams, Michael J. S. *A World of Words: Language and Displacement in the Fiction of Edgar Allan Poe*. Durham, NC: Duke UP, 1988.
Williams, William Carlos. *In the American Grain*. 1925. New York: New Directions, 1956.
Wilson, Ivy. "'No Soul Above': Labor and the 'Law in Art' in Melville's 'The Bell-Tower.'" *Arizona Quarterly: A Journal of American Literature, Culture, and Theory* 63.1 (Spring 2007): 24–47.
Žižek, Slavoj. *The Metastases of Enjoyment: Six Essays on Woman and Causality*. London: Verso, 1994.

# INDEX

Abrams, M. H., 91
Adler, George: influence on Melville, 177–80, 181–82, 183, 190, 266n12; *Letters of a Lunatic*, 178, 180–81; lexicon, 178, 179; literary criticism, 178, 181–82; mental illness, 178–79, 180–81, 182–84, 187
Adorno, Theodor W., 18, 19, 253n19
Aesthetic theories: affect and, 107–9, 247; Kantian, 88, 89–90, 98, 99, 106; of Poe, 75–76, 106–7, 108, 109, 116–17; pragmatist, 100; terror in, 107–9
Affect: aesthetics and, 107–9, 247; Edwards on, 18, 47, 55–56, 60, 61–62, 63–64, 73; in Poe's confessional tales, 155; in "The Raven," 85–87. *See also* Emotions; Feeling; Terror
Affect theory, 6–7, 11, 251–52n7
Agamben, Giorgio, 221
Albrecht, James M., 253n24
"All" feeling, 168, 170, 182, 192
Alterton, Margaret, 257n6, 258n19
Altieri, Charles, 11, 14, 251n5
Analytical method: in algebra, 126, 127, 261n11; analysis of, 123–24, 125–26, 128, 133–34; history, 126–27; perversity and, 155–56; of Poe, 119, 121–34, 149, 159; regress, 126, 127–28, 129, 133–34; scientific method, 7, 126, 136–37. *See also* Composition; Resolution
Anderson, Amanda, 19, 21
Anderson, Mark, 265n3
Anderson, Wallace, 256n28
Antinomies, 172–74, 175, 176, 190–96
Anxiety, 5–6, 210, 268–69n7. *See also* Dread
Aristotle, 9, 10, 12, 17, 175, 176, 252n9
Arminianism, 41, 44
Arnauld, Antoine, 256n29. *See also* Port-Royal Logic
Arsić, Branka, 8, 9, 21, 221, 222, 269–70n14
"Art" (Melville), 265n2

Atheism, 180, 181, 198
Auerbach, Jonathan, 131, 264n31
Automatons, 229–30, 233–34, 235–36, 237–40, 242–43, 271nn25–26
Awakening, *see* Great Awakening

Balance, 167, 190, 192, 202. *See also* Uneven balance
"Bartleby, the Scrivener" (Melville), 204, 205–6, 215, 219–22
Baym, Nina, 265n6
Beauty, 62, 80, 84, 89, 98–99. *See also* Aesthetic theories
"The Bell-Tower" (Melville), 205–6, 229–36, 237–44
Benesch, Klaus, 271n26
"Benito Cereno" (Melville), 205, 215, 226–28
Benjamin, Walter, 262–63n16
"Berenice" (Poe): attention in, 93–94, 96–98, 99, 101–3; Coleridge and, 88–89, 90–91, 92; literality, 92, 100, 101, 102–4; plot, 88; Poe's defense of, 88–89; pragmatist reading, 100; publication, 76, 257n18; themes, 76, 77, 95–96, 100–101, 176
Berkovitch, Sacvan, 38, 39, 254n1
Bezanson, Walter E., 266n12
"The Black Cat" (Poe), 146–48, 150–51, 152, 155–57
Blackness, 1–2, 163–65, 166, 194–95. *See also* Darkness
Blindness, *see* Vision
Bloomingdale Insane Asylum, 178, 180, 183–86, 187, 190
Bodies: consciousness and, 235–36; machines resembling human, 238; mind and, 94
Bonaparte, Marie, 257n1
Breitwieser, Mitchell Robert, 254n4
Brockden Brown, Charles, 25

Brodtkorb, Paul, Jr., 201, 265n1, 267n27, 268n6
Brown, Bill, 270n22
Buell, Lawrence, 251n4

Calvinism: determinism, 2, 3, 164, 207–8; original sin, 163, 165–66. *See also* Puritans
Cameron, Sharon, 36, 37, 69, 70, 209
Carlyle, Thomas, "The State of German Literature," 94–95, 96, 259n24
Cartesian logic, 70–73, 74, 256nn28–29. *See also* Logic
Carton, Evan, 265n36
Case, Kristin, 253n24
Castronovo, Russ, 230
Cavell, Stanley, 20–21, 22, 23, 29, 253nn22–24Chai, Leon, 255–56n20
Chappe optical telegraph, 238–40, 239 (fig.)
Chauncy, Charles, 26, 37, 58–59, 60, 61, 76, 246, 248
Cheever, George, 89–92, 94, 98, 258n18
Clark, Carol, 187, 266n16, 267n20
Colacurcio, Michael, 36, 37, 254n3
Coleridge, Samuel Taylor, 75, 88–92, 93, 94, 96, 97, 98, 259n21
Colman, Benjamin, 58
Color, 199–200, 219, 268n30
Composition: history, 126–27, 262n11; in Poe's detective tales, 124–26, 127–28; in Poe's tales, 129, 130, 131–35, 149, 150–52, 155–56, 159; in *Port-Royal Logic*, 126, 262n10. *See also* Analytical method
"The Conquerer Worm" (Poe), 104–6
Conversion: calls for hellfire sermons, 43, 44–46, 58, 61; conventional order, 58; of Edwards, 66–69; fear and, 58
Cooper, William, 39, 44
Cope, Charlotte, 211, 269n8
Culler, Jonathan, 264n32
*Cyclopaedia* (Rees), 127

Dällenbach, Lucien, 260nn31–32
Damasio, Antonio, 251–52n7
Darkness, 3–4, 166, 177, 194–95, 204. *See also* Blackness; Terror
Dasein, 215, 216–17, 222, 225, 226, 269n11
Daston, Lorraine, 252n8
Davenport, James, 31–34, 37, 41, 45, 47
Davidson, Cathy, 4
Davidson, Edward, 258n19, 263n19
Davis, Colin, 271n1
Dayan, Colin (Joan), 23, 75, 92, 93, 100
Deas, Charles, 266–67n17; *The Death-Struggle*, 183–84, 185 (fig.), 187–90; mental illness, 183–87; *A Vision*, 184–87, 267n20
Death: being-toward-, 223–25, 226, 227–28; dread of, 223–25; Melville on, 168–69; Poe's dead woman tales, 77–78, 87–88, 106–7; terror of, 193–94; understandings, 224. *See also* Hell
*The Death-Struggle* (Deas), 183–84, 185 (fig.), 187–90
Deconstruction, 28, 109–10, 117, 248. *See also* Poststructuralism
Delattre, Roland André, 256nn21–22
Delbanco, Andrew, 41, 254–55n8
Deleuze, Gilles, 221
Derrida, Jacques, 23, 99, 101, 119, 123, 248, 260–61n3
Descartes, René, 70, 172. *See also* Cartesian logic
"A Descent into the Maelstrom" (Poe), 137, 138–41, 142
Detective fiction, 261n4
Determinism, 2, 3, 164, 207–8, 214
Dialectical method: antinomies, 172–74, 175, 176; of Hawthorne, 169; of Hegel, 175–76, 177, 181, 182, 183, 195; in Kant, 172–73; Melville's use of, 168–71; in *Moby-Dick*, 167–68, 173–75, 176–77, 181, 183, 191–96, 201–2. *See also* Uneven balance
Dickinson, Emily, 2, 25
Donaldson, Scott, 204
Dread: distinction from fear, 213; Heidegger on, 215–17, 222, 223–25; Kierkegaard on, 210–13, 214, 268–69n7; in *The Piazza Tales*, 204, 215, 218–19, 221, 226–30, 233–34, 242–43; space and time and, 215–17, 222–24, 228–30
Dryden, Edgar, 269nn12–13
Duquette, Elizabeth, 24, 265–66n7, 266n9, 267n24
Duyckinck, Evert, 183, 184, 186–87
Duyckinck, George, 179, 183, 184

Edwards, Jonathan: on affect, 18, 47, 55–56, 60, 61–62, 63–64, 73; on color, 268n30; conversion, 66–69; debate with Chauncy, 59–62; on hell, 48–57, 255n14; hellfire sermons, 34–35, 39, 46, 47–48, 62, 73; idealism, 35–36, 75, 80; on infinite, 51–52, 56–57, 64–66, 68–69, 72–73, 256n30; letters to Colman, 58; logic and, 69–73, 74, 256nn28–29; philosophy of experience, 35; Poe's affinities with, 75, 81; pragmatism, 35;

relation to terror, 34–36, 37; science and, 63–64; on sin, 35–36, 57, 63, 64–65; on terror, 25–26, 60–61, 62–63, 64, 65–69, 73–74
Edwards, Jonathan, works: *The Distinguishing Marks of a Work of the Spirit of God*, 59–60; *A Faithful Narrative*, 58; *The Nature of True Virtue*, 69; "Of the Prejudices of the Imagination," 64, 65; *Personal Narrative*, 64–65, 66–69; "Sinners in the Hands of an Angry God," 34, 46, 47, 60, 73; "The torments of hell will be eternal," 51–57; *Treatise on the Religious Affections*, 47, 61–62, 73–74; *The Value of Salvation*, 48, 255n14
Edwards, Justin D., 251n3
Egan, Kenneth V., Jr., 263n25
Eliot, T. S., 257n7
Elliot, Emory, 254n5
Elmer, Jonathan, 149, 259n23, 264–65n33, 270n18
Emerson, Ralph Waldo: darkness and, 8; optimism, 2–3, 8, 9, 22; pragmatism and, 20, 21, 22; transcendentalism, 35–36, 140
Emery, Allan, 268n4
Emotions: Hegel on, 266n10; poststructuralist view, 99–100, 102, 236; reason and, 7, 59, 63; signs and, 99; whiteness and, 201. *See also* Affect; Fear; Feeling
"The Encantadas" (Melville), 162, 205, 215, 223, 224–26, 267n26
Engel, William E., 262n14
Enlightenment: empirical science, 63, 232; fear of fear, 233; myth, 231; reason, 4, 120, 121
Epistemology: authors' interest in, 18–19, 25; Edwards and, 48, 63, 80–81; Melville and, 28, 161–62; scientific, 19, 20; skepticism, 21, 22–23, 69–70, 217
Erkkila, Betsy, 253n18, 257n5
Eternity, 51–57, 73. *See also* Hell
*Eureka* (Poe), 127, 261n6, 264n27
Evangelism, 206. *See also* Great Awakening
Evans, K. L., 190, 254n27, 267n24
Evil, 211. *See also* Sin

"The Fall of the House of Usher" (Poe), 77, 87, 106–10, 111–17, 158
Fate, *see* Determinism
Fear: of Adler, 180, 181; aesthetics, 9–10, 17; conversion and, 58; of fear, 233; freedom and, 214, 233; function, 10–11; in Melville's works, 161–63, 205–9, 213–14, 215, 220, 231–34; Puritan view, 32; transcendence, 231–33. *See also* Dread; Terror

Feedback loops, 74, 85, 102, 105–6, 107, 109, 260n34
Feeling: beliefs and, 11–12; of thinking, 7–8, 9, 20, 122; thinking about, 9–18, 90–91. *See also* Affect; Emotions
Feidelson, Charles, Jr., 3, 264n29
Ferris, Isaac, 181, 182
Fichte, J. G., 78, 104, 259n27
Fiedler, Leslie A., 3, 245–46
Fiering, Norman, 34, 37
First Corinthians, 94, 95
Fisher, Benjamin Franklin, 264n28
Fisher, Marvin, 204, 208, 268n2, 270n19
Fisher, Philip, 10
*Flâneur*, 262–63n16
Fleissner, Jennifer, 152–53, 154
Foucault, Michel, 40
Freedom: debates on determinism vs. free will, 164, 169, 179, 207–8, 214; fear and, 210, 214, 233; Hegel on, 266n10; Kant on, 172–73; Kierkegaard on, 210–12, 214; limits, 209–10; resistance to coercion, 210, 220–21; sin and, 211
Freud, Sigmund, 112, 113, 213
Fried, Debra, 257–58n10
Frye, Steven, 268n3

Galison, Peter, 252n8
Gaustad, Edwin, 254n1
German literature: gothic genre, 76, 77–78; Jena school, 80–82, 86, 99, 100, 102, 116; romantic literary criticism, 77, 79–82, 86, 94–95, 116–17
German metaphysics, 179, 180–81
Gide, André, 110, 111
Giles, James, 269n7
Ginzburg, Carlo, 261n8
Glanvill, Joseph, 138
Goddu, Teresa A., 4, 257n1
Goethe, Johann von, 168; *Iphigenia in Tauris*, 181–82
Goodman, Russell B., 253n24
Gordon, Adam, 257n7
Gothic genre, 3–5, 15–16, 76, 77–78, 233–35
Goya, Francisco, 4, 6
Great Awakening, 31–34, 39, 44–47, 58–61, 62
Gregg, Melissa, 251n6
Griffith, Clark, 259n29, 260n38
Grimm brothers, "The Boy Who Left Home to Find Out about the Shivers," 248
Grimstad, Paul, 22, 23, 253n24, 257n9
Guilt, repressed, 2, 4, 6, 38

Gura, Philip, 35, 37

Halliburton, David, 261n5
Halttunen, Karen, 4
Hansen, Thomas S., 257n4
Hawthorne, Nathaniel, 1–2, 22, 25, 163–67, 168–69, 179, 195
"Hawthorne and His Mosses" (Melville), 1–2, 3, 163–67, 195Harrison, Hayford, 267n23
Hegel, G. W. F., 183, 195, 266n10; *Science of Logic*, 175–76, 177, 178, 181, 182
Heidegger, Martin, 210, 213, 215–17, 222, 223–28, 269nn10–11, 270n16
Heimert, Alan, 254n1
Hell: Edwards on reality of, 48–57; eternity of, 51–57, 73; paradoxes, 48
Heller, Terry, 253n15, 253n17
Hellfire sermons: audiences, 40, 41, 46, 47; calls for conversion, 43, 44–46, 58, 61; calls for reformed behavior, 41–44; of Edwards, 34–35, 39, 46, 47–48, 62, 73; in Great Awakening, 39, 44–47; ineffective, 48–54; positive function, 38, 39; prevalence, 254n5; punishments, 40–41; of Puritans, 32–33, 34, 37–47; rhetoric, 39, 41, 42, 43, 48, 254n16; terror in, 32–33, 34, 44, 60–61, 62
Hertz, Neil, 252n12
Hitchcock, Alfred, *Psycho*, 12, 13–14
Hoeveler, Diane, 4–5
Hoffman, Daniel, 257n9, 264n28
Hoffman, Michael J., 264n29
Hofstadter, Douglas, 112, 260n34
Hogle, Jerrold E., 252n14
Hooker, Thomas, 58
Horkheimer, Max, 18, 19, 253n19
Horror, 15–17
Horror stories, 76, 88–89
Houlgate, Stephen, 176
Howard, Leon, 178
Howe, Alexander, 131
Hugo of Siena, 126
Hume, David, 172, 245
Hutchisson, James M., 258n19

Idealism: American, 204; of Coleridge, 90–91, 93; of Edwards, 35–36, 75, 80; German, 80–82, 116–17; Kantian, 75–76, 172; literary criticism, 80; metaphysics, 36; of Poe, 75–76; post-Kantian, 75, 78, 79, 104
"The Imp of the Perverse" (Poe), 12–13, 146–48, 152, 153–55, 156–57

Infinity: Edwards on, 51–52, 56–57, 64–66, 68–69, 72–73, 256n30; of God, 166; paradoxes, 71–72; reflections, 107, 110–11; regression, 72–73, 111, 128, 159. *See also* Eternity; Sublime
Insanity, *see* Madness
*Iphigenia in Tauris* (Goethe), 181–82
Irwin, John T., 23, 109, 110, 123, 124, 261n3, 262n12
"The Island of the Fay" (Poe), 137

Jackman, William G., 184, 187
Jardine, Nicholas, 261–62n9
Jefferson, Ann, 260n31
Jena school, 80–82, 86, 99, 100, 102, 116
Jentsch, Ernst, 234
Johansen, Ib, 260n33, 260n37
Johnson, Barbara, 123–24, 261n3
Justin, Henri, 264n26

Kant, Immanuel: aesthetic theory, 88, 89–90, 98, 99, 106; *Critique of Pure Reason*, 172–73, 176; idealism, 75–76, 172; on safety, 12; sublime, 14–15, 99, 137, 144, 252n12, 263n22
Karcher, Carolyn, 230, 270n19
Kennedy, J. Gerald, 132, 257n8, 259n22
Ketterer, David, 261n5
Kierkegaard, Søren, 210–13, 214, 221, 268–69nn6–7
Kimnach, Wilson H., 254n5, 255nn11–13
Kimpel, Ben D., 268n2
King, Stephen, 15
Kirk, Robert, 271n24
*The Knickerbocker*, 186
Knight, Janice, 255n23
Knutson, Andrea, 21, 253n24, 254n7
Kopley, Richard, 261n5, 262n13

Lacan, Jacques, 119, 122, 123, 248, 261n3
Lacoue-Labarthe, Philippe, 80, 81–82
Lawrence, D. H., 3, 268n5
Lee, Dwight, 178
Lee, Maurice, 24, 120–21, 198, 231, 266n13, 270n20
Lee, Sang Hyun, 254n2, 256n21
Levin, Harry, 3, 245–46
Levine, George, 19, 69–70, 72, 121, 140, 252n8, 260n2
Leys, Ruth, 251–52n7
"Ligeia" (Poe), 77, 87, 104–6, 107
Light, 35, 199–201, 202. *See also* Darkness
Lightning, 68, 207–10

INDEX   295

"The Lightning-Rod Man" (Melville), 205–10, 211, 213–14, 220–21, 228–29, 231
Limon, John, 261n6, 263n18, 264n27
Lippard, George, 25
Literary criticism: by Adler, 178, 181–82; Carlyle on, 94–95; on darkness in American literature, 2, 3–4; German romantic, 77, 79–82, 86, 94–95, 116–17; idealism, 80; Jena school, 80–82, 86, 99, 100, 102, 116; of Poe, 76, 77, 79–80, 85, 89–90
*The Literary World*, 184
Liu, Lydia, 261n3
Ljungquist, Kent, 136, 263n21
Locke, John, 75, 172, 199
Logic: Aristotelian, 175; Cartesian, 70–73, 74, 256nn28–29; Port-Royal Logic, 70–72, 126, 150, 256nn28–29, 262n10; Ramist, 70, 256n28. *See also* Dialectical method
Longaker, Mark Garrett, 255n19
Looby, Christopher, 251n5
Loring, Israel, 39, 44
Lovejoy, David S. 254n1
Lucas, D. W., 252nn9–10

Madness: of Adler, 178–79, 180–81, 182–84, 187; of Deas, 183–87; in Poe's tales, 145–48
"The Man of the Crowd" (Poe), 121, 122–23, 128, 129–34
*Mardi: And a Voyage Thither* (Melville), 169–71, 172–73
Marino, Gordon, 268–69n7
Marovitz, Sanford, 178, 266n12, 266n14
Marty, Martin E., 254n1
Massumi, Brian, 251n6
"The Masque of the Red Death" (Poe), 227–28
Mather, Cotton, 37, 39, 43–44, 45
Mather, Increase, 37, 39, 40, 41–42, 45, 46
Mathews, Cornelius, 79–80
Matthews, Joshua, 268n2
Matthiessen, F. O., 2, 3, 29, 251n1
McAlister, Sean, 100
McCall, Dan, 204, 221
McCarthy, Paul, 178, 267n19
McCarthy, Vincent, 269n7
McGann, Jerome, 257n1
McGurl, Mark, 5, 137–38
"Mellona Tauta" (Poe), 261n6
Melville, Herman: Adler's influence, 177–80, 181–82, 183, 190, 266n12; Deas and, 183–87; European tour, 168, 177–78, 179–80; Hawthorne and, 168–69; pragmatism and, 22, 23; terror in works, 25–26, 161–63, 205–9, 213–14, 215, 220, 231–34; Tuckerman and, 267n20
Melville, Herman, works: "Art," 265n2; "Hawthorne and His Mosses," 1–2, 3, 163–67, 195; *Mardi: And a Voyage Thither*, 169–71, 172–73; *Pierre*, 169, 271n25; *Typee*, 184. *See also Moby-Dick*; *The Piazza Tales*
Merivale, Patricia, 262n15
Metaphysics: German, 179, 180–81; idealist, 36
Milder, Robert, 164–65
Miller, Perry, 34, 38–39, 46–47, 245–46, 254n1
Mind: attention, 93–94, 96–98, 99, 101–3; body and, 94; matter and, 91–93
*Mise en abyme*, 109, 110, 111, 112, 114, 116
*Moby-Dick* (Melville): antinomies, 22–23, 190–96; balance in, 167, 190; climax, 189–90; dialectics, 167–68, 173–75, 176–77, 181, 183, 191–96, 201–2; horror in, 16–17; influence of *The Death-Struggle*, 189–90; "The Line," 190, 193–94, 202; "The Mast-Head," 190–93; terror in, 161, 162, 167, 174–75, 190, 192–95, 196–202; "The Try-Works," 190, 194–96; whale descriptions, 171–72, 173, 174; whiteness of whale, 161, 197–201. *See also* Uneven balance
Moldenhauer, Joseph, 258n16
Moreland, Sean, 257n6, 259n30
"Morella" (Poe), 77, 87, 104, 107
Moretti, Franco, 261n4
Morgan, John, 256n28
Morrison, Toni, 4, 257n1
"The Murders in the Rue Morgue" (Poe), 121, 124–27, 128, 133–34, 261n5
Murison, Justine, 5–6
Murphy, Christina, 264n26

Nagel, Thomas, 19, 69, 253n20
Nancy, Jean-Luc, 80, 81–82
*The Narrative of Arthur Gordon Pym* (Poe), 111
Nature: affect and, 59–60; human relationship to, 138; lightning, 68, 207–10; whirlpools, 138–41, 142. *See also* Sublime
Nelson, Victoria, 5
New, Elisa, 35, 268n6
Newton, Isaac, 35
Ngai, Sianne, 17, 204, 217, 218, 228
Nichol, J. P., 127
Nicole, Pierre, 256n28. *See also* Port-Royal Logic
Niebuhr, Richard R., 73, 256n31
Nietzsche, Friedrich, 20, 264n32
Nifo, Agostino, 128

*North American Review*, 89–92, 94, 98, 258n18
Nothingness, 64, 65, 68, 69–70, 74
Noyes, Joseph, 31–32, 33, 34, 45
Nussbaum, Martha C., 11–12, 14, 17, 18, 21
Nygaard, Loisa, 125

Oakes, Urian, 41, 45
Objectivity, 7, 19, 20
Optical telegraph, Chappe, 238–40, 239 (fig.)
Optimism, 2–3, 8, 9, 21, 22
Otter, Samuel, 251n5, 271n25

Padua medical school, 126, 129
Pease, Donald, 258nn11–12
Peeples, Scott, 260n33
Permenter, Rachela, 266n8
Person, Leland S., Jr., 84, 257n1, 263n24
Perversity: analysis and, 155–56; Poe on, 10–11, 146–48, 152–55, 265n34; reason and, 146–48, 153–55, 156; terror and, 155
"Peter Pendulum, the Business Man" (Poe), 128, 129
Pfau, Thomas, 100, 105, 259nn25–26
"The Philosophy of Composition" (Poe), 78, 81, 82, 83–87
"The Philosophy of Furniture" (Poe), 110–11, 128, 129
"The Piazza" (Melville), 205–6, 217–19
*The Piazza Tales and Other Prose Pieces* (Melville): "Bartleby, the Scrivener," 204, 205–6, 215, 219–22; "The Bell-Tower," 205–6, 229–36, 237–44; "Benito Cereno," 205, 215, 226–28; darkness, 204; diversity of tales, 205; dread in, 204, 215, 218–19, 221, 226–30, 233–34, 242–43; "The Encantadas," 162, 205, 215, 223, 224–26, 267n26; historical context, 204, 206; irony, 208, 213–14; "The Lightning-Rod Man," 205–10, 211, 213–14, 220–21, 228–29, 231; linked motifs, 203, 205; "The Piazza," 205–6, 217–19; publication, 203; space and time, 203–4, 219–20, 221–22, 224–30, 237–42; terror in, 203–4, 205–9, 213–14, 222; tone, 203, 204–5
*Pierre* (Melville), 169, 271n25
"The Pit and the Pendulum" (Poe), 137, 141–45
Plato, 172, 176
Poe, Edgar Allan: aesthetic philosophy, 75–76, 106–7, 108, 109, 116–17; affinities with Edwards, 75, 81; analytical method, 119, 121–34, 149, 159; confessional tales, 119–20, 121–22, 135, 145–59; dead woman tales, 77–78, 87–88, 106–7; detective tales, 119, 120–21, 122–26, 128, 134, 262n13; horror tales, 76–77; idealism, 75–76; irony in tales, 145–46, 147–48, 264n30; literary criticism, 76, 77, 79–80, 85, 89–90; on perversity, 10–11, 146–48, 152–55, 265n34; physical appearance, 76; popular reputation, 76; pragmatism and, 22, 23; skepticism, 23; sublime tales, 119–20, 121, 134–35, 137, 138–41, 145, 159; on terror, 25–26, 76, 77–79, 108–9, 111, 142–45, 157–59
Poe, Edgar Allan, works: "The Black Cat," 146–48, 150–51, 152, 155–57; "The Conquerer Worm," 104–6; "A Descent into the Maelstrom," 137, 138–41, 142; *Eureka*, 127, 261n6, 264n27; "The Fall of the House of Usher," 77, 87, 106–10, 111–17, 158; "The Imp of the Perverse," 12–13, 146–48, 152, 153–55, 156–57; "Instinct vs. Reason," 128–29; "The Island of the Fay," 137; "Ligeia," 77, 87, 104–6, 107; "The Man of the Crowd," 121, 122–23, 128, 129–34; "The Masque of the Red Death," 227–28; "Mellona Tauta," 261n6; "Morella," 77, 87, 104, 107; "The Murders in the Rue Morgue," 121, 124–27, 128, 133–34, 261n5; *The Narrative of Arthur Gordon Pym*, 111; "Peter Pendulum, the Business Man," 128, 129; "The Philosophy of Composition," 78, 81, 82, 83–87; "The Philosophy of Furniture," 110–11, 128, 129; "The Pit and the Pendulum," 137, 141–45; "The Purloined Letter," 109, 119, 120–21, 122, 123–24, 128, 134; "The Raven," 78, 81, 82–87; "Sonnet—To Science," 135–36, 138; *The Tales of the Grotesque and Arabesque*, 77–78; "The Tell-Tale Heart," 145–48, 150, 152, 156, 157–59. *See also* "Berenice"
Poirier, Richard, 21, 253n24
Pollin, Burton R., 257n4
Polonsky, Rachel, 258n19
*Port-Royal Logic*, 70–72, 126, 150, 256nn28–29, 262n10
Poststructuralism: American literature as prelude, 9, 23–24, 29–30, 247–48; distinction from pragmatism, 9; on emotion, 99–100, 102, 236; on Poe, 110, 119, 120–21, 122–24, 128, 248; readings of American literature, 24, 28; terror and, 23, 24, 110
Pragmatism: aesthetics, 100; American literature and, 2, 20, 21–23, 247–48; balance theory, 202; distinction from poststructuralism, 9; of Edwards, 35; Emerson and, 8

*Psycho* (Hitchcock), 12, 13–14
Punishment, 40–41, 50. *See also* Hell
Puritans: Hawthorne's writing on, 163–64; hellfire sermons, 32–33, 34, 37–47; theology, 45, 67; view of fear and terror, 32
"The Purloined Letter" (Poe), 109, 119, 120–21, 122, 123–24, 128, 134

Quinn, Patrick, 131, 262n15

Radcliffe, Anne, 253n15
Randall, John, 126, 261n7
Rationality, *see* Reason
"The Raven" (Poe), 78, 81, 82–87
Reason: antinomies, 172–74, 175, 176; emotion and, 7, 59, 63; as highest faculty, 59; imagination and, 124–26; nature and, 60; perversity and, 146–48, 153–55, 156; in Poe's tales, 120, 128–29; power, 7–8; stability, 120–21; terror and, 4, 18, 120, 121–22, 139–45, 156–57, 159, 248–49. *See also* Analytical method; Thinking
Recursion, *see* Dialectical method; Feedback loops; Self-recursion; Uneven balance
Rees, Abraham, 127
Reflections, 107, 108–9, 110–11, 131–33, 159
Religion, *see* Calvinism; Evangelism; Great Awakening; Hellfire sermons; Puritans
Repression, 4, 5–6, 113, 236. *See also* Guilt, repressed
Resolution: history, 126–27, 262n11; in Poe's tales, 124–26, 127–28, 129–30, 131–35, 149, 152, 159; in *Port-Royal Logic*, 126, 262n10. *See also* Analytical method
Revivals, *see* Great Awakening
Richards, Eliza, 258n13, 258n15
Richardson, Joan, 21–22, 23, 35, 202
Riddel, Joseph N., 24, 85, 109–10, 116, 254n28, 258n14, 260n33, 260n39
Rivett, Sarah, 63, 255n17, 256n24
Roberts-Miller, Patricia, 255n16
Robinson, Douglas, 253n26
Robinson, Marilynne, 36
Romantic literary criticism, German, 77, 79–82, 86, 94–95, 116–17
Rosenheim, Shawn, 260n1, 263n17
Rousseau, Jean-Jacques, 99
Ruttenburg, Nancy, 33, 268n1

Safety, 12–14, 153–54
Savoy, 251n2
Sbriglia, Russell, 265n35

Schelling, Friedrich Wilhelm Joseph, 78, 80, 104, 113, 259n27, 260n35, 264n27
Schlegel, August Wilhelm, 78, 80, 106
Schlegel, Friedrich, 78, 80, 106
Schouls, Peter, 129
Science: affect and, 63–64; epistemology, 19, 20; objectivity, 7; Poe's poem on, 135–36, 138; religion and, 4, 5, 64, 207–8; scientific method, 7, 126, 136–37. *See also* Analytical method; Nature
Science studies, 7
Sealts, Merton, 265nn3–4, 267n24
Security, *see* Safety
Sedgwick, Eve Kofosky, 234–35, 251n6
Seigworth, Gregory J., 251n6
Self-difference, 212–13, 214, 215, 221, 237
Self-inclusion, 109–10, 111, 112. *See also* Mise en abyme
Self-recursion, 109, 110–11, 112–14, 115–17
Sensory perception, 199–201, 202. *See also* Sublime; Vision
Sermons, *see* Hellfire sermons
Shapin, Steven, 252n8
Shaw, Devin Zane, 257n6
Shepard, Thomas, 45, 254–55n8
Shneidman, Edwin S., 266n9
Silver, Sean, 268nn2–3
Silverman, Kenneth, 257n1
Sin: Edwards on, 35–36, 57, 63, 64–65; free will and, 211; growth, 51; individual, 45; Kierkegaard on, 221; original, 36, 163, 165–66; Puritan view, 41, 43, 45. *See also* Hell
Skepticism, 20, 21, 22–23, 69–70, 217
Slavery, 4, 230–31, 234, 270nn19–20
"Sonnet—To Science" (Poe), 135–36, 138
*Southern Literary Messenger*, 76, 79, 89, 258n18
Space and time: dread and, 215–17, 222–24, 228–30; in *The Piazza Tales*, 203–4, 219–20, 221–22, 224–30, 237–42; terror and, 203–4. *See also* Time
Stern, Milton R., 265n36
Stoddard, Solomon, 39, 42–43, 58
Stout, Harry S., 255n10
Subjectivity: of automaton, 229–30, 242; dread and, 214–15, 221, 228–29; emotion and, 208; idealized, 205; postmodern, 236
Sublime: affect and, 86–87; distinction from terror, 15; Kant on, 14–15, 99, 137, 144, 252n12, 263n22; Poe's sublime tales, 119–20, 121, 135, 137, 138–41, 145, 159; psychoanalysis and, 252n12; third stage, 137–38
Sweeney, Susan, 133

*The Tales of the Grotesque and Arabesque* (Poe), 77–78
Taylor, Matthew, 140, 253n16, 263n23
Telegraph, Chappe optical, 238–40, 239 (fig.)
"The Tell-Tale Heart" (Poe), 145–48, 150, 152, 156, 157–59
Terada, Rei, 28, 99, 110, 236–37, 242, 254n29
Terror: in aesthetic theory, 107–9; in American literature, 1–3, 6, 7, 20, 245–49; benefits of studying, 30; of God, 62; horror and, 16–17; natural, 59–60, 68; in nature, 138–41; perversity and, 155; poststructuralism and, 110; Puritan view, 32; reason and, 4, 120, 121–22, 139–45, 156–57, 159, 248–49; space and time and, 203–4; sublime and, 15; tone of, 2, 7, 8–9, 17–18, 23, 30, 246; whiteness and, 197–201
Terror, religious, *see* Hellfire sermons
Thinking: about feeling, 9–18, 90–91; about thinking, 18–19, 247; feeling of, 7–8, 9, 20, 122. *See also* Analytical method; Mind; Reason
Thacker, Eugene, 20, 253n21
Thompson, G. R., 257n6, 264nn29–30
Thoreau, Henry David, 2, 20
Thrownness, 215, 216, 217, 219, 222, 223, 227, 237–38
Thuesen, Peter J., 256n26
Time: clocks, 222, 224, 225, 226–27, 228; Heidegger on, 223–28, 270n16; measurement, 222, 225, 226, 228, 230, 240, 243; now-, 224, 225–28, 240–42, 243, 270n16; primordial, 215–16, 224, 225, 226, 227, 240, 242. *See also* Eternity; Space and time
Tone: definition, 17; of terror, 2, 7, 8–9, 17–18, 23, 30, 246
Torture, *see* "The Pit and the Pendulum"
Transcendentalism, 20–21, 35–36, 140, 191–93
Tuckerman, Henry, 267n20

*Typee* (Melville), 184

Uncanny, 112, 113–14, 234, 235, 236, 260n35, 270n22
Uneven balance: in *The Death-Struggle*, 188–89; Kant on, 173; Melville on, 163–67, 169; in *Moby-Dick*, 165, 167, 171–72, 175, 176–77, 190, 196–97, 199, 202
*Unheimlich*, 112, 113–14, 260n35. *See also* Uncanny

Veils, 234–36, 237
Vision, 199–201, 237
Voller, Jack, 259n30
Voloshin, Beverly R., 257n6, 258n19

Wallace, Robert K., 267nn21–22
Warner, Michael, 45, 255n9
Webb, John, 39
Weinstein, Cindy, 251n5, 270n17
Weiskel, Thomas, 252nn12–13
Wenke, John, 265n3, 265n5, 266n12, 267n28
Wertheimer, Eric, 268n3
West, Cornel, 253n25
Whalen, Terence, 257n1, 258n17
White, Eugene, 254n1, 255n10
White, Thomas, 76, 77, 88, 257n3
Whiteness, 161, 197–201
Whitman, Walt, 2
Williams, Anne, 252n14
Williams, Dennis, 267–68n29
Williams, John, 267nn24–25
Williams, Michael J. S., 103–4, 259n28
Williams, William Carlos, 3, 257n5
Wilson, Ivy, 270n19

Zabarellae Patavini, Jacobi, 126
Žižek, Slavoj, 265n34
Zombies, 236–37

The authorized representative in the EU for product safety and compliance is:
Mare Nostrum Group
B.V Doelen 72
4831 GR Breda
The Netherlands